We are used to the idea of people believing in Christ, but did the early church consider that Jesus also had faith in God? This book evaluates the evidence, starting with a survey of the meaning of faith in Judaism and Graeco-Roman literature and proceeding to a detailed exegesis of the relevant New Testament material from the Synoptic Gospels, the Pauline and deutero-Pauline epistles, Hebrews and Revelation. Two trajectories of interest in Jesus' faith are identified: the paradigmatic, concerned with matters of discipleship, and the theological, relating Christ to God's gift of salvation. The examination is then broadened to trace the progress of these trajectories through the literature of the first four Christian centuries and concludes by identifying the Arian controversy as the christological development which rendered reference to Jesus' faith untenable within the emergent orthodoxy.

SOCIETY FOR NEW TESTAMENT STUDIES

MONOGRAPH SERIES

General Editor: Margaret E. Thrall

84

THE FAITH OF JESUS CHRIST IN EARLY CHRISTIAN TRADITIONS

The faith of Jesus Christ in early Christian Traditions

IAN G. WALLIS

Chaplain and
Director of Studies in Theology
Sidney Sussex College, Cambridge

CAMBRIDGE
UNIVERSITY PRESS

CAMBRIDGE UNIVERSITY PRESS
Cambridge, New York, Melbourne, Madrid, Cape Town, Singapore, São Paulo

Cambridge University Press
The Edinburgh Building, Cambridge CB2 2RU, UK

Published in the United States of America by Cambridge University Press, New York

www.cambridge.org
Information on this title: www.cambridge.org/9780521473521

First published 1995
This digitally printed first paperback version 2005

A catalogue record for this publication is available from the British Library

Library of Congress Cataloguing in Publication data

Wallis, Ian G.
The faith of Jesus Christ in early Christian traditions / Ian G. Wallis.
p. cm. – (Monograph series / Society for New Testament Studies: 84)
Revision of the author's thesis (doctoral), University of Sheffield, 1991.
Includes bibliographical references and index.
ISBN 0 521 47352 7 (hardback)
1. Jesus Christ – History of doctrines – Early church, ca. 30–600.
2. Jesus Christ – Spiritual life. 3. Bible. N.T. – Criticism, interpretation, etc. I. Title. II. Series: Monograph series (Society for New Testament Studies): 84.
BT590.S65W35 1995
232′.09′0 15–dc20 94–16358 CIP

ISBN-13 978-0-521-47352-1 hardback
ISBN-10 0-521-47352-7 hardback

ISBN-13 978-0-521-01884-5 paperback
ISBN-10 0-521-01884-6 paperback

MARY THERESE WALLIS

in gratitude for a life shared . . .

. . . in anticipation of future reunions . . .

'from her core faith's flame kindled strong'.

CONTENTS

PREFACE

This project has been my travelling companion through a number of significant transitions in life: much of the ground work was undertaken when employed in the business world, it subsequently took shape during theological college training and parochial ministry, and has finally come to fruition in the midst of a chaplaincy in Cambridge. Throughout this journey, many people have helped and in different ways. On a financial level, the trustees of the Sheffield Grammar School Exhibition Fund and the C. F. D. Moule Scholarship Fund made generous contributions, whilst access to libraries in Cambridge (Divinity Faculty, Federation of Theological Colleges, Tyndale House and the University) and Sheffield (University) have proved invaluable.

I have attempted in the footnotes to indicate my debt to those scholars whose work has informed my thinking and I trust that their views have been faithfully represented. Special thanks, however, are due to my doctoral supervisor, Dr Loveday Alexander, and examiners, Professor Richard Bauckham and Dr Andrew Lincoln. Dr Margaret Thrall and Mr Alex Wright, together with the production staff at Cambridge University Press, have also been most helpful in preparing the work for publication.

Family and friends have also played a big part in keeping the 'show on the road' and I am most grateful for their interest, encouragement and prayers. In particular, my father has faithfully monitored progress and offered help where possible. As always, my wife Liz has been a constant source of inspiration and assistance; both she and our good friend Mr Harvey Hames read the entire manuscript and made helpful comments.

I have a vivid memory of a milestone passed in early childhood when it became obvious that I would struggle with matters academic; on that occasion it was reading – later it would be theology. My mother had the unenviable task of trying to comfort me then and in the coming years she carried on believing in me long after I and many others had given up. It is my deepest regret that she did not live long enough to witness my ordination to the priesthood. This work is but a small 'thank you' for her love and faith in me.

CONVENTION FOR REFERRING TO PRIMARY AND SECONDARY LITERATURE

Primary sources

Unless otherwise indicated, biblical translations are taken from the *Revised Standard Version*. Editions of primary sources and translations are cited wherever possible by series rather than by individual volume; details of these are provided in the list of abbreviations. If a reference does not indicate which edition has been used, the standard versions as defined in the primary sources section of the bibliography should be assumed. References to non-biblical primary sources adopt the following format; context determines how much of this information is relevant:

Primary source – author; work; book; chapter, section or page; verse, sub-section or line (e.g. Irenaeus, *Haer.* IV.37.5).

Edition (in square brackets): edition of text, usually by series; volume; page or column (e.g. Irenaeus, *Haer.* IV.37.5. [SC 100.933]).

Translation (preceded by trans.; an asterisk * indicates that the translation has been revised in some way): translation, usually by series; volume; page (e.g. Irenaeus, *Haer.* IV.37.5. [SC 100.933]; trans.* ANCL 9.39).

Secondary literature

Secondary literature is cited in the text and footnotes in abbreviated form, using the author, short title and page number convention. Full details are provided in the bibliography at the end.

ABBREVIATIONS

Primary sources – texts, translations and series

ACW — Ancient Christian Writers: The Works of the Fathers in Translation, edited by J. Quasten and J. C. Plumpe, many vols. (London: Longmans, Green and Co, 1952).

AF — *The Apostolic Fathers*, edited by J. B. Lightfoot (London: Macmillan, 1891).

ANCL — Ante-Nicene Christian Library: Translations of the Writings of the Fathers Down to AD 325, edited by A. Roberts and J. Donaldson, 24 vols. (Edinburgh: T. & T. Clark, 1884–8).

ANF — The Ante-Nicene Fathers: Translations of the Writings of the Fathers Down to AD 325, edited by A. Roberts and J. Donaldson, 10 vols. (Grand Rapids: Eerdmans, 1951–3).

APOT — *The Apocrypha and Pseudepigrapha of the Old Testament in English*, edited by R. H. Charles, 2 vols. (Oxford: Clarendon Press, 1913).

ApV — *Die Apostolischen Väter*, edited by K. Bihlmeyer (Tübingen: J. C. B. Mohr [Paul Siebeck], 1956).

CC — *Origen: Contra Celsum*, edited by H. Chadwick (Cambridge: Cambridge University Press, 1953).

CCG — Corpus Christianorum, Series Graeca, many vols. (Breplos, Turnhout: Leuven University Press, 1977–).

CCL — Corpus Christianorum, Series Latina, many vols. (Breplos, Turnhout: Leuven University Press, 1954–).

DSSU — *The Dead Sea Scrolls Uncovered*, edited by R. Eisenman and M. Wise (Shaftesbury: Element Books, 1992).

ECF — *The Early Christian Fathers*, edited by H. Bettenson (Oxford: Oxford University Press, 1956).

EIA	*Epistula Iacobi Apocrypha*, edited by M. Malinine, H.-C. Puech, G. Quispel, W. Till and R. Kasser (Zürich: Rascher Verlag, 1968).
EV	*Evangelium Veritas*, edited by M. Malinine, H.-C. Puech and G. Quispel (Zürich: Rascher Verlag, 1956).
EWQ	*The Essene Writings from Qumran*, edited by A. Dupont-Sommer (trans. G. Vermes; Gloucester, Mass: Peter Smith, 1973).
GCS	Die griechischen christlichen Schriftsteller der ersten drei Jahrhunderte, many vols. (Berlin: Akadamie Verlag, 1897–).
IG	*Inscriptiones Graecae*, edited by Preussische Akademie der Wissenschaften zu Berlin, many vols. (1873–)
LCC	The Library of Christian Classics, edited by J. Baillie, J. T. McNeill and P. van Dusen, 26 vols. (London: SCM Press, 1953–66).
LCL	Loeb Classical Library, many vols. (London/Cambridge, Mass: Heinemann/ Harvard, 1912–).
NPNF	A Select Library of the Nicene and Post-Nicene Fathers of the Christian Church, edited by P. Schaff and H. Wace, 2 series, many vols. (Grand Rapids: Eerdmans, 1956).
NTA	*New Testament Apocrypha*, edited by E. Hennecke and W. Schneemelcher, 2 vols. (trans. R. McL. Wilson; London: Lutterworth, 1963 & 1965).
OECT	Oxford Early Christian Texts, edited by H. Chadwick, many vols. (Oxford: Clarendon Press, 1971–).
OrAth	*The Orations of St Athanasius against the Arians – According to the Benedictine Text*, edited by W. Bright (Oxford: Clarendon Press, 1873).
OrS	*Die Oracula Sibyllina*, edited by J. Geffcken (Leipzig: J. C. Hinrichs'sche Verlag, 1902).
OSol	*The Odes of Solomon*, edited by J. H. Charlesworth (Oxford: Clarendon Press, 1973).
OTP	*Old Testament Pseudepigrapha*, edited by J. H. Charlesworth, 2 vols. (London: Darton, Longman & Todd, 1983 & 1985).
PG	Patrologiae Graeca, edited by J. P. Migne, 162 vols. (Paris, 1857–66).

PJer *Paraleipomena Jeremiou*, edited by R. A. Kraft and A.-E. Purintun (Missoula: SBL, 1972).

PL Patrologiae Latinae, edited by J. P. Migne, 221 vols. (Paris, 1844–64).

SC Sources chrétiennes, edited by H. de Lubac and J. Daniélou, many vols. (Paris: Éditions du Cerf, 1945–).

Secondary literature – publishers, periodicals and works of reference

BAGD *A Greek-English Lexicon of the New Testament and Other Early Christian Literature*, initial translation and adaptation of W. Bauer's original by W. F. Arndt and F. W. Gingrich, subsequently revised and augmented by F. W. Gingrich and F. W Danker, 2nd edn. (Chicago/London: Chicago University Press, 1979).

BFD *A Greek Grammar of the New Testament and Other Early Christian Literature*, by F. Blass and A. Debrunner (trans. R. Funk; Cambridge: Cambridge University Press, 1961).

CBQ *Catholic Biblical Quarterly*.

EWNT *Exegetisches Wörterbuch zum Neuen Testament*, edited by H. Balz and G. Schneider, many vols. (Stuttgart: Kohlhammer, 1978–).

ExpT *Expository Times*.

GNTG *A Grammar of New Testament Greek*, edited by J. H. Moulton (vol. 1), W. F. Howard (vol. 2), N. Turner (vols. 3 & 4), 4 vols. (Edinburgh: T. & T. Clark, 1906–76).

HeyJ *Heythrop Journal*.

HTR *Harvard Theological Review*.

JBL *Journal of Biblical Literature*.

JBR *Journal of Bible and Religion*.

JES *Journal of Ecumenical Studies*.

JJS *Journal of Jewish Studies*.

JSNT *Journal for the Study of the New Testament*.

JSOT *Journal for the Study of the Old Testament*.

JTS *Journal of Theological Studies*.

NIDNTT *The New International Dictionary of New Testament Theology*, edited by C. Brown, 3 vols. (Exeter: Paternoster, 1975–8).

NKZ — *Neue kirchliche Zeitschrift.*
NovT — *Novum Testamentum.*
NTS — *New Testament Studies.*
RAC — *Reallexikon für Antike und Christentum: Sachwörterbuch zur Auseinandersetzung des Christentums mit der antiken Welt*, edited by T. Klausner, many vols. (Stuttgart: Hiersemann, 1950–).
RGG — *Die Religion in Geschichte und Gegenwart*, edited by K. Galling, 3rd edn., 7 vols. (Tübingen: J. C. B. Mohr [Paul Siebeck], 1957–65).
RTR — *Reformed Theological Review.*
SB — *Kommentar zum Neuen Testament*, by H. Strack and P. Billerbeck, 6 vols. (Munich: Beck, 1922–61).
SBL — Society of Biblical Literature.
SJT — *Scottish Journal of Theology.*
SPCK — Society for Promoting Christian Knowledge.
TDNT — *Theological Dictionary of the New Testament*, edited by G. Kittel and G. Friedrich, 10 vols. (trans. G. W. Bromiley; Grand Rapids: Eerdmans, 1964–76).
TDOT — *Theological Dictionary of the Old Testament*, edited by G. J. Botterweck and H. Ringgren, many vols. (trans. J. T. Willis, G. W. Bromiley and D. E. Green; Grand Rapids: Eerdmans, 1974–).
TLG — *Thesaurus Linguae Graecae*, edited by L. Berkowitz and K. A. Squitier, 2nd edn. (Oxford: Oxford University Press, 1986).
ZAW — *Zeitschrift für alttestamentliche Wissenschaft.*
ZNW — *Zeitschrift für neutestamentliche Wissenschaft.*
ZST — *Zeitschrift für systematische Theologie.*
ZTK — *Zeitschrift für Theologie und Kirche.*

Secondary literature – series

AGJU — Arbeiten zur Geschichte des antiken Judentums und des Urchristentums.
ALGHJ — Arbeiten zur Literatur und Geschichte des hellenistischen Judentums.

ANTJ	Arbeiten zum Neuen Testament und Judentum.
BETL	Bibliotheca ephemeridum theologicarum Lovaniensium.
BGBE	Beiträge zur Geschichte der biblischen Exegese.
BNTC	Black's New Testament Commentaries.
BZNW	Beihefte zur Zeitschrift für die neutestamentliche Wissenschaft.
CGNT	Cambridge Greek Testament Commentaries.
EKKNT	Evangelisch-Katholischer Kommentar zum Neuen Testament.
FRLANT	Forschungen zur Religion und Literatur des Alten und Neuen Testaments.
HNT	Handbuch zum Neuen Testament.
HTKNT	Herders theologischer Kommentar zum Neuen Testament.
ICC	International Critical Commentary.
JSNTSS	*Journal for the Study of the New Testament* – Supplementary Series.
KEK	Kritisch-Exegetischer Kommentar über das Neue Testament.
NICNT	New International Commentary on the New Testament.
NIGTC	New International Greek Testament Commentary.
NovTSup	Supplements to *Novum Testamentum.*
NTL	New Testament Library.
OTL	Old Testament Library.
ÖTNT	Ökumenischer Taschenbuchkommentar zum Neuen Testament.
SANT	Studien zum Alten und Neuen Testament.
SBLDS	Society of Biblical Literature Dissertation Series.
SBLMS	Society of Biblical Literature Monograph Series.
SBT	Studies in Biblical Theology.
SNTSMS	Society for New Testament Studies Monograph Series.
SNTU	Studien zum Neuen Testament und seiner Unwelt.
SNTW	Studies of the New Testament and its World.
THKNT	Theologischer Handkommentar zum Neuen Testament.
TNTC	Tyndale New Testament Commentaries.
TSK	Theologische Studien und Kritiken.
TU	Texte und Untersuchungen.
WBC	Word Biblical Commentary.

WMANT	Wissenschaftliche Monographien zum Alten und Neuen Testament.
WUNT	Wissenschaftliche Untersuchungen zum Neuen Testament.
ZB	Züricher Bibelkommentare.

1

SETTING THE SCENE

1 The context for the present study

The issue of Jesus' faith, as opposed to faith in or directed towards him, is not a new one. It has been raised previously by theologians and biblical exegetes alike, but seemingly the matter has never been conclusively resolved one way or the other. From one perspective, we have Thomas Aquinas' celebrated refutation of faith as an attribute of the human condition assumed by the Son of God. Having presented a case for Christ's faith, which cites Romans 1.17 and Hebrews 12.2 in support, he then demonstrates its untenability:

> The field of faith is divine reality that is hidden from sight. This we maintained in the *Secunda Pars*. Now, a virtue, like any other habit, takes its character from its field of action. Hence, where divine reality is not hidden from sight there is no point in faith. But from the moment of conception Christ had the full vision of the very being of God, as we will hold later on. Therefore he could not have had faith.
>
> Hence: (i) The reason faith ranks higher than the moral virtues is that it deals with more important affairs than they do. Yet it handles these affairs with certain limitations. Now Christ suffered no such limitations. And so, even though he did have moral virtues he could not have had faith. For the moral virtues do not carry the kind of limitation faith does in dealing with their own particular material. (ii) The moral value of faith comes from accepting, out of obedience to God, things which are not clearly seen. Thus, St Paul speaks of *the obedience of faith for the sake of his name among all the nations*. But Christ practised the ultimate obedience to God, as is written, *He became obedient*

> *unto death*. So, he taught no moral values which he himself had not already achieved in a higher way.[1]

We may note here how theological considerations prove determinative as Aquinas assumes that the nature of the incarnate Son's relationship with God excludes the possibility of his demonstrating faith, regardless of scriptural precedent.[2] In contrast to this, however, emphasis upon Christ's identification with humanity has led to the opposite conclusion. Maurice Wiles expresses it thus:

> But the vision to which Jesus gives rise is not only a vision of God. If Jesus is the 'image of God', that implies not only that to see him is to see the Father, but also that to see him is to see man as he is intended to be in the design of God's creation . . . So in reading the story of Jesus not merely as a historian but with the concern of faith, I am seeking to see in it a way of faith for myself as a believer too.[3]

In this case, focus upon the nature of the relationship between Jesus and others permits, if not requires, the former to be seen as one who shares faith. Further, the perspective of a common humanity, articulated this time in terms of an existential correspondence between the experience of Jesus and that of others, has also yielded fruit in the domain of biblical exegesis, both in terms of specific texts which speak of Jesus' faith[4] and of broader conceptions of Jesus' relationship to God as expressed in the Gospels.[5] But here again there have been problems and not only in terms of interpretation of key references, but also at the level of presupposition. In this latter respect, Rudolf Bultmann criticises Gerhard Ebeling for using the bridge of faith, linking believers with Jesus, to speak in a historicising manner of the latter's personal disposition:

[1] Aquinas, *Summa Theologiae*, 3a.7.3.

[2] 'In the first case, that of Aquinas, it is probably not so much the neat either-or distinction between faith and vision (read: faith and revelation) that finds an echo in so many minds, not so much this as the more general unreflecting conviction that belief in the divinity of Jesus rules out all possibility of envisaging a personal faith of Jesus himself.' (Mackey, 'Historical Jesus', 162–3)

[3] Wiles, *Faith*, 61–2; also Baillie, *Faith*, 231–63; Cook, 'Call', 679–700; Ebeling, *Nature*, 44–57; Gogarten, *Christ*, 38–4, 235–53; Mackey, *Jesus*, 159–71.

[4] The seminal work here is still Gerhard Ebeling's article, 'Jesus and Faith', in *Word*, 201–46; also Mackey, 'Historical Jesus', 155–74, and Thüsing, 'New Testament', 143–59.

[5] Especially, Sobrino, *Christology*, 79–145; also Cairns, *Faith*, esp. 218–23; E. Fuchs, *Studies*, 48–64; Schoonenberg, *Christ*, 146–52; cf. Braun, 'Meaning', 89–127.

> The Gospels do not speak of Jesus' own faith, nor does the kerygma make reference to it. To be sure, Ebeling most appropriately describes the structure of faith as an existential stance. When he says, however, that 'it would be impossible to exempt Jesus himself from an act of faith in view of the way in which he speaks of it,' then like Fuchs he deduces the personal attitude of the historical Jesus from an understanding of existence present in his activity and becoming audible in his words. He thus confuses the existential encounter with an objectifying view. When he states that 'a structural uniqueness of faith' lies in the fact 'that the origin of faith is directed to an encounter with the witnesses of faith,' then by 'witnesses of faith' he evidently means believers who witness to their faith, whereas the kerygma does not permit any inquiry into the personal faith of the preacher.[6]

Whilst much of the discussion about Jesus' faith has focussed upon the significance of his life and ministry for understanding the nature and content of human response to God and, as such, has tended to revolve around references gleaned from the Synoptic Gospels and the Epistle to the Hebrews,[7] the issue has also come to expression within more overtly theological contexts. In this respect, recent years have witnessed a renewed interest[8] in the question of whether the apostle Paul draws attention to the faith of Christ either as the basis for Christ's obedience – and, indeed, all human response – to God or as a channel for God's faithfulness in Christ to all people.[9] But once again differences in exegesis and, indeed, presupposition have prevented a consensus being reached.

[6] Bultmann, 'Primitive', 34. That Bultmann's stance here is not informed by critical exegesis is evident from a footnote accompanying this quotation: 'In Heb. 12.2, Jesus is described as the "pioneer and perfector of our faith". But this is not a description of Jesus as a believer, as Ebeling would suppose, for he does not appear in the "cloud of witnesses" in Heb. 11.'

[7] Key passages include: Matt. 17.14–20/Mark 9.14–29; Matt. 21.18–22/Mark 11.12–14, 20–25; Heb. 3.1–6; 12.1–2; also Rev. 1.5; 2.13; 3.14; 14.12; 19.11.

[8] It should be noted, however, that the question of whether the πίστις Χριστοῦ constructions in Paul (e.g. Rom. 3.22, 26; Gal. 2.16, 20; 3.22; Phil. 3.9; cf. Gal. 3:26 [𝔓46]; Eph. 3:12) refer to Christ's personal faith was raised by German-speaking scholars at the turn of the century: Haussleiter, 'Glaube', 109–45, and 205–30; Kittel, 'Πίστις', 419–36; cf. Schläger, 'Bemerkungen', 356–8.

[9] As we shall see in chapter 3, the contemporary debate is considerably more nuanced than these two alternatives suggest, although most if not all positions can be accommodated within the proposed anthropological–theological polarity.

One drawback with most discussions of Jesus' faith to date is that they fail to give adequate consideration to the extent of the early church's interest in this theme or to assess its significance in relation to other christological development. On the one hand, theological studies cite scriptural precedent to support rather than provide the point of departure for consideration of Jesus' faith; on the other hand, biblical exegesis identifies reference to Jesus' faith in certain passages, whilst the broader theological implications remain largely unexplored. As a result, the basis for interpreting Jesus as one who demonstrated faith remains both incoherent and inconclusive.[10] It is in response to this unsatisfactory situation that the present study is offered.

2 The scope of the present study

The purpose of this investigation is to assess whether early Christian traditions bear witness to interest in the faith of Jesus Christ and, if they do, to ask why.[11] Our approach is primarily exegetical with emphasis upon the theological issues raised by the texts considered. The larger part of the study is devoted to the New Testament, but relevant antecedent material together with extra-canonical sources suggestive of our theme will also be discussed. We aim, therefore, to trace the early church's concern with Jesus' faith from inception to conclusion or decline and, as part of this exercise, we shall attempt

10 For example, J. D. G. Dunn, commenting on whether Mark 11.23 speaks of Jesus' faith, claims that, as the more primitive versions of Matt. 17.20 and Luke 17.6 do not permit this interpretation, this possibility is certainly not original and at best originates in Markan redaction. He then concludes that, as there are no other substantial data in the Synoptic Gospels suggestive of Jesus' faith, 'Jesus is the witness of grace not the witness of faith.' (*Jesus*, 75) It seems strange, firstly, that there is no mention of Mark 9.23 in this context, to say nothing of the relevant texts in Paul, Hebrews and Revelation mentioned earlier, and, secondly, that the origins of Mark's interest in Jesus' faith does not merit further consideration. And again, during his discussion of Rom. 3.22, Professor Dunn maintains that the likelihood of the verse referring to Christ's faith(fulness) is rendered less probable as this theme receives no further consideration in the letter (*Romans*, vol. 1, 166); but this assumes that other possible references should not be taken in this way (e.g. Rom. 1.17; 3.25–26; also Gal. 2.16, 20; 3.22; Phil. 3.9). This atomising approach inevitably shrouds the cumulative force of the case for Jesus' faith; see also 'Once More', 737.

11 It should be noted that we are not concerned directly with whether the earthly figure of Jesus demonstrated faith; however, it would be naïve to suppose that our findings have no bearing upon this issue. For example, if it can be shown that the early church was interested in the faith of Jesus, the question of where that interest originated becomes pertinent.

to identify areas of correspondence or similarity between traditions reflecting such interest.

In order to provide a framework within which evidence can be understood and its cumulative significance assessed, we have adopted the notion of a trajectory.[12] Thus, in addition to assessing the contribution of individual sources, we shall also consider each one as a node on a trajectory running through Christian tradition and, as such, as part of a broader trend or concern. The model of a trajectory is helpful here in that it accommodates the ideas of progression and correlation without ignoring the particularity of individual texts or requiring us to demonstrate either literary dependency or a precise path of development. It must be emphasised that we are not trying to superimpose a degree of homogeneity upon otherwise divergent material, but to provide a fresh perspective on evidence suggestive of interest in Jesus' faith which, when viewed in isolation, lacks coherence against the broader backcloth of development in Christian thought. In consequence, it may prove necessary to consider a more complex pattern than a single linear progression and entertain, for example, a number of parallel trajectories.

There are, however, ramifications implicit within this methodology which should be recognised from the outset. Firstly, the study is not exhaustive in that we have not been able to survey every relevant source nor, indeed, to discuss fully those included. As a result, the emphasis has been upon establishing the existence of and basis for interest in Jesus' faith by focusing upon representative instances. The issue of Jesus' faith is such that, once a case has been made, a much greater selection of evidence becomes pertinent.

Secondly, our case is ultimately a cumulative one. Whilst each chapter is an independent unit and may be judged on its own merits, evaluation of whether the early church was interested in Jesus' faith rests upon assessing the trajectory or trajectories as a whole. Without this perspective, it is impossible to do justice to the evidence since however eloquently a text may speak of Jesus' faith, it will always appear to be a solitary island in a sea of silence. To this end, it is hoped that by adopting a broader outlook we shall be able to suggest contexts in the life of nascent Christianity where talk of Jesus' faith would have been meaningful.

[12] The notion of trajectory as a means of understanding developments in early Christianity was introduced by Robinson and Köster, *Trajectories*; see also, for example: Dunn, *Unity*; Köster, *Introduction*; Kloppenborg, *Formation*.

Thirdly, there is inevitably a degree of circularity involved in our approach: a trajectory is only the sum of constituent nodes, the grouping and significance of which may only exist as part of that trajectory, which then contributes towards the meaning of each individual node. However, we maintain that this dialectical relationship between phenomena and hermeneutical framework is integral to all interpretation and cannot be circumvented;[13] we do not believe, therefore, that our method is qualitatively more or less subjective than those underpinning views which will be challenged in the course of this investigation. As with all interpretation, we ask that our conclusions be judged in terms of their adequacy in relation to the phenomena they purport to explain and their coherence with respect to broader canons of understanding.

One further presupposition which has been adopted is that Christian believers in the early centuries could have considered the figure of Jesus to be important not only for what he revealed of God, but also for what he revealed of human response to God. This point hardly needs substantiation, but is none the less easily overlooked when evaluating traditions in which the primary focus is Jesus' theological significance. However, the nature of the gospel form,[14] the correspondence between Jesus and the disciples as characterised by the Synoptic Evangelists[15] and the parallels between the ministries of Jesus and those of the apostles as seen in Luke-Acts,[16] all suggest reflection upon Jesus in terms of Christian discipleship.

How then are we going to identify interest in Jesus' faith? On the one hand, faith is a polymorphous concept which cannot simply be

[13] For example, consider two current interpretative models drawn from the philosophical writings of H.-G. Gadamer (e.g. *Truth*, esp. 267–74, 333–41) and L. Wittgenstein (e.g. *Investigations*). Firstly, the notion of interpretation as a dialectical process leading to a fusion between the horizons of the early Christian author and the modern exegete. Secondly, the construction of a 'language game' on the part of the interpreter which gives meaning or significance to the ancient text. Both these methodologies recognise the substantial contribution of the interpreter within the process and, in this respect, are similar to the 'trajectory approach'. All three acknowledge that we have no access to early Christian or other ancient traditions apart from our own 'subjective' apprehension of them; to this end, 'objective' interpretation is a matter of providing a hermeneutic in which a text can be heard, given meaning and understood. See the discussion of Thiselton, *Two Horizons*, esp. 293–325 and 386–427.

[14] Stanton, *Jesus*, 117–36; also Burridge, *Gospels*, esp. 191–219, 240–59.

[15] Hengel, *Leader*, 38–88, and Riesner, *Jesus*, 408–98.

[16] Franklin, *Christ*, 145–72; Miller, Character, 231; Neirynck, 'Miracle Stories', 182–8.

equated with a particular word group;[17] on the other hand, the πιστεύω root, which is the principal referent to faith for Christian traditions written in Greek, has a broader semantic field than is relevant to our study.[18] It seems that we need to be both more specific than a word study and more encompassing at the same time. Our primary concern is with faith as a relational phenomenon normally demonstrated by a human being in response to God; by investigating Jesus' faith, therefore, we are looking for evidence suggesting interest in or reflection upon Jesus' faith-relationship with God.[19]

Clearly, there are many aspects of Jesus' life which could be considered characteristic of his faith, such as his prayer life[20] and his miracle-working ability.[21] Whilst such phenomena can be interpreted in this light, they need not be and, as a result, prove inconclusive for our purpose. We shall, therefore, focus primarily upon contexts where the πιστεύω group is present.[22] This approach has at least two advantages: firstly, it removes much of the ambiguity regarding whether reference to Jesus' faith is intended and,

[17] Good introductions to the philosophical and theological dimensions of faith are provided by: Binder, *Glaube*, 11–28; Bogdan, *Belief*; Evans, 'Faith', 1–19 and 199–212; Hick, *Faith*; Mackey, 'Theology', 207–37; Swinburne, *Faith*. On faith as a phenomenon in the Christian tradition, see especially: Baillie, *Faith*; Buber, *Two Types*; Hahn and Klein, *Glaube*; Hermisson and Lohse, *Faith*; Lührmann, *Glaube*; Schlatter, *Glaube*.

[18] The classic treatment is that of Bultmann and Weiser, 'πιστεύω', 174–228; additional material is presented in: Burton, *Galatians*, 475–85; Ebeling, *Word*, 201–46; Jepsen, 'אָמַן', 292–323; Lampe, *Lexicon*, 1082–8; Lohse, 'Emuna', 147–63; Lührmann, 'Pistis', 19–38.

[19] Much of the difficulty regarding the possibility of Jesus demonstrating faith stems from a failure to distinguish between the phenomenon of faith and the belief structure through which it is articulated. However, the fact that Jesus Christ was considered central to Christian belief after the resurrection, does not mean that he may not have been thought to share in faith at a stage when it was expressed in more theological (as opposed to christological) terms. On faith as a phenomenon prior to belief, see: Cook, 'Call', 679–700; Panikkar, 'Faith', 223–54; Smith, *History*, esp. 36–99; *Faith*, esp. 128–72; cf. Wainwright's criticism of Smith ('Wilfred Cantwell Smith', 353–66). Whilst the distinction between 'faith' as a mode of being and 'belief' as a means of communicating such faith can be helpful, the relation between these two elements is intimate and two-way.

[20] E. Fuchs, *Studies*, esp. 61–4, and Theunissen, 'Gebetsglaube', 13–68.

[21] Ebeling, *Word*, esp. 230–2, and Nolan, *Jesus*, 30–6. In a more general sense, Vermes, *Jesus*, esp. 49–54, suggests that much of Jesus' life is suggestive of a climate of *'emûnâh*.

[22] A similar starting point is adopted by C. D. Marshall in his investigation of faith in Mark's Gospel (*Faith*, 30–3). It should be noted that where sources are not written in Greek, the equivalent word-group/s will be considered (e.g. *'āman* in Hebrew, *fides* or *credo* in Latin).

secondly, as our concern is to establish whether the early church was specifically interested in the faith of Jesus, we shall be on firmer ground when concentrating on instances where attention is drawn to it.

We have already indicated that our controlling interest is the disposition of faith and not the πιστεύω word group, although the latter has been adopted as a means to the former. We are concerned, in particular, with faith in its relational sense. This encompasses two sets of characteristics: the characteristics of the basis for the relationship (e.g. trust, belief, hope, conviction, etc.) and those of the outworkings of the relationship (e.g. faithfulness, obedience, action, petition, etc.). Where texts permit specificity, we shall indicate in what sense Jesus' faith is conceived; where this is not possible, a more general comment will be made. Unless otherwise indicated, the word *faith* is used throughout this study to embrace the overall phenomenon and not a particular element or characteristic of it.[23]

Before commencing our investigation, it will be helpful to explore some of the ways in which faith was understood and expressed in Jewish, Classical and Hellenistic sources prior to and contemporaneous with the early Christian traditions we shall be considering. This is an important exercise for whilst Christianity would, in due course, bring a new definition to faith and, arguably, invest it with a new level of importance as a religious response, it would be wrong to think of the resurrection of Jesus Christ as the birth of faith. Faith was already an integral part of the religious mind-set at the time when the books of the New Testament were being written and it would be quite impossible to grasp the meaning of faith in early Christian traditions without an appreciation of how it was understood in Judaism and elsewhere. Our concern at this stage is not to establish firm lines of development or dependency, but to illustrate a *milieu* by offering a number of preliminary observations, supported by examples from a range of primary sources, about how the phenomenon of faith was understood and how the πιστεύω group was used.

23 On the range of meaning of the English words 'faith' and 'belief', see: O'Connor, *Faith*, xi-xx; Smith, *History*, 36–69; *Faith*, 105–27.

3 The meanings of faith in early Christian times

The phenomenon of faith as an interpersonal relationship between human beings or between humanity and God is by no means a Christian innovation. For instance, within the Jewish tradition it is amply attested throughout the Old Testament and is often articulated by means of the *'āman* root. It also comes to expression via more narrative forms in stories of faith relating crucial events in Israel's history or incidents in the lives of her central figures.[24] In this latter respect, Abraham is particularly prominent as can be seen by the way in which later interpretations often explicitly identify him as a man of faith or emphasise references to his faith attested in the pentateuchal traditions.[25] For example:

> ' . . . that words came in heaven concerning Abraham that he was faithful in everything which was told him and he loved the Lord and was faithful in all affliction . . . And I have made known to all that you are faithful to me in everything which I say to you. Go in peace.' (Jub. 17.15 and 18.16) 'Was not Abraham found faithful when tested, and it was reckoned to him as righteousness?' (1 Macc. 2.52) 'Shema'yah says: "The faith with which their father Abraham believed in Me is deserving that I should divide the sea for them." For it is said: "And he believed in the Lord . . ." . . . And so also you find that our father Abraham inherited both this world and the world beyond only as a reward for the faith with which he believed, as it is said: "And he believed in the Lord . . ."' (Mek., Beshallah on Exod. 14.15 and 14.31) 'That God marvelling at Abraham's faith in Him repaid him with faithfulness by confirming with an oath the gifts which He had promised, and here He no longer talked with him as God with man but as a friend with a familiar.' (Philo, *Abr*. 273; trans. LCL 289.133) 'And he had faith in the word of the Lord and it was reckoned to him for merit because he did not argue before him with words.' (Tg. Ps.-J. on Gen. 15.6; trans. Bowker, *Targums*,

[24] In this respect, the foremost event is the Exodus, whilst Abraham, Moses and David are well used personnel. The use of these and other stories to inform the Jewish view of faith is explored by: Brueggemann, *Man*, *passim*; *Hope*, esp. 7–26; Hermisson and Lohse, *Faith*, 10–46.

[25] For fuller discussions of Abraham in Jewish traditions, see: Clements, *Abraham*, 52–8; Hansen, *Abraham*, 175–99; Jeremias, ''Αβραάμ', 8–9; SB, vol. 3, 186–201.

201; also: 2 Macc. 1.2; Neh. 9.7–8; Philo, *Rer. Div. Her.* 94; Sir. 44.19–21; Tg. Onq. on Gen. 15.6; cf. Rom. 4; Gal. 3; Heb. 12)

The use of narrative as a vehicle for exploring the meaning of faith in the Old Testament and other Jewish literature alerts us to the importance attributed to praxis in this sphere. It suggests that the definition of faith was conceived as a reactive process of reflection upon events and characters in Jewish history, rather than as a proactive construction of belief patterns dependent upon more philosophical or abstracted thinking. Whilst not necessarily indicating a polarisation between intellectual and expressive dimensions of faith,[26] this does indicate that certain aspects of the phenomenon of faith were considered to be most adequately communicated by the lives and conduct of key exponents. We are not denying here the hagiographical significance of literature relating the lives of the great Jewish heroes, but identifying an additional didactic or emulative function in which these figures incarnate what it means to live by faith and, by doing so, provide tangible and concrete examples for others to follow. Thus, together with more formal declarations of belief and conduct,[27] the substance of faith within Jewish traditions prior to and around the time of the New Testament is developed primarily in terms of people and situations rather than abstract propositions.[28]

General support for this assessment is provided by the case-law approach adopted in the Mishnah and other Jewish writings, whereby the conduct and utterances of figures in Israel's past act as precedents for particular directions or injunctions.[29] More specific-

26 Cf. Martin Buber's rigid distinction between Jewish faith, characterised by a relationship of trust, and Christian faith, characterised by a relationship of acknowledgement (*Two Types*, 7–12 and *passim*); on the inadequacy of this stance, see: Lindsay, *Josephus*, esp. 165–89; Lohse, 'Emuna', 147–63; Oesterreicher, *Dialogue*, 74–98.

27 Within the Old Testament these can be found, for example, in the *Shema* and the *Decalogue* (Deut. 6.4–5 and Exod. 20.1–17). On the significance and later development of statements of faith in Judaism, see Urbach, *Sages*, esp. 1–36.

28 This is also apparent, for example, in the ways in which the Psalms provide a language for faith rooted in the experiences of the people; knowledge of God results from reflection upon divine encounter and absence.

29 This technique is too extensive to annotate in detail, but the following examples, which are taken from the Mishnah and indicate how support for particular courses of action is provided by Abraham and Moses, should be illustrative: 'R Nehorai says [in a debate about the relative value of different occupations]: I would set aside all the crafts in the world and teach my son naught save the Law, for a man enjoys the reward thereof in this world and its whole worth remains for

ally and somewhat later, we find this technique in the Mekilta de Rabbi Ishmael, where the need for each Israelite to have faith is both substantiated by and illustrated from the lives of Abraham and Moses:

> Great indeed is faith before Him who spoke and the world came into being. For as a reward for the faith with which Israel believed in God, the Holy Spirit rested upon them and they uttered the song; as it was said: 'And they believed in the Lord ... Then sang Moses and the children of Israel' (Ex. 14.3; 15.1). R. Nehemiah says: Whence can you prove that whosoever accepts even one single commandment with true faith is deserving of having the Holy Spirit rest upon him? We find this to have been the case with our fathers. For as a reward for the faith with which they believed, they were considered worthy of having the Holy Spirit rest upon them, so that they could utter the song, as it is said: 'And they believed in the Lord ... Then sang Moses and the children of Israel.' And so also you find that our father Abraham inherited both this world and the world beyond only as a reward for the faith with which he believed, as it is said: 'And he believed in the Lord,' etc. (Gen. 15.6). And so also you find that Israel was redeemed from Egypt only as a reward for the faith with which they believed, as it is said: 'And the people believed' (Ex. 4.31). And thus it says: 'The Lord preserveth the faithful' (Ps. 31.24) – He keeps in remembrance the faith of the fathers ... What does it say about the people of faith? 'Open ye the gates, that the righteous nation that keepeth faithfulness may enter in'

the world to come. But with all other crafts it is not so; for when a man falls into sickness or old age or troubles and cannot engage in his work, lo, he dies in hunger. But with the Law it is not so; for it guards him from all evil while he is young, and in old age it grants him a future and a hope. Of his youth, what does it say? *They that wait upon the Lord shall renew their strength.* Of his old age, what does it say? *They shall still bring forth fruit in old age.* So, too, it says of our father Abraham, *And Abraham was old and well stricken in years, and the Lord had blessed Abraham in all things.* And we find that Abraham our father had performed the whole Law before it was given, for it is written, *Because that Abraham obeyed my voice and kept my charge, my commandments, my statutes, and my laws.*' (m. Kidd. 4.14; also m. Aboth 5.19) 'The greater Sanhedrin was made up of one and seventy [judges] and the lesser [Sanhedrin] of three and twenty. Whence do we learn that the greater Sanhedrin should be made up of one and seventy? It is written, *Gather unto me seventy men of the elders of Israel*; and Moses added to them makes one and seventy.' (m. Sanh. 1.6; also m. Yoma 3.8; 4.2; 6.2; m. Ros. Has. 2.9; m. Meg. 3.4; m. Aboth 5.18)

(Isa. 26.2). In this gate, then, all people of faith shall enter. (Mek., Beshallah on Exod. 14.31)

In this extract we can discern how Abraham, Moses and the Israelites participating in the Exodus are presented as exemplars of faith who receive the concomitant benefits. Whilst these figures are spoken of in generous terms, it is clear that their conduct or attitude of faith is not simply something to be venerated, but to be followed and put into practice.[30]

One difficulty with the narrative form as a vehicle for articulating faith is the question of definition: how are we able to delimit faith and determine where it is present? In this respect, it is helpful to consider stories of faith in conjunction with lexical stock closely identified with the phenomenon and, as we have already indicated, *'āman* is the principal root utilised for this purpose in Hebrew.[31] Review of the usage of this stem in the Old Testament, however, reveals a broad range of meaning and in many cases it doesn't denote a relationship between God and humanity at all.[32] In other contexts, the *'āman* group describes a relationship between fellow human beings[33] and, on occasion, the setting for this is where one party acts as God's messenger and, as a result, response to them indirectly determines response to God.[34]

30 The emulative function of key figures has also been identified as a determinative influence for the composition of certain of the so-called 'divine man' characterisations in Classical and Hellenistic literature: 'Whether the figure in question is Plato's Socrates, Dio of Prusa's Diogenes, Plutarch's Alexander, or Philo's Moses, the elevated or even divine status of the charismatic figure rests upon his characterization as a sage and possessor of virtue who can serve as a paradigm for moral edification.' (Tiede, *Charismatic*, 291) D. L. Tiede offers a detailed treatment of these portrayals, especially Philo's Moses (101–37), but see also the assessment of C. H. Holladay (*THEIOS ANER*, 103–98).

31 A. Weiser also considers the following roots: *bāṭaḥ ḥāḵâh ḥāsâh, yāḥal, qāwâh* ('πιστεύω', 182–96).

32 In addition to Jepsen, 'אָמַן', 292–323 and the literature cited there, see: Lindsay, *Josephus*, 21–38; Lührmann, 'Pistis', 19–38; *Glaube*, 31–45; Meyer, *Rätsel*, 118–41. Although it is often difficult to give the precise meaning, the following ideas are conveyed by the *'āman* root: confirm, establish (e.g. Gen. 42.20; 1 Sam. 3.20; 1 Kings 8.26; 1 Chron. 17.23, 24; 2 Chron. 6.17; 2.20b; Job 29.24); firm, permanent, secure, steadfast, sure (e.g. Exod. 17.12; Deut. 28.59; 1 Sam. 25.28; 2 Sam. 7.16; 1 Kings 11.38; 2 Chron. 31.12, 15; 34.12; Neh. 13.13; Pss. 37.3; 89.28, 37; 93.5; 119.86; Isa. 22.23, 25; 33.6, 16; 55.3; Jer. 15.18; Hos. 5.9); honest, reliable, trustworthy, truthful (e.g. 2 Kings 12.15; 22.7; Ps. 96.13; Prov. 11.13; 12.17; 13.17; 14.5; 20.6; 25.13; 27.6; Isa. 8.2; 59.4; Jer. 5.1, 3; 7.28; 9.2); assurance, pledge (e.g. Deut. 28.66). Clearly, there is a considerable degree of overlap in these categories.

33 'But Sihon did not trust Israel to pass through the territory . . .' (Judg. 11.20; also 1 Sam. 27.12; 2 Chron. 32.15; Jer. 12.6; 40.14; Lam. 4.12; cf. relationship between humanity and animals in Job 39.12, 24)

34 'Believe in the Lord your God, and you will be established; believe his prophets, and you will succeed.' (2 Chron. 20.20c; also Exod. 4.1; 19.9)

Cases where the *'āman* root describes a relationship between God and humanity are both numerous and difficult to classify. Often it is not possible to distinguish clearly between, for example, faith as intellectual acceptance and faith as personal trust, in that both aspects are present in most occurrences, although in different proportions. This is perhaps inevitable, given that the nature of faith is such that most propositional beliefs have behavioural implications and most expressions of faith have their source in intellectual belief.[35] For example, Abraham's acceptance of God's promise that he would be the father of a great nation required him, amongst other things, to venture forth from his homeland (Gen. 12.1–3; 15.1–6); on the other hand, Isaiah's exhortation that King Ahaz should demonstrate faith by dismantling his contingency plans in the face of political disaster, assumes a certain understanding of God and his ability to help (Isa. 7.1–9).

Rather than attempting to distinguish between active and passive or intellectual and trust-like dimensions of faith, a more profitable distinction is between cases where *'āman* is used to denote response which initiates a relationship or develops it further and cases where it denotes the maintenance of an existing relationship. In the first category, *'āman* is used only of human response to divine initiative, which may take the form of miracle, promise or commandment, often resulting in the reception of salvific benefit of some kind and leading to the establishment of covenant (e.g. Gen. 15; Exod. 4):

General: 'But they would not listen, but were stubborn, as their fathers had been, who did not believe in the Lord their God.' (2 Kings 17.14; also: Deut. 1.32; 2 Chron. 20.20a; Pss. 78.22; 106.12; Isa. 7.9; 28.16; 43.10; Jonah 3.5)

Miracle: 'Then Moses answered, "But behold, they will not believe me or listen to my voice, for they will say, 'The Lord did not appear to you.'" . . . "that they may believe that the Lord, the God of their fathers, the God of Abraham, the God of Isaac, and the God of Jacob, has appeared to you." . . . "If they will not believe you," God said, "or heed the first sign, they may believe the latter sign. If they will not

[35] Although this sounds more like a philosophical judgement (cf. Swinburne, *Faith*, 3–32, 104–24) than an exegetical deduction, it does seem to accord with what we find in the Bible: James informs his readers that even the demons' belief in God causes them to shudder (Jas. 3.19), whilst the stretcher-bearers, whose faith is identified with their initiatives in bringing their friend to Jesus, must have had some prior understanding of why this endeavour was worthwhile (Matt. 9.1–8/Mark 2.1–12/Luke 5.17–26).

believe even these two signs or heed your voice" . . . And the people believed; and when they had heard that the Lord had visited the people of Israel and that he had seen their affliction, they bowed their heads and worshiped.' (Exod. 4.1, 5, 8, 9, 31; also: Exod. 14.31; Num. 14.11; Ps. 78.32)

Promise: 'And he believed the Lord; and he reckoned it to him as righteousness.' (Gen. 15.6; also: Num. 20.12; Ps. 106.24)

Commandment: '"Go up and take possession of the land which I have given you," then you rebelled against the commandment of the Lord your God, and did not believe him or obey his voice.' (Deut. 9.23)

Salvific Benefit: 'If you will not believe, surely you shall not be established.' (Isa. 7.9; also: 2 Chron. 20.20a)

Faith in these contexts constitutes the means by which people enter into relationship with God in the terms dictated by God's prior action. In the second category, *'āman* denotes both divine and human conduct with reference to an existing relationship which is usually defined in terms of covenant. Thus, God is faithful to his prior promises, actions or commitments and may entrust certain aspects of his faithfulness to others; for its part, humankind is expected likewise to respond in faithfulness:

God is faithful: 'Know therefore that the Lord your God is God, the faithful God who keeps covenant and steadfast love with those who love him and keep his commandments, to a thousand generations.' (Deut. 7.9; also: Deut. 32.4; Pss. 19.17; 33.4; 36.5; 40.10; 88.11; 89.1, 2, 5, 8, 25, 33, 49; 92.2; 98.3; 100.5; 111.7–8; 119.75, 90, 138; 143.1; Isa. 25.1; 49.7; Jer. 42.5; Lam. 3.23; Hos. 2.22)

God entrusts: 'Not so with my servant Moses; he is entrusted with all my house.' (Num. 12.7; cf. Job 4.18; 12.20; 15.15)

Humankind is faithful: 'The Lord rewards every man for his righteousness and his faithfulness; for the Lord gave you into my hand today, and I would not put out my hand against the Lord's anointed.' (1 Sam. 26.23; also: Deut. 32.20; 1 Sam. 22.14; 2 Sam. 20.19; 2 Chron. 19.9; Pss. 12.1; 31.23; 78.8, 37; 101.6; 116.10; 119.30, 66; Prov. 12.22; Isa. 26.2; Hos. 11.12; Hab. 2.4)

The significance of faith for divine–human encounter is developed further during the intertestamental period and beyond, where it increasingly characterises human response to God.[36] What is more, faith becomes the determinative factor not primarily for the maintenance of existing covenantal obligation, but for the appropriation of God's salvific benefits in the present and, especially, in the future. This trend is evident in many types of literature, including:

Apocalyptic: 'For at the end of the world, a retribution will be demanded with regard to those who have done wickedly in accordance with their wickedness, and you will glorify the faithful ones in accordance with their faith.' (2 Bar. 54.21) 'And it shall be that everyone who will be saved and will be able to escape on account of his works, or on account of the faith by which he has believed.' (4 Ezra 9.7; also: 2 Bar. 54.16; 4 Bar. 6.6–7; 2 Enoch 62.1–2 [J]; 4 Ezra 6.5)

Midrash: 'Do not fear on his [i.e. Jacob's] account, my sister [i.e. Rachel], because he is upright in his way and he is a perfect man. And he is faithful. And he will not perish. Do not weep.' (Jub. 27.17)

Liturgical: 'For fire shall burn up the foundations of the mountains and fire shall consume nethermost Sheol. But they that hope in Thy laws Thou wilt deliver, and bring aid to them that serve Thee with faith that their seed may be before Thee for ever.' (1QH 17.13; trans. *EWQ* 249–50; textual uncertainty)

Missionary: 'And when Achior saw all that the God of Israel had done, he believed firmly in God, and was circumcised, and joined unto the house of Israel, remaining so to this day.' (Jdt. 14.10; cf. Jonah 3.5)

Pesher: 'But the righteous will live by his faith. The explanation of this concerns all those who observe the Law in the House of Judah. God will deliver them from the House of Judgement

[36] Adam and Eve 29.7; 2 Bar. 54.16, 21; 4 Bar. 6.7–8; 1 Enoch 43.4; 46.8; 58.5; 61.4, 11; 63.5, 7; 69.24; 108.11, 13; 2 Enoch 35.2 (A)/35.3(B); 51.2, 5; 61.5–62.1(A); Ep. Arist. 261; 4 Ezra 6.5, 28; 7.33–4; 9.7; 13.23; Jdt. 14.10; Jub. 14.21; 17.15; 18.16; 27.17; 1 Macc. 3.13; 2 Macc. 15.7; 3 Macc. 2.7, 11; 4 Macc. 16.18–23; 17.1–2; Mart. Isa. 1.9; 2.9; 6.3, 6; Odes Sol. 29.6; 1QpHab 8.1–3b; 1QH 17.13; 1QM 13.2–3; Sib. Or. 3.69, 74, 284, 376, 584–5, 724, 775; 4.40, 52; 5.161, 284–5, 462; 8.251–9; Sir. 1.14–15, 27; 2.6–10, 13; 4.16; 6.7; 7.26; 11.21; 12.10; 16.3; 17.14; 25.12; 32.24; 45.4; 48.22; 49.10; 51.1; Test. Asher 7.7; Test. Dan 5.13; 6.4; Test. Isaac 1.6–8; Test. Jacob 7.11; Tob. 14.4; Wis. 1.2; 3.9, 14; 12.2, 17; 14.5, 28; 16.26. See, especially: Binder, *Glaube*, 31–5; Hatch, *Pauline Idea*, 1–19; Lindsay, *Josephus*, 39–51; Lohse, 'Emuna', 147–63; Lührmann, 'Pistis', 19–38; Reitzenstein, *Mystery-Religions*, 293–5.

because of their affliction and their faith in the Teacher of Righteousness.' (1QpHab 8.1–3b; trans. *EWQ* 263)

Sapiential: 'Those who trust in him [i.e. the Lord] will understand truth, and the faithful will abide with him in love . . . ' (Wis. 3.9; also: Sir. 4.16; Wis. 16.26)

Testamentary: 'Because the way of God goes on forever, hear not only with chaste bodily ears, but also with the depth of the heart and with true faith without any doubt . . . then how much the advantage of the one who has been firm in the faith in the word of God, and has held fast without doubt and with an upright heart to the knowledge of the commandments of God and the stories of the saints; for he will be the inheritor of the kingdom of God.' (Test. Isaac 1.6–7 [Christian interpolation?]; also Test. Dan 5.13; 6.4)

There is also evidence to suggest that within eschatological contexts faith, rather than being the responsibility of the believer, could actually constitute a gift from God:

> I shall bring them out into the bright light, those who have loved my holy name, and seat them each one by one upon the throne of his honor; and they shall be resplendent for ages that cannot be numbered; for the judgement of God is righteousness, because he will give faith – as well as the paths of truth – to the faithful ones in the resting place. (1 Enoch 108.13; also: Sib. Or. 3.584–5; Test. Isaac 1.8)

One final observation relating to the development of the concept of faith in Judaism prior to or contemporaneous with the New Testament concerns the expectation that God's anointed ones or his eschatological messiah would possess faith or demonstrate faithfulness. This motif has its origin in the Old Testament (e.g. 1 Sam. 2.35; Isa. 11.5; 16.5; 42.3) and of particular interest here is the relationship between God and David attested in Psalm 89. In the opening verses, God is praised for his *'ᵉmûnâh* (vv. 2, 3, 6, 9), but later on this divine prerogative is bestowed upon David his anointed one (v. 25). In the face of Israelite infidelity, God's covenant stands firm with David and is established forever (v. 30; cf. v. 38); his *'ᵉmûnâh* will remain with him throughout (v. 34). The psalm draws to a conclusion ruefully with the question, 'Lord, where is thy steadfast love of old, which by thy *'ᵉmûnâh* thou didst swear to David?' (v. 50). A similar flow of thought is present in the Psalms of Solomon, chapter

17, where the son of David is the Lord's instrument upon earth for the implementation of God's rule. As the Lord is faithful in his conduct and promises so is his chosen one: 'The Lord himself is his [i.e. the son of David's] king, the hope of the one who has a strong hope in God (ἐλπὶς τοῦ δυνατοῦ ἐλπίδι θεοῦ) ... His hope will be in the Lord (ἡ ἐλπὶς αὐτοῦ ἐπὶ κύριον) ... Shepherding the Lord's flock in faith and righteousness (ἐν πίστει καὶ δικαιοσύνῃ), he will not let any of them stumble in their pasture.' (Pss. Sol. 17.34, 39, 40; trans.*)

Amongst other extra-biblical references,[37] a passage from 1 Maccabees is particularly interesting in this respect. It describes the process by which Simon is elected to office and draws attention to the criteria upon which this decision is made. The mention of πίστις in this context is all the more significant given that Simon's appointment takes place within the expectation that a faithful prophet would soon appear:

> And when the people saw the faith of Simon (τὴν πίστιν τοῦ Σιμωνος), and the glory which he sought to bring upon his nation, they made him leader and high-priest, because he had done all these things, and because of the justice and the faith (τὴν δικαιοσύνην καὶ τὴν πίστιν) which he kept to his nation ... And the Jews and the priests were well pleased that Simon should be their leader and high-priest for ever, until a faithful prophet should arise (ἕως τοῦ ἀναστῆναι προφήτην πιστὸν) ... (1 Macc. 14.35, 41; trans. *APOT* 1.119)

4 The meanings of the πιστεύω group in early Christian times

Having offered a number of general observations about the phenomenon of faith, we move on next to consider the πιστεύω

[37] 'And in those days my eyes saw the Elect One of righteousness and of faith.' (1 Enoch 39.6; also 83.8) 'R. Isaac b. Marion said: "But the righteous shall live by his faith" (Hab. II, 4) means that even the Righteous One who lives for ever lives from His faith.' (Eccles. R. III.9.1 [on Eccles. 3.9]) 'But those who cross them in faith shall not be disturbed ... And the Way has been appointed for those who cross over after him [i.e. the Lord's messiah], and for those who adhere to the path of his faith, and those who adore his name.' (Odes Sol. 39.5, 13; trans.* *OSol* 136; also 4.3, 5; 8.10) 'And Thou didst renew for them Thy Covenant ... [Thou didst raise up] for them a faithful shepherd.' (Fragment of a liturgical prayer from Qumran Cave 1) '... but in truth he [i.e. the Lord's messiah] will judge the poor, and reprove with faithfulness for the needy of the people ...' (Tg. Isa. on 11.4)

group and, in particular, on how it was utilised before and around the New Testament era, both in Jewish and in Graeco-Roman environments, to describe the human side of relationship with the divine. Starting with the Jewish setting, it is clear from the Septuagint that the translators considered πιστεύω cognates to provide suitable equivalents for much of the semantic content of the *'āman* root,[38] with the ἀληθεύω group constituting the only alternative well represented in the case of certain substantive forms.[39] This tendency to use the πιστεύω group for human response to God is also attested in much of the intertestamental literature, the works of the Jewish historian Josephus and, in more nuanced form, in Philo of Alexandria:[40]

[38] Consider the following statistics relating to verbal forms of *'āman*: (i) Niphal: ἀξιόπιστος Prov. 27.6; ἐμπιστεύω 2 Chron. 20.20b; πιστεύω Gen. 42.20; πίστις Jer. 15.18; πιστός Num. 12.7; Deut. 7.9; 28.59b; 1 Sam. 2.35; 3.20; 22.14; 25.28; 1 Kings 11.38; Neh. 9.8; 13.13; Job 12.20; Pss. 19.8; 89.29, 38; 101.6; 111.7b; Prov. 11.13; 25.13; Isa. 1.21, 26; 8.2; 22.23, 25; 33.16; 49.7; 55.3; Jer. 42.5; Hos. 5.9; πιστόω 2 Sam. 7.16; 1 Kings 8.26; 1 Chron. 17.23, 24; 2 Chron. 1.9; 6.17; Pss. 78.8, 37; 93.5; αἶρω Isa. 60.4; θαυμαστός Deut. 28.59a; καλέω Hos. 12.1(?); συνίημι Isa. 7.9b; (ii) Hiphil: ἐμπιστεύω Deut. 1.32; Judg. 11.20 (var); 1 Chron. 20.20 [x2]; Jonah 3.5; καταπιστεύω Micah 7.5; πιστεύω Gen. 15.6; 45.26; Exod. 4.1, 5, 8, 9, 31; 14.31; 19.9; Num. 14.11; 20.12; Deut. 9.23; 28.66; 1 Sam. 27.12; 1 Kings 10.7; 2 Kings 17.14 (var); 2 Chron. 9.6; 32.15; Job 4.18; 9.16; 15.15, 22, 31 (var); 24.22; 29.24; 39.12, 24; Pss. 27.13; 78.22, 32; 106.12, 24; 116.10; 119.66; Prov. 14.15; Isa. 7.9a; 28.16; 43.10; 53.1; Jer. 12.6; 40.14; Lam. 4.12; Hab. 1.5; θέλω Judg. 11.20 (var); πείθω Prov. 26.25.

[39] E.g. (i) *'emûnâh*: ἀλήθεια 2 Chron. 19.9; Pss. 36.6; 40.11; 88.12; 89.2, 3, 6, 9, 25, 34, 50; 92.3; 96.13; 98.3; 100.5; 119.30, 75, 86, 90, 138; 143.1; Isa. 11.5; 26.2; ἀληθινός Isa. 25.1; 59.4; ἀξιόπιστος Prov. 28.20; πίστις 1 Sam. 26.23; 2 Kings 12.16; 22.7; 1 Chron. 9.22, 26, 31; 2 Chron. 31.12, 15, 18; 34.12; Ps. 33.4; Prov. 12.17, 22; Jer. 5.1, 3; 7.28; 9.2; Hos. 2.22; Hab. 2.4; πιστός Deut. 32.4; Prov. 13.17; 14.5; 20.6; ποιμαίνω Ps. 37.3; στηρίζω Exod. 17.12; (ii) *'emet*: ἀλήθεια Gen. 24.27, 48; 32.11; 47.29; Deut. 22.20; Jos. 2.14; Judg. 9.15, 16, 19; 1 Sam. 12.24; 2 Sam. 2.6; 15.20; 1 Kings 2.4; 3.6; 22.16; 2 Kings 20.3, 19; 2 Chron. 18.15; 32.1; Neh. 9.13, 33; Pss. 15.2; 25.5, 10; 26.3; 30.10; 31.6; 40.11, 12; 43.3; 45.5; 51.8; 57.4, 11; 61.8; 69.14; 71.22; 85.11, 12; 86.11; 89.15; 91.4; 108.5; 111.7, 8; 115.1; 117.2; 119.43, 142, 151, 160; 132.11; 138.2; 145.18; 146.6; Prov. 8.7; 11.18; 14.22; 20.28; 22.21; 29.14; Eccles. 12.10; Isa. 10.20; 16.5; 38.3; 42.3; 48.1; 59.14, 15; Jer. 4.2; 9.4; 14.13; 23.28; Dan. 8.26; 9.13; 10.21; 11.2; Hos. 4.1; Micah 7.20; Mal. 2.6; Zech. 8.8, 16, 19; ἀληθεύω Gen. 42.16; ἀληθής Deut. 13.15; Neh. 7.2; Isa. 43.9; ἀληθινός Exod. 34.6; 2 Sam. 7.28; 1 Kings 10.6; 17.24; 2 Chron. 9.5; 15.3; Pss. 19.10; 86.15; Prov. 12.19; Jer. 2.21; Dan. 10.1; Zech. 8.3; ἀληθῶς Deut. 13.15; 17.4; Dan. 8.26 (var); δίκαιος Exod. 18.21; Ezek. 18.8, 9; Zech. 7.9; δικαιοσύνη Gen. 24.49; Jos. 24.14; Isa. 38.19; 39.8; 61.8; Dan. 8.12; ἐλεημοσύνη Isa. 38.18; πίστις Prov. 3.3; 16.6; Jer. 28.9; 32.41; 33.6; πιστός Prov. 14.25; Jer. 42.5.

[40] For more detailed discussions, see: Hay, 'Pistis', 463–8; Lindsay, *Josephus*, 53–163; Peisker, Glaubensbegriff; Schlatter, *Glaube*, 275–83; Williamson, *Philo*, 309–85.

Intertestamental: 'For the fear of the Lord is wisdom and instruction, and faith and meekness (πίστις καὶ πραότης) are his delight.' (Sir. 1.27; author's trans.) 'The Holy One of Israel will rule over them in humility and poverty, and he who believes on him (ὁ πιστεύων ἐπ' αὐτῷ) shall reign in truth in the heavens . . . because he [i.e. the Lord] knows that on the day in which Israel believes (πιστεύσει), the enemy's kingdom will be brought to an end.' (Test. Dan 5.13; 6.4; trans.*) 'Those who trust (οἱ πεποιθότες) in him [i.e. the Lord] will understand truth, and the faithful (οἱ πιστοὶ) will abide with him in love.' (Wis. 3.9; also: Jdt. 14.10; 1 Macc. 3.13; 3 Macc. 2.7; 4 Macc. 16.22; 17.2; Tob. 14.4; Sib. Or. 3.69, 74, 284; 4.40, 52; 5.161, 284; Sir. 1.14–15; 2.6–10, 13; 4.16; 11.21; 25.12[var]; 32.24; 45.4; 49.10; 51.1; Wis. 1.2; 3.14; 12.2, 17; 16.26)

Josephus: 'However, their [i.e. Amram and Jochebed's] belief in the promises of God was confirmed (προκατηγγελμένοις ὑπὸ τοῦ θεοῦ πίστιν) by the manner of the woman's delivery . . .' (*Ant.* II.218 [LCL 242.258–9]) '. . . and He [i.e. God] bade him [i.e. Moses] cast his staff to the ground and to have faith (πίστιν) in His promises.' (*Ant.* II.272 [LCL 242.282–3]) 'Furthermore, what had befallen him [i.e. Moses] on Mount Sinai, the utterances of God and the miraculous signs which He had shown him to inspire faith (πίστιν) in His injunctions.' (*Ant.* II.283 [LCL 242.286–9]; trans.*) '. . . their faith in God (πίστιν τοῦ θείου) . . . by his faith in God (πίστει τοῦ θείου) . . .' (*Ant.* XVII.179, 284 [LCL 410.454–5, 504–5])

Philo: 'Faith in God (ἡ πρὸς θεὸν πίστις), then, is the one sure and infallible good, consolation of life, fulfilment of bright hopes, dearth of ills, harvest of goods, inacquaintance with misery, acquaintance with piety, heritage of happiness . . .' (*Abr.* 268 [LCL 289.130–1]) '. . . that surest and most stable quality, faith (πίστιν).' (*Conf. Ling.* 31 [LCL 261.26–7]) 'The leader in adopting the godly creed, who first passed over from vanity to truth, came to his consummation by virtue gained through instruction, and he received for his reward belief in God (τὴν πρὸς θεὸν πίστιν) . . . Belief in God (τοῦ δὲ πιστεύειν θεῷ), life-long joy, the perpetual vision of the Existent – what can anyone conceive more profitable or more august than these?' (*Praem.* 27 [LCL

341.326–9]) 'The words "Abraham believed God (ἐπίστευσεν Ἀβραὰμ τῷ θεῷ)" are a necessary addition to speak the praise due him who has believed (τοῦ πεπιστευκότος) ... the most perfect of virtues, faith (τὴν τελειοτάτην ἀρετῶν, πίστιν) ...' (*Rer. Div. Her.* 90–1 [LCL 261.326–7]; cf. *Abr.* 270)

Outside of the Judaeo-Christian tradition, the πιστεύω group is also associated with human response or reaction to the divine.[41] In some cases the emphasis falls upon credulity in or proof with respect to whether the gods exist.[42] More commonly, however, it is found in relation to oracles or the miraculous, although it can denote trust in the divine and describe the religious response in more general and encompassing terms:

Oracles: 'What I have told you, Asclepius, you will deem true if you apply your thought to it; but if not, you will find it incredible (ἄπιστα); for belief follows on thinking, and disbelief follows on want of thinking (τῷ γὰρ νοῆσαι ἕπεται τὸ πιστεῦσαι, τὸ ἀπιστῆσαι δὲ τῷ μὴ νοῆσαι).' (*Corp. Herm.* IX.10 [Scott, *Hermetica*, vol. 1, 184–5]; trans.*) 'Athena, Queen, who hears the words of Gods, And disbelieveth (ἄπιστος) them, is sense-bereft.' (Euripides, *Iph. Taur.* 1475–6 [LCL 10.406–7]) '... for he disbelieved the oracle (ἀπιστέων τε τῷ χρησμῷ) and thought that those who had inquired of the god spoke untruly.' (Herodotus I.158 [LCL 117.198–9]) 'But since both of them saw that most men neither readily accept anything unfamiliar to them, nor venture on great risks without the hope of divine help (χωρὶς τῆς ἐκ τῶν θεῶν ἐλπίδος), Lycurgus made his own scheme more acceptable and more easily believed in (εὐπαραδεκτοτέρας καὶ πιστοτέρας) by invoking the oracles of the Pythia in support of projects due to himself.' (Polybius, *Hist.* X.2.10–11 [LCL 159.104–5]) 'However, do not believe the god (πιστεύσητε τῷ θεῷ) even in this without due grounds, but examine the god's utterance in detail.' (Xenophon, *Ap.* 15 [LCL 168. 650–1]; also *Mem.* I.1.5)

Miracles: 'A man whose fingers, with the exception of one, were

[41] G. Barth, 'Pistis', 110–26, and Hatch, *Pauline Idea*, 67–81.

[42] E.g. 'Tis the God: I may not doubt him (τῷ θεῷ γοῦν οὐκ ἀπιστεῖν εἰκός).' (Euripides, *Ion* 557 [LCL 12.60–1])

paralysed, came as a suppliant to the god. While looking at the tablets in the temple he expressed disbelief (ἀπίστει) regarding the cures and scoffed at the inscriptions . . . When he had straightened them all, the god asked him if he would still be disbelieving (ἀπιστησοῖ) of the inscriptions on the tablets in the Temple. He answered that he would not. "Since, then, formerly you did not believe (ἀπίστεις) the cures though they were not beyond belief (ἀπίστοις), for the future," he said, "your name shall be 'Unbeliever (ἄπιστος)'." When day dawned he walked out sound.' (*IG* IV.1.121.A.3 [Edelstein, *Asclepius*, 222–6]; trans.*) 'If the Greeks are to be believed (πιστεύειν) in these matters [i.e. Dionysus' bi-annual changing of the water into wine], one might with equal reason accept what the Aethiopians above Syene say about the table of the sun.' (Pausanias, *Descriptio Graeciae* VI.26.2 [LCL 272.158–9]) 'Epidauros, too, is an important city, particularly because of the fame of Asclepius, who is believed to cure diseases of every kind (θεραπεύειν νόσους παντοδαπὰς πεπιστευμένου) and always has his temple full of the sick, and also of the votive tablets on which the treatments are recorded, just as at Cos and Trica.' (Strabo, *Geog.* VIII.6.15 [LCL 196.176–7])

Trust: 'Fortunate men stand in a certain relation to the divinity and love the gods, believing on the basis of the benefits they have received from fortune (πιστεύοντες διὰ τὰ γιγνόμενα ἀγαθὰ ἀπὸ τῆς τύχης).' (Aristotle, *Rhet.* II.17 [LCL 193.260–1]; trans.*) 'Thy words are reasonable; natheless I would have thee trust my promise and the god's (θεοῖς τε πιστεύσαντα τοῖς τ' ἐμοῖς λόγοις) and confidently sail with me . . .' (Sophocles, *Phil.* 1374–7 [LCL 21.482–3]) '. . . but trusting (πιστεύοντες) to the fortune (τύχῃ) which by divine favour has preserved her hitherto, and to such help as men, even the Lacedaemonians, can give we shall try to win our deliverance.' (Thucydides, *Hist.* V.112.2; [LCL 110.174–5]; also: IV.92.7; V.104)

General: 'Piety, through faith which they had in the gods (εὐσεβείας μὲν διὰ τὴν πίστιν ἣν ἐν τοῖς θεοῖς εἶχον).' (Aristides, *Pan. Or.* 155 [LCL 458.122–3]) 'Holy is God the Father of all . . . Wherefore I believe and bear witness <that> I enter into Life and Light (διὸ πιστεύω καὶ μαρτυρῶ <ὅτι> εἰς ζωὴν καὶ φῶς χωρῶ).' (*Corp. Herm.*

I.26, 31 [Scott, *Hermetica*, vol. 1, 130–3]) 'If the deity is faithful, he also must be faithful (εἰ πιστόν ἐστι τὸ θεῖον, καὶ τοῦτον εἶναι πιστόν); if free, he also must be free ... therefore, in everything he says and does, he must act as an imitator of God.' (Epictetus, *Diss.* II.14.13 [LCL 131.308–9]; also I.4.18–19; II.4.1–3; 22.25–7; IV.1.126; 3.7) 'Your children lack fathers, your youth lack old men, your wives husbands, your husbands rulers, your rulers laws, your laws philosophers, your philosophers gods, your gods faith (οἱ θεοὶ πίστεως).' (Philostratus, *Ep.* 33 [LCL 17.430–1])

The most helpful exponent with reference to theological usage of πιστεύω and one contemporaneous with the composition of certain New Testament books is Plutarch (*circa* AD 50–120). His voluminous writings bear witness to the broad spectrum of meaning and applications already mentioned.[43] Of particular significance is the way in which he can, on occasion, use πίστις to describe the mode of existence of those who live in relation to the divine: 'Now we should, I grant you, remove superstition from our belief in the gods (τῆς περὶ θεῶν δόξης) like a rheum from the eye; but if this proves impossible, we should not cut away both together and kill the faith that most men have in the gods (τὴν πίστιν ἣν οἱ πλεῖστοι περὶ θεῶν ἔχουσιν).' The following lines go on to expound certain elements of that faith in greater detail:

[43] Cf. πιστεύω group in relation to (i) existence of gods: 'The atheist thinks there are no gods; the superstitious man wishes there were none, but believes in them against his will; for he is afraid not to believe (πιστεύει δ' ἄκων· φοβεῖται γὰρ ἀπιστεῖν).' (*Moralia* 170–1 [LCL 222.490–1]; also 17b and 165b); (ii) oracles: 'Then do we believe (πιστεύοντες) these verses to be the god's, and yet dare to say that in beauty they fall short of the verses of Homer and Hesiod?' (*Moralia* 396d [LCL 306.268–9]; cf. 166d, 377c, 402b, 407a, 549b, 756b) 'At all events, during the journey which he made at this time, the assistance rendered him by Heaven in his perplexities met with more belief (ἐπιστεύθη) than the oracles which he afterwards received, nay, in a way, the oracles obtained belief (ἡ πίστις) in consequence of such assistance ... So, you see, while it is a dire thing to be incredulous towards indications of the divine will (ἡ ἀπιστία πρὸς τὰ θεῖα) ...' (*Alex.* 27.1 and 75.2 [LCL 99.302–3 and 430–1]; trans.*); (iii) miracles: 'Such things [i.e. miraculous happenings in nature] if they come to pass, it is hard to believe (πιστεῦσαι), to say nothing of foretelling them, without divine inspiration.' (*Moralia*, 398e [LCL 306.282–3]) 'However, those who cherish strong feelings of goodwill and affection for the Deity, and are therefore unable to reject or deny anything of this kind, have a strong argument for their faith in the wonderful and transcendent character of the divine power (μέγα πρὸς πίστιν ἐστὶ τὸ θαυμάσιον καὶ μὴ καθ' ἡμᾶς τῆς τοῦ θεοῦ δυνάμεως).' (*Cor.* 38.3 [LCL 80.212–3]) G. Barth offers a fuller treatment of the religious application of the πιστεύω group in Plutarch ('Pistis', esp. 115–23).

> This is no terrifying or grim faith . . . No; among mankind a few are afraid of God who would not be better off without that fear; for since they fear him as a ruler mild to the good and hating the wicked, by this one fear, which keeps them from doing wrong, they are freed from the many that attend to crime . . . On the other hand the attitude towards God that we find in the ignorant but not greatly wicked majority of mankind contains no doubt along with the sense of reverence and honour an element of tremulous fear . . . but outweighing this a thousand times is the element of cheerful hope, or exultant joy, and whether in prayer or in thanksgiving of ascribing every furtherance of felicity to the gods. (*Moralia* 1101c [LCL 428.110–13])[44]

5 Concluding remarks

Having attempted to sketch out the *milieu* of faith within which early Christian traditions took shape, we must now summarise our principal findings. Firstly, faith as a relation between human and divine had come to expression both within and outside Judaism prior to the Christian era. The range of meanings for this disposition runs from credulity over the existence of the divine to a fully-fledged personal relationship based upon God's perceived initiatives. In addition, there is considerable evidence to suggest that faith could describe God's maintenance of covenantal relationships with Israel. Within the Jewish heritage, we also noted how faith was often expounded in narrative form, using key figures or events from Israel's past to serve as examples. Further, whilst faith cannot be limited to word groups, both the *'āman* and πιστεύω roots provided the primary lexical stock for referring explicitly to this phenomenon. The growing prominence of faith as indicative of human attitude or response to the divine is also worthy of mention. In particular, its eschatological associations and function with reference to the re-establishing of God's kingdom or covenant demonstrate that faith had become an essential element within Jewish expectation and understanding of salvation. Finally, one aspect of this was the belief that God's messiah would himself be a man of faith.

[44] Plutarch, *Moralia* 1101c [LCL 428.110ff]; also '. . . who are possessed by a feeling of piety towards these gods, and thus we should not stop short of transplanting such names from the heavens to the earth, and eliminating and dissipating the reverence and faith (τιμὴν καὶ πίστιν) implanted in nearly all mankind at birth.' (*Moralia* 359–60 [LCL 306.56–7]; cf. 402e; 756a-b)

2

JESUS' FAITH IN THE SYNOPTIC GOSPELS

1 Preliminary considerations

In the previous chapter, we observed how nascent Christianity inherited certain ways of articulating faith. Faith already had its own vocabulary in the form of the πιστεύω group and the *'āman* root, which could denote – amongst other things – various aspects of human–divine relationship. We also noted how faith could be expounded in narrative form by reflecting on the lives of Israel's great exemplars. And following on from this, we recognised the importance within Jewish traditions of the phenomenal dimension of faith, which was rooted in experience rather than in abstract thinking.

These then are some of the characteristics delimiting the background against which early Christian traditions should be interpreted. We shall, therefore, make recourse to this heritage throughout our investigation and, in order to gain perspective for the present chapter, a number of corollaries need to be made. Firstly, although the resurrection certainly influenced the way in which faith came to be understood and articulated in Christianity, it is not the birth of faith. For one thing, we have seen how faith had already come to expression in Jewish and Graeco-Roman environments; for another, the resurrection itself assumes the existence of a community of faith without which its effects could not have been received or interpreted. Had there been no disciples of the earthly Jesus, post-crucifixion experiences of that same person raised from the dead would have been impossible.[1] Further, the fact that New Testament authors adopted the same basic vocabulary for faith and

[1] The christological implications of this are spelt out by Marxsen, *Beginnings*, esp. 77–85, and Moule, *Origin*, esp. 1–10. For the existence and function of disciple groupings before Easter, see: Gerhardsson, *Origins*, esp. 51–77; Riesner, *Jesus*, esp. 499–502; Schürmann, 'Anfänge', 342–70; Stanton, *Jesus*, 13–27.

used figures such as Abraham to exemplarise it, indicates that they acknowledged a degree of continuity between Jewish and Christian understandings.[2]

Further, although the resurrection undoubtedly altered the nature of the relation between Jesus and faith, it is unlikely to be the source of all such associations.[3] For instance, in a climate where faith was part of the religious currency and where Jewish expectation maintained that God's messiah would share this quality, assessments of Jesus would, at least initially, tend to be framed in terms of a profound man of faith, who demonstrated many of the phenomena associated with God's eschaton. In this respect, it cannot be without significance that the portrayals of Jesus in the Synoptic Gospels correspond in many details with Old Testament descriptions of Moses, one of the great Jewish exemplars of faith, and David, from whose stock the faithful messiah would come.[4] In addition, the way in which the Synoptics depict the disciples as those called to follow in Jesus' footsteps,[5] suggests that his ministry was considered – at least in certain respects – to be emulative.[6]

By suggesting that the ministry of Jesus was considered a fruitful seedbed for understanding faith, we neither wish to deny the post-resurrection perspective of the Synoptic Gospels nor their theological evaluation of Jesus. Nor, for that matter, do we wish to posit a historicising interest in the life of Jesus *per se*.[7] On the contrary, we are claiming that theological and anthropological perspectives on Jesus may not have been considered mutually exclusive. There is,

[2] Lohse, 'Emuna', 147–63; *contra* Buber, *Two Types*, who maintains that the resurrection delimits Jewish (including Jesus) and Christian understandings of faith.

[3] See, for example, Ebeling's insights into Jesus as the awakener of faith (*Word*, esp. 232–46); also Marxsen, *Beginnings*, 57–68.

[4] This point will be taken up again in section 4.

[5] Clearly this is a complicated area and one which the Synoptic Evangelists handle differently. However, in all three cases, the disciples are called to minister in similar ways to Jesus. For example, they are required to preach, heal, exorcise (e.g. Matt. 10.1/Mark 6.7–13/Luke 9.1–6) and give up their lives for the Gospel (e.g. Matt. 16.24–8/Mark 8.34–9.1/Luke 9.23–7). On this whole area, see: Hengel, *Leader*, 38–88; Riesner, *Jesus*, 408–98; Robbins, *Jesus*.

[6] This has been explored by J. Sobrino, specifically in terms of the relevance of Jesus' faith for discipleship: 'The most radical and most orthodox affirmation of *faith in Jesus* is affirming that the *faith of Jesus* is the correct way to draw nearer to God and realize his kingdom, and then acting accordingly.' (*Christology*, 108; Sobrino's italics)

[7] There is a subtle but none the less real difference between attempting, on the one hand, to recover details from post-resurrection documents of Jesus' faith as an aspect of his personal history and, on the other, to see what interest those same documents reflect in Jesus' faith as it relates to Christian discipleship.

after all, no *a priori* reason why Jesus' significance for faith could not have embraced what he disclosed of God in and through his life of faith. In this respect, we must be careful not to confuse the post-resurrection perspective of the Synoptists with one informed by later Christian debate in which certain aspects of Jesus' humanity proved to be a stumbling block for establishing his divine status.[8]

Evidence for this dual perspective is supplied by the miracle traditions attested in the first three Gospels. In their present form, many of them fulfil an epiphanic function by revealing something of Jesus' theological significance.[9] This is especially apparent in those exorcisms where Jesus is addressed in christologically explicit terms by the one possessing the patient,[10] as the event is contextualised within the broader struggle between God and Satan.[11] There are cases, however, where correspondence between Jesus' conduct and that expected from his disciples can be discerned. Four of these traditions will be discussed in detail later,[12] but here we should note that, although these accounts portray the disciples as impotent, they also indicate that Jesus intended them to follow his example. In this way, these pericopae appear to reflect an interest in what Jesus reveals about discipleship as well as about the nature and salvific purpose of God.

The resurrection, therefore, does not necessarily preclude interest in Jesus as one who was thought to incarnate faith and, as such, to provide a model for those wishing to commit their lives to the God revealed in and through Jesus Christ. Further, when elements of the synoptic tradition are considered in light of the background material presented above and the correspondence between the ministries of Jesus and his disciples just noted, we discover that this was in fact

8 We shall pick this issue up again in chapter 6.

9 For example, Jesus is the one who has authority to forgive sins (Matt. 9.1–8/Mark 2.1–12/Luke 5.17–26), to control the natural elements (e.g. Matt. 8.23–7/Mark 4.35–41/Luke 8.22–5; Matt. 14.13–21/Mark 6.30–4/Luke 9.10–17) and to overcome the powers of evil (e.g. Matt. 8.28–34/Mark 5.1–20/Luke 8.26–39; Mark 1.21–8/Luke 4.36–7). He also performs those healings characteristic of the messiah or the messianic era (Matt. 11.2–6/Luke 7.18–23; Matt. 8.17; Luke 4.18; 7.16). On this aspect of the miracle traditions: Fuller, *Interpreting*, 46–68; van der Loos, *Miracles*, esp. 233–54; Richardson, *Miracle-Stories*, 38–74.

10 E.g. 'Jesus, Son of the Most High God' (Mark 5.7/Luke 8.28; cf. Matt. 8.29); 'the Holy One of God' (Mark 1.24/Luke 4.34); 'You are the Son of God' (Mark 3.11; Luke 4.41).

11 Kertelge, *Wunder*, 50–89; Theissen, *Miracle Stories*, 85–90; Twelftree, *Christ*, 72–86.

12 I.e. 'healing of the possessed boy', 'stilling of the storm', 'Peter's walking on water' and 'withering of the fig tree'.

the case. And it is to this material that we must now turn. We shall start by examining four traditions reflecting the view that Jesus performed miracles by faith (section 2). Attention will then shift to the areas of correspondence between Jesus' teaching on faith and aspects of his thaumaturgic technique (section 3). Finally, we shall take a broader look at the Synoptic Evangelists' portrayal of Jesus in the light of Jewish conceptions of the life of faith (section 4).[13]

2 References to Jesus' faith in the miracle traditions

There are no unambiguous references to Jesus' faith in the synoptic miracle stories, but at least four traditions are highly suggestive in this respect. Each case demonstrates a level of correspondence between Jesus' conduct and the intended conduct of his disciples which invites comparison.

2.1 Healing of the possessed boy

The narrative relating the healing of the possessed boy is attested in all three Synoptic Gospels (Matt. 17.14–20[21]/Mark 9.14–29/Luke 9.37–43), although we only need to focus upon the Matthean and Markan versions.[14] Whilst Markan priority is generally recognised,[15] the *traditionsgeschichtliche* problems of the pericope are substantial and have been rehearsed at length elsewhere.[16] We shall

[13] Owing to possible ambiguities arising from the biographical nature of the gospel material, it may be helpful to reiterate precisely what is and is not being attempted in this chapter. It is our intention to address the following question: Do the Synoptic Gospels furnish evidence of the early church's interest in the faith of Jesus and, if they do, why were the evangelists or their sources so interested?

[14] Luke's version contains neither of the key faith texts found in Matthew and Mark (Matt. 17.20–1; Mark 9.23–4). Further, in a manner uncharacteristic of his treatment of miracles elsewhere, Luke's account on this occasion is even shorter than Matthew's. It seems that he has played down the didactic function of this healing, which is based on a comparison between Jesus' conduct and that of his disciples, and preferred instead to use the tradition to confirm the theological significance of Jesus suggested by the preceding transfiguration story. Thus, after Jesus' exorcism of the boy, there is no *post mortem* with the disciples; rather, we are simply informed that 'all were astonished at the majesty of God' (Luke 9.43; cf. Luke 5.25–6; 13.13; 17.15; 18.43; 19.37; Acts 3.8–9). For a fuller treatment of Luke's version, see Busse, *Wunder*, 249–67.

[15] E.g. Fitzmyer, *Luke*, vol. 1, 805; Gundry, *Matthew*, 348; Theissen, *Miracle Stories*, 177.

[16] 'The standard critical explanations for these features are essentially variants on two basic hypotheses. The first maintains that the present format of the story is the product of the amalgamation of two separate traditions, one centring on the

confine ourselves to indicators of interest in Jesus' faith which emerge from the texts as they stand and conclude by commenting on their traditional or redactional provenance.[17]

Mark's version of the story is by far the longest of the three accounts and includes two dialogues involving Jesus. The first, with the boy's father, contains a key logion for our investigation (τὸ εἰ δύνῃ, πάντα δυνατὰ τῷ πιστεύοντι, 9.23) and seems to disclose the means by which the exorcism is performed. This is partially contradicted by the second, however, where Jesus explains the disciples' failure to execute the deliverance by drawing attention to the difficulty of this particular case (τοῦτο τὸ γένος, 9.29); how this squares with Jesus' cry of exasperation in verse 19 (ὦ γενεὰ ἄπιστος) and with the prominence given to faith elsewhere in the narrative requires additional clarification. Finally, it is prayer (v. 29) and not faith which Jesus singles out as the key factor for success in this instance, even though there is little in the narrative to suggest that he followed his own advice.

One of the distinguishing features about this miracle is that it records an attempt by the disciples to put into practice the commission they had received earlier to assist Jesus in making the kingdom known through proclamation and demonstration.[18] This characteristic receives further emphasis by the placement of the pericope within the section of the Gospel in which Mark explores many

inability of the disciples to perform a miracle, the other on the father and the paradox of unbelieving belief. Some think they were originally independent miracle stories; others that they were two versions of the same episode. Some ascribe the combination to the pre-Markan phase, others to Mark himself, and opinions on how the narrative should be distributed between each source and what is attributable to Markan redaction, differ considerably. The second hypothesis, more favoured in recent research, conjectures one basic story that has been considerably expanded in the process of oral transmission and/or Markan redaction. Whether the traditional kernel focused on the inability of the disciples to heal (vv. 14–19), the discussion with the father (vv. 20–7), or was a basic exorcism story elaborated to highlight discipleship failure and the importance of faith (e.g. vv 16–18, 20–2, 25b-27), is a matter of dispute.' (C. D. Marshall, *Faith*, 122) In addition to literature cited in this work, see: Aichinger, 'Epileptiker-Perikope', 114–43; Dautzenberg, 'Jesusüberlieferung', 41–62; Schmithals, 'Heilung', 211–33. D.-A. Koch tabulates the main areas of tension in the narrative as it stands (*Bedeutung*, 115); L. Schenke, however, considers these to be more apparent than real (*Wundererzählungen*, 317–20).

17 It should be noted that our findings militate against the view that Mark was responsible for joining together two independent miracle traditions or for inserting the dialogue between Jesus and the father narrated in Mark 9.21–4.

18 E.g. Mark 3.14–15; 6.7–13; cf. Matt. 10.1–15; Luke 9.1–6; 10.1–20.

aspects of discipleship (8.22–10.52);[19] it seems reasonable, therefore, to expect the story under review to have a bearing upon this theme as well. Mark's use of the disciples' incomprehension or partial understanding as a didactic technique can be seen prior to this narrative in the exposition about Jesus' messiahship (8.27–9.1) and again afterwards in relation to teaching on humility and ambition (9.33–7; 10.35–45).[20] In each of these cases, the incompleteness or incorrectness of the disciples' response provides Jesus with the opportunity to develop these themes in terms of his ministry.[21] A similar process also seems to be operating in the *Puer Lunaticus* pericope, where their failure to perform a cure not only results in Jesus' having to do it, but also, and perhaps more importantly, in Jesus' explaining something of the healer's role in this process.

With these general observations about Mark's theological concerns and literary devices in mind, we can appreciate more fully the changing dynamics of the story as it unfolds. Initially, the father of the patient seeks Jesus to help his son and, in his absence, makes a similar request to those commissioned to assist Jesus in his ministry, namely, the disciples. They are unable to perform the necessary deliverance and become enmeshed in some sort of discussion within the context of the gathered crowd. Jesus, on his return, inquires of those present what is going on and is subsequently put in the picture by the father, who explains how he brought his son to Jesus' disciples ἵνα αὐτὸ ἐκβάλωσιν, καὶ οὐκ ἴσχυσαν. In this way, the answer to Jesus' question, which was initially put to the group as a whole (καὶ ἐπηρώτησεν αὐτούς), directs attention towards his impotent followers who then become the primary focus for Jesus' following exclamation (ὦ γενεὰ ἄπιστος κτλ).[22]

Whilst it is possible that the crowd are also included within the compass of γενεὰ ἄπιστος, it is unlikely that the father is implicated;[23] his omission seems necessary on a number of counts.

[19] Best, 'Mark 8:22–10:52', 323–37, and Reploh, *Markus*, esp. 211–26; see also the review of Black, *Disciples*.

[20] Best, *Following*, *ad loc*, and Reploh, *Markus*, 123–72.

[21] 'In so far as the disciples appear in a bad light it is because Mark wishes to use them as a foil: their failure to understand is sometimes introduced in order to allow Jesus to give further and fuller instruction; their fearfulness is brought out in order that Jesus may show them the sources of calm and courage; their desire for positions of importance is stressed in order that Jesus may teach them about the meaning of service.' (Best, 'Role', 399)

[22] Cranfield, *Saint Mark*, 301; Koch, *Bedeutung*, 122–6; van de Loos, *Miracles*, 399.

[23] C. D. Marshall puts a strong case for the inclusion of the father among the γενεὰ ἄπιστος on the basis that: (i) Jesus' answer in 9.19 is part of a conversation

Elsewhere in the second Gospel, faith in relation to miracles is associated specifically with action.[24] For example, Jesus sees (ἰδὼν) the faith of the stretcher-bearers as they go to great lengths to deliver their patient to him (2.5), he draws attention to the haemorrhaging woman's faith after she has struggled through the crowd to touch him and later to make her public confession (5.34), he rewards blind Bartimaeus with an audience after his concerted endeavours to make his petition heard (10.52). This motif of faith-in-action encourages us to identify the father's faith with his initiative in seeking Jesus for a healing in the first place. Further, granting that the narrative suggests his faith is tested by attendant circumstances,[25] there is little to indicate an initial coming to faith within the confines of the story. In this respect, his retort, πιστεύω· βοήθει μου τῇ ἀπιστίᾳ (v. 24), is more consistent with the undermining of his faith as a result of his encounter with the disciples than with its birth or development.[26] We may deduce, therefore, that the determinative factor for this healing is more likely to be associated with the healer than with the suppliant or patient. That is to say, the successful deliverance of the boy results from Jesus' replacing his disciples as exorcist and not from any discernible change in the disposition of the father or anyone else for that matter.[27]

involving all those assembled (cf. 9.16, αὐτούς); (ii) by maintaining that the disciples' impotence resulted from their lack of strength (οὐκ ἴσχυσαν), the father misapprehended the nature of miraculous power; (iii) the father's appeal βοήθει μου τῇ ἀπιστίᾳ (9.24) suggests a self-identification with the faithless (*Faith*, 117–18). Each of these observations, however, is open to question. As we have noted, the father's response to Jesus' initial question (9.17–18) moves the narrative forward and focuses attention specifically on the disciples; is it not more likely, therefore, that the αὐτοῖς in 9.19 refers back to τοῖς μαθηταῖς σου in the previous verse rather than the αὐτούς of 9.16? The use of ἰσχύω in 9.18 may simply denote that – for whatever reason – the disciples could not perform the deliverance; further, if the father's understanding of miracles was misguided, Jesus' instructions to the disciples in 9.29 does little to shift attention from technique to God. Finally, whilst it is possible that βοήθει μου τῇ ἀπιστίᾳ places the father among the γενεὰ ἄπιστος, it is just as likely that his ἀπιστία results from his experience at the hands of the disciples.

24 This is not to deny that Mark understood the various forms of action to be based upon some prior assessment of Jesus; see Hahn, 'Verständnis', 54–7.

25 'Faith is faith tested by difficulties ... In all the Marcan miracle stories the motifs of faith and difficulty are associated.' Theissen, *Miracle Stories*, 134, 136.

26 Cranfield, 'St Mark 9.14–29', 64–5; Hooker, *Mark*, 224; Lane, *Mark*, 332.

27 'If then this pericope is oriented towards the instruction of the disciples in exorcism, and probably in all healing activity since exorcism as such is not expressly emphasised, this instruction does not take the form "Exorcise as Jesus did (does)", i.e. it is not a passage teaching imitation of Christ.' (Best, *Following*, 69). E. Best's assessment may capture the intention of Mark's redactional hand-

In the light of these observations, we may now consider the *crux interpretum* to assess whether it implicates Jesus as a believer: τὸ εἰ δύνῃ, πάντα δυνατὰ τῷ πιστεύοντι (v. 23).[28] This saying constitutes Jesus' reply to the father's petition in the previous verse which is couched in conditional language (ἀλλ' εἴ τι δύνῃ), presumably as a result of his experience at the hands of the disciples.[29] Jesus' response is not initially to grant the request, but rather – in the aftermath of the disciples' failure – to explain or perhaps even defend the means by which acts of God can be performed (cf. 10.27; 14.36). Jesus reiterates the hesitant words of the father (cf. τὸ εἰ δύνῃ) and then, by affirming the potential of the person practising that faith which the disciples lacked, reveals the channel by which God's power can flow. The father then makes a second request in language reminiscent of the first, but in this case he is the prospective recipient: πιστεύω· βοήθει μου τῇ ἀπιστίᾳ (v. 24). Even after this veiled affirmation, it is the imminent arrival of the crowd which prompts Jesus into action as he fulfils both petitions by healing the boy and, in doing so, strengthening the father's wavering faith.

Although the father's explicit confession (i.e. πιστεύω) follows Jesus' πάντα δυνατὰ τῷ πιστεύοντι, it is unlikely for the reasons outlined above that his faith was the means for success where previously there had been failure; this is not to conclude that his faith was superfluous, but to recognise that it had been present throughout.[30] We should also note that within the Synoptic

ling of the pericope, but it does not reflect the narrative progression of the tradition. In structural terms, Jesus replaces the disciples in the role of exorcist, whilst all other participants remain the same.

28 'The extreme compression of the sentence has given trouble to copyists. Not seeing that in τὸ εἰ δύνῃ Jesus is repeating the words of the father in order to challenge them, a variety of witnesses have inserted πιστεῦσαι, which has the effect of changing the subject of the verb 'can' from Jesus to the father. As a result the τό now seemed more awkward than ever, and many of these witnesses omit it.' (Metzger, *Commentary*, 100) The secondary nature of πιστεῦσαι is generally accepted and may well reflect an attempt to distance Jesus from the demonstration of faith (Pesch, *Markusevangelium*, vol. 2, 85).

29 It is quite possible that the father's words should be interpreted as a sign of his continuing faith in the face of difficulties and not as indicative of ἀπιστία (Martin, *Mark*, 56, and Roloff, *Kerygma*, 151).

30 It is important that the development of the story is not overlooked at this stage. There is a tendency to interpret 9.22 in the light of verse 24: the father's ἀπιστία comes to expression in his tentative approach of Jesus (ἀλλ' εἴ τι δύνῃ κτλ) and it is only after Jesus' response in verse 23 that he finds even a wavering faith. However, the flow of the narrative indicates that the father's hesitancy resulted from the disciples' failure to heal his son; πιστεύω· βοήθει μου τῇ ἀπιστίᾳ

Gospels, a patient or petitioner's faith is never explicitly mentioned in the context of exorcism.[31] This reflects a tendency for exorcism to be seen by the evangelists as a discrete category of release, characterised by direct confrontation between God's minister and evil, taking place within the possessed person, but over which that person has little or no control.[32] Under such circumstances, the faith of a patient or indeed other supportive roles is inappropriate. In consequence, it seems that the nature of the healing provides further support for the conclusion that, whilst πάντα δυνατὰ τῷ πιστεύοντι may have a secondary application with respect to discipleship,[33] it relates within the miracle itself to Jesus, the teacher of disciples.[34] He is the variable factor, absent from the first attempt but present for the second, who shows the father and the faithless disciples that πάντα δυνατὰ τῷ πιστεύοντι.

Confirmation of this interpretation is found at the conclusion of the narrative where a *post mortem* is conducted privately in which the disciples ask Jesus why they were unable to perform the exorcism. Their question not only emphasises the didactic function of the pericope, but also underlines that they were responsible for the previous abortive attempt. Jesus' answer, τοῦτο τὸ γένος ἐν οὐδενὶ δύναται ἐξελθεῖν εἰ μὴ ἐν προσευχῇ (v. 29), initially appears to be in conflict with the priority given to faith elsewhere in the story. However, recourse to another context where Jesus is once again instructing the disciples on faith reveals that Mark – and possibly his sources – recognised an intimate relationship between these two phenomena. We shall explore Mark 11.22–25 in detail

therefore, reflects a resolve – in the light of Jesus' affirmation (v. 23) – to stand by his faith which, whilst present from the beginning, had been compromised by ἀπιστίᾳ in the light of the initial failure.

31 See, however, Twelftree, *Christ*, 121–2, on Mark 7.24–30; but Hull, *Magic*, 73–4.

32 This is particularly apparent in the second Gospel; see Dunn, *Jesus*, 44–53, and Koch, *Bedeutung*, 55–61.

33 It is highly likely that the secondary application of πάντα δυνατὰ τῷ πιστεύοντι to the father, the disciples and, possibly, the crowd is intended by Mark. All parties need to realise such faith, but this insight does not necessarily negate the view that it was Jesus' faith which constituted the missing ingredient for this particular miracle. A number of scholars recognise this distinction and, as a result, consider πάντα δυνατὰ τῷ πιστεύοντι in terms of Jesus' faith on exegetical grounds, but acknowledge the broader application of the logion in the light of the evangelist's didactic concerns (e.g. Anderson, *Mark*, 230–1, and Schweizer, *Mark*, 187–9).

34 Achtemeier, 'Mark 9.14–29', 480–81; Ebeling, *Word*, 234; Hooker, *Mark*, 224; Lohmeyer, *Markus*, 187–91; Martin, *Evangelist*, 109; *Mark*, 56; Schreiber, *Theologie*, 240–1; Thüsing, *New Testament*, 145.

later, but here it should be noted that prayer is portrayed within these verses as an expression of faith.[35] It is possible, therefore, that Jesus' exorcistic command in Mark 9.25 should be understood as a form of prayer and, as such, the channel for or expression of his faith.[36]

Turning to Matthew's version of the pericope (Matt. 17.14–20[21]) we notice how, in keeping with his treatment of miracle stories elsewhere,[37] the account is considerably shorter than Mark's and fails to attest much of the detail found in the latter, including the discussion between Jesus and the patient's father concerning faith (cf. Mark 9.22b-24). In contrast to Luke, Matthew does record a *post mortem* conversation relating the disciples' inability to perform the exorcism, but it is completely different from Mark's and incorporates a form of the mountain-moving logion (Matt. 17.19–20).[38] The absence of Mark 9.22b-24, including πάντα δυνατὰ τῷ πιστεύοντι, and the presence of another faith logion in verse 20[39]

[35] Lane, *Mark*, 335; Pesch, *Markusevangelium*, vol. 2, 97; Schenke, *Wundererzählungen*, 346; Thüsing, *New Testament*, 145.

[36] 'The central part of the story is devoted to the way Jesus elicits a prayer of faith from the father (vv. 21–4) because it exemplifies the attitude required of the disciples in their own exercise of healing power, and also the requisite attitude they must seek in those to whom they minister.' (C. D. Marshall, *Faith*, 223) C. D. Marshall's identification of the father's petition with Jesus' direction that his disciples must pray if they are to exorcise successfully (9.29) is difficult to sustain. Presumably, the father must have made a similar request to Jesus' disciples in the first place; in which case, his faith cannot have been the determinative factor for the miracle. Further, Jesus' words in verse 29 constitute an answer to the disciples' question concerning their inability to perform the exorcism; it seems highly unlikely, therefore, that a reference to the suppliant's conduct would be included at this stage. Clearly, Mark will have presented the pericope under review in such a way as to illuminate the role of faith in the life of his community and, to this end, the narrative serves a broader purpose. However, the roles of exorcist and suppliant are equally valid in a post-resurrection situation and, as a result, we must be cautious about subsuming all the evangelist's teaching about faith under the same all-encompassing umbrella.

[37] Gatzweiler, 'Miracles', 210–14; Greeven, 'Heilung', 65–78; Held, 'Interpreter', esp. 168–92.

[38] The readings constituting verse 21 (cf. τοῦτο δὲ τὸ γένος οὐκ ἐκπορεύεται εἰ μὴ ἐν προσευχῇ καὶ νηστείᾳ and minor variants) seem redundant after the mountain-moving logion and probably represent a secondary assimilation to Mark 9.29 (see Metzger, *Commentary*, 43).

[39] W. R. Telford puts a strong case forward for considering the *Puer Lunaticus* pericope as the earliest discernible context for the mountain-moving logion; it is possible, therefore, that its presence in the Matthean version is traditional and not the result of redaction (*Temple*, 104–9).

significantly clarify the 'mechanics' of the miracle and, in particular, the cause of the disciples' failure.[40]

As Jesus returns from the scene of the transfiguration and joins the crowd, he encounters the sick boy's father who petitions him concerning his son and informs Jesus of the disciples' impotence. The form of address, κύριε, ἐλέησόν μου τὸν υἱόν (v. 15), is found elsewhere in the first Gospel[41] and is considered to be characteristic of the evangelist;[42] here it communicates the christologically alert and petitionary nature of the suppliant's faith. Comparable forms of address are found on the lips of those to whom faith is explicitly attributed (e.g. Matt. 8.5–13; 9.27–31; 15.21–28; cf. 8.25; 14.30), whilst in other contexts Jesus is presented as the focus for belief.[43] Further, the three faith logia unique to Matthew[44] betray a similar conception of faith as petition to Jesus, the Davidic messiah and the church's Lord.[45]

The father's supplication at the beginning of the story (κύριε, ἐλέησόν μου τὸν υἱόν, 17.15) distances him from Jesus' subsequent admonition, which is introduced by the words ὦ γενεὰ ἄπιστος (v. 17).[46] Without further discussion or delay, Jesus performs the exorcism by means of a rebuke which is not recorded and, after the healing, the disciples approach him in private to ascertain why they

40 Matthew's tendency to clarify the relationship between Jesus and suppliants within the miracle traditions is generally recognised: Gerhardsson, *Mighty Acts*, 45–51; Held, 'Interpreter', 187–91, 233–7; Kingsbury, 'Observations', 570.

41 E.g. ἐλέησον ἡμᾶς υἱὸς Δαυίδ (9.27); ἐλέησόν με, κύριε υἱὸς Δαυίδ (15.22); ἐλέησον ἡμᾶς, [κύριε] υἱὸς Δαυίδ (20.30, 31).

42 W. D. Davies, *Setting*, 95; Gerhardsson, *Mighty Acts*, 45–9; Held, 'Interpreter', esp. 284–8; Klein, 'Glaubensverständnis', 38; Lohse, 'Glaube', 343; Theissen, *Miracle Stories*, 138.

43 E.g. πιστευόντων εἰς ἐμέ (Matt. 18.6, 10 [var]; cf. Mark 9.42 πιστευόντων [εἰς ἐμέ]) and καὶ πιστεύσομεν ἐπ' αὐτόν (Matt. 27.42; cf. Mark 15.32 πιστεύσωμεν).

44 I.e. ὕπαγε, ὡς ἐπίστευσας γενηθήτω σοι (8.13; cf. 8.6, 8 κύριε); κατὰ τὴν πίστιν ὑμῶν γενηθήτω ὑμῖν (9.29; cf. 9.27 υἱὸς Δαυίδ and 9.28 κύριε); ὦ γύναι, μεγάλη σου ἡ πίστις· γενηθήτω σοι ὡς θέλεις (15.28; cf. 15.22 κύριε υἱὸς Δαυίδ and 15.25, 27 κύριε). The Matthean provenance of these logia is supported by: G. Barth, 'Πίστις', 224; A. Fuchs, *Untersuchungen*, 150–5, Gundry, *Matthew*, 147; Held, 'Interpreter', 239–41; Roloff, *Kerygma*, 159–61.

45 On the relationship between these titles and miracles, see: Berger, 'Messiastraditionen', esp. 3–9; Bornkamm, 'Stilling', 52–7; Duling, 'Therapeutic', 392–410; Ellis, *Matthew*, 40–46; Held, 'Interpreter', 246–75; more generally, Kingsbury, 'Kyrios', 246–55, and 'Son of David', 591–602.

46 In contrast to Mark's presentation, Matthew's reference to the disciples as those demonstrating ὀλιγόπιστια (17.20) calls into question their identification with the faithless and suggests that the crowd may be the principal target for his admonition (cf. 17.14, τὸν ὄχλον). On the distinction between the disciples and the crowd in Matthew, see Minear, 'Disciples', 28–44.

had been unsuccessful.[47] Jesus' response to the disciples is unambiguous: διὰ τὴν ὀλιγοπιστίαν ὑμῶν (v. 20).[48] They were unable to carry out the deliverance because of their ὀλιγοπιστία. We have already drawn attention to the christologically orientated faith of the father and the crowd's lack of faith, but how does the disciples' ὀλιγοπιστία relate to these poles? Elsewhere in the first Gospel, Matthew uses ὀλιγόπιστος or ὀλιγοπιστία in relation to the disciples' failure to perform or discern the miraculous.[49] A similar understanding is evident here; but rather than indicating a total lack of faith, it seems more likely that Matthew is drawing attention to a deficiency of a particular kind.[50] This is suggested by the presence of the mountain-moving logion which speaks specifically about the power and effectiveness of faith. In contrast to the faith of a suppliant who petitions Jesus for mercy (cf. κύριε, ἐλέησόν μου τὸν υἱὸν κτλ), the disciples must possess a more performatory type of faith which comes to expression in explicit command and is the means by which the power of God is actualised.[51]

The nature of faith attested by the mountain-moving logion will be discussed later, but here we note that, in spite of the christological perspective of faith evident in this pericope and elsewhere, it is difficult not to interpret verse 20 as a commentary on Jesus' previous exorcism, underlining the exemplary significance of his

[47] It is clear that Matthew's redaction of this tradition is intended to clarify the role of the disciples in the healing process. This desire may well constitute a response to a live church situation for the evangelist in which members (perhaps leaders) were either abusing or ignoring this aspect of ministry; see: Dautzenberg, 'Jesusüberlieferung', 45–50; Hill, 'Matthew 7.15–23', 327–48; Schweizer, 'Church', 130–3.

[48] The textual variant ἀπιστίαν probably represents an attempt to harmonise with ἄπιστος in verse 17; it seems unlikely that the *hapax* ὀλιγοπιστία would have been substituted for the more common ἀπιστία; see Metzger, *Commentary*, 43.

[49] E.g. Matt. 8.26 (calming the storm); 14.31 (Peter's walking on water); 16.8 (the miraculous feeding); see: Gerhardsson, *Mighty Acts*, 62; Held, 'Interpreter', 291; Luz, 'Disciples', 107. The only exception is an occurrence which Matthew inherits from tradition (Matt. 6.30/Luke 12.28). On the likely Semitic background of ὀλιγόπιστος and ὀλιγοπιστία, see Ebeling, *Word*, 227–8.

[50] W. D. Davies and Allison, *Saint Matthew*, vol. 2, 727; Gerhardsson, *Mighty Acts*, 63; Luz, 'Disciples', 107; Klein, 'Glaubensverständnis', 39–42; Künzel, *Gemeindeverständnis*, 207.

[51] This interpretation gains support from Paul's allusion to the mountain-moving logion during his discussion of faith as a charismatic gift (1 Cor. 13.2, πᾶσαν τὴν πίστιν ὥστε ὄρη μεθιστάναι cf. 1 Cor. 12.9), given to some Christians for a particular purpose and on behalf of the whole body. It is clear that the apostle is not referring at this juncture to faith as a universal response to God, but to a special kind of faith which was required for the performance of various demonstrations of Christ's presence.

conduct (cf. καί ἐπετίμησεν αὐτῷ ὁ Ἰησοῦς, 17.18).[52] The disciples may have been ineffectual (καὶ οὐκ ἠδυνήθησαν αὐτὸν θεραπεῦσαι, 17.16) owing to their ὀλιγοπιστία, but Jesus was successful because he demonstrated that faith which says τῷ ὄρει τούτῳ· μετάβα ἔνθεν ἐκεῖ, καὶ μεταβήσεται· και οὐδὲν ἀδυνατήσει ὑμῖν – a faith which all who intend to fulfil Christ's commission must demonstrate.

We have now considered Matthew's and Mark's versions of the *Puer Lunaticus* pericope in some detail and identified evidence of interest in Jesus' faith relating to the training and enabling of disciples. Both accounts imply that the disciples would have successfully performed the exorcism if they had demonstrated the kind of faith exhibited by Jesus. What is less clear is whether this perspective originates with the evangelists themselves. Given that it comes to expression through elements of the story unique to each account, it is apparent, on the one hand, that neither of them proved successful in suppressing traditional material if this was their intention and, on the other, that such evidence is consistent with redactional activity. It is unlikely, however, that Matthew and Mark would have independently revised their sources in such a way as to implicate Jesus with faith; in any case, Jesus' faith is not the primary focus for their accounts. Further, our surveys in chapter 1 uncovered little to suggest that Jesus' faith would have been considered a particularly contentious or noteworthy issue at the time when the gospels were composed. In the light of these factors, the motif of Jesus' faith should probably be understood as something which the evangelists inherited, utilised and perhaps even developed from tradition.[53]

2.2 Stilling of the storm and walking on the water

Having recognised the function of Jesus' faith vis-à-vis the training of the disciples in the *Puer Lunaticus* pericope, we now move on to

52 Matthew does distinguish between the faith of the patient or advocate (e.g. 8.5–13; 9.1–8; 9.27–31; 15.21–8) and that of the miracle worker (e.g. 17.14–20; 21.18–22), although he considers both categories to be in some sense petitionary in nature. We shall return later in this chapter to the tensions caused by maintaining that the first Gospel portrays Jesus as an exemplar of miracle-working faith whilst, at the same time, maintaining that, as messianic Lord, he is also the focus for that faith.

53 In the light of these conclusions, the comments of P. J. Achtemeier are particularly interesting: 'Into this account, the discussion about faith has been inserted (vss 23–24). The point of this insert, however, is unique in the gospel literature, in that the clear implication of vs 23 is that Jesus can do this act because he has the requisite faith ... The story, with its insertion, thus clearly belongs to a level of theological reflection other than, and, as our analysis has shown, quite likely prior

consider two further miracle traditions which possibly share this understanding. In their present form, the 'stilling of the storm' and the 'walking on the water' narratives fulfil an epiphanic role through which Jesus' lordship over nature is revealed.[54] And yet another motif worthy of attention can also be discerned. Starting with the 'stilling of the storm' (Matt. 8.23–7/Mark 4.35–41/Luke 8.22–5), we note that all three accounts describe how the disciples find themselves 'at sea' in the midst of a raging storm and with Jesus asleep in the boat. Fearful for their lives, they wake Jesus and inform him of the predicament and request his assistance.[55] In each case, Jesus rebukes (ἐπιτίμησεν) the elements and tranquillity (γαλήνη) returns, with the result that the disciples are left awestruck concerning their master's true identity.

Prior to his rebuke in Matthew and afterwards in Mark and Luke, Jesus questions his disciples concerning their faith: τί δειλοί ἐστε, ὀλιγόπιστοι; (Matt. 8.26); τί δειλοί ἐστε, οὔπω ἔχετε πίστιν; (Mark 4.40); ποῦ ἡ πίστις ὑμῶν; (Luke 8.25). Given that their response to the miracle relates to the one who is able to control the natural elements (Matt. 8.27/Mark 4.41/Luke 8.25), it is usually thought that Jesus was challenging his disciples about their lack of trust in him and his ability to keep them safe.[56] This interpretation,

to, that of the synoptic authors ... This implication about the source of Jesus' power (his faith) found little support in the continuing theological and Christological reflections of the primitive church, as its absence in other gospel traditions clearly shows.' ('Mark 9.14–29', 480–1)

[54] E.g. 'What sort of man is this, that even winds and sea obey (ὑπακούουσιν) him?' (Matt. 8.27); 'Who then is this, that even wind and sea obey (ὑπακούει) him?' (Mark 4.41); 'Who then is this, that he commands even wind and water, and they obey (ὑπακούουσιν) him?' (Luke 8.25); 'And those in the boat worshipped him, saying, "Truly you are the Son of God."' (Matt. 14.33). See: Achtemeier, 'Person', 169–76; Bornkamm, 'Stilling', 53–7; Busse, *Wunder*, 202–4; Koch, *Bedeutung*, 92–9; van der Loos, *Miracles*, esp. 646–9; Nineham, *St Mark*, 148–9; Schenke, *Wundererzählungen*, 55–9.

[55] Only Matthew records a positive request for help; in the others it is implied: κύριε, σῶσον, ἀπολλύμεθα. (Matt. 8.25); cf. διδάσκαλε, οὐ μέλει σοι ὅτι ἀπολλύμεθα (Mark 4.38) and ἐπιστάτα ἐπιστάτα, ἀπολλύμεθα. (Luke 8.24). On the significance and nature of the disciples' request, see Guelich, *Mark*, vol. 1, 266–7.

[56] Anderson, *Mark*, 145–6, and Cranfield, *Saint Mark*, 174. A number of scholars understand the focus to be more in terms of faith in God's provision which is channelled through Jesus: Lane, *Mark*, 177–8; Pesch, *Markusevangelium*, vol. 2, 275–7; Schweizer, *Mark*, 109. L. Schenke views the disciples' lack of faith in terms of their unpreparedness to perish with him (*Wundererzählungen*, 83–93), whilst M. Dibelius considers the focus to be upon confidence in Jesus as a great miracle worker (*Tradition*, 77–80) and V. Taylor maintains that the disciples lacked faith in the fatherly care of God which Jesus exhibited when asleep in the boat (*St*

however, accommodates certain details in the story, but conflicts with others. Firstly, within the Synoptics, faith is often associated with an approach to Jesus for assistance;[57] here, on the contrary, this action is indicative of the disciples' faithlessness or lack of faith. Secondly, δειλός is a strange choice to express the disciples' fear of perishing. It is only attested here in the Synoptics[58] and in comparable contexts, φοβέω and its derivatives are used to express fear and similar emotions;[59] indeed, fear seems an entirely natural response under such circumstances. Why then are the disciples challenged in diction more indicative of cowardice or timidity? Thirdly, we have already drawn attention to the way in which ὀλιγόπιστος is associated in the first Gospel with the disciples' inability to perform or discern the miraculous; in the present context, this may indicate that the evangelist intended that they should be considered in relation to the performance of the stilling. Fourthly, each account records the disciples' amazement at how the natural elements obey (ὑπακούω) Jesus when he issues a command; the parallel with Luke's version of how faith as a grain of mustard seed can say to the sycamine tree ἐκριζώθητι καὶ φυτεύθητι ἐν τῇ θαλάσσῃ· καὶ ὑπήκουσεν ἂν ὑμῖν (17.6) is striking. Finally and in more general terms, the means by which Jesus performs this miracle are remarkably consistent with certain characteristics of mountain-moving faith spoken of elsewhere (Matt. 17.20; 21.20; Mark 11.23; cf. Luke 17.6). For example, faith comes to expression in a specific and unambiguous command addressed to the natural order which secures the prescribed end.[60]

Mark, 276); on the various interpretations of faith in this pericope, see C. D. Marshall, *Faith*, 215–9.

57 E.g. Matt. 9.1–8/Mark 2.1–12/Luke 5.17–26; Matt. 9.18–26/Mark 5.21–43/Luke 8.40–56; Matt. 8.5–13/Luke 7.1–10; Mark 10.46–52/Luke 18.35–43; Matt. 9.27–31; 15.21–8; Luke 7.36–50; 17.11–19. See the discussion of faith as 'a boundary-crossing motif (ein grenzüberschreitendes Motiv)' in Theissen, *Miracle Stories*, 129–40.

58 Δειλός, Matt. 8.26/Mark 4.40; Rev. 21.8; δειλία, 2 Tim. 1.7; δειλιάω, John 14.27; cf. the association with the πιστεύω group in Rev. 21.8, 'But as for the cowardly, the faithless (τοῖς δὲ δειλοῖς καὶ ἀπίστοις) ... their lot shall be in the lake that burns with fire and sulphur, which is the second death.'

59 In addition to the traditions under review (Mark 4.41/Luke 8.25; Matt. 14.26/ Mark 6.50; Matt. 14.27, 30), Jesus' answer to Jairus after the healing of the haemorrhaging woman and news of his daughter's death is particularly significant (μὴ φοβοῦ, μόνον πίστευε/πίστευσον Mark 5.36/Luke 8.50). Also Matt. 9.8; 17.6, 7; 27.54; 28.4, 8; Mark 5.15; 16.8; Luke 1.12, 65; 2.9; 5.26; 7.16; 8.37; 9.34; 21.26.

60 Cf. 'Then he arose and rebuked (ἐπετίμησεν) the winds and the sea; and there was a great calm.' (Matt. 8.26); 'And he awoke and rebuked (ἐπετίμησεν) the wind, and said to the sea, "Peace! Be still!" And the wind ceased, and there was a great calm.' (Mark 4.39); 'And he awoke and rebuked (ἐπετίμησεν) the wind and the

The cumulative force of these observations points towards an alternative interpretation for the disciples' lack of faith and for the significance of the pericope as a whole. From this perspective, Jesus admonishes the disciples because they fail to demonstrate that kind of miracle-working faith which has power over the natural elements.[61] He then replaces them in the role of miracle worker, stills the storm by exhibiting that faith which they lacked and thereby provides the disciples and the early church with another example of faith in action.[62]

A similar function can be discerned in Matthew's inclusion of Peter's attempt to walk on water (Matt. 14.28–31) within the tradition narrating Jesus' performance of the same feat (Matt. 14.22–33/Mark 6.45–52; cf. John 6.16–21).[63] In this case, Peter, initially successful in joining his Lord upon the sea, is soon overcome with fear and begins to sink. He cries out for assistance and receives help as Jesus once more challenges a disciple concerning faith (ὀλιγόπιστε, εἰς τί ἐδίστασας), although this time the link between faith and performance of miraculous activity is more direct.[64] The implication is that Peter initially demonstrates faith and is able to walk on water,[65] but subsequently sinks when

raging waves; and they ceased, and there was a calm.' (Luke 8.24). These areas of correspondence will be discussed further in section 3.

61 'The contrast between their [i.e. the disciples'] behaviour and his [i.e. Jesus'] demonstrates their different attitudes to God: Jesus trusts, while the disciples panic.' (Hooker, *Mark*, 140; also Coutts, 'Authority', 112–13) M. D. Hooker does, however, acknowledge that the story in Mark's redaction functions to underline the disciples' failure to believe in Jesus' true significance.

62 The importance of this pericope for instruction on discipleship, as well as christology, is recognised by many (e.g. Busse, *Wunder*, 202–5; Gnilka, *Markus*, vol. 1, 195–8; Guelich, *Mark*, vol. 1, 267–70; Pesch, *Markusevangelium*, vol. 2, 275–7), although its contribution tends to be understood in terms of what the story reveals of the early church's trust in her risen Lord.

63 On Matthew's involvement in this section of the gospel, see Gundry, *Matthew*, 295–302.

64 'Peter, one of those who were afraid, overcomes his anxiety and is ready for the highest faith. That he is able to walk on the water like Jesus proves that he had this faith.' Held, 'Interpreter', 206.

65 Once again, as an early reference to this tradition and one in which Peter is challenged by the penitent Senator Marcellus concerning the machinations of Simon Magus indicates, there are strong parallels with Jesus' teaching concerning mountain-moving faith: 'So I beg you, do not resent what I am about to say: that Christ our Lord, whom you preach in truth, said to your fellow-apostles in your presence, "If you have faith like a grain of mustard seed, you shall say to this mountain, Remove yourself, and at once it will remove (*Si habueritis fidem sicut granum sinapis, dicitis monti huic: transfer te et continuo se transferet*)." But, Peter, this Simon called you an unbeliever (*infidelem*), since you lost faith (*dubitantem*) when upon the water; indeed I heard that he also had said, "Those who are with

overwhelmed by doubt.[66] By describing how Peter is able to imitate Jesus, the narrative invites comparison between these two figures: the disciple sees his master doing something and, at his beckoning, attempts to follow his example.[67] Further, whilst not overlooking its christological significance,[68] the episode does seem to favour the conclusion that if Peter was able to walk on water by faith, then Jesus was successful for the same reason.[69] Certainly, we find this assessment in later Christian reflection; for example, the Sibylline Oracles allude to Christ as one who 'will stop the winds with a word. He will calm the raging sea by walking on it with feet of peace and with faith (τοὺς ἀνέμους παύσειε λόγῳ, στορέσει δὲ θάλασσαν μαινομένην ποσὶν εἰρήνης πίστει τε πατήσας).' (8.273–4 [*OrS* 161]). And again, the Odes of Solomon speak of how the Lord was able to breach the rivers of tribulation and provide an example for others to follow:

> The Lord has bridged them [i.e. the rivers of tribulation]
> by His Word,

me have not understood me." Therefore if you lost faith (*dubitabatis*), you on whom he laid his hands, whom he also chose, and with whom he worked miracles ...' (Act. Pet. 10) This and the following extra-biblical texts are discussed in chapter 6.

66 Matthew records that Jesus interprets Peter's fear (ἐφοβήθη, 14.30) as doubt (εἰς τί ἐδίστασας, 14.31); the only other occurrence of διστάζω in the New Testament is Matt. 28.17. On the significance of the doubting motif in this narrative, see G. Barth, 'Glaube', 287–9.

67 The importance of the pericope for discipleship has been noted, but usually this is envisaged in terms of the need for Christians to recognise the presence of their Lord in situations of difficulty and to place their trust in him (Beare, *Matthew*, 330; Hill, *Matthew*, 247; Schweizer, *Matthew*, 323). Whilst this outlook is congruent with the evangelist's intentions elsewhere, it neither exhausts the significance of the story under consideration, nor provides the most obvious meaning for it; as we shall note later, it is possible that Matthew intended both perspectives. Although W. D. Davies and D. C. Allison consider that ὀλιγοπιστία in Matt. 17 may reflect a 'special faith required to perform great miracles' (*Saint Matthew*, vol. 2, 727), this option is not considered in Matt. 14.28–31 (vol. 2, 509).

68 'And those in the boat worshipped him, saying, "Truly you are the Son of God (ἀληθῶς θεοῦ υἱὸς εἶ)".' (Matt. 14.33; cf. κύριε, Matt. 14.28; κύριε, σῶσον με, Matt. 14.30).

69 'The Christology provides the basis for what is told. Peter cannot walk on the water but Jesus – who can – gives him the command and the ability.' (*Mighty Acts*, 57) B. Gerhardsson allows Matthew's theological assessment of Jesus to provide the interpretative key for the significance of the overall pericope; in doing so, however, he fails to consider the areas of comparison between Jesus and Peter which are also evident. These, too, have christological implications, but in terms of Jesus' significance for discipleship rather than his importance for knowledge of God.

And He walked and crossed them on foot.
And His footsteps were standing firm upon the waters,
  and were not destroyed;
But they are like a beam of wood that is constructed on
  truth.
On this side and that the waves were lifted up,
But the footsteps of our Lord Messiah stand firm.
And they are neither blotted out,
Nor destroyed.
And the Way has been appointed for those who cross over
  after Him,
And for those who adhere to the path of His faith
  (*dhymnwth*);
And who adore His name.
Hallelujah. (Odes Sol. 39.9–13 [*OSol* 135–6])

As we concluded in the case of the *Puer Lunaticus* narrative, allusions to Jesus' faith in the stilling of the storm pericope probably originate in tradition. The epiphanic function concerning Jesus' identity is very much to the fore in all three versions, whilst there is little sign that Mark or Luke wished to develop any implicit reference to Jesus' faith. However, the transposition of the disciples' reprimand concerning their lack of faith to before the miracle and the presence of ὀλιγόπιστοι in the first Gospel may be indicative of a desire to underline the correspondence between the miracle-working ability of Jesus and that of his followers. We have already seen how Matthew's account of the exorcism in Matthew 17.14–20 clarifies this very relationship and a similar parallel is created in the walking on the water episode by the inclusion of Peter's attempt. It may well be, therefore, that in addition to the christological focus of faith in his Gospel, Matthew also wished to acknowledge the place of Jesus' faith within the performance of miracles and to exploit its exemplary function for the life of the community. If this was the case, it seems that Matthew did not consider faith in Jesus and the faith of Jesus to be mutually exclusive. A disciple must follow Jesus' example in the life of faith; but even where faith comes to expression in performatory miracle-working conduct, its source and object is still the person of Jesus who is messiah, Lord and son of God.

2.3 Withering of the fig tree

The 'withering of the fig tree' is the final miracle to be considered in this section. It is only attested in the first two Gospels[70] and there are significant differences in the evangelists' handling of the tradition. Part of this may result from the strangeness of the event, Jesus' punitive response to a fruitless fig tree, and its seeming incongruity with the other miracles recorded in the Gospels.[71] As such, it invites a more symbolic or discursive interpretation and this approach is clearly evident in Mark's redaction, where the narrative frames the 'cleansing of the temple' pericope. Intercalation is a characteristically Markan technique[72] and here it encourages the reader to view the cursing alongside Jesus' conduct in the temple as judgement upon the corrupt cultus.[73] Further, when Jesus illustrates the power of faith in terms of levelling τῷ ὄρει τούτῳ, attention is once again drawn to the temple mount and to the seat of corruption.[74]

Although Mark undoubtedly puts the fig tree tradition to good use as a vehicle for developing central concerns, his handling has the effect of interrupting the flow of the story. In particular, with reference to our own investigations, it loosens the link between Jesus' performance of the miracle and the ensuing teaching on faith. As a consequence, faith becomes the key to discerning the source and significance of Jesus' actions in the temple, rather than

[70] Matt. 21.18–22/Mark 11.12–14, 20–5; whilst not recording this miracle, Luke does include a parable on the same subject and with a similar message which may constitute a variant (Luke 13.6–9; see Beare, *Matthew*, 419, and I. H. Marshall, *Luke*, 552). The other parable of the fig tree is recorded in all three Synoptics and clearly has a different application (Matt. 24.32–5/Mark 13.28–31/Luke 21.29–33).

[71] This is the only punitive miracle attributed to Jesus in the New Testament (cf. Act 5.1–11; see Theissen, *Miracle Stories*, 109), although this type is more prevalent in the apocryphal literature and especially the infancy gospels (e.g. Infancy Gospel of Thomas).

[72] Cf. Mark 3.20–35; 5.21–43; 6.7–32; 8.22–10.52; 14.1–11; 14.54–72. See: Achtemeier, *Mark*, 32–33; Dewey, *Debate*, 21–2; von Dobschütz, 'Erzählerkunst', 195–6; Kee, *Community*, 54–6; Stein, 'Methodology', 193–4. Anderson, *Mark*, 263, and Schweizer, *Mark*, 230 are amongst those who consider the current example as Markan.

[73] Although the fig tree can be a symbol for Israel, especially with reference to her punishment (e.g. Isa. 28.3; Jer. 5.17; 8.13; Hos. 2.12; 9.10, 16; Amos 4.9; Micah 7.1; Joel 1.7, 12), it is probable that Mark intends a narrower focus here in terms of Israel's Temple and its cultus. On this interpretation, C. D. Marshall, *Faith*, 159–74, and Telford, *Temple*, 39–68.

[74] Given the context, it seems that if a particular mountain is intended, the Temple Mount is more probable than the Mount of Olives (cf. Zech. 14.4).

the prerequisite for accomplishing miraculous acts of God.[75] Thus, within Mark's redaction, mountain-levelling faith is identified with the means by which those people and structures corrupting the worship of God will be overthrown (11.23), and praying faith characterises those who worship God authentically and wish to return the Lord's house to a house of prayer (11.24–5; cf. 11.17).[76]

In spite of Mark's presentation of the fig tree incident, an implicit comparison between Jesus' action of cursing and those who (ὃς ἂν) demonstrate mountain-levelling faith is discernible.[77] Even with the insertion of the cleansing, it is still Peter's comment concerning the withered tree in verse 21 which precipitates Jesus' teaching about faith. Further, the kind of faith which is described by Jesus as having authority over the natural order (cf. ἄρθητι καὶ βλήθητι εἰς τὴν θάλασσαν) seems remarkably similar to that which enables Jesus to say to another part of creation, μηκέτι εἰς τὸν αἰῶνα ἐκ σοῦ μηδεὶς καρπὸν φάγοι (v. 14). Thus, although Mark shows little signs of wishing to develop this line of thinking, his account nevertheless indicates some degree of correspondence between Jesus' act of cursing and the possibilities open to those who exhibit faith.[78] One conclusion suggested by this association is that Jesus also performed the miracle by faith, a faith which the disciples must share if they are to perform comparable acts of God.[79]

The relation between the fig tree incident and Jesus' teaching on faith is much more pronounced in Matthew's version, where the cleansing of the temple constitutes an independent section (Matt. 21.12–13). The eschatological dimensions of the latter are underlined by the report that, once he had purged the temple of those corrupting its purpose as a house of prayer, Jesus healed the blind and crippled.[80] In the light of David's banning of such invalids from

75 Throughout the Gospel, the πιστεύω group is associated with understanding. Consider, for example, the role of faith as the means of discerning Jesus' significance in relation to God's forgiveness (2.5), the gospel (1.15), healing (6.6), the messiah (9.42; 10.52; 15.32) and the personal nature of salvation (5.34); cf. John the Baptist (11.31) and false messiahs (13.21). See: Hahn, 'Verständnis', 54–7; Martin, *Evangelist*, 110; Schmithals, *Markus*, vol. 1, 156–8; Telford, *Temple*, 82.

76 See especially Hooker, *Mark*, 269, and C. D. Marshall, *Faith*, 163–74.

77 It is probable that the reference to fig trees, as well as to mountain-levelling, has an eschatological significance in this context; so Derrett, 'Figtrees', 249–65, and Hiers, 'Season', 394–400.

78 Pesch, *Markusevangelium*, vol. 2, 204–6, and Schmithals, *Markus*, vol. 2, 501.

79 Gnilka, *Markus*, vol. 2, 134, and Hooker, *Mark*, 269.

80 Cf. Isa. 35.5; 61.1; Gen. R. XCV.1 (on Gen. 46.28); Eccles. R. I.4.2 (on Eccles. 1.4); Tanh. B. on Ps. 146.8. The purification of the Temple, of course, also had eschatological implications in Jewish expectation; see Sanders, *Jesus*, 77–90.

the temple (2 Sam. 5.6–8), it is difficult not to interpret their inclusion here as signal of the arrival in Jerusalem of the messianic son of David (Matt. 21.9, 15; cf. 11.2–6).[81] After spending the night in Bethany, Jesus and his disciples return to Jerusalem and on their way encounter a fig tree which fails to provide sustenance for the messiah. Jesus then pronounces 'May no fruit ever come from you again!' and immediately the tree withers.

Although the symbolism of this act within the broader messianic context is not excluded, the attention remains focussed on the event itself by the disciples' question, 'How did the fig tree wither at once?' (v. 20). In this way, rather than encouraging the reader to view the withering in relation to, for example, the cleansing of the temple, Matthew uses the withering as an opportunity to present teaching on the means by which acts of God are performed.[82] In response to his followers' question, therefore, Jesus encourages them to exhibit undoubting, miracle-working faith. At this point the conduct of Jesus in the withering and that which he intends the disciples to display are brought into close proximity: 'Truly, I say to you, if you have faith and never doubt, you will not only do what has been done to the fig tree, but even if you say to this mountain, "Be taken up and cast into the sea," it will be done. And whatever you ask in prayer, you will receive, if you have faith.' (vv. 21–2)

Not only will they be able to mimic Jesus in the destruction of the fig tree, but they will also participate in that dimension of God's sovereign activity which is characteristic of the eschatological era, namely, the levelling of mountains.[83] In the light of this, it seems highly unlikely that Matthew would have brought Jesus' action in the withering and his teaching on the power of faith into such an intimate relationship if he had not intended Jesus' conduct to be interpreted in terms of faith: Jesus, who renders the fig tree barren by faith, explains the nature of that faith to his disciples and uses his own example as a means of encouraging them to perform similar and more far reaching miracles.[84]

81 Duling, 'Therapeutic', 404; Gibbs, 'Purpose', 460; Schweizer, *Matthew*, 408.

82 Held, 'Interpreter', 288–91; Gerhardsson, *Mighty Acts*, 58–9; Lohmeyer, *Markus*, 302–3; Telford, *Temple*, 78.

83 It is improbable that mountain-levelling is to be understood literally in this context; rather, the emphasis is upon God's action in the eschaton (see section 3.1).

84 '"Not only will you do what was done to the fig tree" is unique to the first gospel. Basically, Matthew constructs it by taking the fig tree from the context and using two of his favourite words, μόνον and ποιήσετε. The new line links the saying

An initial difficulty with this proposal concerns the suitability of the fig tree tradition for such a didactic purpose. Unlike the healing of the possessed boy considered earlier, the current miracle appears tangential to Jesus' primary concerns and unrepresentative of the ministry for which the disciples were being prepared; as such, it seems an inappropriate point of departure for instruction on the dynamics of faith. Further, as we have noted, Matthew does not exploit the symbolic significance of the withering to the same extent as Mark; on the contrary, he emphasises the withering as an event[85] although, characteristically, records few details concerning the miracle itself. This suggests that Matthew had little substantive interest in the nature of this particular miracle, but simply used it as a context for presenting teaching on faith.

A more significant objection and one which applies to Matthew's redaction of the other traditions considered in section 2 arises from the recognition that within this pericope faith is not only described in terms of miracle-working performatory utterances, but also of petition (cf. 'And whatever you ask in prayer, you will receive, if you have faith.'). If, as we have indicated in section 2.1, the evangelist understands faith as supplication directed towards Jesus, the church's messiah and Lord,[86] how could he also attribute such faith to Jesus himself?[87] The issue here revolves around whether Matthew, writing in a post-resurrection situation, could present

about the disciples' faith with Jesus' causing the fig tree to wither. In this way Matthew makes Jesus a paradigm in the exercise of faith.' (Gundry, *Matthew*, 417)

85 Gerhardsson, *Mighty Acts*, 58.

86 The classic miracle tradition from this point of view is Matt. 9.27–31, which is only recorded in the first Gospel. The blind men, who address Jesus in messianic terms (υἱὸς Δαυίδ), affirm their commitment to the Lord (ναί, κύριε) when asked by him, πιστεύετε ὅτι δύναμαι τοῦτο ποιῆσαι? In response, Jesus says, κατὰ τὴν πίστιν ὑμῶν γενηθήτω ὑμῖν.

87 This dilemma may well be reflected in the reluctance of scholars to see a reference to Jesus' faith in Matthew's redaction. For example, W. R. Telford, who comments that 'What is of prime concern is the means whereby the tree has withered' and who points out Matthew's emphasis upon 'supplicating faith' in Matt. 21.22, concludes: 'Hence the story, which nowhere speaks of Jesus either exercising faith in his cursing of the tree nor of praying for its withering, is taken as a paradigm for the power of supplicating faith, a power available to the disciples, and thereby to Christian believers in general.' (*Temple*, 78–9) What is not clear from this assessment is how, given the evangelist's intention to explain the means by which the miracle reported in Matt. 21.20 took place, the references to faith in the following verses (which actually refer to the withering) can exclude Jesus. Matthew certainly intended to demonstrate the significance and broader application of the faith evident in the fig tree incident, but not at the cost of denying the exemplary function of Jesus for that faith.

Jesus as an exemplar of a faith of which he had become in some sense the substance or content. Clearly, the proposal that Matthew envisaged Jesus as both the model believer and the object of faith may seem strange or unfamiliar, but it is questionable whether these categories are mutually exclusive. Rather, their resolution is a matter of perspective: viewed anthropologically (e.g. in terms of human response to God), Jesus is understood as one with faith in God; viewed theologically (e.g. in terms of God's salvific initiatives), he is interpreted as God's messiah who encompasses salvation and, as such, is the legitimate focus of faith.

These two christological perspectives represented by the faith of Jesus and faith in Jesus or, in more contemporary terms, christology 'from below' and 'from above', receive considerable attention from the early church fathers.[88] There is no reason, however, why Matthew could not also have explored the significance of Jesus in these terms as well; certainly, the findings of the current section point in that direction. A further indication of this process may be supplied by the evangelist's understanding of Jesus' suffering: on the one hand, Jesus' suffering provides an example for others to follow (e.g. 16.21–6; 20.20–7); on the other, it constitutes the means by which God secures the salvation of all (20.28; 26.26–9).

3 Correspondence between Jesus' faith logia and his miracles

Most of Jesus' sayings concerning faith occur in association with miraculous activity of one sort or another. The distinctive understanding of faith which emerges from these logia has been recognised by many and considered indicative of their dominical pedigree.[89] An equally significant observation, however, concerns the striking correspondence between certain characteristics of this view of faith and Jesus' conduct in relation to the performance of miracles.[90] In order to demonstrate this, we shall present the

[88] This matter is taken up again in chapter 6.

[89] Esp. Matt. 17.20; 21.21; Mark 11.23; Luke 17.6. Bultmann, *Jesus*, 189–91; Hermisson and Lohse, *Faith*, 121–4; Goppelt, *Theology*, vol. 1, 149–54; Jeremias, *Theology*, 159–66; Lührmann, *Glaube*, 17–30; Perrin, *Rediscovering*, 130–42; Zmijewski, 'Glaube', 95–6.

[90] 'But now, the concept of faith testified to above all in the saying about the faith that moves mountains is strikingly similar to the extremely marked use of the concept of faith in the healing miracles.' (Ebeling, *Word*, 230) The most thorough discussion of the relationship between the synoptic miracle and saying traditions is probably still that of Perels, *Wunderüberlieferung*.

relevant faith logia[91] and then introduce the major areas of convergence.

Matt. 8.10/Luke 7.9 (Jesus to the centurion): ἀμὴν λέγω ὑμῖν, παρ' οὐδενὶ τοσαύτην πίστιν ἐν τῷ Ἰσραὴλ εὗρον./λέγω ὑμῖν, οὐδὲ ἐν τῷ Ἰσραὴλ τοσαύτην πίστιν εὗρον.

Matt. 8.13 (Jesus to the centurion): ὕπαγε, ὡς ἐπίστευσας γενηθήτω σοι.

Matt. 8.26/Mark 4.40/Luke 8.25 (Jesus to the disciples in the boat): τί δειλοί ἐστε, ὀλιγόπιστοι;/τί δειλοί ἐστε; οὔπω ἔχετε πίστιν;/ποῦ ἡ πίστις ὑμῶν;

Matt. 9.22/Mark 5.34/Luke 8.48; Mark 10.52/Luke 18.42; Luke 17.19; cf. Luke 7.50 (to the haemorrhaging woman, blind Bartimaeus and the leper who returned): ἡ πίστις σου σέσωκέν σε.

Mark 5.36/Luke 8.50 (Jesus to Jairus after news that his daughter had died): μὴ φοβοῦ, μόνον πίστευε./μὴ φοβοῦ, μόνον πίστευσον, καὶ σωθήσεται.

Matt. 9.28–9 (Jesus to the blind men): πιστεύετε ὅτι δύναμαι τοῦτο ποιῆσαι; . . . κατὰ τὴν πίστιν ὑμῶν γενηθήτω ὑμῖν.

Matt. 14.31 (Jesus to Peter on the water): ὀλιγόπιστε, εἰς τί ἐδίστασας;

Matt. 15.28 (Jesus to the Canaanite woman): ὦ γύναι, μεγάλη σου ἡ πίστις· γενηθήτω σοι ὡς θέλεις.

Matt. 16.8 (Jesus to the disciples, who were reflecting on his miraculous feeding): τί διαλογίζεσθε ἐν ἑαυτοῖς, ὀλιγόπιστοι, ὅτι ἄρτους οὐκ ἔχετε;

Mark 9.23 (Jesus to the possessed boy's father): τὸ εἰ δύνῃ, πάντα δυνατὰ τῷ πιστεύοντι.

Matt. 17.20 (Jesus to the disciples after they had failed to heal the possessed boy): διὰ τὴν ὀλιγοπιστίαν ὑμῶν· ἀμὴν γὰρ λέγω ὑμῖν, ἐὰν ἔχητε πίστιν ὡς κόκκον σινάπεως, ἐρεῖτε τῷ ὄρει τούτῳ· μετάβα ἔνθεν ἐκεῖ, καὶ μεταβήσεται· καὶ οὐδὲν ἀδυνατήσει ὑμῖν.

Matt. 21.21–2 (Jesus to the disciples after the fig tree had with-

[91] There is no special significance to the structure of this list; it has been compiled for ease of reference during the rest of section 3. In addition to the logia included, see also ὦ γενεὰ ἄπιστος (Matt. 17.17/Mark 9.19/Luke 9.41) and σημεῖα δὲ τοῖς πιστεύσασιν ταῦτα παρακολουθήσει· ἐν τῷ ὀνόματί μου δαιμόνια ἐκβαλοῦσιν, γλώσσαις λαλήσουσιν καιναῖς, [καὶ ἐν ταῖς χερσὶν] ὄφεις ἀροῦσιν, κἂν θανάσιμόν τι πίωσιν οὐ μὴ αὐτοὺς βλάψῃ, ἐπὶ ἀρρώστους χεῖρας ἐπιθήσουσιν καὶ καλῶς ἕξουσιν (Mark 16.17–18).

ered): ἀμὴν λέγω ὑμῖν, ἐὰν ἔχητε πίστιν καὶ μὴ διακριθῆτε, οὐ μόνον τὸ τῆς συκῆς ποιήσετε, ἀλλὰ κἂν τῷ ὄρει τούτῳ εἴπητε· ἄρθητι καὶ βλήθητι εἰς τὴν θάλασσαν, γενήσεται· καὶ πάντα ὅσα ἂν αἰτήσητε ἐν τῇ προσευχῇ πιστεύοντες λήμψεσθε.

Mark 11.22–4 (Jesus to the disciples after the fig tree had withered): ἔχετε πίστιν θεοῦ. ἀμὴν λέγω ὑμῖν ὅτι ὃς ἂν εἴπῃ τῷ ὄρει τούτῳ· ἄρθητι καὶ βλήθητι εἰς τὴν θάλασσαν, καὶ μὴ διακριθῇ ἐν τῇ καρδίᾳ αὐτοῦ ἀλλὰ πιστεύῃ ὅτι ὃ λαλεῖ γίνεται, ἔσται αὐτῷ. διὰ τοῦτο λέγω ὑμῖν, πάντα ὅσα προσεύχεσθε καὶ αἰτεῖσθε, πιστεύετε ὅτι ἐλάβετε, καὶ ἔσται ὑμῖν.

Luke 17.6 (Jesus to the apostles after they asked him, πρόσθες ἡμῖν πίστιν): εἰ ἔχετε πίστιν ὡς κόκκον σινάπεως, ἐλέγετε ἂν τῇ συκαμίνῳ [ταύτῃ]· ἐκριζώθητι καὶ φυτεύθητι ἐν τῇ θαλάσσῃ· καὶ ὑπήκουσεν ἂν ὑμῖν.

3.1 The eschatological and salvific context of faith

Most of the sayings listed above offer little description of the substance and context of faith. The major exceptions to this are provided by those which speak of mountain-levelling (Matt. 17.20; 21.21; Mark 11.23; cf. 1 Cor. 13.2) or tree-uprooting (Luke 17.6) faith.[92] The former image has, in particular, attracted a range of interpretations[93] and although such expressions are difficult to define, three factors seem determinative. Firstly, within the Jewish tradition prior to the New Testament, mountains were considered to be the prerogative of God.[94] God existed before them, he made them and has authority over them.[95] They tremble before God and are demolished by him either through divine intent or simply as a

[92] The relationship between these different versions is complex. Recent studies have tended to conclude that Matt. 17.20 represents the earliest version (G. Barth, 'Glaube', 269–72; Hahn, 'Wort', 149–69; Telford, *Temple*, 95–127), although there is still disagreement concerning whether Luke 17.6 is an independent logion (so Perrin, *Rediscovering*, 138; Manson, *Sayings*, 141; see also W. D. Davies and Allison, *Saint Matthew*, vol. 2, 727–8; Derrett, 'Mountains', esp. 243–4, and Zmijewski, 'Glaube', 81–103). Schwarz, 'πιστιν', 27–35, considers possible Semitic *Vorlagen*.

[93] See SB, vol. 1, 759, and Telford, *Temple*, 109–17.

[94] The following works have informed much of what is said here: Donaldson, *Jesus*, 25–83; Foerster, 'ὄρος', 475–87; Talmon, 'הַר', 427–47.

[95] E.g. Job 9.5; Pss. 65.6; 90.2; 95.4; Isa. 40.12.

consequence of his presence.[96] By implication, therefore, a faith which is able to move mountains is one which participates in the actions of God (cf. τὸ εἰ δύνῃ, πάντα δυνατὰ τῷ πιστεύοντι, Mark 9.23; Matt. 19.26/Mark 10.27/Luke 18.27).[97]

Secondly, mountains are associated specifically with God's presence. He is often encountered there[98] and, in particular, has chosen to reveal himself on Mount Sinai or Horeb[99] and to make his dwelling on Mount Zion.[100] The sayings under review may well speak of a particular mountain (τῷ ὄρει τούτῳ) and, given the context of the withering of the fig tree pericope, the Temple Mount or Mount Zion, the peak supremely identified with God's dwelling, seems the most likely candidate.[101] Further, one version of the logion defines faith as levelling and not simply moving mountains (Matt. 21.21/Mark 11.23): that is to say, a mountain which is cast into the sea is one which removes the extremes of topography and returns the terrain to a plain. Whilst the overthrowing of the mountains could indicate an attempt to displace or remove God, their levelling is more suggestive of God's presence, previously concentrated on certain high places, becoming manifest on a more universal basis (cf. Isa. 11.9). Against this background, mountain-levelling faith is a faith which is particularly associated with the means by which God's presence is known on earth.[102]

Thirdly, although much Jewish eschatological hope revolves around Mount Zion (e.g. Isa. 2.2–4; 25.6–10; 35.5–6; Micah 4.1–3), there is also a strong expectation that other mountains would be destroyed in the time of consummation.[103] Their levelling would facilitate the return of the exiles:

> 'In the wilderness prepare the way of the Lord, make straight in the desert a highway for our God. Every valley

[96] E.g. Deut. 32.22; Judg. 5.5; 1 Kings 19.11; Pss. 83.14; 104.32; Isa. 41.15; Jer. 4.24; Ezek. 38.20; Micah 1.4; Nah 4.24; Hab. 3.6; 4 Ezra 8.23.

[97] Ebeling, *Word*, 241–3; Stauffer, *Theology*, 168–72; Suhl, *Wunder*, 35–7.

[98] Gen. 22.2; Exod. 17.9; 1 Sam. 7.1; 9.12; 19.25; 2 Sam. 6.3; 1 Kings 18.42; 1 Chron. 16.39; cf. Deut. 12.2–9; 1 Kings 20.23, 28.

[99] Esp. Exod. 19; also Exod. 3.1; 4.27; 18.5; 24.13; Num. 10.33.

[100] Pss. 9.11; 14.7; 20.2; 53.6; 43.4; 68.16; 74.2; 76.2; 78.67–71; 84.5; 128.5; 132.11–13; 133.3; 134.3.

[101] The Mount of Olives is another alternative (cf. Zech. 14.1–5). See C. D. Marshall, *Faith*, 168, and the literature cited there.

[102] Derrett, 'Mountains', 235–43.

[103] 'Even the frequent prophetic theme that the mountains and valleys would be levelled on that day (e.g. Is 40.3–4) is brought into service in this motif: only Jerusalem will remain aloft (Zech 14.10).' (Donaldson, *Jesus*, 48)

> shall be lifted up and every mountain and hill made low; the uneven ground shall become level, and the rough places a plain. And the glory of the Lord shall be revealed . . .' (Isa. 40.3–5) 'For God has ordered that every high mountain and the everlasting hills be made low and the valleys filled up, to make level ground, so that Israel may walk safely in the glory of God.' (1 Bar. 5.7; also Isa. 45.2; 49.11; Pss. Sol. 11.1–6)

And their removal furnishes an unambiguous indication of God's presence in power:

> 'Behold, a day of the Lord is coming . . . On that day his feet shall stand on the Mount of Olives which lies between Jerusalem on the east; and the Mount of Olives shall be split in two from east to west by a very wide valley; so that one half of the Mount shall withdraw northward, and the other half southward. And the valley of my mountains shall be stopped up, for the valley of the mountains shall touch the side of it . . . Then the Lord your God will come, and all the holy ones with him.' (Zech. 14.1, 4–5) 'The God of the universe, the Holy Great One, will come forth from his dwelling. And from there he will march upon Mount Sinai and appear in his camp emerging from heaven with a mighty power . . . Mountains and high places will fall down and be frightened. And high hills shall be made low; and they shall melt like a honeycomb before the flame.' (1 Enoch 1.3, 6; also 1 Enoch 52.6; Test. Mos. 10.1, 3–4)

A different and patently metaphorical application is found in Daniel, where a mountain representing God's eternal kingdom overcomes all opposition and fills the entire earth:

> 'As you looked, a stone was cut out by no human hand, and it smote the image on its feet of iron and clay, and broke them in pieces . . . But the stone that struck the image became a great mountain and filled the whole earth . . . And in the days of those kings the God of heaven will set up a kingdom which shall never be destroyed, nor shall its sovereignty be left to another people. It shall break in pieces all these kingdoms and bring them to an end, and it shall stand for ever; just as you saw that a stone was cut from a

mountain by no human hand, and that it broke in pieces ...' (Dan. 2.34–5, 44–6)

Against this background, a faith that moves mountains is a faith which comes to expression in God's eschaton.[104] From this perspective, it is interesting that later Jewish sources actually suggest the involvement of human agency within these divine operations:[105]

> R. Samuel b. Nahman said: When the Holy Spirit began to ring in Samson, it began in three places, as it is said, *And the spirit of the Lord began to ring within him in Mahaneh-Dan, between Zorah and Eshtaol* (*ib.* xiii, 25). R. Samuel b. Nahman said: Scripture here informs us that he took two mountains and knocked them one against the other, just as a man takes two stones and knocks them one against another. (Lev. R. VIII.2, commenting on Judg. 13.25; also b. Sota 9b)

In the light of these three factors, namely, mountain-moving or levelling as indicative, firstly, of God's prerogative; secondly, of his presence and, thirdly, of his salvific power, we may propose – albeit tentatively – an interpretative frame for the relevant faith logia (Matt. 17.20; 21.21–22; Mark 11.22–24; cf. Luke 17.6). By speaking about faith in relation to phenomena characteristic of the consummation of time, the reader is encouraged to understand this disposition as the channel by which God's purposes for this period will not only be discerned but also come about.[106] If the removal of

[104] Hahn, 'Wort', 157; Lohmeyer, *Matthäus*, 304; Lührmann, *Glaube*, 18; Zmijewski, 'Glaube', 95.

[105] In an entirely different context, we may note those cases where the distressed request that the mountains fall on them to bring relief (e.g. Hos. 10.8; Apoc. Elijah 2.34; cf. Luke 23.30; Rev. 6.16). Attention should also be drawn to a tradition concerning Rabbi Eliezer ben Hyrcanus, who requested that the uprooting of a carob-tree would substantiate his teaching (i.e. 'If the halachah agrees with me, let this carob-tree prove it! Thereupon the carob-tree was torn a hundred cubits out of its place – others affirm, four hundred cubits. "No proof can be brought from a carob-tree," they retorted.' b. Baba Metzia 59a-59b) The parallel with Luke 17.6 is obvious and the rabbinic ruling may be intended to demonstrate that the 'obedience' of the carob-tree resulted not simply from the correctness of Eliezer's halakah, but also because it came from God. On this interpretation, see Vermes, 'Hanina', 30.

[106] 'It is this eschatological background that gives to the image something more than the force of a simple metaphor, that makes it more than a figure signifying, in the vivid imagery of the oriental mind, that men can do the impossible if only they try hard enough. What is in view is actual thaumaturgy, the belief that men will do the impossible, and will do it in the New Age. Wonder-working, indeed, is the

mountains is indicative of the eschaton, faith is the means by which the eschaton will be realised.

We switch next to consider the significance of Jesus' miracles as portrayed in the Synoptics. It is clear from many Jewish sources that the re-establishment of God's kingdom would encompass miraculous acts of healing, resuscitation and other phenomena:

> 'Then the eyes of the blind shall be opened, and the ears of the deaf unstopped; then shall the lame man leap like a hart, and the tongue of the dumb sing for joy.' (Isa. 35.5–6) 'And many of those who sleep in the dust of the earth shall awake, some to everlasting life, and some to shame and everlasting contempt.' (Dan. 12.2) 'And it will happen after he has brought down everything which is in the world, and has sat down in eternal peace on the throne of the kingdom, then joy will be revealed and the rest will appear. And then health will descend like a dew, and illness will vanish, and fear and tribulation and lamentation will pass away from among men, and joy will encompass the earth.' (2 Bar. 73.1–2) 'He [i.e. the Lord] shall release the captives, make the blind see, raise up the do[wntrodden.] ... then He will heal the sick, resurrect the dead, and to the Meek announce glad tidings.' (4Q521; trans. *DSSU* 23; also Isa. 26.19; 29.18; 53.5; 61.1–2; Jer. 30.17; 31.7–9; Ezek. 37.12–14 Joel 2.28–32; Micah 7.15; Mal. 4.2; 4 Ezra 7.123; 9.6; 13.50; Jub. 23.29–30; Test. Zeb. 9.8)

It comes, therefore, as no surprise that the evangelists and, in particular, Matthew and Luke have presented Jesus' miracles in this light as well.[107] In many cases miracles, especially healings and exorcisms, accompany Jesus' preaching of the kingdom.[108] They

visible sign of the Kingdom's advent and presence in the gospel tradition (cf. Matt. 11.2ff and parallels). In the Messianic Age, the impossible becomes possible, the metaphor becomes reality, men themselves in that beatific time will find nature respond to them in undreamt-of ways!' (Telford, *Temple*, 116; also Dautzenberg, 'Jesusüberlieferung', 52–7; Derrett, 'Figtrees', 255–7) R. M. Grant notes that some of the church fathers took the disciples' failure to move mountains as indicative of their lack of faith ('Coming', 301–2).

107 On this and the following points, see: Beasley-Murray, *Jesus, ad loc*; Berger, 'Messiastraditionen', 3–9; Busse, *Wunder*, esp. 428–33; Dulling, 'Therapeutic', 392–410; Fuller, *Mission*, 35–43; Miller, Character, 188–237

108 E.g. Matt. 4.23/Mark 1.39; Matt. 9.23; Matt. 12.9–14/Mark 3.1–6/Luke 6.6–11; Matt. 13.53–8/Mark 6.1–6; Mark 1.21–8/Luke 4.31–7; Mark 2.1–12/Luke 5.17–26; cf. Matt. 12.38; 16.1; 27.42; Mark 8.11; 15.32; Luke 11.16.

furnish John the Baptist with evidence of Jesus' messianic identity (Matt. 11.2–6/Luke 7.18–23) and the Jewish authorities with signs of God's kingdom (Matt. 12.22–9/Luke 11.14–22; cf. Mark 3.22–7). Jesus' Jubilee sermon in Luke 4.16–21 makes reference to acts of healing and release (cf. Isa. 58.6; 61.1–2), whilst Matthew interprets Jesus' healing ministry in the light of Isaiah's suffering servant (Matt. 8.17; 12.15–21).[109] It is apparent, therefore, that Jesus' acts of healing and exorcism were interpreted within the context of God's messianic reign. They were understood as tangible demonstrations of God's presence and the proximity of his kingdom.[110] They were considered eschatological in significance and, as such, indicative of the availablity of God's salvation.[111] In consequence, it seems legitimate to draw a parallel between Jesus' miracles so interpreted and the category of phenomena denoted by the levelling or removal of mountains in the faith logia considered above.

3.2 Emphasis upon the disposition rather than the object of faith

Unlike many later Christian constructions involving the πιστεύω group, the faith logia attributed to Jesus in relation to miracles are remarkably silent concerning the object of faith.[112] With the possible exceptions of πιστεύετε ὅτι δύναμαι τοῦτο ποιῆσαι in Matthew 9.28 and the ambiguous ἔχετε πίστιν θεοῦ in Mark 11.22,[113] the object of faith is never specified. Whilst this may indi-

109 The same pattern is reflected in the ministry of the disciples. Miracles of healing and exorcism accompany their work of proclaiming the kingdom (Matt. 10.5–15/ Mark 3.13–15/Luke 9.1–6; Luke 10.1–12), but they must also be careful not to fall foul of false messiahs who perform signs and wonders to substantiate their claims (Matt. 24.24/Mark 13.22).

110 Delling, 'Verstandnis', 267–75; Goppelt, *Theology*, vol. 1, 139–57; Harvey, *Constraints*, 98–119; Kee, *World*, 156–73; B. F. Meyer, *Aims*, 154–8; Mussner, *Miracles*, esp. 48; Polhill, 'Perspectives', 389–99; Sabourin, *Miracles*, 76–9.

111 This dimension needs to be balanced against the synoptic traditions which indicate that Jesus was not prepared to legitimate himself by means of miracles (e.g. Matt. 12.38; Matt. 16.1/Mark 8.11/Luke 11.16; Matt. 27.42/Mark 15.32). Within an eschatological context, Jesus' miracles furnish tangible evidence of God's salvation and not proof of his identity; however, it is difficult to deny them at least an implicit christological significance.

112 Cook, 'Call', 688–96, and Ebeling, *Word*, 323. There are cases in the Synoptics, however, where faith is explicitly directed towards Jesus (Matt. 18.6/Mark 9.42; Matt. 27.42/Mark 15.32), the gospel (Mark 1.15), John the Baptist (Matt. 21.32/ Mark 11.31/Luke 20.5), false Christs (Matt. 24.23, 26/Mark 13.21) and the word of God (Luke 1.20, 45).

113 Although πίστιν θεοῦ is often taken as an objective genitive (i.e. faith in God), it is possible that a genitive of origin should be preferred (i.e. 'faith from God'; see

cate that Jesus was thought to conceive of faith as an autonomous and independent source of power,[114] it more likely betrays the recognition that he did not redefine the object of faith but accepted the traditional Jewish understanding, namely, faith in the one creating, sustaining and saving God.[115] It is true that certain of the traditions supporting these sayings exert a christologising influence upon the meaning of faith (cf. section 2), but the reluctance to speak overtly of faith in Jesus is significant and militates against assuming him as the object where the πιστεύω group is used absolutely.[116]

It is the phenomenon of faith itself and not its object, however, which provides the focus for many of these logia, suggesting that Jesus was considered to have made an innovative or substantial contribution in this sphere. For example, the personal appropriation of faith is often stressed, indicating the importance of the disposition.[117] And yet faith is not portrayed as a general mode of existence, for it requires context, direction and openness to the potentialities and possibilities of a given situation.[118] In a number of cases, faith is identified with a particular course of action or initiative on the part of the exponent and may be described in narrative form or made explicit in the sayings themselves. Jesus responds to the haemorrhaging woman, who struggles to make contact with him and is healed in the process, with the words ἡ πίστις σου σέσωκέν σε.[119] The same logion greets blind Bartimaeus in response to his perseverance (Mark 10.52/Luke 18.42) and the grateful leper who returns to Jesus having been healed (Luke 17.19). The Canaanite woman's determination that Jesus would attend to her child results in the exclamation, ὦ γύναι, μεγάλη σου ἡ πίστις. Faith also comes

also Mark 1.14; Acts 19.20[D]; Rom. 1.1, 17; 3.21–2; 4.11, 13; 15.16; Phil. 3.9). We have already drawn attention to references in Jewish literature suggesting that faith was conceived of as an eschatological gift from God (e.g. 1 Enoch 108.13; Sib. Or. 3.584–5; Test. Isaac. 1.8) and this background would be consistent with the Markan context of πίστιν θεοῦ, where faith is portrayed as the means by which acts of God are performed.

114 See the literature discussed by van der Loos, *Miracles*, 265–70.

115 Buber, *Two Types*, esp. 17–23.

116 Marxsen, *Beginnings*, 65, and Perrin, *Rediscovering*, 138.

117 E.g. ἡ πίστις σου; κατὰ τὴν πίστιν ὑμῶν; μεγάλη σου ἡ πίστις; ποῦ ἡ πίστις ὑμῶν; see Goppelt, *Theology*, vol. 1, 152.

118 Bornkamm, *Jesus*, 131; Bultmann, *Jesus*, 189–90; Ebeling, *Word*, 232.

119 Matt. 9.20–22/Mark 5.21, 24–34/Luke 8.42–8. The declaratory force of ἡ πίστις σου σέσωκέν σε has been modified in Matthew's version where the woman's healing is only recorded after Jesus' pronouncement (Matt. 8.22; cf. Mark 5.29/Luke 8.44). For a detailed investigation of this logion and the relevant traditions see, Wallis, Faith.

to expression in specific injunctions as mountains are commanded ἄρθητι καὶ βλήθητι εἰς τὴν θάλασσαν and trees ἐκριζώθητι καὶ φυτεύθητι ἐν τῇ θαλάσσῃ. In each of these instances, faith is identified neither with propositional belief nor with an implicit trust in Jesus; rather, it comes to expression through initiatives betraying a high level of resolve focussed upon predetermined goals and with specific outcomes in mind.

The disposition of faith is also in view when faith is likened to a κόκκον σινάπεως (Matt. 17.20; Luke 17.6). This turn of phrase may constitute a quantitative assessment, indicating the significance of even the smallest amount, but faith's incompatibility in relation to other aspects of human response renders this unlikely (e.g. δειλός, διακρίνω, διστάζω, φόβος): if only the smallest amount of faith is required, why should this necessarily exclude timidity, doubt and fear?[120] In addition to its size, the mustard seed was noted for its creative potential, an observation which may be reflected in the parable where the kingdom of God is likened to one (Matt. 13.21/ Mark 4.31/Luke 13.19).[121] Against this background, πίστιν ὡς κόκκον σινάπεως assumes a qualitative force indicating the dynamics and potency of a particular kind of faith.[122] A similar approach makes good sense of Jesus' reply to the centurion, in which he celebrates the suppliant's faith (Matt. 8.10/Luke 7.9): in the light of the soldier's insight concerning the parallel between his own authority and that of Jesus, τοσαύτην πίστιν would seem to refer not simply to the amount but also to the nature of the centurion's faith.[123]

When we turn our attention to Jesus' miracles we notice that, although many aspects of his ministry are characterised by a prayerful reliance upon God,[124] this feature is almost entirely missing from

[120] The quantitative interpretation of the comparison between faith and κόκκον σινάπεως is also rendered doubtful by the juxtaposition of ὀλιγοπιστία and the mountain-moving logion in Matt. 17.20; if only the smallest amount of faith is required to heal the possessed boy, why are those who possessed ὀλιγοπιστία unsuccessful?

[121] Beasley-Murray, *Jesus*, 122–4, and Dahl, 'Parables', 148.

[122] Hahn, 'Wort', 159–60, 165–6; Peloni, 'Faith', 207–15; Simon, 'Faith', 307–16. Paul's reference to *πᾶσαν* τὴν πίστιν (1 Cor. 13.2) also supports this interpretation.

[123] BAGD, 823. The emphasis elsewhere upon the potential of even the smallest amount of faith gives credibility to this interpretation (Matt. 17.20; Luke 17.6), as does the way in which ὀλιγόπιστος and ὀλιγοπιστία can be used by Matthew to indicate deficiency in a particular kind of faith.

[124] Dunn, *Jesus*, 11–40, and Jeremias, *Prayers*, 11–107.

his conduct in relation to the performance of healings, exorcisms and other supernatural acts. In general, Luke emphasises this element more than the other Synoptic Evangelists,[125] but all three portray Jesus as one who maintains a daily discipline of prayer[126] and who turns to God in times of particular import or crisis.[127] This general impression of Jesus, however, gains almost no support from the miracle traditions.[128] In the 'feeding of the five thousand' and in the 'healing of the deaf and dumb person', it is recorded that Jesus looks up to heaven before performing the miracles (Matt. 14.19/ Mark 6.41/Luke 9.16; ἀναβλέψας εἰς τὸν οὐρανὸν, Mark 7.34). In the former, he also blesses (εὐλόγησεν) the elements, a gesture repeated over the fishes in the feeding of the four thousand, where he additionally gives thanks (εὐχαριστήσας, Mark 8.6) for the bread. But in spite of Jesus' advice to the disciples concerning the need for prayer in the case of certain types of deliverance (cf. Mark 9.29), there is no record in the synoptic tradition of his petitioning or invoking the assistance of God with respect to miracles. On the contrary, the focus remains firmly trained upon Jesus' resources, actions and utterances.

Jesus has power and authority to heal.[129] His touch[130] brings wholeness, whilst his rebuke[131] expels the powers of evil and controls the natural elements. On occasion he uses therapeutically

125 A. A. Trites provides a concise summary of the data in 'Prayer Motif', 168–86.

126 The relevant evidence includes: occasional references to Jesus at prayer (Mark 1.35; Matt. 14.23/Mark 6.46; Luke 5.16; 9.18; 11.1); his regular attendance at synagogues, albeit for mixed motives (e.g. Matt. 12.9/Mark 3.1/Luke 6.6; Matt. 13.54/Mark 6.2/Luke 4.15–16; Mark 1.21/Luke 4.33; Mark 1.39/Luke 4.44; Matt. 4.23; 9.35); his presence and teaching in the temple (Matt. 21.13/Mark 11.17/ Luke 19.46); and the father–son nature of his relationship with God (Mark 14.36; Matt. 6.9/Luke 11.2; Matt. 11.25–6/Luke 10.21; Matt. 26.42; Luke 23.34, 46).

127 The best attested occasion is Gethsemane (Matt. 26.36–46/Mark 14.32–42/Luke 22.39–46), but see also Matt. 11.25–7/Luke 10.21–2; Luke 3.21; 6.12; 9.28–9; 23.34, 46.

128 Theissen, *Miracle Stories*, 65.

129 E.g. Power (δύναμις): Mark 5.30/Luke 8.46; Luke 4.36; 5.17; 6.19; cf. Matt. 11.20, 21, 23/Luke 10.13; Matt. 13.54, 58/Mark 6.2, 5; Matt. 14.2/Mark 6.14; Matt. 7.22; Mark 9.39; Luke 1.35; 4.14; 9.1; 10.19; 19.37; 24.49. Authority (ἐξουσία): Matt. 9.6, 8/Mark 2.10/Luke 5.24; Mark 1.27/Luke 4.36; by implication Matt. 8.9/Luke 7.8; cf. Matt. 10.1/Mark 3.15/Mark 6.7/Luke 9.1; Matt. 21.23, 24, 27/Mark 10.28, 29, 33/Luke 20.2, 8; Matt. 28.18; Luke 10.19.

130 Usually ἅπτω; e.g. Matt. 8.3/Mark 1.41/Luke 5.13; Matt. 8.15/Mark 1.31; Mark 3.10/Luke 6.19; Mark 6.5; 7.33; 8.23; Luke 4.40; 7.14; 13.13; 22.51.

131 'Επιτιμάω; e.g. Matt. 8.26/Mark 4.39/Luke 8.24; Matt. 17.18/Mark 9.25/Luke 9.42; Mark 1.25/Luke 4.35; Luke 4.39; cf. Matt. 12.16/Mark 3.12; Luke 4.41.

beneficial substances,[132] but it is Jesus' *Heilungswort*[133] which constitutes the principal effector of miracle and, in most cases, takes the form of a command.[134] The contribution of patients or their advocates is not overlooked: some petition Jesus,[135] often in christologically explicit terms;[136] others seem to be held responsible for their own healings.[137] Whatever the precise circumstances, the healing dynamic does not explicitly include Jesus' relationship with God, but remains firmly anchored in his response to the situation under consideration. Further, although Luke emphasises human response to Jesus' miracles in terms of praising God,[138] we should be cautious of assuming that the evangelists intended Jesus' conduct to be interpreted in terms of his theological identity: hence, they did not mention God's contribution to miracles independently of Jesus' because they were considered the same. In the first place, it is doubtful whether the christology of the Synoptics is sufficiently developed that this could be taken for granted. Secondly, as we noted in section 3.1, Jesus' miracles are not primarily portrayed in the first three Gospels as acts of divine authentication, but as manifestations of God's kingdom.[139] Thirdly, Jesus' performance of miracles takes place within a discipling environment where his followers are required to emulate his ministry; and it is clear that they are not considered by the evangelists to be divine.

From what has been said so far, it should be apparent that the means by which Jesus is portrayed as performing miracles demonstrate a fundamental consistency with his teaching on the function of faith within similar situations. Particularly significant are the non-objectified nature of faith, paralleled in Jesus' lack of prayerful

[132] E.g. spittle (πτύω); Mark 7.33; 8.23; cf. John 9.6.

[133] E.g. Matt. 8.3/Mark 1.41/Luke 5.13; Matt. 9.6/Mark 2.11/Luke 5.24; Matt. 12.13/Mark 3.5/Luke 6.10; Matt. 21.19/Mark 11.14; Mark 1.25/Luke 4.35; Mark 5.41/Luke 8.54; Matt. 8.13 (cf. Luke 7.7); Matt. 8.16; 9.29; Matt. 15.28; Mark 4.39 (cf. Matt. 8.26/Luke 8.24); Mark 7.34; Mark 9.25 (cf. Matt. 17.18/Luke 9.42); Luke 5.4; Luke 7.14; Luke 18.42 (cf. Mark 10.52).

[134] Van der Loos, *Miracles*, 321–5, and Theissen, *Miracle Stories*, 63–5.

[135] E.g. Matt. 8.2/Mark 1.40/Luke 5.12; Matt. 17.15/Mark 9.17–25/Luke 9.38–40; Matt. 20.30–1/Mark 10.47–8/ Luke 18.38–9; Matt. 8.6, 8/Luke 7.6; Matt. 15.22, 25/Mark 7.26; Matt. 9.27; Mark 7.32, 8.22; Luke 17.13; cf. Matt. 9.2/Mark 2.4–5/Luke 5.18–19.

[136] E.g. κύριε: Matt. 8.2/Luke 5.12; Matt. 8.6, 8/Luke 7.6; Matt. 15.22, 25; 17.15; 20:[30], 31; υἱὸς Δαυίδ: Matt. 20.30, 31/Mark 10.47, 48/Luke 18.38, 39; Matt. 9.27; 15.22.

[137] E.g. Mark 5.24–34/Luke 8.42–8; cf. Matt. 13.53–8/Mark 6.1–6.

[138] E.g. Luke 7.16; 9.43; 13.13; 18.43; 19.37; cf. Matt. 9.8/Mark 2.12/Luke 5.25–6.

[139] Cf. John 2.11, 23; 5.17; 7.31; 20.30, 31.

petition to God, and the definition of faith in concrete, pragmatic and dynamic terms, which finds its counterpart in the ways Jesus chooses to heal, exorcise and execute other supernatural acts. The correspondence in these areas is sufficiently profound that it requires us to consider whether Jesus' utterances concerning faith were envisaged as, so to speak, the theory which was exemplified or incarnated in his ministry as a miracle worker.

3.3 Focus on the performatory nature of faith

In the previous section we saw how faith is often identified with specific behavioural initiatives determined by each situation. One category of particular interest is where faith comes to expression in a command which leads to the goal of faith being realised. The most profound cases of this are the mountain and tree-moving sayings, where faith is equated with specific imperatives: μετάβα ἔνθεν ἐκεῖ (Matt. 17.20); ἄρθητι καὶ βλήθητι εἰς τὴν θάλασσαν (Matt. 21.21/ Mark 11.23); ἐκριζώθητι καὶ φυτεύθητι ἐν τῇ θαλάσσῃ (Luke 17.6). The language here is uncompromising and assumes a performatory force as faith invests everything in a single, tightly prescribed outcome. Faith is similarly depicted in the interpretations of the healing of the possessed boy and the stilling of the storm presented above. In the former, Jesus, who claims that πάντα δυνατὰ τῷ πιστεύοντι (Mark 9.23) or who subsequently informs his disciples of the power of faith (Matt. 17.20), exorcises the boy himself with a command: ἐγὼ ἐπιτάσσω σοι, ἔξελθε ἐξ αὐτοῦ καὶ μηκέτι εἰσέλθῃς εἰς αὐτόν (Mark 9.25; cf. Matt. 17.18). In the latter, Jesus admonishes the disciples for their lack of faith and then, taking their place, calms the storm by rebuking the elements: σιώπα, πεφίμωσο (Mark 4.39; cf. ἐπετίμησεν, Matt. 8.26/Mark 4.39/Luke 8.24). Finally, it is possible that in Luke's version of the healing of the centurion's servant, the soldier's faith (Luke 7.9) should be identified with a confidence in Jesus which simply requires that he speak the word καὶ ἰαθήτω ὁ παῖς μου (Luke 7.7).[140]

In the light of these examples, it is apparent that most of the logia espousing or consistent with the imperatory nature of faith are

[140] Busse, *Wunder*, 445–7. The textual variant ἰαθήσεται probably represents a later assimilation to the Matthean version (cf. Matt. 8.8; so Metzger, *Commentary*, 142).

closely associated with Jesus' conduct as a miracle worker.[141] In some of these cases, there is a striking similarity between the performatory language of faith and the healing-words of Jesus: as faith issues forth in command, so Jesus performs miracles in the same way. Further, a broader review of Jesus' thaumaturgic pursuits recorded in the Synoptics reveals how miracles are regularly effected by Jesus' commands:

> θέλω, καθαρίσθητι (Mark 1.41/Matt. 8.3/Luke 5.13); ἔγειρε ἆρον τὸν κράβαττόν σου καὶ ὕπαγε εἰς τὸν οἶκόν σου/ἐγερθεὶς ἆρόν σου τὴν κλίνην καὶ ὕπαγε εἰς τὸν οικόν σου/ἔγειρε καὶ ἄρας τὸ κλινίδιόν σου πορεύου εἰς τὸν οἶκόν σου (Mark 2.11/Matt. 9.6/Luke 5.24); ἔγειρε [καὶ στῆθι, Luke] εἰς τὸ μέσον ... ἔκτεινον [σου, Matt.] τὴν χεῖρα [σου, Luke] (Mark 3.3, 5/Luke 6.8, 10/Matt. 12.13); φιμώθητι καὶ ἔξελθε ἐξ [ἀπ', Luke] αὐτοῦ (Mark 1.25/Luke 4.35); ταλιθα κουμ, ὅ ἐστιν μεθερμηνευόμενον· τὸ κοράσιον, σοὶ λέγω, ἔγειρε/ἡ παῖς, ἔγειρε (Mark 5.41/Luke 8.54); ὕπαγε, ὡς ἐπίστευσας γενηθήτω σοι (Matt. 8.13); κατὰ τὴν πίστιν ὑμῶν γενηθήτω ὑμῖν (Matt. 9.29); ὦ γύναι, μεγάλη σου ἡ πίστις· γενηθήτω σοι ὡς θέλεις (Matt. 15.28); σιώπα, πεφίμωσο (Mark 4.39); ἔξελθε τὸ πνεῦμα τὸ ἀκάθαρτον ἐκ τοῦ ἀνθρώπου (Mark 5.8); εφφαθα, ὅ ἐστιν διανοίχθητι (Mark 7.34); τὸ ἄλαλον καὶ κωφὸν πνεῦμα, ἐγὼ ἐπιτάσσω σοι, ἔξελθε ἐξ αὐτοῦ καὶ μηκέτι εἰσέλθῃς εἰς αὐτόν (Mark 9.25); νεανίσκε, σοὶ λέγω, ἐγέρθητι (Luke 7.14); ἀνάβλεψον· ἡ πίστις σου σέσωκέν σε (Luke 18.42).

Although this correspondence between Jesus' faith logia and his performance of miracles may be coincidental, it more likely reflects a belief that Jesus was thought to perform miracles by faith.[142]

[141] E.g. Matt. 17.20 – exorcism of the possessed boy; Matt. 21.21/Mark 11.23 – withering of the fig tree; Matt. 8.26/Mark 4.40/Luke 8.25 – stilling the storm; Luke 7.9 – healing the centurion's servant; cf. Luke 17.6.

[142] In this respect, it is interesting that the disciples, who follow Jesus in his ministry of proclaiming the kingdom in word and deed, can be depicted as performing miracles by, amongst other things, faith. In addition to the references discussed in section 2, see Mark 16.17; John 14.12–14; Acts 3.16; 6.5–8; 1 Cor. 13.2; Jas. 5.15; Act. Pet. 10 (quoted in section 2.2); Act. Thom. 20, 'But his [i.e. Thomas'] works of compassion, and the healings which are wrought by him without reward, and moreover his simplicity and kindness and the quality of his faith (τῆς πίστεως αὐτοῦ) show that he is righteous or an apostle of the new God whom he preaches.'

3.4 Final comments

We have seen that in the areas of context, disposition and potential there are significant similarities between certain of Jesus' faith logia and the means by which he is portrayed in the Synoptics as performing miracles. The cumulative force of this evidence is sufficiently strong to suggest that the latter may have been interpreted in terms of the former, implying that Jesus' ability to perform mighty works was due, at least in part, to his faith. This correlation almost certainly predates the current form of the synoptic compositions, where Jesus' miracles serve primarily to illuminate the nature of his mission and identity. From this perspective, the phenomena we have examined in this section serve a different purpose: the Jewish expectation that the messianic era would be characterised by miraculous happenings demonstrates the proximity of God's kingdom in Jesus, whilst his lack of petition to God and the performatory nature of his *Heilungsworten* indicate Jesus' authority in relation to that kingdom. However, the overriding concerns of the synoptic evangelists have not completely obscured the significance of these traditions in earlier contexts where the same characteristics, interpreted in terms of his faith logia, indicate that Jesus was thought to exhibit miracle-working faith.

4 Additional corroborative evidence: Jesus the man of faith

In sections 2 and 3 we have presented the more substantial and explicit evidence suggesting interest in Jesus' faith. Having identified this motif, however, additional areas of correspondence between the portrayal of Jesus in the Synoptic Gospels and Jewish definitions of the life of faith become significant and worthy of attention.[143] Once again, we are dealing here with associations and thematic presentations which on the whole pre-date the contributions of the evangelists. The πιστεύω root is not attested in these cases, although the possibility that faith is in view and that a narrative presentation of Jesus as the one fulfilling the Jewish life of faith may be intended can be shown by recourse to extra-biblical sources where a similar

[143] Apart from the Old Testament references, some of the Jewish material mentioned below reached its extant form after the Synoptic Evangelists composed their Gospels. These traditions have been selected because they specifically mention faith, but they bear witness to a way of life which is rooted in and can be traced back to much earlier Jewish expressions; see Bowker, *Targums*, 3–92.

phenomenon is described using faith vocabulary.[144] For example, Jesus' directions concerning the benefits of simplicity in lifestyle[145] betray a trust in God which is entirely in keeping with Rabbi Eliezer the Great's declaration, 'Whoever has a piece of bread in his basket and says, "What shall I eat tomorrow?" belongs only to them who are little in faith (*mqṭny 'mnh*).'[146] This trust is also implicit within Jesus' confidence, based upon God's graciousness, that prayers will be answered. As a result, prayer is not a matter of rehearsing religiosity before others,[147] but of expectant and specific petitioning of God as Father.[148]

Other allusions to Jesus' life of faith may be discerned in his fidelity to the Torah[149] and faithfulness to God's calling.[150] This latter point comes into particular focus with respect to Jesus' trust in God's faithfulness as he prepares to face suffering and death.[151] Once again, the way in which this is depicted in the Synoptics is consistent with Jewish references where faith is explicitly mentioned.[152] Finally, it is interesting how many of the characteristics of

144 On this possibility, see Buber, *Two Types*, 28–9, and Vermes, *Jesus*, 49–51.

145 Matt. 6.25–34/Luke 12.22–31; Matt. 10.9–10/Mark 6.8–9/Luke 9.3; Luke 10.4.

146 b. Sot. 48b; cf. m. Sot. 9.12 (ref. to Ps. 12.1); also Mek., Vayassa on Exod. 16.4 and 16.27.

147 Matt. 14.23/Mark 6.46; Matt. 6.7; Mark 1.35; Luke 5.16; 9.18; cf. 'One who says the Tefillah so that it can be heard is of the small of faith (*mqṭny 'mnh*).' (b. Ber. 24b)

148 Matt. 6.7–14/Luke 11.2–4; Matt. 7.1–6/Luke 11.9–13; Matt. 21.22/Mark 11.24; cf. 'R Ammi said: A man's prayer is only answered if he takes his heart into his hand, as it is said, "Let us lift up our heart with our hands." ... R Ammi said: Rain falls only for the sake of Men of Faith (*ḇ'ly 'mnh*), as it is said, Truth springeth out of the earth and righteousness hath looked down from heaven.' (b. Taan. 8a)

149 Matt. 8.4/Mark 1.44/Luke 5.14; Matt. 22.34–40/Mark 12.28–31; Matt. 26.17–20/ Mark 14.12–17/Luke 22.7–14; Matt. 5.17–20; cf. 'I have chosen the way of faithfulness (*derek 'ᵉmûnâh*), I set thy ordinances before me ... Teach me good judgement and knowledge, for I believe (*he'ᵉ mānti*) in your commandments.' (Ps. 119.30, 66) 'Blessed be the God of Israel because of all His plan of holiness and His works of truth! And blessed be all those who serve Him in righteousness (and) know Him by faith (*be'ᵉmûnâh*)!' (1QM 13.2–3; trans. *EWQ*, 188)

150 Matt. 26.36–46/Mark 14.32–42/Luke 22.39–46; cf. 'A bad messenger plunges men into trouble, but a faithful envoy (*'emûnîm*) brings healing.' (Prov. 13.17; also Prov. 14.4); 'Behold, he whose soul is not upright in him shall fail, but the righteous shall live by his faith (*be'ᵉmûnāṯô*)' (Hab. 2.4)

151 Matt. 16.21–8/Mark 8.31–9.1/Luke 9.22–7; Matt. 17.22–3/Mark 9.30–2/Luke 9.43–5; Matt. 20.17–19/Mark 10.32–4/Luke 18.31–4; Matt. 22.31–2/Mark 12.26–7/Luke 20.36–8; Matt. 24.9–14/Mark 13.9–13/Luke 21.12–19; Matt. 26.26–9/ Mark 14.22–5.

152 E.g., 'Remember that it is for God's sake you were given a share in the world and the benefit of life, and accordingly you owe it to God to endure all hardship for his sake, for whom our father Abraham ventured boldly to sacrifice his son Isaac, the father of our nation; and Isaac, seeing his father's hand, with knife in it, fall

Jesus' ministry as portrayed in the first three Gospels can be paralleled in the lives of Israel's great men of faith. Given the prominence of Davidic pedigree within messianic expectation, a comparison with the depiction of King David in the Old Testament suitably illustrates the point:[153]

> Both Jesus and David receive the Holy Spirit (Matt. 3.16/Mark 1.10/Luke 3.22; 1 Sam. 16.13), are involved in an exorcism after their anointing (Mark 1.23–8/Luke 4.33–7; 1 Sam. 16.14–23), violate the Jewish law in order to provide food (Matt. 12.1–8/Mark 2.23–8/Luke 6.1–5; 1 Sam. 21.1–6), are depicted as shepherds (Matt. 26.31/Mark 14.27; 2 Sam. 5.2), receive acknowledgement from the blind as they enter Jerusalem (Matt. 20.29–34/Mark 10.46–52/ Luke 18.35–43; 2 Sam. 5.6–8), make a sorrowful ascent of the Mount of Olives (Matt. 26.30/Mark 14.26/Luke 22.39; 2 Sam. 15.30), face a time of trial accompanied by three comrades (Matt. 26.37/Mark 14.33; 2 Sam. 15.19–24), witness a protest of enduring fidelity by one of their number (Matt. 26.33/Mark 14.29/Luke 22.33; 2 Sam. 15.19–21), suffer betrayal by a trusted follower (Matt. 26.46/Mark 14.42; 2 Sam. 15.31) and utter a cry of abandonment at a moment of desperation (Matt. 27.46/Mark 15.34; Ps. 22.2).

The catalogue could be extended, but hopefully sufficient information has been presented to indicate that the depiction of Jesus in the Synoptics correlates with the way in which King David is described in Old Testament traditions. Although this evidence does not necessarily demonstrate a desire to frame Jesus in a Davidic stereotype, it does suggest some sort of relation between these two figures and one which could be explained in terms of their belonging to the stock of Israel's great men of faith. As David is celebrated as a man of faith (e.g. 1 Sam. 22.14; 26.23) and as the Davidic messiah is

down against him, did not flinch. Daniel also, the righteous one, was thrown to the lions, and Hananiah and Azariah and Mishael were cast in the fiery furnace, and all endured for the sake of God. Therefore, you who have the same faith in God (τὴν αὐτὴν πίστιν πρὸς τὸν θεὸν) must not be dismayed. For it would be unreasonable for you who know true religion not to withstand hardships.' (4 Macc. 16.18–23; also Midr. Ps. on Ps. 31.23)

153 Donahue, 'Temple', 75–8, and Goppelt, *Typos*, 82–90; cf. Brueggemann, 'David', 156–81; 'Dust', 1–18; Wifall, 'David', 93–107. A similar exercise could be done for other Old Testament figures (e.g. Elijah, Moses); for instance, see W. D. Davies', *Setting*, 25–108, assessment of Matthew's presentation of Jesus in Mosaic categories.

expected to exhibit a similar disposition (e.g. Pss. Sol. 17.34, 39–40), so Jesus is of Davidic stock and belongs to the continuum of faith.

5 Concluding remarks

In this chapter we have surveyed the synoptic records for evidence of interest in Jesus' faith. We focussed upon traditions associated with the miracles of Jesus and, in particular, upon two areas. Firstly, narratives suggesting a degree of correspondence between Jesus' conduct as miracle worker and his disciples and, secondly, Jesus' faith logia associated with miraculous activity and their relation to the means by which he performed such acts. The latter led us to conclude that a particular kind of faith was considered to be exemplified by Jesus and to constitute an effective means for his accomplishment of miracles; the former illustrated the way in which Jesus' practical exposition of faith in executing miracles was used as an example and means of instruction for the disciples. Finally, we also drew attention to a number of motifs or themes from the ministry of Jesus which indicate that these two more substantial areas might form part of a broader narrative characterisation of Jesus as a man of faith.

Why then was the early church interested in Jesus' faith? The synoptic material reviewed in this chapter is concerned almost exclusively with discipleship, as the exemplary function of Jesus' life for those called to follow his way is explored. This would suggest that at least certain aspects of his ministry were interpreted as expressions of his faith in God and, consequently, as something to be emulated. It seems reasonable to conclude, therefore, that such traditions reflect an early assessment of Jesus in which he was considered as a man of profound faith who elucidated the way of faith for others. We should not, however, overlook the theological framework of the Gospels in which his example is now contextualised, for it is this which delimits and, in a sense, legitimises the comparison between Jesus and his followers. As Jesus proclaims the kingdom through word and deed and calls others to do the same, so his disciples find guidance and an authoritative definition of the life of faith in his earthly ministry. Yet in as much as Jesus, the crucified and risen one, fulfils a unique role within God's salvation, he ceases to be the one to emulate and becomes the one to revere and, ultimately, to worship. As we intimated earlier, the tension between these two responses is reflected in the epiphanic and exemplary functions exhibited by certain of the synoptic miracle stories: Jesus' miracles can substantiate his unique role or they can illustrate the life of discipleship.

The way in which these two approaches coexist in the Synoptics is of considerable importance for understanding early christological reflection in that they suggest how Jesus' significance in relation to, on the one hand, God and his offer of salvation and, on the other, human response to that offer were related. Further, recognition of this favours the conclusion that assessments of Jesus as proclaimer of the kingdom, who was thought to live by faith, and as the one proclaimed to be God's messiah or son, on whom the faith of others should be focussed, were not necessarily considered to be mutually exclusive. Although the ontological implications of this association were not fully explored at this stage, the first three canonical Gospels furnish evidence that, in functional terms, Jesus the exemplar of faith, who provides a model for others to follow, could coexist with Jesus the focus for faith, who mediates God's offer of salvation.

3

JESUS' FAITH IN THE PAULINE EPISTLES

1 Preliminary considerations

Over the past two or three decades the question of whether Paul refers to the faith of Jesus Christ has received considerable attention. It constituted the subject matter for the presidential address delivered to the 43rd General Meeting of the Society for New Testament Studies in 1988[1] and it seems that the question still remains largely unresolved.[2] The debate, which can be traced back with certainty to the previous century,[3] revolves around a number of genitival constructions exhibiting a form of Christ's name qualifying the substantive πίστις:[4]

Romans 3.22	διὰ πίστεως Ἰησοῦ Χριστοῦ
Romans 3.26	τὸν ἐκ πίστεως Ἰησοῦ
Galatians 2.16a	διὰ πίστεως Ἰησοῦ Χριστοῦ
Galatians 2.16b	ἐκ πίστεως Χριστοῦ
Galatians 2.20	ἐν πίστει ζῶ τῇ τοῦ υἱοῦ τοῦ θεοῦ
Galatians 3.22	ἐκ πίστεως Ἰησοῦ Χριστοῦ
Philippians 3.9	τὴν διὰ πίστεως Χριστοῦ

The crucial issue is whether one or more of these constructions refers, either exclusively or in conjunction with another party,[5] to

[1] Hooker, 'ΠΙΣΤΙΣ', 321–42.

[2] See the contributions of Dunn ('Once More', 730–44) and Hays ('ΠΙΣΤΙΣ', 714–19) at the 1991 meeting of the Society of Biblical Literature.

[3] Detailed defences of the subjective genitive come towards the end of the nineteenth and beginning of the twentieth centuries (e.g. Haussleiter, 'Glaube', 109–45, 205–30; Kittel, 'Πίστις', 419–36); but see also the literature cited by Campbell, *Rhetoric*, 58–62, and Howard, 'On the "Faith of Christ"', 461.

[4] Cf. Gal. 3.26 [𝔓46], διὰ τῆς πίστεως Χριστοῦ Ἰησοῦ and Eph. 3.12, διὰ τῆς πίστεως αὐτοῦ. Only Romans, 1 and 2 Corinthians, Galatians, Philippians, 1 Thessalonians and Philemon are considered Pauline in the present study. On occasion, πίστις Χριστοῦ will be used as a shorthand for referring to all seven occurrences.

[5] As we shall see, it is possible that Jesus' faith is referred to in conjunction with the faithfulness of God or the faith of believers.

the faith of Jesus Christ. Each of these occurrences will be discussed in detail below, but we shall start by introducing the theological issues central to the debate and surveying the pertinent grammatical data. Before doing this, however, it is worth noting that the burden of proof can no longer be thought to rest with those claiming the apostle had Christ's own faith in view.[6] It is true that most modern English versions adopt the objective genitive translation for the relevant πίστις Χριστοῦ constructions without comment,[7] but it is questionable whether earlier interpretative traditions are so supportive. For example, in terms of general Greek usage, recent surveys have concluded that there are no unambiguous cases of πίστις with the objective genitive of person in the Septuagint, Apocrypha, Pseudepigrapha, Josephus or Philo.[8] Further, it has been pointed out that a number of the key reference works covering the New Testament period do not cite any examples of this usage.[9] The subjective genitive option also gains support from early translations and, particularly, the Peshitta, Vulgate and Sahidic Coptic.[10] In more recent centuries, the *Authorised Version* accommodates this interpretation,[11] whilst Martin Luther opted decisively for the objective genitive (*Glaube an Christum*) and seemingly set the trend for future European translations.[12]

[6] *Contra* Cranfield, *Romans*, vol. 1, 203; Käsemann, *Romans*, 94, 101; Moule, 'Concept', 222; Wilckens, *Römer*, vol. 1, 188.

[7] The *New Revised Standard Version* gives the subjective genitive reading in the margin for all seven occurrences.

[8] Howard, 'The "Faith of Christ"', 214–15, and D. W. B. Robinson, 'Faith', 78; G. Howard points out that the only possible exception in the literature surveyed is found in Josephus: 'I have another particular motive in that the story provides good evidence of God's power (καὶ πολλὴν ἔχει πίστιν τοῦ θεοῦ τῆς δυνάμεως).' *Ant*. XIX.16 [LCL 433.222–3].

[9] D. W. B. Robinson, 'Faith', 78.

[10] Howard, 'The "Faith of Christ"', 213.

[11] E.g. Gal. 2.16, 'Knowing that a man is not justified by the works of the law, but by the faith of Jesus Christ, even we have believed in Jesus Christ, that we might be justified by the faith of Jesus Christ, and not by the works of the law: for by the works of the law shall no flesh be justified.' Cf. Rom. 3.26, 'To declare, I say, at this time his righteousness: that he might be just, and the justifier of him which believeth in Jesus.'

[12] It may well be the case, therefore, that the Reformation proved to be the determinative period for the shift from subjective to objective genitive. Characterised by a desire to rediscover scripture and to study the text in the original languages, it certainly provides an appropriate context for such a modification; and yet it cannot be entirely coincidental that the Reformation is also noteworthy for its emphasis upon justification by grace and the need for personal repentance and faith in Christ. See Dunn, 'Perspective', 185–7; Hooker, 'ΠΙΣΤΙΣ', 322; Stendahl, *Paul*, esp. 78–96.

1.1 Central theological issues

Detailed theological discussion will accompany the following exegetical sections. At this stage, we simply need to draw attention to three issues which have proved central to the debate so far in order to provide a framework for more thoroughgoing analysis.[13]

Could Paul have made reference to the faith of Jesus Christ?

Two aspects of the apostle's thinking have been influential for those answering this question in the affirmative. Firstly, Paul's interpretation of Christ's death as an act of obedience (e.g. Rom. 5.17–19; Phil. 2.8), understood in the light of the intimate relationship between faith and obedience in his writings (e.g. Rom. 1.5; 10.16; 16.26), has led to the conclusion that when the apostle speaks of πίστις Χριστοῦ he must have the faith of Christ in mind.[14] Secondly, those who discern in Paul's rejection of 'works of the law' as a means of securing standing before God a more fundamental attitude towards the impotence of all human initiative or response, recognise that the apostle would be unlikely to advocate salvation through the faith of believers alone. In consequence, when Paul speaks of faith as a new initiative in relation to Christ he must have Christ's own faith in mind, otherwise faith would in effect become another 'work'.[15] The apostle's interest in Christ's faith is generally thought to be soteriologically motivated in the sense that, being identified with his death on the cross, it provides the means by which God's salvation is made available.[16] Others, however, stress its exemplary function.[17]

What is the relationship between God's faithfulness and Jesus' faith?

In addition to textual studies, the matter of Christ's faith has also arisen in more systematic discussions of Paul's soteriology and, in

[13] The following surveys offer a more detailed overview: Campbell, *Rhetoric*, 58–69; Hays, *Faith*, 158–62; Hultgren, 'PISTIS', 248–53; Kertelge, *Rechtfertigung*, 162–6.

[14] Hays, *Faith*, 166–76; 'ΠΙΣΤΙΣ', 714–29; Johnson, 'Rom. 3:21–26', 85–90; Keck, 'Jesus', 457–60; R. N. Longenecker, *Paul*, 149–53; 'Obedience', 145; S. K. Williams, *Saving Event*, 47–51; 'Righteousness', 274–7.

[15] Goodenough, 'Paul', 43–8; Howard, *Paul*, 57–65; Hooker, 'ΠΙΣΤΙΣ', 339–41.

[16] Haussleiter, 'Glaube', 128–45, 205–30; S. K. Williams, *Saving Event*, 47–51.

[17] Hays, 'ΠΙΣΤΙΣ', 728; Johnson, 'Rom. 3:21–26', 87–9; S. K. Williams, 'Again', 443.

particular, his understanding of faith and righteousness. For example, a number of scholars[18] note the correspondence in the Old Testament between God's righteousness and faithfulness, usually in relation to the covenant, and recognise a similar correlation in the apostle's thinking.[19] In the light of this, when Paul associates God's πίστις and δικαιοσύνη intimately with Christ, he presents Christ as the incarnation of or channel for divine righteousness and covenantal faithfulness.[20]

What is the relationship between Jesus' faith and the faith of Christians?

One of the criticisms levelled against subjective interpretations of πίστις Χριστοῦ is that they undermine the place of the believer's faith within the salvation process.[21] Although this is questionable linguistically,[22] it does bring into focus another problem: if Paul maintains that salvation is mediated by a Christian's faith, faith is in danger of becoming yet another meritorious 'work'; however, if salvation is wrought by the faith of Christ, where is the place for human response? As this dilemma corresponds closely to the objective and subjective interpretations for the πίστις Χριστοῦ con-

18 M. Barth, 'Faith', 365–6; *Justification*, esp. 35–48; Gaston, 'Abraham', 39–59; 'Believers', 116–34; Hays, 'Psalm 143', 107–15; Hebert, 'Faithfulness', 373–9; Ljungman, *Pistis*, 37–47; Stuhlmacher, *Gerechtigkeit*, esp. 113–45; T. F. Torrance, 'One Aspect', 111–14; Vallotton, *Christ*, esp. 13–29, 121–8.

19 'On the basis of this pattern, I think it is not incautious to claim that Paul intends "the faithfulness of God," "righteousness of God" and "the truthfulness of God" as virtual equivalents ... When he talks about the faithfulness, truthfulness and righteousness of God in Rom. 3.1–7, then, he is referring to God's fidelity to the promises given to Abraham, the promises that on the basis of faith God will justify all peoples of the earth.' (S. K. Williams, 'Righteousness', 268–9)

20 The classic theological statement of this position is that of K. Barth: 'The righteousness of God is manifested – through his faithfulness in Jesus Christ. The faithfulness of God is the divine patience according to which He provides, at sundry times and in many divers points in human history, occasions and possibilities and witnesses of the knowledge of His righteousness. Jesus of Nazareth is the point at which it can be seen that all the other points form one line of supreme significance. He is the point at which is perceived the crimson thread which runs through all history. Christ – the righteousness of God Himself – is the theme of this perception. The faithfulness of God and Jesus the Christ confirm one another. The faithfulness of God is established when we meet the Christ in Jesus.' (*Romans*, 96)

21 Dunn, *Romans*, vol. 1, 166–7; 'Once More', 735–7; Hultgren, 'PISTIS', 258–62; Moule, 'Concept', 157; Murray, *Romans*, vol. 1, 370–4.

22 As we shall see, all seven cases of πίστις Χριστοῦ are accompanied by at least one further occurrence of the πιστεύω group, referring to the faith of believers.

structions, it has led some to question whether these two positions are mutually exclusive. Reflection upon the corporate and inclusive nature of Christ's humanity in Paul suggests that, although all faith ultimately originates in Christ, at the point of conversion believers participate in that faith and, in some sense, make it their own.[23]

1.2 Relevant grammatical data

We shall return to these and other theological issues in the following sections, but first we need to consider the relevant grammatical information around which much of the debate has revolved.[24] If we concentrate on the relatively undisputed letters of Paul (i.e. Rom., 1 and 2 Cor., Gal., Phil., 1 Thess. and Phlm.) and exclude the seven πίστις Χριστοῦ occurrences already noted, πίστις is followed by a genitive on twenty occasions all of which favour, if not demand, a subjective interpretation. In most cases, it is attested with the article and qualified by the personal pronoun in the genitive case, which usually refers to Christian believers, although the πίστις of God and Abraham are also represented.[25]

Πίστις is not the only personal disposition qualified by a form of Christ's name in the genitive case used by Paul, and many of those attested are without doubt subjective in application. The evidence here favours the view that the presence of the article signals a subjective genitive, but there is too much variation to be conclu-

[23] Deissmann, Paul, 162–4; Hooker, 'ΠΙΣΤΙΣ', esp. 336–42; Ljungman, *Pistis*, 43–4; J. A. T. Robinson, *Body*, esp. 63; Schmidt, *Römer*, 71–2; S. K. Williams, 'Again', 442–6; 'Hearing', 89–93; cf. Hultgren, 'PISTIS', 262–3. T. F. Torrance maintains that God's faithfulness, Christ's faith(fulness) and the believers' faith are all represented in the expression: 'In most of these passages the *pistis Iesou Christou* does not refer only either to the faithfulness of Christ or to the answering faithfulness of man, but is essentially a polarized expression denoting the faithfulness of Christ as its main ingredient but also involving or at least suggesting the answering faithfulness of man, and so his belief in Christ, but even within itself the faithfulness of Christ involves both the faithfulness of God and the faithfulness of the man Jesus . . . Jesus Christ is thus not only the incarnation of the Divine *pistis*, but He is the embodiment and actualization of man's *pistis* in covenant with God.' ('Biblical Concept', 113)

[24] The most important studies on grammatical issues are, in support of the objective genitive: Dunn, 'Once More', esp. 231–5; 'Hultgren, 'PISTIS', 248–63; Murray, *Romans*, vol. 1, 363–74; and of the subjective genitive: Campbell, *Rhetoric*, 214–18; Haussleiter, 'Glaube', 110–27; O'Brien, *Philippians*, 398–400; S. K. Williams, 'Again', 431–47.

[25] Rom. 1.8, 12; 3.3 (God) 4.5, 12, 16 (Abraham); 1 Cor. 2.5; 15.14, 17; 2 Cor. 1.24; 10.15; Phil. 2.17; 1 Thess. 1.3 (your work of faith), 8; 3.2, 5, 6, 7, 10; Phlm. 6; cf. Eph. 3.12 (Christ Jesus our Lord); Col. 1.4; 2.5; 2 Thess. 1.3 and Tit 1.1.

sive.[26] For example, Paul usually refers to the grace of Christ in articular form, but there are possible exceptions;[27] this pattern is also evident with reference to the Spirit.[28] The article is included when mentioning Christ's love, power and sufferings, but is absent where his emotions and mind are in focus.[29] A similar pattern emerges from a broader review of genitival constructions including Christ's name.[30]

There is also the question of why Paul did not use πίστις followed by a dative or one of the prepositions εἰς, ἐν, ἐπί or πρός, rather than a simple genitive, had he wished to denote faith in Christ. With the exception of πρός, all these are attested in the case of the verbal form πιστεύω,[31] and on a number of occasions Jesus or God define the objects of belief.[32] The problematic διὰ [τῆς] πίστεως ἐν τῷ αὔτου αἵματι (Rom. 3.25) must also be considered,[33] whilst both πίστις ἐν and πίστις εἰς followed by Christ are attested in the

[26] The contrary position has been defended, however, on the basis that 'when Paul uses the term *pistis* followed by a genitive which is clearly to be understood as subjective, the article is invariably present before *pistis*'. (Hultgren, 'PISTIS', 253; cf. Phil. 1.27, τῇ πίστει τοῦ εὐαγγελίου!) Thus, just as the apostle wrote τὴν πίστιν τοῦ θεοῦ (Rom. 3.3), τῆς πίστεως τοῦ 'Αβραάμ (Rom. 4.12) and ἡ πίστις ὑμῶν (Rom. 1.8; etc.) when referring to the πίστις of God, Abraham and fellow believers respectively, he would have written ἡ πίστις τοῦ Χριστοῦ had he wished to refer to Christ's πίστις; but this is not the case. Further, J. D. G. Dunn cites Jas. 2.1, Rev. 2.13 and 14.12 as evidence for the articular usage with the sense of 'the faith of Christ' in early Christianity ('Once More', 732–4). In response, D. A. Campbell (*Rhetoric*, 214–18) and S. K. Williams ('Again', 432–3) indicate why the presence or absence of the article cannot be determinative in this instance; perhaps the most conclusive reason, however, is that Paul seems able to use articular and anarthrous genitival phrases with broadly the same meaning (e.g. grace of God – arthrous: Rom. 5.15; 1 Cor. 1.4; 3.10; 15.10; 2 Cor. 6.1; 8.1; 9.14; Gal. 2.21; anarthrous: 1 Cor. 15.10; 2 Cor. 1.12; righteousness of God – arthrous: Rom. 10.3; anarthrous: Rom. 1.17; 3.5, 21, 22; 2 Cor. 5.21; Spirit of God – arthrous: 1 Cor. 2.11, 14; 3.16; 6.11; anarthrous: Rom. 8.14, [15.19]; 1 Cor. 7.40; 12.3; 2 Cor. 3.3, 17 [κυρίου]; Phil. 3.3).

[27] Rom. 16.20, [24]; 1 Cor. 16.23; 2 Cor. 8.9; 13.13; Gal. [1.6]; 6.18; Phil. 4.23; 1 Thess. 5.28.

[28] Arthrous: Gal. 4.6; Phil. 1.19; anarthrous: Rom. 8.9.

[29] Arthrous: love (Rom. 8.35; 2 Cor. 5.14); power (2 Cor. 12.9); suffering (2 Cor. 1.5); anarthrous: emotion (Phil. 1.8); mind (1 Cor. 2.16).

[30] Cross – arthrous: Gal. 6.12, 14; Phil. 3.18; death – arthrous: 2 Cor. 4.10; gospel – arthrous: Phil. 1.27; law – arthrous: Gal. 6.2; anarthrous: 1 Cor. 9.21; life – arthrous: 2 Cor. 4.10; power – arthrous: 2 Cor. 12.9; truth – anarthrous: 2 Cor. 11.10.

[31] Simple dative: Rom. 4.3; 10.16; Gal. 3.6; εἰς: Rom. 10.10; Gal. 2.16; Phil. 1.29; ἐν: 1 Thess. 1.7; ἐπί: Rom. 4.5, (18), 24; 9.33; 10.11; cf. ὅτι: Rom. 6.8; 10.9; 1 Thess. 4.14.

[32] Jesus: Rom. 9.33; Gal. 2.16; [3.26]; Phil. 1.29; God: Rom. 4.3, 5, [17], 24; Gal. 3.6.

[33] The meaning of this phrase will be discussed in section 2.

deutero-Pauline epistles.[34] It should also be noted that apart from Paul, there are no unambiguous cases in the New Testament where πίστις followed by Christ or God in the genitive case must be interpreted objectively.[35]

Finally, a glance at most recent English translations alerts us to another difficulty, namely, the pleonasm attested in Romans 3.22, Galatians 2.16 and 3.22 when verbal and substantive constructions involving πιστεύω cognates are treated as semantically equivalent. Consider, for example, the *Revised Standard Version's* rendering of Galatians 2.16:

> We ourselves, who are Jews by birth and not Gentile sinners, yet who know that a man is not justified by works of the law but through faith in Jesus Christ (διὰ πίστεως Ἰησοῦ Χριστοῦ), even we have believed in Christ Jesus (εἰς Χριστὸν Ἰησοῦν ἐπιστεύσαμεν), in order to be justified by faith in Christ (ἐκ πίστεως Χριστοῦ), and not by works of the law, because by works of the law shall no man be justified.

Why include the construction involving πιστεύω? Surely three references in as many lines to the same human disposition is at least strained?[36] Indeed, references to the faith of believers are present in all contexts under review in addition to the πίστις Χριστοῦ constructions.[37]

In the light of these observations, we may conclude with some confidence that the question of whether πίστις Χριστοῦ and its variants should be interpreted subjectively or objectively cannot be

[34] Πίστις ἐν: Eph. 1.15; Col. 1.4; cf. 1 Tim. 1.14; 3.13; 2 Tim. 1.13; 3.15; πίστις εἰς: Col. 2.5. See also πίστις πρός: 1 Thess. 1.8 (God); Phlm. 5 (Christ).

[35] Cf. Mark 11.22; Jas. 2.1; Rev. 2.13; 14.12; also Acts 3.16; Col. 2.12; 2 Thess. 2.13. On the ambiguous nature of these texts see D. W. B. Robinson, 'Faith', 78–9.

[36] Exponents of the objective genitive interpretation for πίστις Χριστοῦ draw attention to the fact that repetition can be used as a form of emphasis (e.g. Dunn, *Romans*, vol. 1, 166–7). As we shall see, however, it is questionable whether Paul intended to emphasise the faith of believers in the relevant contexts and, even if he did, the triple reference in Gal. 2.16 is still problematic.

[37] Εἰς πάντας τοὺς πιστεύοντας in Rom. 3.22 for Rom. 3.22, 26 (cf. διὰ [τῆς] πίστεως in Rom. 3.25); καὶ ἡμεῖς εἰς Χριστὸν Ἰησοῦν ἐπιστεύσαμεν in Gal. 2.16 for Gal. 2.16, 20; τοῖς πιστεύουσιν in Gal. 3.22 for the same verse; and ἐπὶ τῇ πίστει in Phil. 3.9 for the same verse. Given the importance of the relevant passages for understanding Pauline soteriology, it cannot be overstated that subjective genitive interpretations for πίστις Χριστοῦ do not exclude the faith of believers.

decided on grammatical grounds alone.[38] Moreover, the evidence is sufficiently ambiguous that neither option carries the burden of proof; rather, the matter remains open and must be decided on contextual and theological grounds.

2 The Epistle to the Romans

Rom. 3.22 and 26: δικαιοσύνη δὲ θεοῦ διὰ πίστεως °'Ιησοῦ Χριστοῦ ‘εἰς πάντας’ τοὺς πιστεύοντας ... πρὸς τὴν ἔνδειξιν τῆς δικαιοσύνης αὐτοῦ ἐν τῷ νῦν καιρῷ, εἰς τὸ εἶναι αὐτὸν δίκαιον καὶ δικαιοῦντα τὸν ἐκ πίστεως ⌜'Ιησοῦ.

Textual Notes: (°) the omission of 'Ιησοῦ by B & Marcion, which makes little difference to the sense of the verse, may be original; (‘) some witnesses attest ἐπὶ πάντας instead of εἰς πάντας, whilst the variant εἰς πάντας καὶ ἐπὶ πάντας looks like a conflation; (⌜) the form 'Ιησοῦ Χριστοῦ in a number of authorities is probably a scribal accretion.

Translation:[39] <3.21> But now God's righteousness [*or* covenantal faithfulness], attested by the law and the prophets, has been disclosed apart from the law, <22> [that is,] the righteousness of God through Jesus Christ's faith for all those believing. For there is no distinction, <23> since all have sinned and lack the glory of God, <24> being justified [*or* brought into a right relation with God] freely by his grace through the redemption which is in Christ Jesus, <25> whom God put forward as a means of expiation through [Jesus'] faith at the cost of [*or* by means of] his blood, to demonstrate [*or* prove] his righteousness in overlooking past sins <26> in the forebearance of God; to demonstrate his righteousness in the present time, in order to be righteous even in justifying the one [who lives] from Jesus' faith [*or* the one participating in Jesus' faith].

Having introduced one of the central thrusts of the letter in

38 ‘... it would be fairer to say that if any kind of conclusion has been reached, it is that the question cannot be settled on the basis of appeals to grammatical construction alone. This issue can be settled only by exegesis, and because New Testament scholars approach the texts with widely differing presuppositions, they are likely to interpret the phrase in very different ways.’ (Hooker, ‘ΠΙΣΤΙΣ’, 321)

39 The translations provided at the beginning of the sections on Romans, Galatians and Philippians have been prepared so as to reflect the results of the accompanying exegesis.

Romans 1.16–17,[40] Paul commences his detailed exposition of how God's mercy and justice can be seen through all his dealings with humankind.[41] He explains that all people – whether Gentile or Jew – have enjoyed the opportunity to respond positively to the prevenient and providential goodness of God. The history of humankind before the coming of Christ, however, is the story of the exploitation of that divine graciousness. As a consequence, God has left people to their own resources (e.g. 1.24, 26, 28) and to the power of sin (cf. 5.13), in the knowledge that all would ultimately have to face the judgement of God (e.g. 2.2, 5–11, 16) and the revelation of the divine wrath (e.g. 1.18).[42] The giving of the law did not substantially alter this basic predicament for, irrespective of whether it could be practised and fulfilled, its primary function was not to provide a means of salvation but to identify sin (e.g. 3.20; 4.15) and, presumably, to delimit appropriate response to God's covenantal initiatives.[43]

Into this situation of divine–human estrangement under the power of sin, Paul claims that the righteousness of God has been revealed apart from the law (3.21). But how is the righteousness of God revealed? The passive voice of φανερόω suggests divine action or origin, whilst the choice of the perfect tense over the aorist indicates an initial and continuing disclosure. The following verses

[40] Cranfield, *Romans*, vol. 1, 87–102; Dunn, *Romans*, vol. 1, 36–49; Nygren, *Romans*, 65–92.

[41] The view that the opening chapters of Romans are concerned primarily with vindicating God, rather than with establishing the universality of human sin, is defended by Hays, *Echoes*, esp. 41–57, and Snodgrass, 'Justification', 72–93.

[42] On this approach, for example: Hays, 'ΠΙΣΤΙΣ', 720; Martin, *Reconciliation*, 48–67; Räisänen, *Paul*, 94–113; Sanders, *Palestinian Judaism*, esp. 474–511.

[43] Paul's attitude to the law has been the focus of much scholarly endeavour in recent years; see the surveys of Barclay, 'Paul', 5–15, and Moo, 'Paul', 287–307. Our assessment of Paul's treatment of the law in the early chapters of Romans can be summarised as follows: in the light of the universalising of God's gift of salvation in Christ, Paul does not present the provision of and response to the law as an independent soteriological system which is able to deal with the fundamental estrangement between God and humankind (this may well have been a conviction he shared with many Jews as well). To this end, he is entirely negative towards those who maintain that they can secure their standing before God simply in terms of 'works of the law'; however, the law itself can fulfil a positive function in establishing from both ethical (i.e. no one seeking God) and forensic (i.e. under God's judgement) perspectives, the nature and implications of the human predicament outside of grace (especially, Sanders, *Palestinian Judaism*, 474–97, and *Jewish People*, 70–86, 143–8). As we shall see, Paul is keen to maintain the continuity between God's covenantal graciousness extended, on the one hand, to Abraham and the Jewish lineage and, on the other, to all people in Christ; on this, see Dunn, 'Light', 89–128, and Wright, *Climax*.

give rise to many interpretative difficulties, but there can be little doubt that Paul understands the origin of the revelation to be in the redemptive death of Christ (3.24–5; cf. 1.17), although it is less obvious whether the emphasis falls on the initial manifestation or subsequent 'revelations' through the gospel. However, the presence of διὰ πίστεως Ἰησοῦ Χριστοῦ (cf. εἰς πάντας τοὺς πιστεύοντας) in verse 22 has led many scholars to qualify this revelation in terms of human response and, by doing so, to come down on the side of the latter.[44] But emphasis upon the faith of believers at this stage in Paul's argument seems unlikely for a number of reasons.[45]

As we have already remarked, Paul offers a diagnosis in the early chapters of Romans of the human predicament in relation to God before the coming of Christ. It is one characterised by humanity's unwillingness to respond appropriately to God.[46] At the beginning of the third chapter, the apostle notes that τὰ λόγια τοῦ θεοῦ were entrusted (ἐπιστεύθησαν) to the Jews; but what if they proved unfaithful (ἠπίστησαν) as well?[47] He affirms that their ἀπιστία does

[44] E.g. '... the righteousness of God through faith in Jesus Christ for all who believe'. (RSV) See, for example, the commentaries of Barrett, Cranfield, Käsemann, Sanday and Headlam, and Wilckens.

[45] J. D. G. Dunn appears to recognise this when he comments that taking διὰ πίστεως Ἰησοῦ Χριστοῦ as an objective genitive 'does not mean that Paul regarded man's faith as the manifestation of God's righteousness. What Paul says is that God's righteousness comes to expression *through* faith in Christ (rather than through those acts which set Jews apart in their national distinctiveness).' (*Romans*, vol. 1, 167) Yet Paul's understanding of God's righteousness in Christ not only abrogates the salvific priority enjoyed by the Jews on the basis of the law, but also undermines all human endeavour in this respect. To claim that Paul replaces God's righteousness mediated through the law with God's righteousness mediated through faith in Christ does not remove the human boast, for both constitute responses to God's prior initiative.

[46] The question whether Paul believed the rift between God and humanity prior to the coming of Christ to be absolute is not easy to answer, although a number of scholars would now maintain that he did not (e.g. G. N. Davies, *Faith*, 35–71; Dunn, 'Perspective', 95–122; Gaston, 'Believers', 116–34; 'Paul and the Torah', 15–34). The opening chapters of Romans suggest Paul recognised that all people had the opportunity to know God; he also views Abraham positively and acknowledges the special provision made by God for the Jews and, possibly, through them for the Gentiles. All this favours the view that he must have considered the possibility of experiencing the salvation of God prior to Christ as real. But this has to be balanced against his conviction that a 'quantum leap' took place in Christ; it is not simply that the nature of human response changed from keeping the law to faith, or even that it was always faith, but that the context and initiative for all human response is now determined by Christ.

[47] 'We take it then that the thought conveyed by ἠπίστησαν in relation to the ἐπιστεύθησαν of the previous verse is not that these Jews have proved unfaithful to their trust but that they have failed to believe the λόγια τοῦ θεοῦ entrusted to them ... The Jews' unbelief was also, as a matter of fact, unfaithfulness to the

not nullify τὴν πίστιν τοῦ θεοῦ; clearly God's πίστις is not mediated or controlled by humanity's lack of response.[48] It seems improbable, therefore, that in Romans 3.21 he would maintain that the revelation of God's righteousness was dependent upon or mediated by the faith of believers on hearing the gospel.[49] Such an interpretation detracts not only from the sufficiency of God's grace manifested in Christ[50] and contradicts Paul's previous assessment of humanity's unwillingness to respond to God, but also fails to accommodate the 'pastness' of the initial revelation of God's righteousness attested in 3.21 and reiterated in 5.6–11.[51] It should also be noted that the righteousness of God in 3.21–2 belongs to a series of synonymous expressions which characterise God's conduct in relation to his covenant[52] and stand in contrast to the obduracy of the recipients. Finally, given that εἰς πάντας τοὺς πιστεύοντας (3.22) relates to human faith in Jesus Christ,[53] if διὰ πίστεως Ἰησοῦ Χριστοῦ is similarly interpreted, then the resulting repetition may well indicate unnecessary redundancy in style[54] and certainly places the emphasis in the disclosure of God's righteousness upon human response rather than divine initiative.

Taken cumulatively, these observations call into question those

covenant; and Paul may well, while referring primarily to their unbelief, have also had in mind the thought of their unfaithfulness.' (Cranfield, *Romans*, vol. 1, 180)

48 G. N. Davies, *Faith*, 75–80; Goodenough, 'Paul', 43–5; Ljungman, *Pistis*, 38–41; Stuhlmacher, *Gerechtigkeit*, 85.

49 'Man's unfaithfulness in no way destroys the faithfulness of God – but the faithfulness of God should have been answered by the faithfulness of man. A priori, we may expect the Second Adam to be obedient, to give glory to God, and to be faithful.' (Hooker, 'ΠΙΣΤΙΣ', 324; also Campbell, *Rhetoric*, 63–4, and Hays, 'ΠΙΣΤΙΣ', 720)

50 Keck, 'Jesus', 456–7. Some scholars have equated πίστις here with the gospel itself and, in this way, have shifted the emphasis from the personal act of faith onto the whole event in which the righteousness of God is encountered (Kertelge, *Rechtfertigung*, 77, and Wissmann, *Verhältnis*, 30–3, 81–3). Whilst this interpretation recognises the theological context of human response, it is still open to some of the criticisms levelled against equating πίστις simply with human faith.

51 Campbell, *Rhetoric*, 63–4; Hays, *Faith*, 172–4; S. K. Williams, *Saving Event*, 48.

52 R. B. Hays notes the following string: τὴν πίστιν τοῦ θεοῦ ... ὁ θεὸς ἀληθής ... θεοῦ δικαιοσύνη ... ἡ ἀλήθεια τοῦ θεοῦ; he observes that 'these expressions function interchangeably in this passage and therefore interpret one another'. ('Psalm 143', 110; also S. K. Williams, 'Righteousness', 265–73)

53 Cf. S. K. Williams, who questions whether Paul considers Jesus as an appropriate object of faith (*Saving Event*, 43, and 'Again', 434–5); but Dunn, *Romans*, vol. 1, 167.

54 M. Barth, 'Faith', 368; Johnson, 'Rom. 3:21–26', 79; Schmidt, *Römer*, 66; *contra* Mundle, who takes εἰς πάντας τοὺς πιστεύοντας as the basis for understanding διὰ πίστεως Ἰησοῦ Χριστοῦ (*Glaubensbegriff*, 75–83).

interpretations which take διὰ πίστεως Ἰησοῦ Χριστοῦ as an objective genitive referring exclusively or at least primarily to the faith of believers. Consideration of the subjective genitive option, however, suggests an alternative understanding in which the righteousness of God and, particularly, its initial revelation is mediated by Jesus Christ's πίστις.[55] Yet before this can be taken as a viable alternative, we must explore the relationship between Christ's πίστις and the revelation of God's righteousness. It is striking how frequently God's righteousness and faithfulness are used synonymously in the Old Testament,[56] an observation which invites consideration of the relationship between God's faithfulness and Christ's πίστις. Furthermore, given that the Old Testament is a likely source for Paul's thinking in this sphere, it is not inconceivable that reflection upon the significance of Christ within God's dispensation of salvation would lead the apostle to interpret Jesus' life and death as a channel for God's faithfulness.[57]

This pattern of thinking is evident in the Old Testament, where the faithfulness of God towards his people is a strong theme, especially in the Psalms.[58] God's conduct, which can also be described in terms of *ṣᵉḏāqâh, mišpaṭ, ḥeseḏ* or *ᵉmûnâh*, is always determined by the covenant between himself and his people. His faithfulness should not, however, be interpreted as an exclusively passive state of being or level of activity through which the covenant is simply maintained; on the contrary, it comes to expression in fresh initiatives either of direct or mediated revelation through which God's continuing covenantal promises and purposes are made known.[59] Consider again Psalm 89, which in Christian and later

55 This position is adopted by an ever increasing number of scholars; see, especially, Campbell, *Rhetoric*, 58–69, 214–18, and Hays, 'ΠΙΣΤΙΣ', 714–29.

56 S. K. Williams, 'Righteousness', 260–73; also Kertelge, *Rechtfertigung*, 67, and Stuhlmacher, *Gerechtigkeit*, 116.

57 Hays underlines the centrality of the Hebrew Scriptures for understanding Paul's writings (*Echoes*, esp. 1–33). That the apostle was thinking along the lines suggested here gains support from Hays' assessment of the allusion to Ps. 143 in Rom. 3.20: 'The psalmist's appeal to God's truthfulness (*alêtheia*; cf. Rom. 3:4, 7) and righteousness (*dikaiosunê*; cf. Rom. 3:5, 21–22) as ground of hope and instrument of deliverance provides the background against which all of Romans 3 can be read. The psalm provides Paul not only with the language for a blanket indictment of humankind but also with the expectant language of prayer that looks to God's righteousness as the source of salvation.' (*Echoes*, 52)

58 E.g. Deut. 32.4; Pss. 19.8–9; 33.4; 36.5–6; 40.10; 88.11–12; 92.3; 96.13; 100.5; 111.7; 119.75, 86, 90, 138, 143.1: Isa. 11.5; 25.1; Jer. 42.5.

59 J. V. Taylor, *Christlike God*, 124–9. God's faithfulness is not a question of his ceasing to act, but of his acting within the terms of his revealed character or

Jewish thought came to be interpreted messianically.[60] It speaks of God's *'emûnâh* in terms of establishing a covenant with David, but there is evidence that this was later linked with the covenant of Abraham as well.[61] God's *'emûnâh* is with David (v. 24) and remains with him even when Israel must be punished for her rebellion (vv. 30–3). The psalm concludes with a lament concerning God's seeming absence in the face of the Davidic king's misfortunes and culminates with a petition to God for assistance, 'Lord, where is thy steadfast love (*ḥasādeykā*) of old, which by thy faithfulness (*be'emûnāṯekā*) thou didst swear to David'. In this way, Psalm 89 articulates God's faithfulness in terms of his covenantal initiatives towards the Davidic kingly line and, in times when his chosen one suffers rejection and humiliation, God is petitioned in order that his *'emûnâh* may be seen once more. Although *'emûnâh* is rendered in the Septuagint by ἀλήθεια,[62] the conceptual link between God's faithfulness and its expression through a human being is established.

The manifestation of God's faithfulness through his chosen one is developed further in the Psalms of Solomon. Once again the Lord is faithful in his actions (e.g. πιστός, Pss. Sol. 8.28; 14.1; 17.10) and his messiah of Davidic stock will act on his behalf. In a similar way to other Jews, his hope is in God[63] and he will shepherd the Lord's flock – those who are descendants of Abraham (Pss. Sol. 18.3): 'The Lord himself is his [i.e. the son of David's] king, the hope of the one

being-in-relation. The tendency to overlook this dynamic nature of God's continuing covenantal faithfulness may well result from either a desire to stress the link between God's faithfulness and truth (e.g. Hebert, 'Faithfulness', 373–9) or an over-emphasis upon the active nature of human faith (e.g. Turner, *Words*, 154–7).

60 Juel, *Exegesis*, 104–10; on Ps. 89, Vallotton, *Christ*, 24–5, and chapter 1, section 3.

61 'R. Aha said: [Abraham wondered]: Surely Thou too indulgest in prevarication! Yesterday Thou saidest, *For in Isaac shall seed be called to thee* (Gen. 21.12); Thou didst then retract and say, *Take now thy son* (*ib.* 22.2); while now Thou biddest me, LAY NOT THY HAND UPON THE LAD! Said the Holy One, blessed be He, to him: "O Abraham, My covenant will I not profane (Ps. LXXXIX, 35), *And I* will *establish My covenant with Isaac* (Gen. XVII, 21). When I bade thee, '*Take now thy son*,' etc., *I will not alter that which is gone out of My lips* (Ps. *loc. cit.*). Did I tell thee, Slaughter him? No! but, '*Take him up*.' Thou hast taken him up. Now take him down."' Gen. R. LVI.8 (on Gen. 22.11).

62 Ps. 89 [LXX, Ps. 88]:2, 3, 6, 9, 25, 34, 50; cf. Ps. 89.29 and 38 where πιστός translates the niphal of *'āman*. 'What is too easily missed is the fact that for a Jew like Paul talk of "the truth of God" carried the same connotation, since *'emûnâh* and *'emeṯ* could be translated equally by ἀλήθεια or πίστις.' (Dunn, 'Once More', 742)

63 The ἐλπίζω group is used to express the hope of both the messiah (17.34, 39) and others (5.14; 6.6; 8.31; 9.10; 15.1; 17.3).

who has a strong hope in God (ἐλπὶς τοῦ δυνατοῦ ἐλπίδι θεοῦ) ... His hope will be in the Lord (ἡ ἐλπὶς αὐτοῦ ἐπὶ κύριον) ... Shepherding the Lord's flock in faith and righteousness (ἐν πίστει καὶ δικαιοσύνῃ), he will not let any of them stumble in their pasture.' (Pss. Sol. 17.34, 39, 40; trans.*)

These and other traditions discussed in chapter 1 (section 3) bear witness to the expectation that the messiah would be a man of faith and that through his faith, God's covenantal faithfulness would continue to be made known. Furthermore, this background does seem to provide a context in which Paul's διὰ πίστεως Ἰησοῦ Χριστοῦ in Romans 3.22 can be interpreted meaningfully as a subjective genitive, referring to the πίστις of Jesus Christ, the messiah, through which the covenantal faithfulness or righteousness of God is revealed. As we shall see, Christ's πίστις is not identical with God's πίστις; rather, God's covenantal faithfulness to the Abrahamic promise is revealed in and through the faith of Jesus.

The relationship between God's faithfulness and Christ's πίστις will be explored further at a later stage,[64] but here the point to note is that the semantics of the πιστεύω group do not permit any simple solution. A neat lexical distinction cannot be drawn, either from general usage or from the Pauline writings, between faith and faithfulness.[65] For instance, Paul refers to τὴν πίστιν τοῦ θεοῦ (Rom. 3.3)[66] and lists πίστις (Gal. 5.22) amongst the fruit of the Spirit, where a sense of faithfulness must be intended. In addition, he frequently attributes πιστός to God and humans alike,[67] and can use this form to mean, on the one hand, 'trustworthy' or 'dependable' (e.g. 1 Cor. 1.9; 4.2; 10.13; 2 Cor. 1.18) and, on the other, 'trusting' or 'faith-ful' (e.g. 2 Cor. 6.15; Gal. 3.9).

The Interpretation of Habakkuk 2.4 in Romans 1.17

Before returning to Romans 3, it will be helpful to consider the meaning of Paul's rendering of Habakkuk 2.4 in Romans 1.17, ὁ δὲ

64 Previous attempts to interpret πίστις Χριστοῦ in the light of God's faithfulness have tended to equate the former with the latter and, by doing so, have interpreted Christ's πίστις in predominantly passive and static terms. Consider, for example, Hebert, 'Faithfulness', 373–9, and T. F. Torrance, 'One Aspect', 111–14, in the light of Barr, *Semantics*, 161–205.

65 See the material surveyed in BAGD, 662–5, and Bultmann, 'πιστεύω', 204–22.

66 Πίστις is also used of God in the Septuagint (Ps. 32.4; Hab. 2.4; Jer. 15.18; 39.41; 40.6; Lam. 3.23 [R]; cf. Hos. 2.22).

67 God: 1 Cor. 1.9; 10.13; 2 Cor. 1.18; 1 Thess. 5.24; humans: 1 Cor. 4.2, 17; 7.25.

δίκαιος ἐκ πίστεως ζήσεται. Unlike the Masoretic Text and the Habakkuk Commentary from Qumran, which speak of the righteous one's faith(fulness), and most versions of the Septuagint, which refer to God's faith(fulness),[68] Paul does not qualify πίστις with a personal pronoun. Although this is ambiguous grammatically, there is little reason to doubt that the apostle intended ὁ δίκαιος as the exponent of faith. But how should the quotation as a whole be understood and to whom does it refer? One major problem revolves around whether ἐκ πίστεως should be connected with ζήσεται, as in the Masoretic Text and the Septuagint, or with ὁ δίκαιος, as proposed by Beza and followed by numerous interpreters of Paul ever since.[69] Both options can be defended linguistically, with the result that the issue must be decided on contextual and theological grounds.

The majority but by no means consensus view is that ἐκ πίστεως qualifies ὁ δίκαιος (i.e. 'The righteous-by-faith shall live') and that ὁ δίκαιος refers to all those who, by exercising faith, become partakers in God's justification graciously made available through Christ. This interpretation seems unlikely, however, for it is not only contrary to the original Hebrew and subsequent Greek renderings of Habakkuk 2.4, but also and more importantly seems to be at variance with Paul's soteriology developed throughout the epistle. By maintaining that πίστις should be taken with ὁ δίκαιος, it is claimed that the verse reflects Paul's conviction that justification is personally appropriated through faith in Christ alone and that righteousness cannot be secured by human effort.[70] But unless a prior and more fundamental theological truth is presupposed, these options are structurally very similar and ostensibly the same: justi-

[68] MT and 1QpHab, *wᵉṣadîq beʾᵉmûnāṯô yiḥyeh*; LXX (most MSS): ὁ δὲ δίκαιος ἐκ πίστεως μου ζήσεται; cf. LXX (A and C) and Heb. 10.38, ὁ δὲ δίκαιος μου ἐκ πίστεως ζήσεται.

[69] C. E. B. Cranfield (*Romans*, vol. 1, 100–2) and G. N. Davies (*Faith*, 39–42) cite the relevant literature. G. N. Davies follows C. K. Barrett and others in seeing an intentional ambiguity in Paul's expression; see also Ziesler, *Meaning*, 175–7.

[70] Consider, for example J. D. G. Dunn's comments on Paul's version of Hab. 2.4 and, in particular, the omission of the personal pronoun: 'When πίστις is understood as "trust," better sense can be made of *both* the chief alternative text forms: that is to say, for Paul the counterpart of God's faithfulness is not man's *faithfulness* (at any rate as understood within Judaism), but *faith*, his trust in and total reliance upon God. If man's faithfulness is a consistent expression of that faith, good and well. But Paul's charge against Israel will be that the definition of faithfulness as observance of the law amounts to a serious misunderstanding of faith – and so of righteousness (both God's and man's), and so also of the life which follows from it.' (*Romans*, vol. 1, 46)

fication appropriated by responding to the revelation of God's law in the life of covenantal faithfulness and justification appropriated by believing in God's work in Christ proclaimed through the gospel. In both cases, the emphasis falls upon the individual and his or her response to God's provision; whilst Paul does not ignore the importance of a believer's faith within the salvation process, and readily distinguishes it from performing 'works of the law', the major innovation within his understanding of salvation is God's prevenient grace, initially extended to Abraham and fulfilled in Christ.[71] As a result, it seems more in keeping with Paul's intention in Romans to frame the contrasting approaches to justification not in terms of the 'works-faith' dichotomy, but rather of justification on the basis of human response versus justification on the basis of God's universal grace in Christ[72] or, expressed another way, of human righteousness versus God's righteousness and covenantal faithfulness.

The priority of grace within Paul's theology is, of course, generally accepted, but its relationship to faith remains an area of considerable debate and will need to be explored later on. At this stage, it is sufficient to note that as long as ὁ δίκαιος in Romans 1.17 is identified with each believer, this verse, which is considered by many commentators to set out the theme for at least the first half of the epistle, places the emphasis upon humanity's response to God and not on God's initiative in Christ. Not only does this seem unlikely in the light of what has been said above, but in doing so it permits – if not encourages – a meritorious understanding of faith.[73] Further, it is questionable whether Paul would refer to a believer as ὁ δίκαιος. In the first place, it suggests that righteousness is a personal possession and, from this perspective, conflicts with the apostle's discussion of the impossibility of righteousness being achieved by human initiative.

Secondly, even when both the forensic and the ethical dimensions of justification are taken into consideration, Paul does not claim that believers are righteous but that they receive righteousness from

[71] On the centrality of grace for Paul's soteriology see: Doughty, 'Priority', 163–80; Kim, *Origin*, esp. 269–311; Sanders, *Palestinian Judaism*, 447–523.

[72] Hooker, 'ΠΙΣΤΙΣ', 341, and Howard, 'Romans 10.4ff', 335.

[73] That such an understanding was entertained is evident from Qumran: 'The explanation of this [i.e. Hab. 2.4] concerns all those who observe the Law in the House of Judah. God will deliver them from the House of Judgement because of their affliction and their faith in the Teacher of Righteousness.' (1QpHab 8.1–3; trans. *EWQ*, 263)

God.[74] This point is developed in Romans 4 with reference to Abraham. Like the rest of humankind, the patriarch is a sinner (cf. 4.5) who is incapable of being righteous and who, through his faith in God, has righteousness reckoned to him; in the same way, righteousness is reckoned to those who have faith (e.g. 4.23–5).[75]

For Paul, there is only one person who, in addition to God, is truly righteous and that is Christ. It is he alone who does not need to have righteousness reckoned to him for he knew no sin (2 Cor. 5.21) and, through his δικαίωμα, secured justification for all (Rom. 5.18). Righteousness in relation to humanity, therefore, can never be dissociated from the life and death of Christ, for he embodies what it is to be righteous and the righteousness of humanity resides within him.[76] In the light of these comments, an alternative interpretation for ὁ δίκαιος in Romans 1.17 becomes apparent, namely, that it refers primarily to Christ who lived by faith.[77] This proposal has the advantage of placing Christ at the heart of this programmatic verse and, given the significance of Jesus' faith and its relationship to that of each believer, provides a suitable summary for the first part of the epistle. The 'Righteous One' as an epithet for the messiah is attested in both Jewish and Christian sources,[78] whilst there is evidence to suggest that Habakkuk 2.4 was interpreted messianically in the Septuagint.[79] It is possible, therefore, that Paul draws upon Habakkuk 2.4 to explain how the righteousness of God is revealed ἐκ

[74] This is clearly a highly complex and much debated area, but the point to emphasise here is that for Paul all righteousness has its origin in God – whether understood in a forensic sense, by which all are justified before God through Christ's atoning death, or in an ethical sense, by which members of Christ's body are transformed by the indwelling presence of the Spirit. Righteousness is never the personal property of the believer; rather, it is a function of their relation to God in Christ.

[75] A. T. Hanson, *Studies*, 52–66. The significance of λογίζομαι in relation to faith and righteousness will be discussed below.

[76] Kertelge, *Rechtfertigung*, 83.

[77] Bligh, 'Jesus', 418–19; Campbell, *Rhetoric*, 204–13; A. T. Hanson, *Studies*, 39–51; Haussleiter, 'Glaube', 205–13. Others prefer to identify here a reference to God's faithfulness (e.g. G. N. Davies, *Faith*, 42–6; Gaston, 'Abraham', 59–60); as we shall see, however, given the close relationship between the revelation of God's righteousness or faithfulness and Christ these alternatives may be more apparent than real (cf. K. Barth, *Romans*, 39–42, and Vallotton, *Christ*, 63–70).

[78] E.g. 1 Enoch 38.2; cf. 'the Elect One of righteousness and of faith' 1 Enoch 39.6; Acts 3.14; 7.52; 22.14; Jas. 5.6; cf. no article in 1 Pet. 3.18; 1 John 2.1. See Hays, 'Righteous One', 191–215.

[79] 'The LXX, by translating the Hebrew of verse 3d as ἐρχόμενος, instead of making it apply to the vision, has imported the idea of a coming one and therefore given a messianic tone to the whole passage.' (A. T. Hanson, *Studies*, 42). Also Hays, *Faith*, 150–8; Koch, 'Text', esp. 69–74.

πίστεως εἰς πίστιν. It is initially revealed in Jesus the Righteous One, whose life of faith (ἐκ πίστεως) provides the basis for the righteousness and faith (εἰς πίστιν) of all people – Jew and Gentile alike.[80]

Having suggested that the motif of the messiah's faith may have been introduced by Paul from the outset, we return again to chapter 3 to see how this theme is developed in relation to the revealing of God's righteousness (3.22). In verse 23, the apostle reaffirms the sinful state of humankind and then, in stark contrast, moves on to speak of God's grace evident through the redemption secured in Christ Jesus (v. 24). Once again, the emphasis is upon God's salvific initiative prior to and independent of human response, which is further developed in the following two verses. There is as yet no scholarly consensus concerning the existence or extent of pre-Pauline traditions in Romans 3.24–6,[81] although it is interesting that the problematic διὰ [τῆς] πίστεως of verse 25 is often considered a Pauline addition to traditional material;[82] an observation which, if early material is being revised, underlines both the presence and the positioning of this phrase within the apostle's presentation.

The difficulties in maintaining that the revelation of God's righteousness is in some way mediated by human faith have already been introduced; the presence of διὰ [τῆς] πίστεως[83] in verse 25 suggests that similar issues are evident once again in relation to the 'mechanics of salvation' or the way in which God's righteousness operates through Christ. Whether ἱλαστήριον is understood as the 'means' or the 'place' of redemption,[84] it seems theologically incoherent for Paul to maintain that the efficacy of Christ's sacrificial

80 A number of scholars (e.g. K. Barth, *Romans*, 41; Dunn, *Romans*, vol. 1, 44; Hebert, 'Faithfulness', 375) understand ἐκ πίστεως εἰς πίστιν along the lines of 'from God's faithfulness to man's faith'. As we have already noted, if Jesus' faith constitutes the channel for God's faithfulness, this alternative is remarkably similar to the one proposed here.

81 A convenient summary of alternatives is provided by Stuhlmacher, *Reconciliation*, 94–109.

82 See the discussion of Kertelge, *Rechtfertigung*, 48–53; 71–85. B. W. Longenecker defends the integrity of διὰ [τῆς] πίστεως within the pre-Pauline formula in Rom. 3:24–6 and claims that the apostle inherited the subjective genitive interpretation ('ΠΙΣΤΙΣ', 478–80).

83 The provenance of the article in διὰ [τῆς] πίστεως remains unresolved: 'On the one hand, the article may have been added by copyists who wished to point back to διὰ πίστεως Ἰησοῦ Χριστοῦ in ver. 22. On the other hand, later in the chapter when Paul uses πίστις absolutely (i.e. without a modifier), διά is followed by the article (cf. verses 30 and 31).' (Metzger, *Commentary*, 508)

84 The distinction is that of Dunn, *Romans*, vol. 1, 170–2.

death is dependent upon human faith. Not only does such an interpretation detract from the completeness of God's revelation in Christ, but it also contradicts much of the apostle's teaching elsewhere. Consider, for example, Romans 5.6–11 where he underlines, in similar language and concepts, that justification and reconciliation are established in the death of Christ whilst all remain sinners or enemies. Clearly, there are matters relating to the forensic and ethical dimensions of justification and the place of a believer's faith within the salvific process which must be considered, but these are implications of and not controlling factors within the revelation and achievement of God's salvific work in Christ: 'But God shows his love for us in that while we were yet sinners Christ died for us' (5.8). Further, this understanding seems to be rooted and may well originate in Paul's own christophany: as he reports in Galatians 1.11–17, it was the prevenient, enabling grace of God in disclosing to him the risen Jesus, whilst he remained committed to persecuting the church, which liberated him to acknowledge and respond to Jesus as Lord and messiah.[85]

In consequence, the preliminary question relating to διὰ [τῆς] πίστεως in Romans 3.25 concerns the identification of the exponent of faith and not how it relates to ἐν τῷ αὐτοῦ αἵματι. But if there are grounds to question whether human faith was foremost in the apostle's mind at this juncture, why would he speak of Christ's or God's faith? A context which helps make sense of the former is provided by the interpretation of the martyrdom of Eleazar, the seven sons and their mother expounded in 4 Maccabees.[86] The following passage, which explores the soteriological significance of their deaths, has proved influential for interpretations of Romans 3[87] and, in particular, for understanding Christ's death:

> These then, having consecrated themselves for the sake of God, are now honored not only with this distinction but also by the fact that through them our enemies did not prevail against the nation, and the tyrant was punished and our land purified, since they became, as it were, a ransom

[85] Beker, *Paul*, 260–2; Bornkamm, 'Revelation', 90–103; Dupont, 'Conversion', 176–94; Kim, *Origin*, 269–311.

[86] See, especially, van Henten, 'Background', 101–28, and S. K. Williams, *Saving Event*, 59–202; also Pobee, *Persecution*, 13–46; Swetnam, *Jesus*, 23–79; van Henten, *Entstehung*.

[87] E.g. Barrett, *First Adam*, 27; Hill, *Words*, 41–5; Michel, *Römer*, 107–8; Wilckens, *Römer*, 190–6; S. K. Williams, *Saving Event*, 34–56, 165–202.

> for the sin of our nation (ὥσπερ ἀντίψυχον γεγονότας τῆς τοῦ ἔθνους ἁμαρτίας). Through the blood of these righteous ones and through the propitiation of their death (καὶ διὰ τοῦ αἵματος τῶν εὐσεβῶν ἐκείνων καὶ τοῦ ἱλαστηρίου τοῦ θανάτου αὐτῶν) the divine providence rescued Israel, which had been shamefully treated. (4 Macc. 17.20–2; also 1.11; 6:28–9)

Parallels are usually identified in the latter half of this quotation revolving around ἱλαστήριον and the sacrifical nature of their demise. In addition, it is interesting to note that in several places throughout the book reference is made to the faith of these martyrs. Consider, for example:

> Remember that it is for God's sake you were given a share in the world and the benefit of life, and accordingly you owe it to God to endure all hardship for his sake, for whom our father Abraham ventured boldly to sacrifice his son Isaac, the father of our nation; and Isaac, seeing his father's hand, with knife in it, fall down against him, did not flinch. Daniel also, the righteous one (ὁ δίκαιος), was thrown to the lions, and Hananiah and Azariah and Mishael were cast in the fiery furnace, and all endured for the sake of God. Therefore, you who have the same faith in God (καὶ ὑμεῖς οὖν τὴν αὐτὴν πίστιν πρὸς τὸν θεὸν ἔχοντες) must not be dismayed. For it would be unreasonable for you who know true religion not to withstand hardships. (4 Macc. 16.18–23; also 5.25; 7.19, 21; 15.24; 17.2; cf. 7.9; 5.16)

Although no attempt is made in this passage or elsewhere in 4 Maccabees to establish the efficacy of faith within the salvific process, it is clear that the martyrs stood firm in the face of death through a faith which they shared with some of the great figures from Israel's history who also confronted death.[88] A more causal relationship between faith and salvation can be found in 1 Mac-

[88] 'The parallel passage at 16.20–23 mentions Abraham and Isaac at the Aqedah, Daniel amid the lions, and Hananiah, Mishael, and Azariah as examples of "faith in God" (v. 22), showing that 4 Maccabees looks upon faith as trust in God's power to save (cf. also 15.24 and 17.2).' (Swetnam, *Jesus*, 46; also van Henten, 'Background', 26–7) It is interesting how the sacrifice of the Maccabean martyrs is linked in this passage with the offering of Isaac, especially as some scholars have identified the presence of Akedah theology at this juncture (see Daly, 'Significance', 56–7, and Schoeps, *Paul*, 142; cf. the revised tradition-history by P. R. Davies and B. D. Chilton, 'Aqedah', 514–46).

cabees (e.g. Ανανιας, Αζαριας, Μισαηλ πιστεύσαντες ἐσώθησαν ἐκ φλογός, 1 Macc. 2.59) and is developed much further in Rabbinic circles with particular reference to Abraham and Moses. The important point at this stage, however, is not whether the faith of Eleazar, the seven sons and their mother merited salvation, but simply that 4 Maccabees bears witness to a tradition in which the disposition of those who were martyred and whose deaths were considered to have redemptive significance was characterised as faith. This observation, when taken in consideration with the evidence for the messiah as a man of faith surveyed in section 1.3, provides a basis for understanding διὰ [τῆς] πίστεως in terms of Christ's faith.

The relationship of διὰ [τῆς] πίστεως to the rest of Romans 3.25 remains unclear. The notion of salvation ἐν τῷ αὐτοῦ αἵματι is paralleled in Romans 5.9 and is often interpreted against the background of Leviticus 16–17 or, as noted above, 4 Maccabees 17. Although Christ is clearly central to 3.25, it is the righteousness of God in overlooking former sins which is the controlling motif, and the soteriological moment within this redemptive initiative is the death of Christ or, more precisely, the shedding of his blood.[89] But does the verse explain how Christ's death acts as an ἱλαστήριον for God? Could it be because of his faith (διὰ [τῆς] πίστεως)? Grammatically speaking, ἐν τῷ αὐτοῦ αἵματι can be taken as an instrumental dative of price[90] with the sense that atonement is achieved 'through [i.e. Christ's] faith at the cost of his blood'.

The obedience of Christ

Support for this interpretation comes from Paul's understanding of Jesus' obedience.[91] In Romans 5, the apostle illustrates the significance of Christ within the history of salvation by comparing and contrasting him with Adam.[92] At one stage in the discussion, he maintains that as Adam's disobedience (παρακοή) resulted in many becoming sinners, so Christ's obedience (ὑπακοή) supersedes that initial act and secures the righteousness of many (Rom. 5.19).

[89] Kertelge, *Rechtfertigung*, 81–3, and Ziesler, *Meaning*, 191–5.

[90] *GNTG*, III, 252; also BFD § 219.3; Rom. 5.9; Rev. 5.9; cf. Acts 20.28.

[91] On the relationship between Christ's faith and obedience: Grundmann, 'Teacher', 107–13; Johnson, 'Rom. 3:21–26', 85–90; Keck, 'Jesus', 457–60; R. N. Longenecker, 'Obedience', 142–52.

[92] W. D. Davies, *Paul*, 36–57; Scroggs, *Last Adam*, esp. 76–82; Shedd, *Man*, 93–199; Wright, *Climax*, esp. 35–40.

Whilst the precise meaning of δικαίωμα in Romans 5.18, which parallels ὑπακοῆς in the following verse, remains unclear, it certainly includes Jesus' obedience revealed on the cross and quite probably refers to his life in more general terms.[93] The obedience of Jesus also features in the Christ-hymn of Philippians, where the kenosis of Christ is epitomised by his death on the cross (Phil. 2.8).[94] In the light of these passages alone, it is evident that Paul can not only speak of Christ's obedience as an aspect of his humanity, but also attribute soteriological significance to it: Christ's radical obedience to God is the grounds for the justification of humankind.

The intimate relationship between faith and obedience in Paul[95] is captured within the phrase ὑπακοὴν πίστεως (Rom. 1.5; 16.26), which presently envelops his letter to the Romans. The precise relationship between these elements remains a matter of debate.[96] On occasion, it seems as if Paul considers faith and obedience as equivalent,[97] but the setting of Romans 1.5 suggests that this is not always the case. At the beginning of the epistle, the apostle expounds his commission in terms of establishing ὑπακοὴν πίστεως amongst the nations, including the Christians at Rome. Clearly, the latter group had already come to faith (e.g. 1.8, 12) with the result that, if obedience and faith are identical, the apostle would by his own confession have little reason to visit them. The believers at Rome, however, still needed to let that faith find expression in every aspect of their lives through obedience. It is possible, therefore, that ὑπακοὴν πίστεως denotes obedience which is a consequence or expression of faith and not simply identical with it. Thus, although the apostle maintains that faith constitutes the fundamental human response to God, obedience is a necessary outworking of that disposition.[98]

93 On δικαίωμα in Paul, see Cranfield, *Romans*, vol. 1, 289, and Hooker, 'Atonement', 462–70.

94 A number of scholars recognise the presence of 'Adam-christology' in Phil. 2.6–11 as well as Rom. 5; see Dunn, *Christology*, 114–21, and Wright, *Climax*, 56–98.

95 Bultmann, *Theology*, vol. 1, 314–24, and G. N. Davies, *Faith*, 25–30, 167–72.

96 Cranfield, *Romans*, vol. 1, 66, lists seven possibilities: obedience to the faith *(fides quae creditur)*; obedience to (the authority of) faith; obedience to God's faithfulness attested in the gospel; the obedience which works faith; the obedience required by faith; believing obedience; the obedience which consists of faith.

97 E.g. Rom. 1.8 and 16.19; 10.16a and 10.16b; 11.23 and 11.30–1; 1.5 and 15.18.

98 G. N. Davies, *Faith*, 25–30. A similar dynamic may be present in Gal. 5.6 with reference to faith and love: ἀλλὰ πίστις δι' ἀγάπης ἐνεργουμένη; see also τοῦ ἔργου τῆς πίστεως in 1 Thess. 1.3.

The attribution of obedience to Jesus Christ, together with this close relationship between faith and obedience, renders the proposed interpretation of 'through [Christ's] faith at the cost of his blood' for the difficult διὰ [τῆς] πίστεως ἐν τῷ αὐτοῦ αἵματι in Romans 3.25 a distinct possibility.[99] The faith of Jesus is demonstrated in his act of obedient self-giving on the cross in the shedding of his blood and, on the basis of this, God's ἱλαστήριον has been established.[100] Additional support for this understanding can be found in 4 Maccabees, where the principal expression of the martyrs, who it is noted possess faith, is obedience to the Torah.[101] Furthermore, it is because of their obedience in not eating unclean food that they are tortured and put to death.

If Romans 3.24–5 summarises both the grounds for and the mechanics of justification, verse 26 introduces the implications.[102] The temporal frame of reference (ἐν τῷ νῦν καιρῷ) is reminiscent of 3.21 where God's righteousness is initially revealed in Christ and subsequently through the gospel; in this case, a similar timeframe is intended, not least because the source of ἔνδειξις is once again Christ. In addition, Paul notes that as a consequence of the divine initiative in Christ, God is established as righteous in his justifying τὸν ἐκ πίστεως Ἰησοῦ. This phrase can be understood as an objective genitive providing the focus or object for God's justifying actions: 'that he [i.e. God] himself is righteous and that he justifies him who has faith in Jesus'.[103] However, given that Paul has already demonstrated that God's justifying work in Christ occurred when

[99] On this approach see, especially, S. K. Williams, *Saving Event*, 41–51; also Gaston, *Paul*, 172.

[100] Schmidt, *Römer*, 69. Given that the content of Christ's faith in Romans 3 finds expression in his obedience, the question of why Paul did not speak explicitly of Christ's obedience arises. The most likely reason is that the Hebrew Scriptures and, in particular, the accounts of God's dealings with Abraham define the fundamental response to God's graciousness and covenantal faithfulness in terms of faith (Gen. 15.6; cf. Hab. 2.4).

[101] E.g. 4 Macc. 5.16; 9.2; 15.9–10. Note that 4 Maccabees provides a thematic rather than a linguistic parallel in this respect; in these references, 'obedience' translates εὐπείθεια and not ὑπακοή.

[102] Barrett, *Romans*, 80; Hultgren, 'PISTIS', 259–61; Kertelge, *Rechtfertigung*, 83–4; Wilckens, *Römer*, vol. 1, 197.

[103] So Dunn, *Romans*, vol. 1, 175, and Wilckens, *Römer*, vol. 1, 198; cf. 'I continue to resist the temptation of reading, with D L X 33 614 et al., δικαιοῦντα τὸν ἐκ πίστεως Ἰησοῦν (= "by justifying Jesus ἐκ πίστεως"). This manuscript tradition shows that a significant number of interpreters in the church later found no difficulty with the idea that Jesus was justified by faith . . .' (Hays, 'ΠΙΣΤΙΣ', 722)

all were in sin, attempts to interpret πίστεως 'Ιησοῦ primarily in terms of the believer's faith seem to detract from, if not contradict, the finality of the cross.[104]

It should also be noted that Paul rarely uses 'Ιησοῦς in isolation from Χριστός or κύριος and, when he does, the focus tends to be upon the earthly existence of Jesus.[105] In the light of this, it is difficult to understand why he would speak in verse 26 of faith in the earthly Jesus, rather than the exalted Lord; in contrast, the faith of the earthly Jesus is not only a more natural interpretation grammatically, but also coheres with the development of thought in the previous verses. Further, similar constructions using ὁ/οἱ ἐκ followed by the genitive are attested in Romans 4.12 (τοῖς οὐκ ἐκ περιτομῆς), 4.14 (οἱ ἐκ νόμου) and 4.16 (τῷ ἐκ τοῦ νόμου; τῷ ἐκ πίστεως 'Αβραάμ), where the sense is that of belonging to the circumcision, the law or πίστεως 'Αβραάμ.[106] The last case is particularly interesting because of its striking similarities with τὸν ἐκ πίστεως 'Ιησοῦ in 3.26 and there is little doubt that it should be taken as a subjective genitive.

In order to assess the significance of τῷ ἐκ πίστεως 'Αβραάμ in Romans 4.16 and to understand in more general terms how this patriarch elucidates the significance of faith within salvation, we need to consider the portrayal of Abraham in Romans 4.[107] Before doing this, however, a number of comments relating to the final verses of chapter 3 are relevant. In 3.27–31, Paul considers how God's work in Christ has ramifications for both Jews and Gentiles.[108] Following on from the redemptive and more specifically sacrificial imagery of 3.23–6, the tone is still primarily forensic or declaratory: Paul establishes the theological basis for the removal of human boasting and for the salvation of Gentiles as well as Jews.[109] The contrast between διὰ νόμου τῶν ἐργῶν and διὰ νόμου πίστεως in 3.27 must affirm both these elements. Yet it is difficult to envisage

104 Kertelge, *Rechtfertigung*, 84.

105 Rom. 8.11; 2 Cor. 4.10–11; Gal. 6.17; cf. 1 Cor. 12.3; 2 Cor. 4.5; 11.4; 1 Thess. 1.10. See Haussleiter, 'Glaube', 112–14, and Johnson, 'Rom. 3:21–26', 80–1.

106 *GNTG*, III, 260; in the form ὁ/οἱ ἐκ: Rom. 3.26; 4.16; 9.30; 10.6; 14.23; Gal. 3.7; 3.9; in the form ἐκ πίστεως: Rom. 1.17; 3.30; 5.1; 9.32; Gal. 2.16; 3.11, 12, 22, 24; 5.5.

107 On this area, see: Barrett, *First Adam*, 22–45; G. N. Davies, *Faith*, 143–72; A. T. Hanson, *Studies*, 52–66; Hays, 'Abraham', 76–98; Käsemann, *Perspectives*, 79–101; Watson, *Paul*, 135–6.

108 Beker, *Paul*, 78–83; Gaston, 'Abraham', 60–3; Howard, 'Romans 3:21–31', 223–33.

109 P. Richardson, *Israel*, 137–40, and Sanders, *Palestinian Judaism*, esp. 488–97.

how this can be maintained if the distinction is framed in terms of 'works of the law' versus 'faith in Christ'[110] or 'response to God mediated by the Jewish law' versus 'response to God mediated by a law fulfilled through faith'.[111] Although these alternatives may accommodate the universal scope of redemption, they fail to explain why human boasting is thereby excluded;[112] on the contrary, they affirm that the boast of Jew and Gentile is now the same, both groups participating in God's salvation by faith. Further, Paul does not speak in these verses of the faith of Jews and Gentiles, but of faith in the absolute (ὃς δικαιώσει περιτομὴν ἐκ πίστεως καὶ ἀκροβυστίαν διὰ τῆς πίστεως)[113] or of the 'law of faith' (διὰ νόμου πίστεως). These observations suggest that when Paul refers to faith in this context and indeed in others where it is contrasted with the law or works of the law, he means not simply personal belief but some sort of 'dispensation of faith'.[114]

As Paul expounds in 3.21–6, the dispensation of faith is supremely operative in God's covenantal faithfulness communicated through Jesus' obedience of faith, as God's righteousness embraces all

[110] Käsemann, *Romans*, 102–3, and Sanders, *Jewish People*, 33.

[111] Cranfield, *Romans*, vol. 1, 218–20, and Dunn, *Romans*, vol. 1, 187.

[112] Although the presence of καύχησις in Rom. 3.27 is reminiscent of Rom. 2.17 and 23, where καυχάομαι refers to the boast of the Jewish People, the context here is universal and relates to all human attempts to secure standing before God (cf. Rom. 3.27 reads διὰ νόμου τῶν ἔργων not διὰ ἔργων τοῦ νόμου).

[113] S. K. Stowers, building on the subjective genitive interpretation for πίστις Χριστοῦ and the recognition that Paul understood the justification of all people to be established through Christ's πίστις, maintains that the apostle distinguishes between the ways in which God's salvation in Christ 'applies' to the Jews and Gentiles by means of the prepositions διά and ἐκ: 'I have argued that Paul consistently applies διὰ τῆς πίστεως to the redemption of the Gentiles. The case is different for ἐκ πίστεως, which can refer to both Jews and Gentiles ... With διὰ πίστεως, the perspective is that of God as agent and Christ as means of bringing about righteousness. Thus, God put forward Jesus as an expiation διὰ πίστεως of Jesus (3.25) and God has manifested his righteousness διὰ πίστεως of Jesus Christ (3.22). The Jewish interlocutor questions the idea that God could justify the Gentile peoples διὰ τῆς πίστεως of Christ and yet uphold the law (3.30). The phrases with ἐκ πίστεως express the vicarious benefits of Abraham's and Jesus' heroic faithfulness toward God.' ('Romans 3:30', esp. 672–4; cf. Campbell, 'Meaning', 91–103)

[114] The meaning of this phrase should become clearer as we proceed. In certain respects, the dispensation of faith is the other side of the dispensation of grace. As God's salvific initiative towards humankind is through Christ, so humankind's response to God is enabled by and located within Christ's faith. Our understanding here has much in common with H. Binder's 'Glaubens-Sphäre' (*Glaube*, 84–105) and K. Kertelge's presentation of God's righteousness in Christ as the grounds of faith (*Rechtfertigung*, 161–227).

people: God's grace is the origin and ground for all faith.[115] Moreover, as we shall see when we discuss the relationship between Christ's faith and that of other believers, this has both forensic and ethical dimensions. The revelation of God's righteousness in Christ, therefore, constitutes a prior and totally unmerited act which fundamentally transforms the structure and possibility of divine–human relationship.[116] The establishing of this dispensation of grace is independent of human involvement (Rom. 5.12–21; 1 Cor. 15.21–3; 2 Cor. 5.16–21); however, faith remains the only appropriate response to God's prior and continuing initiative. Thus, when Paul speaks about πίστις in Romans 3.27–31, he does not refer primarily to the faith of believers, but to the salvific provision of God established through the faith of Christ (cf. 3.21–6). In this way, the apostle describes how Christ is not only the channel for God's grace, but also the source and context of response to that grace through faith.

The significance of Abraham

To illustrate response to this dispensation, Paul turns to Abraham. In certain respects, he must have been an obvious choice in that he is depicted in the Old Testament as the recipient of God's promise to

115 Especially, Hay, 'Pistis', 472–6.

116 This issue is still a matter of considerable debate with many scholars engaged (e.g. Dunn, Gaston, Hays, Howard, Kim, Sanders, Räisänen, Watson, Wright, etc.). A number of observations, however, are beginning to find general approval: (i) Paul's soteriology is formulated primarily in relation to the Gentile question; (ii) first century Judaism was on the whole a religion of grace and not self-achievement; (iii) few Jews at Paul's time would have claimed that salvation was mediated through observing the law; (iv) Paul's own 'call experience' was a formative influence for his theology. Clearly, these elements can be interpreted in more ways than one and, as a consequence, can support different evaluations of Paul. But it does seem that approaches to the apostle's soteriology in Romans and Galatians which maintain that the good news of God's righteousness in Christ is that God's covenantal blessings have now been extended to embrace Gentiles, with the result that all people now appropriate salvation through faith, do not adequately explain the centrality of Christ for human response to God. Paul is not only saying that in Christ faith has become a universal currency (surely that had been the case since Abraham), but that all human response to God is enabled by, located in and communicated through Christ. Faith, like righteousness, sanctification, sonship and the indwelling of the Spirit, is a function of being found in Christ. If keeping the law is not an entry requirement for receiving God's covenantal blessings in Judaism, then neither is believing in Christ the way to inheriting God's salvation in Paul; rather, it is Christ who communicates and, in a sense, embodies not only God's gift of righteousness to Jew and Gentile alike, but also humanity's response of faith.

bless his descendants and all people (e.g. Gen. 12.1–3, 7; 13.15–16; 15.5, 18; 17.7–8, 19; 22.17–18), as well as a man of faith associated with righteousness (e.g. Gen. 15.6). Discussion of the patriarch initially revolves around Genesis 15.6, which suitably reflects the themes of faith and righteousness, but also – and less helpfully for Paul – suggests the priority of human belief over the divine reckoning of righteousness and, as a consequence, the efficacy of faith within the salvific process.[117] The efficacious nature of Abraham's faith for himself and others was, of course, developed in later Jewish tradition,[118] as was the tendency to equate his faith with keeping the law or remaining obedient in times of testing,[119] and the inclination to restrict the Abrahamic promises to the Jewish nation.[120]

Although we cannot be sure how much of this interpretative tradition was current when Paul wrote, it is almost certain that his recourse to Abraham and Genesis 15.6 in particular, was motivated by the need not only to present the scriptural foundation for his own thinking, but also to redress Jewish misappropriation of the patriarch. But what aspects of Jewish understanding of Abraham does he attack? One front suggested by the 'faith–works' distinction in Romans 4.1–5 is that Paul rejects the definition of Abraham's faith in terms of his obedience or covenantal faithfulness; the apostle demonstrates that the patriarch responds to God's salvific initiatives

[117] See, especially, Gaston, 'Abraham', 45–63. It should be noted that when verse 6 is seen within the context of Gen. 15.1–6 as a whole, the priority of faith to grace cannot so easily be maintained.

[118] Bowker, *Targums*, 202–3; 213–15; Heidland, 'λογίζομαι', 290. E.g.: 'Shema'yah says: "The faith with which their father Abraham believed in Me is deserving that I should divide the sea for them." For it is said: "And he believed in the Lord" (Gen. 15.6). Abtalyon says: "The faith which they believed in Me is deserving that I should divide the sea for them." For it is said: "And the people believed" (Ex. 4.31).' (Mek., Beshallah on Exod. 14.15; also Beshallah on Exod. 14.31; Test. Asher 7.7; Exod. R. XXIII.1–15 [on Exod. 15.1]; Tg. Onq. and Tg. Ps.-J. on Gen. 15.6; Philo, *Abr.* 273; *Rer. Div. Her.* 94)

[119] Barrett, *First Adam*, 32; G. N. Davies, *Faith*, 155–8; Swetnam, *Jesus*, 31–7. E.g. 'Was not Abraham found faithful when tempted, and it was reckoned to him as righteousness?' (1 Macc. 2.52) 'And the Lord was aware that Abraham was faithful in all of his afflictions because he tested him with his land, and with famine. And he tested him with the wealth of kings. And he tested him again with his wife, when she was taken (from him), and with circumcision. And he tested him with Ishmael and with Hagar, his maidservant, when he sent them away. And in everything in which he tested him, he was found faithful. And his soul was not impatient. And he was not slow to act because he was faithful and a lover of the Lord.' (Jub 17.17–18; also Jub 14.21; 18.16; 19.8–9; 2 Macc. 1.2; Sir. 44.19–21, LXX)

[120] Hansen, *Abraham*, esp. 175–99, and Sutherland, 'Gen. 15.6', 443–56.

with nothing but trust.[121] This approach is certainly on the right lines when it stresses that salvation cannot be earnt, but it is questionable whether the faith-works dichotomy communicates the apostle's intentions in Romans 4.

In the first instance, unless Paul believed in Sarah's immaculate conception, Abraham's faith in the promises of God must have found expression in his continuing to have sexual intercourse with his wife despite their advanced years and Sarah's barrenness.[122] Although Paul does not spell this out explicitly, it is implied in 4.18–21, where he repeatedly refers to Abraham's faith-full perseverance or obedience in the face of impossible circumstances (e.g. 'In hope he believed against hope . . . He did not weaken in faith . . . No distrust made him waver . . .'). Secondly, in the light of what we have said about Romans 3 so far, the faith–works dichotomy only furthers Paul's case to a limited extent in that his principal concern is not to redefine response to God in terms of faith, but to establish that God's righteousness is disclosed in Christ independently of and prior to human response; that is to say, to reaffirm the priority of grace. Finally, it is questionable whether Paul would drive a wedge between faith and works in this way. Putting to one side the meaning of πίστις Χριστοῦ, the apostle opens a number of letters by giving thanks for the expressions of faith evident in his churches (e.g. Rom. 1.8–12; Phil. 1.25–6; 1 Thess. 1.2–3; cf. Eph. 1.15), whilst phrases such as 'obedience of faith' (ὑπακοὴν πίστεως, Rom. 1.5; 16.26), 'work of faith' (τοῦ ἔργου τῆς πίστεως, 1 Thess. 1.3) and 'the sacrificial offering of your faith' (λειτουργίᾳ τῆς πίστεως ὑμῶν, Phil. 2.17) speak of a practical or expressive dimension to faith.

If Paul is not concerned primarily to counter the association of faith with obedience or covenantal faithfulness, what is the significance of his presentation of Abraham in Romans 4?[123] There

121 Especially, Dunn, *Romans*, vol. 1, 238; 'Once More', 741; see G. N. Davies, *Faith*, 147–54, for alternative positions.

122 The issue of Isaac's pedigree was clearly a live one in later Jewish reflection; interpretative traditions counter the challenge that Abraham and Sarah were not his parents by emphasising that Isaac resembled Abraham and commenting on Sarah's seemingly limitless powers of lactation (e.g. b. Baba Metzia 87a; Gen. R. LIII.6–9 [on Gen. 21.2–3]; Tg. Ps.-J. on Gen. 21.2; see Bowker, *Targums*, 220–1). It is crucial for Paul's argument, however, that Abraham is Isaac's father, otherwise God's promise to bless him with an heir to enable its fulfilment would be void.

123 The significance of chapter 4 for understanding Paul's presentation in the previous verses is explored by Hays, 'Abraham', 76–98, and Rhyne, *Faith*, esp. 63–93.

appear to be three main thrusts, each of which reinforces his understanding of God's righteousness in Christ developed in the previous chapter and, at the same time, undermines attempts to interpret the patriarch as a champion of Jewish exclusivism or self-attained righteousness. The first thrust affirms that God's promise to bless Abraham was made prior to and independent of any initiative or response on the part of the patriarch; it was pure grace. To be sure, this understanding is present in the Genesis accounts (e.g. Gen. 12.7; 13.15–16; 15.5), although it seems to have been lost in later Jewish speculation about the 'merits of the fathers'.[124] Paul, however, reinforces the prevenient nature of God's justifying actions by interpreting ἐπίστευσεν δὲ Ἀβραὰμ in terms of πιστεύοντι δὲ ἐπὶ τὸν δικαιοῦντα τὸν ἀσεβῆ.[125]

The second point which Paul illustrates by means of Abraham is that faith is the only appropriate response to God's graciousness. The key factor here is that, in contrast to the interpretative tradition reflected in the Septuagint, Paul does not attribute any meritorious sense to God's reckoning of righteousness to Abraham.[126] It is clear from 4.4, where reckoning κατὰ χάριν stands side by side with reckoning κατὰ ὀφείλημα, that he considers λογίζομαι neutral. Further, Paul emphasises that God's reckoning of Abraham took place when the patriarch was uncircumcised (4.10–12) and thus had nothing to do with his specifically Jewish identity.[127] And again, although the reckoning of righteousness to Abraham is associated with his implied faith-in-action later in the chapter (i.e. intercourse with Sarah), it is clear that his response is on the basis of the promise and not in order to earn it.[128]

124 On the significance of the so-called 'merits of the fathers' (esp. Abraham and Moses) for Paul: W. D. Davies, *Paul*, 268–73; Marmorstein, *Merits*; Stewart, *Theology*, 127–33; Urbach, *Sages*, 496–508; Ziesler, *Meaning*, 122–7; but see the reassessments of G. N. Davies, *Faith*, 155–8, and Sanders, *Palestinian Judaism*, 183–205.

125 Hahn, 'Genesis 15.6', 100–2, and A. T. Hanson, *Studies*, 52–66. Further support for this is found in Rom. 4.24, where the broader implications of ἐλογίσθη αὐτῷ εἰς δικαιοσύνην are for those 'who believe in him that raised from the dead Jesus our Lord'.

126 The MT is grammatically ambiguous on this matter, not least because it is unclear who is the subject of the active *ḥāšab̲* and to whom *ṣᵉdāqāh* belongs. By contrast, the LXX renders the active voice of *ḥāšab̲* with the passive λογίζομαι + εἰς and invites a causal understanding of the relationship between πίστις and δικαιοσύνη (see Cranfield, *Romans*, vol. 1, 231, and Gaston, 'Abraham', 46–56).

127 Even though he describes this rite as σφραγῖδα τῆς δικαιοσύνης τῆς πίστεως, it is likely that Paul wished to distance faith from the notion of circumcision as a condition of God's promise or covenant (cf. Gen. 17.10–14); Barrett, *First Adam*, 33, and A. T. Hanson, *Studies*, 58–62.

128 Hahn, 'Genesis 15.6', 102–3.

All this suggests that, even though Paul follows the Septuagint almost exactly in his rendering of Genesis 15.6,[129] he understands the relationship between faith and righteousness to be one of coincidence rather than consequence. This also seems to be the logic of Genesis 15.1–6 as a whole, where the stress is upon the free election of God, favouring a translation for verse 6 along the following lines: 'Faith is reckoned as righteousness because this is pleasing to the will of Yahweh, not because faith has any value intrinsically.'[130] For Paul, therefore, faith is how Abraham participates in, and not earns, God's salvific blessings; from the human perspective, it is located between God's promise and his fulfilment of the same (4.21). It is the channel or medium through which God's promise comes to fulfilment; God's promise is freely made to Abraham, his faith is then a response to that promise and God, in turn, is faithful to his promise in bringing it to fulfilment.[131]

The third point which Paul emphasises about Abraham is that the content of God's promise to the patriarch was to bless all nations and not just the Jews.[132] One of the central issues here is Paul's understanding of the relationship between God's promise to Abraham and the righteousness which was reckoned to him. Initially, he speaks of the patriarch's belief in 'him who justifies the ungodly' (4.5), with clear parallels to God's justifying initiatives in Christ discussed in the previous chapter. Later on, however, it becomes apparent that God's promise to Abraham also constitutes the basis for his belief: 'In hope he believed against hope, that he should become the father of many nations; as he had been told, "So shall your descendants be."' (4.18; cf. 4.17–22) Moreover, righteousness is reckoned within the context of this believing response

[129] At the beginning the LXX reads, καὶ ἐπίστευσεν Αβραμ, whilst Rom. 4.3 reads, ἐπίστευσεν δὲ 'Αβραὰμ; otherwise they are identical. On the tradition–historical and literary–critical issues revolving around Gen. 15.6, see: Seybold, 'חָשַׁב', 241–4; von Rad, *Problem*, 125–30; Westermann, *Genesis*, vol. 1, 222–33.

[130] Heidland, 'λογίζομαι', 289; also Swetnam, *Jesus*, 37. In this respect, Philo's comment is apt: 'The words "Abraham believed God" are a necessary addition to speak the praise due to him who has believed. Yet, perhaps it may be asked, do you consider this worthy of praise? When it is God who speaks and promises, who would not pay heed, even though he were the most unjust and pious of mankind?' (Philo, *Rer. Div. Her.* 90; trans. LCL 261.327)

[131] Käsemann, *Perspectives*, 83–9; cf. 'Now Abraham was 100 years old when Isaac, his son, was born to him. Then Sarah said, "The Lord has created happiness for me; everyone who hears will rejoice for me." And she said, "Faithful is He that promised Abraham, and fulfilled it, that Sarah would nurse children; for I have given birth to a son in his old age."' (Tg. Onq. on Gen. 21.6–7; also Heb. 11.11)

[132] Sanders, *Jewish People*, 33–6, and Watson, *Paul*, 138–42.

(4.22). These observations suggest a close relationship between ἐπαγγελία and δικαιοσύνη in this context.[133]

Paul, therefore, may have intended δικαιοσύνη in Genesis 15.6 to be understood in terms of the promise to be the father of all nations and, more specifically, of God's fulfilment of that promise by means of his continuing faithfulness. Righteousness here is not a possession or disposition of Abraham, nor does it simply constitute a declaration that God is just in his dealings with humanity or that Abraham is morally upright; rather, it characterises the implementation of the promise by means of divine–human relation. That is to say, it is a righteousness or right-relatedness which originates in God's initiative to bless all people and comes to expression in the relationship between God and Abraham as grace finds faith.[134] The promise is the substance of God's righteousness; God shows himself righteous each time he acts to secure its realisation and humanity through faith participates in that righteousness by entering into the promise.

We can discern in Paul's presentation of Abraham, therefore, a tripartite structure of divine–human relationship in which God's initiative in extending the promise of blessing to Abraham is met by faith on the part of the patriarch which, in turn, is met by God's faithfulness in bringing the promise to fulfilment.[135] On the basis of this analysis, we may paraphrase Paul's understanding of Genesis 15.6 in the following terms: 'In response to God's free-election and promise to make him the father of all nations, Abraham believed in God, who justifies the ungodly independently of their initiatives. Abraham's faith came to expression in his conduct towards Sarah

[133] Cf. Sir. 44.19–21; but see other Jewish sources where *ṣ^eḏāqâh*/δικαιοσύνην is interpreted in terms of a broad spectrum of blessings, including, performing miracles (Mek., Beshallah on Exod. 14.15), being an heir of this and the coming world (Mek., Beshallah on Exod. 14.31) and merit (Tg. Ps.-J. on Gen. 15.6).

[134] 'The righteousness of which Paul is thinking here is not a visible righteousness consisting in just and holy acts and dispositions; it is a righteousness of relationship (between man and God) . . . His [i.e. Abraham's] faith signified no human achievement but corresponded to the divine graciousness in quickening the dead and calling things that are not as if they were – in this case, calling righteousness into being.' (Barrett, *First Adam*, 38–9) The proposal that righteousness in this context is God's rather than Abraham's is at least as old as the book of Nehemiah (see Neh. 9.7–8).

[135] A similar structure is reflected in Philo's assessment: 'That God marvelling at Abraham's faith in Him repaid him with faithfulness by confirming with an oath the gifts which He had promised, and here He no longer talked with him as God with man but as a friend with a familiar.' (Philo, *Abr.* 273; trans. LCL 289.133)

and was met by God's righteousness or right-relatedness in bringing the promise to fulfilment with the gift of an heir.'

With this overview of Paul's understanding of Abraham in mind, we return to τῷ ἐκ πίστεως 'Αβραάμ in Romans 4.16. We have already noted that the construction can reflect the sense of belonging to a group and, in this context, suggests those who share Abraham's faith. Whilst the apostle may intend by this a reliance on the patriarch's faith for standing before God, his portrayal of Abraham as a fellow sinner in need of justification militates against this option. On the contrary, it seems more likely that Paul understands the phrase in the sense of participating in a dispensation of faith which has Abraham as the principal exemplar and first exponent.[136] As Abraham responded in faith to God's promise and was met by God's righteousness or faithfulness to that promise in bringing it to fulfilment, so others are encouraged to share in that dynamic. The significance of Abraham's faith, however, is not identical to that of all future believers for it possesses both a revelatory and a paradigmatic function: revelatory, because through him the priority of God's grace over human initiative or response first becomes apparent;[137] and paradigmatic, because his life incarnates what it is to have faith within the context of God's promise coming to fulfilment.[138] In consequence, although Abraham's faith does not replace or exclude the faith of future believers (cf. τῷ ἐκ πίστεως 'Αβραάμ), it does provide a definition for the life of faith.

Our treatment of τῷ ἐκ πίστεως 'Αβραάμ also provides a useful point of departure for interpreting τὸν ἐκ πίστεως 'Ιησοῦ (Rom. 3.26) in that both phrases exhibit a similar structure and overlap in meaning. For instance, Jesus' faith – like Abraham's – stands at the source of divine initiative; his faith reveals the righteousness or faithfulness of God in bringing salvation to both Jew and Gentile within the dispensation of faith.[139] Although Paul does not describe

136 Hays, 'Abraham', 93–8; Wedderburn, 'Observations', 90–1; *contra* Gaston, 'Abraham', 60–1.

137 This is usually discussed in terms of Abraham as the father of all nations; see G. N. Davies, *Faith*, 162–7, and Watson, *Paul*, 138–42.

138 Barrett, *First Adam*, 42, and Käsemann, *Perspectives*, 85.

139 'Clearly, from Romans and similar expressions in Galatians, ἐκ πίστεως applies to both Jews and Gentiles. Paul uses it especially when he wants to describe faithfulness as a source or foundation of blessing and covenants in which Jews and Gentiles share. The expression ἐκ πίστεως can apply both to Abraham's and Jesus' faithfulness (Rom. 3.26; 4.16; cf. Gal. 3.7, 9). The promises were first made to Abraham and his descendants on the basis of his faithfulness . . . The promised

in detail the relationship between Abraham and Christ in this context, he does affirm a continuity in God's promise.[140] Further, he stresses the universal dimensions of the promise in Christ and how he is the means by which God brings it to fulfilment in the face of the law and sin. Those who share Jesus' faith, therefore, are those who find in his faith the means by which God fulfils his promise. A second area of similarity between τὸν ἐκ πίστεως 'Ιησοῦ and τῷ ἐκ πίστεως 'Αβραάμ is located in the continuity between the exponent and those who share the faith to which they bear witness. For Paul, Jesus' faith is not qualitatively different from that of others; it is the faith of the human Jesus seen in obedience to death on the cross and not of the exalted son of God.

But there appears to be one significant difference between τῷ ἐκ πίστεως 'Αβραάμ and τὸν ἐκ πίστεως 'Ιησοῦ which revolves around the function of their faith within the apostle's thinking.[141] In contrast to Abraham, Paul does not emphasise the exemplary nature of Jesus' faith; rather, the faith of Jesus, the one to whom righteousness did not have to be reckoned, is soteriologically determinative in that it not only bears witness to the priority of grace, but also provides the vehicle through which God's grace is communicated and made available to all.[142] Through Jesus' faith, God's commitment to his promise is confirmed in the justification of or extension of right-relatedness to all humankind. God's righteousness is thereby revealed and the dispensation of grace established by which both Jew and Gentile are freed to respond to God. There is a further dimension to this as well, for Jesus' faith is not simply the means by which God's covenantal faithfulness – that is to say, his faithfulness to the Abrahamic promise – is revealed, but is

seed was Christ, and in him on the basis of Abraham's and Jesus' own faithfulness, totally unmerited by the recipients, the Gentiles are justified.' (Stowers, 'Romans 3.30', 673)

140 Paul works out the 'mechanics' of this continuity between Abraham and Christ in Galatians 3; see Beker, *Paul*, 94–104; Drane, *Paul*, 24–38; Hester, *Concept*, esp. 47–57.

141 Cf. the slightly different assessment of Abraham in Hays, 'Abraham', esp. 94–98.

142 As we shall see, Paul explores the correspondence between Christ and Abraham in these terms within Galatians. Although the patriarch's conduct in relation to the promise that he would be the father of many nations is considered by Paul to be an expression of his faith (Rom. 4.16–22) and, as such, could be interpreted as a vehicle for the fulfilment of God's purposes in a similar way to Christ's death, this is not the apostle's primary concern here. On the contrary, Abraham, the fellow-sinner (Rom. 4.5) and believer in the God of resurrection (Rom. 4.17), incarnates the response of faith within God's dispensation of grace.

also the basis or grounds for all human faith.[143] Men and women, Jew and Gentile, are freed to believe because of what was established through Jesus' faith and, as we shall see, there is a sense in which all faith is encompassed within the faith of Jesus, the messiah.

Human faith in the dispensation of faith–grace

We have already hinted at the intimate relationship between Jesus' faith and that of believers with respect to ἐκ πίστεως εἰς πίστιν in Romans 1.17, but it is 3.22 which provides the focus for this as faith is contextualised within God's salvific provisions in Christ. The first part of the verse affirms that God's righteousness is disclosed through the faith of Jesus Christ and the following verses develop this further in relation to the cross; the second part goes on to claim that this righteousness is εἰς πάντας τοὺς πιστεύοντας. How, then, should this phrase be understood?[144] Paul not infrequently uses constructions including the articular participle of πιστεύω to describe the way in which belief is made possible by a prior salvific initiative on the part of God[145] and this understanding makes good sense here: belief results from or is a consequence of God's righteousness being disclosed through the faith of Christ. But, it may be asked, if God's justification of the ungodly and gift of righteousness or covenantal right-relatedness are secured for all people in Christ, what place is there for belief? Has not Paul's desire to emphasise the extent and implications of God's grace communicated through Christ eroded the need for human response? Indeed, the apostle may

143 On this aspect see, especially, Hay, 'Pistis', esp. 461–76. D. A. Campbell points out that Paul only uses the construction ἐκ πίστεως in those letters where he also cites Hab. 2.4; he suggests that this was intentional on the part of the apostle, who wished all occurrences of ἐκ πίστεως to be interpreted in the light of his messianic understanding of the Habakkuk (*Rhetoric*, 211–13). Campbell also maintains that ἐκ πίστεως and διὰ τῆς πίστεως 'are stylistic variations of the same basic idea, allowing Paul to repeat his point without undue tedium'. ('Meaning', 96)

144 In cases where διὰ πίστεως Ἰησοῦ Χριστοῦ is taken as an objective genitive, this clause is usually understood in terms of emphasis, stressing the universality (πάντας) of belief for both Jews and Greeks; Cranfield, *Romans*, vol. 1, 203; Dunn, *Romans*, vol. 1, 167; Wilckens, *Römer*, vol. 1, 188.

145 E.g. Rom. 1.16 (the gospel); 4.24 (the resurrection of Christ); 9.33 (laying of a foundation stone) and 10.4 (Christ himself; cf. 10.11); 1 Cor. 1.21 (the cross of Christ); Gal. 3.22 (the promise); cf. Rom. 1.16; 4.11, 24; 9.33 [Isa. 28.16]; 10.4, 11 [Isa. 28.16]; 1 Cor. 1.21; 14.22 [x2]; Gal. 3.22; 1 Thess. 1.7; 2.10, 13. Paul's presentation of Abraham in Romans 4 also supports this interpretation in that the patriarch's response of faith is precipitated by God's prior initiative in mediating the promise.

have anticipated such questions (e.g. 6.1, 15).[146] One solution is to distinguish between the forensic and the ethical dimensions of righteousness: whereas the former is wrought through the cross (e.g. 5.12–21), the latter is only appropriated through faith and the ensuing life of obedience.[147] The difficulty with this approach is that it seems alien to Paul's thinking, for the contrast in effect becomes one of potential and actual: righteousness only becomes real in the life of the believer through faith. Further, it is not at all clear that Paul considered believers morally righteous.

A distinction which is more in keeping with Paul's thinking is between divine and human perspectives. Righteousness, whether conceived in forensic or ethical terms, is completely identified with God's work in Christ: he is the Righteous One whose death spells the end of the penalty for sin and discloses the universal scope of God's covenantal graciousness. For Paul, righteousness cannot be approached from the angle of human response however conceived,[148] as if it was something to apprehend, attain or possess; rather, it is a matter of participating in Christ, through whom and in whom God's righteousness – in all its richness – is communicated. The accent rests upon divine initiative and enablement at every stage, and not simply at the cross and its proclamation, where the possibility for new life is established.[149] In consequence, as Abraham's faith in response to the promise was the channel through which God proved faithful to the same by bringing it to fulfilment, so a believer's faith in response to God's justifying work in Christ is

[146] Although it is often thought that Paul's questions in Rom. 6.1, 15 are rhetorical or hypothetical, this may not be the case; it is quite possible that he was aware that God's grace in Christ was open to abuse.

[147] Cranfield, *Romans*, vol. 2, 824–33, and Ziesler, *Meaning*, esp. 168–71.

[148] *Contra* the anthropological perspective of Bultmann, *Theology*, vol. 1, 270–314, and others, where the emphasis is on the appropriation of God's righteousness through faith in response to the kerygma; see the comments of Binder, *Glaube*, 104.

[149] On this approach to righteousness in Paul see especially, Käsemann, *Questions*, 168–87, and, more fully, in the works of Kertelge, *Rechtfertigung*, esp. 305–7, and Stuhlmacher, *Gerechtigkeit*, 203–36. K. Kertelge and Stuhlmacher do not speak explicitly about Christ's personal faith, but of faith which originates, is facilitated by and takes place within the context of Christ. It is questionable, however, whether this conception adequately represents Paul's understanding of how Christ not only creates the possibility of human response to God's righteousness, but is also the substance of that response. Just as by baptism, believers participate within the baptism of Christ's death, so by faith, believers participate within the faith of Christ. See the comments of H. Binder, who recognises the inadequacy of subject–objective approaches to the relationship between Christ and faith (*Glaube*, esp. 84–106); Christ defines and enables faith at every stage.

the vehicle though which the believer participates in that righteousness. God's righteousness, therefore, is not the reward of faith, but encompasses faith at every stage as the faith of Christ becomes the context where human faith meets divine faithfulness.[150]

The relationship in which human faith is grounded upon and participates within the salvific benefits of Christ's faith, exhibits strong structural similarities with other Pauline expressions of what it means to be 'in Christ'.[151] Consider, for example, the apostle's treatment of baptism in Romans 6.[152] His thinking here, as in many other spheres, is guided, firstly, by reflection upon the sufficiency and completeness of Christ's death for justification and, secondly, by a hope of future life based upon the conviction that God raised Jesus from the dead. Paul does not, however, simply associate the overcoming of sin and experiencing of different dimensions of righteousness with the past events of Jesus' death and resurrection; rather, these salvific benefits are inextricably linked to the person of Christ.[153] Human response, therefore, is not simply a matter of belief in a person, but of participation within him who is righteous and who mediates God's righteousness to all.[154] Further, it is this dynamic of participation in Christ which undergirds Paul's statements in the opening verses of Romans 6.

There seems to be intentional ambiguity in Paul's use of baptismal terminology within this chapter which permits a juxtaposition

150 The key here is perspective. When someone comes to faith there is clearly an existential change from the human perspective, but no change from the divine perspective; all that has happened is that the believer has recognised his or her place in Christ, who is the context of all righteousness and faith. This approach should be contrasted with one in which forensic justification is established by Christ and its ethical implications are appropriated by faith; in failing to recognise the different perspectives in what Paul says about salvation, the impression is given that faith activates righteousness in the sense that it either appropriates the potential of the cross and thereby contributes towards its efficacy or is somehow able to change God's attitude from one of deserved wrath to one of unmerited grace. Both these options fail to accommodate the completeness of the entire salvation event in Christ; he is the context of both the God-ward and the human-ward movements in God's righteousness.

151 See the helpful comments of Neugebauer, *In Christus*, esp. 171–4. He identifies a similar relationship between πίστις and ἐν Χριστῷ to the one isolated by K. Kertelge and P. Stuhlmacher in the case of πίστις and δικαιοσύνη.

152 On the interpretation of Romans 6 offered here, see especially Tannehill, *Dying*, 7–43.

153 Bornkamm, *Experience*, 71–86; Dunn, *Baptism*, 139–46; Kertelge, *Rechtfertigung*, 263–75; J. A. T. Robinson, *Body*, 74.

154 Hooker, 'Christ', 349–60; 'Atonement', 462–81; Sanders, *Palestinian Judaism*, 453–74; 502–8. C. F. D. Moule offers a good survey as well as taking the discussion further (*Origin*, 47–96).

with Jesus' death. It is not clear whether he presents the latter as a form of baptism or indeed, if he does, whether there is an additional reference to initiation.[155] In all probability, βάπτισμα (6.4) refers to the baptism of believers and βαπτίζω (6.3) encompasses a metaphorical sense and, by so doing, links those baptised with the Crucified One.[156] Whether such nuance is legitimate or not, Paul's intention is clear: through baptism, believers find their place within the death of Christ. He does not mean by this that everyone must independently suffer their own crucifixion in the likeness of Christ, nor that Christ must be re-crucified in every rite. On the contrary, the language is not of duplication or repetition, but of sharing or participation within that which is already complete, namely, the death of Christ (cf. συνετάφημεν, σύμφυτοι, συνεσταυρώθη).[157]

Through baptism, believers consciously come under the influence of God's salvific work accomplished and located in Christ. The implication is that baptism, as we noted with faith, is of no soteriological significance in isolation; the efficacy resides within the inclusive and all-pervasive nature of God's covenantal graciousness disclosed in Jesus' death. Nor does he see atonement or righteousness as entities which are transferred to the believer at baptism; it is the believer who is encompassed within Christ, the divine ἱλαστήριον and communicator of God's righteousness. Paul focuses almost entirely upon the theological perspective of baptism and expounds its significance in an objective manner. No reference is made to the motives or disposition of the believer at this stage, for God's grace is prior to, independent of, and enables human response. Further, even the hope of resurrection is not based upon

155 The consensus view is that water initiation is in Paul's mind in Romans 6; however, the observation that βάπτισμα is a Christian term without any antecedent connection with water baptism, together with its metaphorical usage in Mark 10.38 and Luke 12.50, where it refers to Jesus' death, has led some to question this (e.g. D. W. B. Robinson, 'Definition', 1–15, and J. A. T. Robinson, 'One Baptism', 257–74).

156 Dunn, 'Birth', 174–5, and Wagner, *Baptism*, 288–90.

157 'If this interpretation is correct, dying and rising with Christ cannot be understood as a repetition of Christ's death and resurrection, or as the result of some subjective or sacramental process by which Christ's death and resurrection are made present, or in any other way which seeks to supplement the death and resurrection of Christ as particular events in the past and thereby make up their deficiencies. Provided that dying and rising with Christ is understood in the context of Paul's eschatology, it is clear both that the death and resurrection of Christ are particular, past events and that the believers participate in them, for these events involve the old and new dominions as wholes, and so also those who are included in these dominions.' (Tannehill, *Dying*, 30)

the quality of discipleship, but upon God's raising Jesus from the dead. It is these indicatives, establishing the reality and shape of God's grace, which constitute the basis – not the precondition – for the ethical imperative (cf. 6.12).[158]

The pneumatology of Romans 8 also reflects this priority of grace, whereby God's initiatives encompass and enable human response and transformation. The futility of human endeavour to secure a positive relationship with God is once again affirmed and articulated on this occasion in terms of a flesh–-spirit polarity. This contrast, especially in the light of Romans 7.7–25, coupled with the observation that no reference has been made since the beginning of chapter 6 to the occurrence of coming to faith, suggests that Paul is not making a temporal distinction between pre- and post-conversion situations, but establishing an existential one in which each person either gives God permission to work through his Spirit or relies on his own resources.[159] Throughout the chapter, Paul projects upon a 'fallen' view of creation and the human predicament without God, the reality of life in the Spirit: liberating from sin and death (v. 2) to give life (vv. 10–11), putting to death the practices of the body so that the experience of sonship can be known (vv. 14–17), confirming hopes of future redemption (v. 23) and interceding for those who are not able to pray (vv. 26–7). Great emphasis is placed throughout this chapter upon the initiative of God working through his Spirit to transform and bring life and, although little is said explicitly about the place of human response within this process, it is implied in verses 13–18 and 24–5 that God only operates where he finds cooperation. Life in the Spirit is certainly about coming within the influence of the Spirit of Christ, but each prompting of the Spirit must be recognised and, so to speak, given permission before the individual participates in the realities secured in the death and resurrection of Jesus.

3 The Epistle to the Galatians

Gal. 2.16 and 20: εἰδότες [δὲ] ὅτι οὐ δικαιοῦται ἄνθρωπος ἐξ ἔργων νόμου ἐὰν μὴ διὰ πίστεως ˢἸησοῦ Χριστοῦˢ, καὶ ἡμεῖς εἰς Χριστὸν Ἰησοῦν ἐπιστεύσαμεν, ἵνα δικαιωθῶμεν ἐκ πίστεως Χριστοῦ καὶ οὐκ ἐξ ἔργων νόμου, ὅτι ἐξ ἔργων

[158] Furnish, *Theology*, 162–81, 194–8, and Tannehill, *Dying*, 77–83.
[159] Dunn, *Jesus*, esp. 312–16.

νόμου οὐ δικαιωθήσεται πᾶσα σάρξ ... ζῶ δὲ οὐκέτι ἐγώ, ζῇ δὲ ἐν ἐμοὶ Χριστός· ὃ δὲ νῦν ζῶ ἐν σαρκί, ἐν πίστει ζῶ τῇ τοῦ ‘υἱοῦ τοῦ θεοῦ’ τοῦ ἀγαπήσαντός με καὶ παραδόντος ἑαυτὸν ὑπὲρ ἐμοῦ.

Gal. 3.22: ἀλλὰ συνέκλεισεν ἡ γραφὴ τὰ πάντα ὑπὸ ἁμαρτίαν, ἵνα ἡ ἐπαγγελία ἐκ πίστεως Ἰησοῦ Χριστοῦ δοθῇ τοῖς πιστεύουσιν.

Textual Notes: (s) the inverted order for Ἰησοῦ Χριστοῦ probably represents an attempt to harmonise with Χριστὸν Ἰησοῦν later in the verse; (‘) there is considerable support for the reading θεοῦ καὶ Χριστοῦ (cf. τοῦ θεοῦ and θεοῦ τοῦ υἱοῦ), although this un-Pauline phrase is generally thought to be secondary (see Metzger, *Commentary*, 593).

Translation: <2.15> We who are Jews by birth and not Gentile sinners, <16> and knowing that no one is justified [*or* put in a right relationship with God] by works of the law, but by Jesus Christ's faith, we also became believers in Christ Jesus, in order that we might be justified on the basis of Christ's faith and not on the basis of works of the law; because no one will be justified on the basis of works of the law ... <19b> I have been crucified with Christ; <20> and no longer do I live, but Christ lives in me. And the life I now live in the body, I live by the faith of the son of God [*or* by participating in the faith of the son of God], who loved me and gave himself for me.

<3.21> Is the law, then, contrary to the promises of God? By no means! For if a law had been given that could give life, then righteousness would indeed be on the basis of law [i.e. human endeavour]. <22> But the scripture has imprisoned all things under [the power] of sin, so that the promise on the basis of Jesus Christ's faith might be given to those who believe [*or* who participate in the dispensation of faith].

The final section of Paul's autobiographical sketch relating his dispute with Cephas at Antioch concerning table-fellowship leads into a defence of humankind's standing before God in relation to Christ and the law. Paul makes it quite clear from the outset that justification and the reception of God's blessings in general do not and have never come through obeying the law (2.16, 21; 3.2, 5, 10–11, 18, 21), even if the law itself fulfilled a positive function by acting as a custodian until the coming of Christ (3.19–20, 23–5) and by bringing sin to light (3.10, 22). It is Christ's death which secures salvation by dealing with the consequences of sin and fulfilling God's promise to bless all people (2.20–1; 3.13–16; 4.4–7). As is often the case, Paul's theology relates directly to the pastoral situation evident in Galatia,[160] and although the characteristics of this predicament alluded to in the letter are by no means homogeneous,[161] there was clearly a tendency amongst Gentile converts to entertain Jewish practices and customs (e.g. 3.1–5; 4.21, 5.1–11; cf. 4.3, 9–10) in addition to the gospel proclaimed by Paul (1.6–9).[162]

Paul reacts strongly against this tendency and interprets it as the desire to secure God's favour by human endeavour, rather than by relying on the mercies of God.[163] He demonstrates with reference to

160 Barrett, *Freedom*, esp. 13–21; Beker, *Paul*, 41–58; Bruce, 'Problems', 253–71; Dunn, *Galatians*, 9–19.

161 Barclay, *Obeying*, 36–74, and Drane, *Paul*, 78–94.

162 In the light of the reassessment of first century Judaism initiated by Sanders' *Paul and Palestinian Judaism*, J. D. G. Dunn, amongst others, offers a re-evaluation of Galatians (see, especially, his collection of essays, *Jesus, Paul and the Law* and his commentary, *Galatians*). Although we cannot examine all his proposals, a number of them are relevant for the present discussion. For instance, he claims that the long-standing interpretation of 'works of the law' in terms of 'good works by which individuals try to gain acceptance by God' is fundamentally flawed in that it is not borne out by the centrality of grace within Jewish understanding of election and covenant; further, he claims that there is little evidence that obedience to the law was understood in Judaism as a means of securing standing before God. In consequence, Professor Dunn maintains that when Paul attacks 'works of the law' in Galatians he is not challenging a legalism of self-attained righteousness, but a nationalism which takes observance of the Torah as a 'badge' of Jewish exclusivism within God's salvation. Although this reconstruction is commendable for its sympathetic assessment of Judaism and offers helpful insights into how Paul's theology reflects his mission to the Gentiles, it is questionable whether it adequately explains the following elements: (i) the central position of Christ within his own experience of God as a practising Jew and for his soteriology which embraces both Jews and Gentiles; (ii) the observation that Paul rejects the works of the law because they fail to secure salvation and not because they indicate an artificial–nationalistic restriction within the dispensation of grace; (iii) the fact that Gentile Christians in Galatia were persuaded to obey the law suggests that they had been persuaded of its salvific efficacy.

163 The issue of whether Paul in Galatians depicts Judaism as a religion of achievement is hotly debated at present, as is the matter of whether he considered the Jewish faith to constitute a means of salvation independent of Christ (see, especially: Dunn, 'Damascus Road', 89–107; Gaston, 'Galatians 2 and 3', 64–79; Räisänen, 'Call Experience', 15–47). Clearly, there are dangers in attempting to construct the apostle's view of Judaism from a letter addressing a particular situation and couched in polemical language. It does seem, however, that the letter requires due consideration be given to the following observations: (i) Paul speaks about the law and works of the law in relation to Gentile Christians persuaded of their soteriological significance for them; (ii) his theology is rooted

personal experience (3.1–5), biblical precedent (3.10–12) and God's actions in Christ (3.13–29), that observing the law does not constitute a way of salvation. He explains that this is not a question of the Jews' inability to fulfil its requirements, but of the law performing a different function within the purposes of God.[164] As we shall see, however, Paul's main argument against Gentile Christians adopting the Jewish practices is not couched in terms of the Torah's soteriological limitations, but of the fulfilment of God's covenantal righteousness in Christ. This will be examined in detail later, but in order to gain perspective, our attention turns initially to the nature of the contrasts articulated by the apostle in Galatians 2.16 and 3.1–5.

Preliminary reflections on Galatians 2.16 and 3.1–5

The phrase ἐξ ἔργων νόμου occurs three times in Galatians 2.16. The first instance is juxtaposed with διὰ πίστεως Ἰησοῦ Χριστοῦ and the second with ἐκ πίστεως Χριστοῦ; many scholars interpret these πίστις-constructions as objective genitives, denoting faith in Christ.[165] Clearly, 2.16 does refer to the faith of believers (καὶ ἡμεῖς εἰς Χριστὸν Ἰησοῦν ἐπιστεύσαμεν), but if all three πιστεύω cognates are understood in this way, the emphasis within this key verse for Paul's soteriology falls rather awkwardly upon the believer rather than Christ. It seems unlikely, however, that Paul would introduce his understanding of the dispensation of salvation established through Christ on the basis of the relative merits of faith in Christ over works of the law.[166] For one thing, Paul knows that faith is not a Christian innovation, but has a longer pedigree in Judaism than observance to the law, characterising Abraham's response to divine grace (cf. 3.6). For another, his own 'call' experience related in Galatians 1.11–17 testifies to the priority of God's

in personal encounter of God's grace in Christ which, although concerned with his commission to the Gentiles, came to him as a Jew.

[164] Hübner, *Law*, 24–42; Räisänen, *Law*, 128–54; Sanders, *Jewish People*, 17–29; Wright, 137–56.

[165] H. D. Betz, *Galatians*, 117–18; Borse, *Galater*, 113; Bruce, *Galatians*, 139–40; Burton, *Galatians*, 121; Dunn, *Galatians*, 138–9; Ebeling, *Truth*, 122–7; Mussner, *Galaterbrief*, 170.

[166] A. Oepke, *Galater*, 59 stresses the arbitrariness of this distinction. H. Räisänen maintains that in Gal. 2.16 Paul does not simply contrast the law with faith, but with faith in Christ; whereas Judaism knows of faith, it is the coming of Christ which is innovative ('Galatians 2.16', esp. 116–21). Räisänen correctly stresses the relationship between faith and Christ, but as we shall indicate below this link is more fundamental.

prevenient, justifying grace disclosed and communicated in Christ, and not to the superiority of faith over works of the law.[167] As Paul goes on to develop in the rest of the letter, it is the coming of Christ which constitutes the new and decisive event in the history of God's dealing with humanity and, as a consequence, it is this reality which one would expect to be central in 2.16. Upon what, then, does Paul encourage the Galatian Christians to base their standing before God? Belief in Christ or works of the law? Or the more fundamental reality of the faith of Christ himself (cf. διὰ πίστεως Ἰησοῦ Χριστοῦ and ἐκ πίστεως Χριστοῦ) through which God's righteousness and covenantal blessings are extended to Jew and Gentile alike?[168]

Ἐξ ἔργων νόμου is attested twice more in Galatians 3.1–5, where it is juxtaposed on both occasions with ἐξ ἀκοῆς πίστεως; as with 2.16, the contrast can be understood in terms of the effectiveness of faith over works for receiving, in this case, the Spirit and its manifestations.[169] Once again, however, this comparison neither reflects the apostle's emphasis elsewhere in the letter upon the divine initiative in Christ, nor corresponds with his christophany in which his own faith played, at best, a secondary role. The meaning of ἐξ ἀκοῆς πίστεως has been much discussed in recent years, although there is as yet little sign of consensus.[170] One difficulty revolves around the degree of parallelism intended with ἐξ ἔργων νόμου, and yet it is often overlooked that the context permits a high degree of correspondence.[171] That is to say, both constructions can be understood as genitives of origin in which human response (i.e. works/hearing) is related to divine initiative (i.e. law/faith). Other instances of ἀκοή denoting the act of hearing, rather than what is heard, can be cited in support;[172] but in what sense can πίστις be understood as a divine initiative? One option is to interpret it in terms of the content of

167 Hooker, 'ΠΙΣΤΙΣ', 341; Howard, *Paul*, 335; Kim, *Origin*, 269–329.

168 'In effect, then, Paul uses πίστις Ἰησοῦ Χριστοῦ in his writings to signal the basis for the Christian gospel: that its objective basis is the perfect response of obedience that Jesus rendered to God the Father, both actively in his life and passively in his death.' (R. N. Longenecker, *Galatians*, 87)

169 H. D. Betz, *Galatians*, 130, and Guthrie, *Galatians*, 92–4.

170 Hays, *Faith*, 143–9, lists four possible interpretations. If ἀκοή means either 'hearing' or 'message/proclamation' and πίστις means either 'believing' or 'the faith', the following options are open: 'by hearing with faith', 'by hearing "the faith"' (= 'by hearing the gospel'), 'from the message that enables faith' and 'from the message of "the faith"' (= 'the gospel message').

171 See the discussions of Friedrich, 'εὐαγγελίζομαι', 100–2, and S. K. Williams, 'Hearing', esp. 86–9.

172 E.g. 'message', Rom. 10.16; 'hearing', 1 Cor. 12.17; 1 Thess. 2.13; cf. Rom. 10.17.

faith, namely, the gospel which came δι' ἀποκαλύψεως Ἰησοῦ Χριστοῦ (1.12). Whilst there is little to suggest that the apostle had in mind a body of teaching or kerygma,[173] the notion of faith being revealed in relation to Christ is attested in 3.23–5. Moreover, as we noted in the discussion of Romans 4.16, faith as the root or source of response may be reflected in the construction οἱ ἐκ πίστεως (3.7, 9),[174] where those who are of or from faith are blessed with Abraham. Consider also Paul's contention that the Gentiles are justified ἐκ πίστεως (3.7) and that one of the reasons why justification cannot be effected through the law is because οὐκ ἔστιν ἐκ πίστεως (3.12).

In the light of these observations, a translation for ἐξ ἀκοῆς πίστεως along the lines of 'hearing stemming from faith' may be more in keeping with Galatians as a whole.[175] It should be noted, however, that ἐξ ἀκοῆς πίστεως is contrasted in 3.5 with ἐξ ἔργων νόμου, a phrase used frequently by the apostle as a 'technical term' or, at least, as shorthand for a particular approach to God (e.g. 2.16 [x3]; 3.2, 5, 10; Rom. 3.20; cf. Rom. 2.15; 3.28). Although we cannot rehearse here the debate over the precise meaning of ἐξ ἔργων νόμου,[176] it does seem likely that the construction is used by Paul as a way of describing response to God outside of grace, that is to say, a dispensation of law characterised by the pursuit of self-attained righteousness.[177] If this is correct, then ἐξ ἀκοῆς πίστεως stands in opposition and denotes response to God (i.e. ἀκοή) engendered by a dispensation of faith which is intimately associated with God's salvific initiatives in Jesus Christ (cf. ἐλθούσης δὲ τῆς πίστεως, 3.25). This proposal makes good sense of the otherwise problematic relationship between reception of the Spirit and faith alluded to in 3.2 and 5. To say that God supplies the Spirit on the basis of human

173 *Contra* Mussner, *Galaterbrief*, 207, and Schenk, 'Gerechtigkeit', 166.

174 Burton, *Galatians*, 155; Schlier, *Galater*, 128; Stowers, 'Romans 3.30', 673.

175 Dunn, *Galatians*, 154; cf. εἰς ὑπακοὴν πίστεως (Rom. 1.5; 16.26); τοῦ ἔργου τῆς πίστεως (1 Thess. 1.3); also πίστις δι' ἀγάπης (Gal. 5.6).

176 One of the key issues at present is whether Paul opposes 'works of the law' because they constitute an alternative system of salvation (i.e. salvation by self-attainment) or because they represent a desire to embrace Jewish identity and/or privilege (i.e. circumcision as a sign of Jewishness, etc.); see Barclay, *Obeying*, 78–82; Dunn, 'Works', esp. 219–25; Räisänen, *Paul*, 162–91; 'Galatians 2.16' 112–26. However, given the intimate link in Judaism between salvation–election and national identity, together with the observation that 'works of the law' place the emphasis upon the 'doer' rather than upon God, it seems likely that Paul would have considered the second option a permutation of the first.

177 H. D. Betz, *Galatians*, 116; Bruce, *Galatians*, 137; Campbell, 'Meaning', 91–103; A. T. Hanson, *Studies*, 48; R. N. Longenecker, *Galatians*, 86.

faith rather than covenantal obedience to the law seems not only arbitrary, but also to be based upon a distinction between the internal disposition and expression of faith which is alien to the apostle. It is also questionable whether Paul would maintain such a strong causal relationship between reception of the Spirit and faith; it is unlikely to have characterised his own experience. On the contrary, it seems more in keeping with the theological tenor of the epistle to say that the Spirit is received within or under the auspices of the dispensation of faith fulfilled in Christ (3.14).[178]

This preliminary overview of Galatians 2.16 and 3.1–5 has alerted us to some of the difficulties faced when the alternative to justification ἐξ ἔργων νόμου is framed in terms of human faith in Christ; but it has also brought into focus a broader conception of faith and one which revolves around the person of Christ. In order to assess the significance of this dispensation of faith, we need to examine the theological heart of the epistle (3.6–4.7) in a more systematic fashion. Paul, having drawn attention to his own experiences (1.11–17) and those of the Galatian Christians (3.1–5), sets about  expressing in theological terms how the new development in humanity's relationship with God is that Christ has come and with Christ, justification for Gentiles as well as Jews.[179] He explains this by focusing initially upon Abraham and, in particular, on his faith. The quotation from Genesis 15.6 in 3.6, which is linked to the previous verses (καθώς) and the means by which the Spirit is received,[180] can be misleading if divorced from what follows. That is to say, Paul does not cite Genesis 15.6 in order to give a universal blueprint for the structure of divine–human relations, but to explain the origins of faith or, expressed more fully, of the dispensation of faith; as  Galatians 3.7 and 3.9 make explicit, it is not Abraham himself, but οἱ ἐκ πίστεως who provide the parallel with or example for the Galatians.[181]

Although Abraham does not fulfil a paradigmatic function within Galatians, his relationship with God exhibits a comparable structure to the relationship of other believers: the divine initiative in communicating the promise enables faith, which in turn is met by

178 Hays, *Faith*, 147–8; Hester, *Concept*, 55; Schlier, *Galater*, 127; S. K. Williams, 'Justification', 91–100.

179 Especially, Howard, *Paul*, 46–65.

180 Bruce, *Galatians*, 152, and, especially, Stanley, 'Curse', 481–511.

181 Barrett, *Freedom*, 23–5; Beker, *Paul*, 95–9; Schlier, *Galater*, 128.

God's faithfulness in bringing the promise to fulfilment. Paul does not use the patriarch, however, to define the precise relationship between faith and salvation; rather, he is concerned to underline that God's blessings are received and propagated through the lineage of faith and not birth.[182] Abraham's faith, therefore, is the basis for the faith of others; but the reception of salvation is not simply an implication of his faith,[183] for those who have faith become υἱοὶ Ἀβραάμ (3.7) and by doing so εὐλογοῦνται σὺν τῷ πιστῷ Ἀβραάμ (3.9). On the one hand, God's blessing and righteousness cannot be dissociated from Abraham and his first act of faith; on the other hand, those who wish to be sons of Abraham and be blessed by God, must personally share his faith and not simply be blood descendants (3.18).[184]

As we noted in section 2, it is unlikely that Paul wished to stress the meritorious nature of Abraham's faith in the sense of earning one's standing before God. His faith is, however, significant soteriologically in that those who are οἱ ἐκ πίστεως receive blessing from God because of their relationship to him who first had faith (3.6–9; cf. Rom. 4.16); in this sense, their standing before God is based upon Abraham's faith and God's promise to bless others through him. Further, Paul is at pains to emphasise that faith has always been the appropriate response to the blessings of God. Even those of Abrahamic descent are not blessed because of this state of affairs, but because of their faith. The importance of Abraham for Paul,

182 On the formal side of Paul's argument, see J. J. Hughes, 'Hebrews 9.15ff', 67–83. G. Howard speaks of Abraham as 'part of a salvific faith-process which works for the salvation of the Gentiles' (*Paul*, 55); also Beker, *Paul*, 48, and Hays, 'Abraham', esp. 97–8.

183 '... although, as we shall see, Abraham was a representative man who had "descendants", his faith was not and could not be as universally effective as Adam's sin.' (Barrett, *First Adam*, 36–7).

184 Paul is not saying that Abraham's faith, rather than his lineage, is the means of salvation for all; on the contrary, he is claiming that it is his 'faith-fulness' and not his 'Jewish-ness' which forms the basis of his relationship with God and that others who wish to share that relationship and its benefits must share his faith; see Dunn, *Galatians*, 163, and A. T. Hanson, *Studies*, 64–5. Dunn maintains that Paul is here driving a wedge between two understandings of πίστις, namely, faith as 'trust in God' and faith as 'covenantal faithfulness and observance of the law' (*loc. cit.*). As we noted in our discussion of Abraham in Romans, this is unlikely to be his principal concern. The latter part of Galatians 3 makes it clear that the fulfilment of the Abrahamic promise to bless all nations is not simply a matter of redefining πίστις, but of re-establishing faith as the only appropriate and universally valid response to God's grace – a step which requires the estrangement between God and humanity, identified by the law, to be overcome through the faith of the messiah.

therefore, resides in the recognition that his faith acts as a channel through which God is able to inaugurate the inheritance, lineage and dispensation of faith.[185]

Having established that God's universal blessing is realised and communicated through faith, Paul shifts his attention to the law and, in particular, to demonstrating its restricted soteriological function within this dispensation of grace.[186] Once again we hear echoes of Paul's own experience of the risen Christ (cf. 1.15–16), but the substance of his presentation consists of a scriptural diagnosis of the human predicament (e.g. 3.10; cf. Deut. 27.26), together with an exposition of how the Abrahamic promise is fulfilled in relation to the Gentiles (e.g. 3.14). Paul is aware that even though the law is not a means of fulfilling the promise, it cannot simply be ignored in an attempt to return to a pre-nomian existence and to believe in God as Abraham believed.[187] He explains that the law brings knowledge of sin (3.22) and sin brings a curse under the law (3.10–13); as a result, all people are constrained by the dispensation of law (cf. 3.23) and the promise is suspended.[188]

In Galatians 3.11–12, Paul juxtaposes the two dispensations of faith and law, and affirms the priority of the former (Hab. 2.4) over the latter (Lev. 18.5).[189] It is important to recognise that faith is established here not simply in contrast to works of the law, but to the dispensation of law and its curse. At this juncture, Paul is not making a general statement about how faith rather than works of the law is the way to righteousness; this would be to ignore the curse of the law and attribute salvific efficacy to one human response over another.[190] If believers are righteous by faith, Jesus need not have

[185] This assessment of Abraham may also be reflected in Jewish interpretations, although mixed up with other more meritorious understandings (e.g. Mek., Beshallah on Exod. 14.31; also Exod. R. XXIII.1–15 [on Exod. 15.1]; b. Shabbath 97a).

[186] Howard, *Paul*, 57, and Sanders, *Jewish People*, esp. 65–70.

[187] This is not to suggest that Paul thought Abraham's faith was defective, but that he recognised the law to be necessary for identifying sin and, as a consequence, to be a prerequisite for the coming of Christ.

[188] It is not clear whether Paul includes the Gentiles under the curse of the law; however, as T. L. Donaldson has pointed out, the Gentiles are in effect constrained by the law one way or another. Either they are directly under its curse or the fulfilment of the Abrahamic promise in their salvation is frustrated by the curse of the law upon the Jewish nation ('Curse', 94–112).

[189] H. D. Betz, *Galatians*, 146–7; A. T. Hanson, *Studies*, 47; Sanders, 'Fulfilling', 105–8.

[190] 'What Paul means is that justification is solely from God apart from any human activity including both faith and works, and since the Mosaic law is something for

been crucified and the Abrahamic covenant would not have been constrained by the law.[191] On the contrary, Paul demonstrates that the reason why reliance must not be placed upon works of the law is because the Righteous One lives by faith (Hab. 2.4), and not because those with faith are righteous.[192] In support of this, he explains that the curse of the law has been dealt with by one who is righteous and whose death on the cross assured that τὴν ἐπαγγελίαν τοῦ πνεύματος λάβωμεν διὰ τῆς πίστεως (3.14).

The messianic interpretation of Habakkuk 2.4 was discussed in relation to Romans 1.17. Although the link between Christ's faith and the cross is not as explicit here as in Romans 3, this association is suggested by the flow of the argument. The promise made to Abraham that all nations would be blessed in him (cf. ἐν σοί, 3.8) was originally received by faith (ἐκ πίστεως, 3.6–9), but the law brought knowledge of sin and a curse upon those unable to live as righteous people.[193] In any case, the law is not a means of justification, because it is not based on faith (ἐκ πίστεως, 3.12).[194] How then is the promise to be fulfilled? Only by means of one who was righteous with respect to the law and yet who chose to embrace the law's curse through death on a cross (cf. Deut. 21.23). All this suggests that Paul understood the righteous one of Habakkuk 2.4 to be Jesus Christ,[195] whose faith was the channel through which God

man to perform it cannot possibly figure in the justification of the Galatians.' (Howard, *Paul*, 57)

191 Paul is not simply concerned to establish the universality of faith, but also to clarify the relationship between grace and faith as revealed in Christ.

192 *Contra* Bruce, *Galatians*, 161: 'How is one justified in the sight of God? Paul has answered this question by pointing to the experience of Abraham (v. 6). It might be argued, however, that Abraham's was a special case; hence Paul cites the statement of justification by faith as a permanent principle in Hab. 2.4b, which in the present context (cf. Rom. 1.17) must be given the sense: "It is the one that is righteous (justified) by faith [not by the law] that will live (find life)."' It is difficult to see how this interpretation adequately reflects the rift caused by the giving of the law, the identification of sin and the suspension of the promise. Further, it suggests that the way of faith remained open after the giving of the law; why then did Christ need to come?

193 N. T. Wright demonstrates that Paul's point here is not that individual Jews have come under the curse of the law, but that the Jewish nation as a whole has been condemned for failing to fulfil its vocation to mediate God's blessing to all people ('Curse', 137–56).

194 Notice how Paul shifts in Gal. 3.11 to talking about the law and not works of the law. Rather than being merely stylistic, this suggests that he was considering the dispensation of the law alongside the dispensation of faith.

195 A. T. Hanson, *Studies*, 39–51. The nature of the relationship between Christ's faith and that of other believers will be discussed below; at this stage we note the judgement of R. B. Hays: 'Thus, three possible interpretations of Gal. 3.11 (=

was able to overcome the curse of the law and extend his covenant blessings to the Gentiles ἐν Χριστῷ Ἰησοῦ so that the promise might be fulfilled διὰ τῆς πίστεως (3.14).[196]

Further support for this interpretation emerges from a closer look at the relationship between Abraham and Christ in Galatians. Although Paul says little about how the death of Christ secures the Abrahamic promise for the Gentiles or, for that matter, of how Abraham inherited the promise in the first place, he does link these figures from the perspective of how the promise, once secured, is propagated. In this respect, Christ is Abraham's one and only true seed (3.16).[197] Little defence of this correlation is offered, although it appears to be deduced from the significance of Christ's death within salvation history: as Gentiles receive the promised Spirit through Christ (3.14; cf. 3.2–5), so Christ must be the offspring through whom the Abrahamic promise is fulfilled.[198]

Paul formalises the relationship between Abraham and Christ by speaking of it in terms of a covenant or testament (διαθήκη, 3.15, 17), thus demonstrating the continuity and the immutable nature of the original promise.[199] It is important to recognise that for Paul it is not a question of God making a new promise in Christ, but of fulfilling an existing one. Although the giving of the law temporarily separates the Abrahamic promise from its consummation, it neither negates nor supersedes it (3.17–18); rather, by bringing transgression to light, the law constrains all humanity – both Jews and Gentiles – under sin until the revelation of the true Abrahamic seed (3.19–24).[200]

Hab. 2.4 as employed by Paul) remain: (a) The Messiah will live by (his own) faith(fulness). (b) The righteous person will live as a result of the Messiah's faith(fulness). (c) The righteous person will live by (his own) faith (in the Messiah). Paul's thought is rendered wholly intelligible only if all three of these interpretations are held together and affirmed as correct.' (*Faith*, 156) This line of interpretation should also be followed for διὰ τῆς πίστεως in Gal. 3.14.

196 This conclusion may gain further support from Gal. 3.23–4, where the coming of Christ is identified with the coming of faith (see below). N. T. Wright stresses that Paul is wanting to demonstrate that the original Abrahamic promise was for one family to experience God's blessings; a family not defined in terms of nationalism, but of faith ('Seed', 157–74).

197 Beker, *Paul*, 37–58, 94–102, and Hester, *Concept*, 47–68.

198 S. K. Williams, 'Justification', 91–100, and Stanley, 'Curse', 481–511. Paul may also have felt justified in linking Abraham and Christ on the basis that they both demonstrated faith.

199 See, especially, Hester, *Concept*, *passim* and J. J. Hughes, 'Hebrews 9:15ff', 66–91.

200 Although Paul may only have had the Jews in mind when he speaks about those under the curse of the law in Gal. 3.10–14, it is both Jews and Gentiles who as

It is into this situation of humankind constrained by the law that Christ comes and, with him, faith (3.23). But how does Paul understand the relationship between Christ and the coming of faith? Does he think that faith as a human response to God first comes into existence with Christ? The case of Abraham and οἱ ἐκ πίστεως discussed in 3.6–9 militates against this possibility.[201] Is, then, the opportunity for faith made possible by Christ (cf. ἐξ ἀκοῆς πίστεως, 3.2, 5)? This may be an implication of its coming, but it does not explain why Paul speaks of faith being revealed at a particular juncture in the past (ἀποκαλυφθῆναι, 3.23). Further, the revelation of faith brings to an end God's provision of a παιδαγωγός in the law and secures justification (3.24–5). For Paul, the coming of faith is not primarily a human response, but a divine initiative corresponding to the breaking of the law's curse (3.10–14).[202] It seems probable, therefore, that Paul identifies the revelation of faith in 3.23 with the coming of Christ.[203] It is Christ's πίστις which inherits the Abrahamic promise and although Paul does not spell out in detail the content of that faith, it is closely related to his death, where the condemnatory effects of the law are embraced (3.13–14, 23–5; cf. 2.19–20).[204]

Corroborative evidence for this interpretation has been located within Roman judicial practice contemporaneous with Paul, where a special testamentary device known as *fidei commissum* existed 'by which the testator (in theory) left it to his heir's good faith to do with

transgressors are constrained by it in verses 19–25; on this, Donaldson, 'Curse', 102–6.

201 Paul's emphasis here is not upon whether there were individual believers before Christ, but upon the dispensation of faith superseding the dispensation of law.

202 H. D. Betz speaks of πίστις as 'the occurrence of a historical phenomenon, not the act of believing of an individual' (*Galatians*, 176; also Bultmann, *Theology*, vol. 1, 319, and Käsemann, *Perspectives*, 83).

203 Bornkamm, 'Revelation', 96–7; Ebeling, *Word*, 204; Hays, *Faith*, 228–33.

204 J. D. G. Dunn concludes that Gal. 3.22 is unlikely to refer to Jesus' faith; instead, he considers that '"faith in Jesus Christ" is the eschatological equivalent of Abraham's faith (cf. Rom. iv.17–24), since the gospel of Jesus Christ is now (for Paul) the place where God's unconditional promise of grace comes to clearest expression.' (*Galatians*, 196) However, as we shall see, Paul does not portray Abraham in Galatians primarily as a paradigmatic believer; as in Jewish tradition, Abraham's faith has a particular place in the realisation of God's promise, and for Paul it is οἱ ἐκ πίστεως (Gal. 3.7, 9), not the patriarch himself, who can be compared with Christian believers. The question of how Paul came to the conclusion that Jesus was Abraham's seed is also relevant here. If, as Professor Dunn would admit, the Abrahamic promise can only be received and propagated through faith and if Christ is his only rightful heir, then presumably he also must have demonstrated faith.

the testamentary property something the testator himself could not do'. The '*fidei commissum* was a device essential to any testament designed to take effect in enjoyment after the death of the first testamentary heir; and essential to any testament designed to benefit persons of alien nationality'.[205] Apparently, this provision was known to later Christian writers and would certainly have supported Paul's case: the *fidei commissum* is identified with the faith of Christ, thereby forging a legitimate non-genealogical link between Abraham and Christ, whilst also explaining how the Gentiles become partakers in the promise.

Christ's πίστις evident on the cross, therefore, is the means by which the promise of blessing made to Abraham is fulfilled. There are clear references to this faith in the form of the subjective genitive constructions of πίστεως Χριστοῦ (2.16; 3.22), and the quotation from Habakkuk in 3.11.[206] Christ's faith is also a part of a broader dispensation of faith noted in 2.20 and 3.23–6, but in these cases – as with 2.16 and 3.22 – the faith of other believers is also in view.[207] These latter references require us to clarify the function of human faith within the salvific process and it is at this juncture that the significance of Abraham within Paul's argument finally becomes evident. He does not present the patriarch as an exemplar of faith, nor does he think that Abraham illustrates how justification is appropriated; rather for Paul, Abraham's faith and the associated blessings are the basis for the faith and blessing of others.[208] That is

205 G. M. Taylor, 'Function', 66; see the comments of S. K. Williams, 'Righteousness', 274–5.

206 G. Howard speaks of 'the faith-act of Christ' (*Paul*, 58); also Goodenough, 'Paul', 45; Keck, 'Jesus', 454–5; Kittel, 'Πίστις', 427–34; R. N. Longenecker, *Galatians*, 78–88, 145; D. W. B. Robinson, 'Faith', 79–80; and many others.

207 At the beginning of the century, A. Deissmann coined the term 'Christusglauben' as an equivalent for πίστις Χριστοῦ expressions because he considered them a special type of genitive 'which might be called the "genitive of fellowship" or the "mystical genitive", because it indicated mystical fellowship with Christ. "Of Jesus Christ" is here in the main identical with "in Christ".' (*Paul*, 163). This 'dual perspective' approach has been picked up by subsequent scholarship with emphasis upon Christ's own faith (e.g. T. F. Torrance's 'polarized expression' ['One Aspect', 111–14] and S. K. Williams' 'Christ-faith' ['Again', 431–7]) or the believer's faith in Christ (e.g. Friedrich's 'Christusglauben' ['Glaube', 93–113] and Hultgren's 'Christic faith' ['PISTIS', 248–63]). Of the numerous works reflecting this approach, special attention should be given to the treatment of Hays, *Faith*, esp. 139–246.

208 'Abraham's faith/obedience (which has vicarious soteriological consequences for those who know him as father) ought to be understood not primarily as a paradigm for the faith of Christian believers but first of all as a prefiguration of the faith of Jesus Christ (cf. Rom. 3.22), whose faith/obedience now has vicarious

to say, Paul uses Abraham to illustrate the relationship between Christ and Christians: Abraham had faith and received the promise from God; οἱ ἐκ πίστεως are blessed not simply because they believe, but because in believing they participate in the faith of him to whom the promise was made (3.6–9). In the same way, Christ had faith and inherited the promise of God made to Abraham; and those who believe in him are also blessed because their faith is grounded in his.

Human faith in the dispensation of faith–grace

As we noted in relation to Abraham, Christ's faith does not remove the need for belief, but the faith of believers is grounded within his faith and is a channel through which God's blessings are received only in as much as their faith is enabled by and relates to Christ's faith.[209] Although the faith of Christ and of other believers are closely interrelated in Galatians (e.g. 2.16; 3.22), Paul does not claim that Christians actually possess Christ's faith – any more than he says that οἱ ἐκ πίστεως possess Abraham's faith – but that through faith they find their place within the blessings secured by Christ's faith.[210] It is significant, however, that references to Christ's faith are associated with discussions of what it means to participate in Christ.[211]

Consider, for example, Galatians 2.20 where Paul claims that he

soteriological consequences for those who know him as Lord. Broadly speaking, then, the relevance of Paul's appeal to the story of Abraham would lie in the fact that he finds there a precedent within Scripture for the idea that the faithfulness of a single divinely-chosen protagonist can bring God's blessing upon 'many' whose destiny is figured forth in that protagonist's action.' (Hays, 'Abraham', 97–8; also Hooker, 'ΠΙΣΤΙΣ', 330)

209 Friedrich, 'Glaube', 104, and Schlier, *Galater*, 167.

210 This corporate nature of Paul's πίστις Χριστοῦ constructions is in many respects the key to the meaning of these expressions and to the dilemma of whether they refer to Christ's own faith or faith in Christ. This is well expressed by M. D. Hooker: 'I suggest that we should think of it [i.e. πίστις Χριστοῦ] not as a polarized expression, which suggests antithesis, but a concentric expression, which begins, always, from the faith of Christ himself, but which includes, necessarily, the answering faith of believers, who claim that faith for their own. Moreover, while exegetes have tended to interpret Paul's statements about faith in individualistic terms, Paul was much more likely to have been thinking primarily of the corporate response of the people of God – of the new community of those who are in Christ, who believe in him and trust in what he is.' ('ΠΙΣΤΙΣ', 341)

211 Deissmann, *Paul*, 161–83; R. N. Longenecker, *Galatians*, 80–96; S. K. Williams, 'Again', 437–42.

has been crucified with Christ and that the life he now lives ἐν πίστει ζῶ τῇ τοῦ υἱοῦ τοῦ θεοῦ. Whereas 2.17–19a describes human initiative in relation to justification and judgement, the emphasis in verses 19b-20 shifts back to God's work in Christ. Unlike Romans 6.1–11, where the metaphor of burial accompanies baptismal terminology, the focus here is very much upon the salvific efficacy of the crucifixion as an event in its own right.[212] Paul's condemnation under the law has been dealt with by the cross and his life is now enabled by the faith of the son of God, whose love for him was epitomised in sacrificial death. Further, given the intimacy of the language (ζῶ δὲ οὐκέτι ἐγώ, ζῇ δὲ ἐν ἐμοὶ Χριστός), it would be difficult to envisage how Paul's response of faith could be meaningfully distinguished from that of the son of God who dwells within him.[213]

The language of participation also characterises the development or unpacking of Galatians 3.22 in the following verses. The law performed a constraining function before the coming or fulfilment of faith in the person of Christ and, with that which was wrought through faith (cf. 3.11–14), the hold of the law is broken. This dispensation of faith fulfilled in Christ opens the possibility of belief to others and reception of the associated blessings promised to Abraham and his seed; indeed, to all who are sons of God διὰ τῆς πίστεως ἐν Χριστῷ Ἰησοῦ (3.26). It is unclear whether ἐν Χριστῷ Ἰησοῦ is meant to qualify 'sons of God' or 'faith'[214] and, although the former yields an unambiguous reference to the faith of believers, both alternatives make very much the same point. On the one hand, sonship in Christ Jesus results from faith, where πίστις encompasses the faith of Christ and believers;[215] on the other, sonship results from faith in Christ Jesus, where the dative ἐν Χριστῷ Ἰησοῦ defines

212 Tannehill, *Dying*, 55–61. *Contra* Schlier, *Galater*, 101–3; there is little to suggest that Paul had Christian baptism in mind at this point.

213 It is also worth noting that even if Gal. 2.20 does refer to faith in the son of God, it is still Christ who dwells within Paul. Who, then, is the Paul – separate from the 'Christ within' – who so believes?

214 Bruce, *Galatians*, 183–4, and Mussner, *Galaterbrief*, 261–2.

215 Whilst it is possible that πίστις refers solely to the faith of believers, this option seems unlikely. As we have seen, faith in Gal. 3.23–5 is identified with the coming of Christ and it is this, rather than human faith, which replaces the law and provides the way to salvation. To say then that faith in Christ secures sonship is to shift the focus from the centrality of what Christ has accomplished on behalf of all onto what believers achieve for themselves in the light of Christ; but sonship – as with the dissolution of human divisions (Gal. 3.28) – is an implication of Christ's death and not of human faith in the crucified one.

the location of faith and not its object (i.e. faith which results from being found in Jesus Christ and his death, etc.).[216] Either way, the thinking is very close to that of 2.16–20 and 3.11–14.[217]

Galatians 3.27 explores the nature of the blessings available through the dispensation of faith by means of βαπτίζω and ἐνδύω. It is probable that both aorists refer to the same event and reflect different perspectives, the passive ἐβαπτίσθητε stressing the 'God-ward' and the middle ἐνεδύσασθε the 'human-ward'.[218] Given Paul's polemic elsewhere in the letter against external rites and ceremonies (e.g. 4.8–11; 5.1–12), it is unlikely that water baptism would be foremost in his mind at this juncture. An alternative interpretation is suggested by the recognition that ἐνδύω is used in the Septuagint as a metaphor for inward change (e.g. Isa. 61.10; Zech. 3.3) and, on occasion, describes reception of the Holy Spirit (e.g. Jdgs. 6.34; 1 Chron. 12.19; 2 Chron. 24.20).[219] This latter usage does seem to resonate with the present context (cf. 1 Cor. 12.13), in that it not only forges a link with the Galatian Christians' experience (cf. Gal. 3.1–5), but also concurs with the identification between receiving sonship and the Spirit noted in Gal. 4.6. Thus, we may note that for Paul the promise is not simply appropriated by faith (τοῖς πιστεύουσιν, 3.22), but by participating – through faith – in Jesus Christ, who inherited the promise through faith (ἐκ πίστεως Ἰησοῦ Χριστοῦ). In consequence, the faith of believers can never be dissociated from the faith of Christ. It is his faith which makes the faith of others possible and enables them to participate in its inheritance.

We may conclude, therefore, that Galatians exhibits a similar relationship between Christ's faith and that of the believer to the one identified in Romans.[220] In both letters, Paul develops his

[216] Most recent commentators understand ἐν Χριστῷ Ἰησοῦ here in a pregnant theological sense; so H. D. Betz, *Galatians*, 186; Bruce, *Galatians*, 184; R. N. Longenecker, *Galatians*, 151–4; Mussner, *Galaterbrief*, 262.

[217] This may also be reflected in the variant διὰ τῆς πίστεως Χριστοῦ Ἰησοῦ for Gal. 3.26, where the subjective genitive interprets ἐν Χριστῷ Ἰησοῦ in terms of faith which originates in Christ's faith.

[218] Dunn, *Baptism*, 109–13, and Bruce, *Galatians*, 185–6.

[219] On the background of ἐνδύω, see H. D. Betz, *Galatians*, 188, and Oepke, 'δύω', 319–20.

[220] Clearly there are differences and, as you would expect, the presentation in Romans is more nuanced and thorough. For example, the definition of Christ's faith in terms of obedience and its significance for the outworkings of the promise are more developed in Romans. Further, whereas Paul uses Abraham in Galatians to illustrate the relationship between Christ and believers, the patriarch serves more as an exemplar of faith in Romans.

understanding of justification and righteousness with the help of a tripartite schema consisting of: (i) God promises to bless all people through Abraham; (ii) Abraham responds in faith; (iii) God is faithful to his promise by bringing it to fulfilment. Within this *Heilsplan*, the law temporarily frustrates the fulfilment of the promise until Christ, the Righteous One, embraces its judgement upon sin by dying on the cross. It is on the cross that his faith-in-obedience is supremely evident as God's faithfulness to the promise reaches out to Jews and Gentiles alike. As a result, both the promise and its fulfilment are encountered in Christ – his faith is at once the grounds for human faith and the channel for its fulfilment.

4 The Epistle to the Philippians

Phil. 3.9: καὶ εὑρεθῶ ἐν αὐτῷ, μὴ ἔχων ἐμὴν δικαιοσύνην τὴν ἐκ νόμου ἀλλὰ τὴν διὰ πίστεως Χριστοῦ, τὴν ἐκ θεοῦ δικαιοσύνην ἐπὶ τῇ πίστει . . .

Translation: <8> And what is more, I continue to regard everything as loss because of the surpassing value of being known by Christ Jesus my Lord [*or* of knowing Christ Jesus my Lord]. For his sake I have suffered the loss of all things and consider them [as no more than] rubbish that I may gain Christ, <9> and be found in him, not having a righteousness of my own which comes from the law, but a righteousness from God through [*or* by means of] Christ's faith which leads to [*or* for the purpose of] faith. <10> [Yes, I have suffered the loss of all things] to know him and [to participate in] the power of his resurrection and the sharing of his sufferings, being continually conformed to his death . . .

The demand that Gentile converts should be circumcised is also in focus at the beginning of Philippians 3.[221] And Paul, having issued a strong exhortation, outlines why circumcision would be of little benefit to the Philippian believers. He explains that circumcision is only of value when it constitutes an inward or spiritual change; the external act simply encourages confidence in the flesh and is fraught with dangers. Paul illustrates this from personal experience as he confides that his own pedigree and endeavours resulted in a situation where he was blameless κατὰ δικαιοσύνην τὴν ἐν νόμῳ (3.6).

[221] On the nature of threat faced by the Philippian Christians, see the reviews in Hawthorne, *Philippians*, xliv–xlvii and O'Brien, *Philippians*, 26–35.

All this changed, however, when his life underwent a radical transformation as he discarded whatever contributed towards a personal righteousness based upon the law in favour of Christ.[222] Paul repeatedly draws attention to this revised attitude towards those things which he once held as gain (κέρδος)[223] by using the verb ἡγέομαι (3.7, 8[x2]) and it cannot be without significance that the same word is used of Christ's kenosis in Philippians 2.6.[224]

The reason for this association becomes apparent in Philippians 3.9, where Paul indicates that it was the abandonment of self which enabled him to be found in Christ, having a righteousness from God διὰ πίστεως Χριστοῦ. But how should this phrase be interpreted? A righteousness through faith in Christ or through Christ's faith? In certain respects, the objective genitive[225] fits with references to Paul's efforts in relation to Christ elsewhere in the chapter (e.g. ἡγέομαι, 3.7–8; διώκω, 3.12, 14), but it should not be overlooked that these endeavours are in turn undergirded and enabled by Christ himself (e.g. 3.12).[226] Without the pre-eminence of God's work in Christ, it is difficult to discern any qualitative difference in terms of soteriological efficacy between Paul's pre- and post-christophany pursuits.[227] In Philippians 3.9, then, Paul is concerned with the origin and appropriation of righteousness in order to explain the basis for his new conduct. Two approaches are contrasted and the comparison is precise:[228]

righteousness ἐκ νόμου	appropriated by human effort (ἐμήν; cf. 3.6)
righteousness ἐκ θεοῦ	appropriated διὰ πίστεως Χριστοῦ

222 Although the occasion of transformation is not named, it is almost certainly the same event as described in Galatians 1; see Ernst, *Philipper*, 96; Martin, *Philippians* (1959), 145; O'Brien, *Philippians*, 384; but Collange, *Philippians*, 129, and Gnilka, *Philipperbrief*, 192.

223 It is probable that overtones of merit and/or self-attained righteousness are present here as well; see Gaventa, *Darkness*, 29–33.

224 Perhaps Paul considered that Christ's self-emptying on the cross informed his own experience; see Hooker, 'ΠΙΣΤΙΣ', 331, and Kurz, 'Imitation', 109–20.

225 Collange, *Philippians*, 130–1; Hawthorne, *Philippians*, 141–2; Vincent, *Philippians*, 116.

226 G. Barth, *Philipper*, 60–1.

227 I.e. beforehand, Paul was using all his energies in pursuit of God's provision in the law; afterwards, he was using all his energies in pursuit of God's provision in Christ.

228 W. Schenk maintains that Paul presents this contrast in the form of a chiasmus (*Philipperbriefe*, 309–10; see also Ernst, *Philipper*, 97–8, and Gnilka, *Philipperbrief*, 194).

If the second approach is taken to mean a 'righteousness from God appropriated by faith in Christ', both options become remarkably similar in their emphasis upon human response.[229] Yet this hardly reflects the centrality of Christ for Paul (e.g. Phil. 2.6–11) and rests upon a dichotomy between 'works of the law' and 'faith in Christ' not evident in Philippians.[230] On the contrary, it seems far more likely that the contrast here is between human righteousness and God's righteousness;[231] the former resting upon human endeavour or response and the latter upon God's work in Christ. Paul does not restrict his kenotic way of life to works of the law, for his whole mode of existence now revolves around self-denial so that God through Christ is able to accomplish in him that which he was unable to accomplish for himself. It is this approach which frees him to be found in Christ and, on the basis of this reality, Paul is able to speak in active terms of pursuing God with all his energy; not because he has fallen back into thinking that righteousness can be earnt, but because God's righteousness is the grounds and motivation for all that he does: 'I can do all things in him who strengthens me.' (4.13)

In the light of these observations, an interpretation for διὰ πίστεως Χριστοῦ in terms of Christ's own faith seems more in keeping with Paul's thinking.[232] From this perspective, each Christian's relationship to God is grounded in a right-relatedness to God communicated through the faith of Christ. But how is this faith to

229 Gnilka *Philipperbrief*, 194, and Ernst, *Philipper*, 98. The problem with the 'grace-gift' approach to faith is that it fails to accommodate Paul's understanding of how Christ is not only the channel for God's righteousness, but also for human response. For Paul, Christ is the locus where God draws close to humanity and humanity draws close to God; his faith is the source of all faith. If God is the giver of faith, then it is through Christ's faith, where all human response is located. To be 'in Christ' is not the result of human faith; faith flows from being 'in Christ'.

230 We also found cause to question whether it is present in Romans and Galatians. J.-P. Collange explains how 'the Law comes to be regarded as a means of salvation and in that way takes the place of God. But faith is not in the same category; it is the anthropological point of contact where the righteousness of God impinges upon man (διὰ πίστεως). Faith has no value in itself; it merely turns one to Christ who is the object of faith (διὰ πίστεως Χριστοῦ).' (*Philippians*, 130) It is questionable, however, whether this distinction can be sustained, for anything which appropriates on an existential level God's righteousness can hardly be considered of 'no value'. Further, could it not also be claimed that for Jews the law is 'the anthropological point of contact where the righteousness of God impinges upon man'?

231 Gundry, 'Grace', 13–16, and O'Brien, *Philippians*, 395–7.

232 Hooker, 'ΠΙΣΤΙΣ', 331–3; Martin, *Philippians* (1976), 132–3; O'Brien, *Philippians*, 379–400; Stowers, 'Romans 3:30', 671.

be understood? We have already drawn attention to the link between chapter 3 and the Christ-hymn of Philippians 2.6–11 (cf. ἡγέομαι) and, previously (cf. section 2), to the relationship between obedience and faith in the apostle's thinking. These associations, together with the flow of the letter, would encourage Paul's readers to interpret the establishing of God's righteousness διὰ πίστεως Χριστοῦ in terms of his obedient self-giving in death mentioned in chapter 2. Through Christ's faith-in-obedience to the divine will and the way of salvation, Paul participates in a right-relatedness to God which is realised in Christ. Christ is where God's righteousness and faith come together; participation in both is a function of his unique relation to both God and humanity. As God comes close to humanity in Christ, so humanity draws close to God in Christ; and both channels of communication are established through Christ's faith-in-obedience.[233]

Interpreting διὰ πίστεως Χριστοῦ in terms of Christ's faith gains further support from Paul's usage of the possessive genitive in relation to Christ elsewhere in the letter.[234] Three additional genitival constructions are worthy of note (e.g. 1.27 [x2]; 3.8). After Paul has explored the merits of remaining in his mortal body or going to be with Christ, he shifts attention to the conduct of the Philippians. He exhorts them to adopt a manner of life worthy τοῦ εὐαγγελίου τοῦ Χριστοῦ[235] and to struggle together τῇ πίστει τοῦ εὐαγγελίου (1.27). The meaning of the first construction is ambiguous as the relation between εὐαγγέλιον and Χριστός is imprecise. Paul may intend to be intentionally vague at this juncture, although the basis for moral exhortation at the beginning of Philippians 2 is not simply the good news about Christ, but Christ himself (ἐν Χριστῷ, κοινωνία πνεύματος, 2.1) and participation in him (τοῦτο φρονεῖτε ἐν ὑμῖν ὃ καὶ ἐν Χριστῷ Ἰησοῦ, 2.5; cf. 3.9); no doubt this explains, at

233 Paul's shift from ὑπακοή in Phil. 2.8 to πίστις in Phil. 3.9 may reflect a broader understanding of faith which encompasses obedience (i.e. obedience as an expression of faith; cf. ὑπακοὴν πίστεως; Rom. 1.5; 16.26) and a desire to provide a link between Christ's faith and that of the Philippians. Further, as we noted earlier, it does seem that Paul considered faith to constitute the fundamental response to God's grace.

234 For example, σπλάγχνοις Χριστοῦ Ἰησοῦ (1.8), τοῦ πνεύματος Ἰησοῦ Χριστοῦ (1.19), τὸ ἔργον Χριστοῦ (2.30), τοῦ σταυροῦ τοῦ Χριστοῦ (3.18) and ἡ χάρις τοῦ κυρίου Ἰησοῦ Χριστοῦ (4.23); ἡμέρας Χριστοῦ Ἰησοῦ (1.6); εἰς ἡμέραν Χριστοῦ (1.10; 2.16).

235 Similar constructions occur frequently in Paul: 'gospel of Christ' – 1 Cor. 9.12; 2 Cor. 2.12; 9.13; 10.14; Gal. 1.7; 1 Thess. 3.2; cf. Rom. 1.9; 2 Cor. 4.4; 2 Thess. 1.8; 'gospel of God' – Rom. 1.1; 15.16; 1 Thess. 2.8–9.

least partially, why Paul goes on to speak of Christ in terms of humility and obedience (2.8).[236] It seems unlikely, therefore, that τοῦ εὐαγγελίου τοῦ Χριστοῦ refers simply to the gospel which has Christ as its object; rather, a genitive of apposition (i.e. 'the gospel which is Christ') fits the context more faithfully.[237]

Consider also τῇ πίστει τοῦ εὐαγγελίου (1.27).[238] There is little support for rendering πίστις here as *fides quae creditur* and although the faith of believers may well be in view, it need not be the main focus.[239] A pointer to Paul's intention here may be provided by Philippians 1.29, where the possibility of belief in Christ and suffering on his behalf is granted on the basis of prior divine initiative (ὅτι ὑμῖν ἐχαρίσθη τὸ ὑπὲρ Χριστοῦ ... πιστεύειν ... πάσχειν).[240] This suggests that τῇ πίστει τοῦ εὐαγγελίου may constitute the motivation and means for the Philippians' discipleship, rather than its object or goal.[241] That is to say, τῇ πίστει may be an instrumental dative[242] which is followed by a possessive genitive: 'by means of the faith belonging to the gospel'. Further, given the close correlation in the verse between Christ and the gospel, the subject of that faith must be firmly grounded in the former. Thus, when Paul writes τῇ πίστει τοῦ εὐαγγελίου he may not be referring simply to something believers do, but to something they become part of in Christ as they share his faith and follow his example (e.g. στήκετε, συναθλοῦντες, πιστεύειν, πάσχειν).

The third construction may well be a simple objective genitive: Paul abandons everything for the superior reality of knowing Christ

236 The significance of Phil. 2.5 and, by implication, of the following Christ-hymn is still a matter of debate; on the ethical or exemplary interpretation, see Kurz, 'Imitation', 103–26; O'Brien, *Philippians*, esp. 253–62; Wright, 'Philippians 2.5–11', 56–98.

237 Collange, *Philippians*, 72–3, and Friedrich, 'εὐαγγελίζομαι', esp. 731; see also Schenk, *Philipperbriefe*, 165–9.

238 This construction has been variously interpreted; for example, 'faith in the gospel', 'the faith brought about by the gospel', 'the faith which is the gospel', 'faithfulness to the apostolic teaching'.

239 Paul's injunction here that the Philippians should pursue the life of discipleship does not seem to rest upon their own initiatives, but on what God provides ἐν ἑνὶ πνεύματι and τῇ πίστει τοῦ εὐαγγελίου. This fits with the way in which the apostle often anchors ethical imperatives upon indicatives denoting what God has done.

240 On the link between χαρίζομαι and divine giving, see Gnilka, *Philipperbrief*, 100, and Hawthorne, *Philippians*, 61.

241 Cf. Ernst, *Philipper*, 61.

242 Cf. Rom. 1.28; 4.19, 20; 5.2; 11.20; 1 Cor. 16.13; 2 Cor. 1.24; Gal. 3.20.

(τῆς γνώσεως Χριστοῦ Ἰησοῦ τοῦ κυρίου μου, 3.8).[243] Whilst this is certainly a viable option, it is perhaps not beyond question. In the first place, it betrays a structure in which knowledge of Christ is dependent upon considering all else as loss. This not only places the emphasis upon human initiative rather than God's grace, but also fails to coincide with Paul's more detailed account of his christophany in Galatians 1. Here it is God's knowledge of him which is the basis for encounter with Christ (Gal. 1.15), a reality which Paul claims also characterises the experience of the Galatian Christians (cf. νῦν δὲ γνόντες θεόν, μᾶλλον δὲ γνωσθέντες ὑπὸ θεοῦ, Gal. 4.9). This suggests an alternative interpretation for Philippians 3.8 in which τῆς γνώσεως Χριστοῦ Ἰησοῦ τοῦ κυρίου μου refers to the knowledge of Christ[244] and constitutes the grounds rather than the goal of Paul's kenosis. The following δι' ὃν confirms the divine initiative implicit within this alternative as Christ's knowledge of Paul enables his knowledge of Christ (3.10).[245] Clearly, this understanding is far from certain, but it does concur with the interpretation of διὰ πίστεως Χριστοῦ outlined above: Christ's faith, like his knowledge of Paul, provides the grounds and basis for Paul's response.

We now return to Philippians 3.9 and, specifically, to the significance of ἐπὶ τῇ πίστει. The contrasting forms of righteousness described in this verse have been presented above, although it must be noted here that God's righteousness is not simply διὰ πίστεως Χριστοῦ, but also ἐπὶ τῇ πίστει. As we have seen, the first of these formulations may well refer to the faith of Christ himself, but what of the second? Paul does not use this construction elsewhere (cf. καὶ ἐπὶ τῇ πίστει τοῦ ὀνόματος αὐτοῦ κτλ, Acts 3.16) and the semantics of ἐπί do not permit precision in interpretation. A conditional sense for ἐπί is favoured by many scholars (i.e. 'depends on faith', 'on the basis of faith'),[246] but only in conjunction with a prior reference to faith in Christ. This option would also work, however,

243 Hawthorne, *Philippians*, 137, and Vincent, *Philippians*, 100; cf. Dunn, 'Once More', 731–2.

244 Cf. Rom. 11.33; 1 Cor. 8.2–3; 13.12; 2 Cor. 2.14; 4.6; 10.5. On the subjective genitive interpretation, see Vallotton, *Christ*, 86–7; others, not wishing to follow this option, emphasise the participatory or mystical dimensions of knowing Christ (e.g. Schenk, *Philipperbriefe*, 307–14; Tannehill, *Dying*, 114–23).

245 A similar relationship between divine initiative and human response may be reflected in Phil. 3.12, διώκω δὲ εἰ καὶ καταλάβω, ἐφ' ᾧ καὶ κατελήμφθην ὑπὸ Χριστοῦ ['Ιησοῦ].

246 Hawthorne, *Philippians*, 142; Lightfoot, *Philippians*, 150; Vincent, *Philippians*, 102.

if διὰ πίστεως Χριστοῦ denoted Christ's faith, although the verse would then not refer explicitly to the faith of believers.[247] Whilst this is possible, it is rendered less likely by the emphasis in the following verses upon personal response to God's righteousness.

A more feasible alternative is to attribute a final rather than a conditional force to ἐπί: 'but a righteousness from God through Christ's faith which leads to [*or* for the purpose of] faith [of believers]'. This gains support from Paul's use of the preposition elsewhere[248] and forges a link with the following verses, where he develops the implications of living within God's righteousness in Christ.[249] Further, as we have already seen, the notion of Christ's faith as the ground for human response is also reflected in Philippians 1.27–9. We may conclude, therefore, that Philippians provides further evidence of Paul's opting to speak about faith within the context of what it means to be in Christ. For him, coming to faith does not signal the commencement of a believer's appropriation of God's righteousness; rather, Christ's faith-in-obedience is the supreme channel for God's righteousness and provides the basis for all faith. That is to say, faith is the response by which believers find their place within the dispensation of grace inaugurated by Christ's faith.

5 Concluding remarks

Our review of the seven πίστις Χριστοῦ constructions is now complete and we have discovered substantial grounds for maintaining that in each case Paul had Christ's own faith in mind. Furthermore, in assessing the significance of these constructions for the apostle, we identified additional πίστις occurrences which may refer to Christ's faith as well.[250] Our investigations also led us to conclude that Paul's principal interest in Christ's faith is soteriologically motivated and that, within his understanding of God's righteousness, two perspectives are evident. Firstly, Christ's faith-in-

[247] The articular form of ἐπὶ τῇ πίστει may indicate the faith of a specific person (i.e. Christ).

[248] E.g. ὑμεῖς γὰρ ἐπ' ἐλευθερίᾳ ἐκλήθητε, Gal. 5.13; οὐ γὰρ ἐκάλεσεν ἡμᾶς ὁ θεὸς ἐπὶ ἀκαθαρσίᾳ ἀλλ' ἐν ἁγιασμῷ, 1 Thess. 4.7; cf. Rom. 8.20; 1 Cor. 9.10.

[249] See, especially, Hooker, 'ΠΙΣΤΙΣ', 331–3; O'Brien, *Philippians*, 381–417; Tannehill, *Dying*, 114–23.

[250] E.g. Rom. 1.17 [Hab. 2.4]; 3.25; Gal. 3.2, 5, 11 [Hab. 2.4], 14, 23–26; Phil. 1.27. In addition, Professor Hooker considers 2 Cor. 1.17–22 and 4.13 likely candidates ('ΠΙΣΤΙΣ', 334–6); see also M. Barth, 'Faith', 364.

obedience interprets Jesus' death from the perspective of his humanity, underlining his solidarity with the human race and his continuity with those who believe.[251] Secondly, by forging a link between God's covenantal faithfulness (i.e. righteousness) and Christ's faith, Paul is able to demonstrate how the latter becomes a channel for the former.

It is important to realise that Paul is not simply saying that Christ's death opens up the possibility of salvation for those who believe and that, in this sense, Christ is the source or grounds of faith. Rather, he is claiming that Christ and, in particular, his death mediates soteriological possibilities not only by providing a channel for God's covenantal faithfulness, but also by establishing an existential continuity between Christ's faith and the faith of believers.[252] That is to say, Christ is the locus where God's righteousness is communicated to humanity and where humanity participates in God's righteousness. For Paul, faith is not something which initially happens outside of, or discrete from God's provision in Christ, constituting an entry requirement or means of appropriation of God's righteousness; rather, faith is a characteristic of Christ's inclusive humanity through which the power of sin is broken on the cross and all people are given a way of responding to God's grace. This, then, is the good news which universalises God's righteousness or covenantal promise and faithfulness: that response to God is no longer determined by race, law-keeping or human endeavour of any other form, but by being found in Christ.

It is in this sense, therefore, that we can speak of a 'dispensation of faith' in Paul's thinking and relate it intimately to a 'dispensation of grace'. Each one constitutes a different dimension to God's salvific work in Christ: the latter adopts a 'theological perspective' and embraces God's righteousness or covenantal faithfulness established for all people in Christ; the former adopts an 'anthropological perspective' and embraces the possibility of responding to God in

[251] On the function of Christ as 'representative human' in Paul's theology, see: Dunn, 'Understanding', 125–41; *Christology*, esp. 98–128; Wright, *Climax*.

[252] See the comments of M. Thompson, who reviews the significance of the example and teaching of Jesus in Rom. 12.1–15.13: 'The example of Christ is not limited to the pre-existent or the risen Christ, but has as its focus the character of Jesus, seen most clearly in his death on the cross . . . The example of Christ does not signify for Paul any kind of mechanical reproduction of Jesus' life and deeds, any more than the teachings of Jesus constituted a new Torah. Imitation means Spirit-enabled following of Jesus' spirit and attitude exemplified and characterized on the cross.' (*Clothed*, 238–9; also 78–86)

faith. Further, in the light of this dual perspective, we should not be surprised that Paul speaks of Christ's faith in terms of disposition (e.g. obedience or faithfulness) rather than content (e.g. in God). For whilst his faith opens the possibility of faith to all, a believer's faith comes to expression in relation to God's provision in Christ; in consequence, Christ exemplarises a faith of which he is, in part, the content.

The relationship between the faith of Christ and believers can, in certain respects, be described as participatory, but not in the sense that the former removes the need for the latter or can be substituted for it. On the contrary, faith is possible because all may participate in a dispensation of faith established by Christ's faith. In a very real sense, therefore, Paul understands Christ's faith as the grounds or guarantee of all faith; and, whilst its soteriological significance renders it beyond emulation, believers are expected to share in faith and, by so doing, to recognise their place within the dispensation established by Christ's faith. Further, it was in this context that we noticed similarities with other aspects of the apostle's understanding of what it means to be 'in Christ'. For example, Paul does not consider baptism as a means of actualising or repeating Christ's death so that it becomes efficacious for the initiate; that would undermine his emphasis upon the completeness of God's work in Christ. Rather, baptism is the acknowledgement or demonstration that Christ's death and its salvific implications encompass – and always have done – the person baptised.

Before drawing this chapter to a close, we should say something about the origin of Paul's thinking concerning Christ's faith. It is possible that he inherited certain elements from tradition (e.g. Rom. 3.24–6, interpretations of Christ's death, etc.).[253] He may also have been aware of the expectation that the messiah would be a man of faith[254] and will almost certainly have been conversant with traditions associating God's covenantal faithfulness with the faith of his chosen one (e.g. Pss. Sol. 17). Further, the portrayal of Jewish martyrs, whose suffering and death were deemed sacrificial and

253 Paul appears to have been familiar with some of Jesus' teaching concerning faith (1 Cor. 13.2; cf. Matt. 17.20; 21.21; Mark 11.23). Further, it is possible that the tradition encapsulated in Phil. 2.6–11 may also have been formative, with the emphasis upon the salvific efficacy of Jesus' obedience (cf. Howard, 'Phil. 2:6–11', 368–87, and Murphy-O'Connor, 'Anthropology', 25–50).

254 E.g. 1 Sam. 2.35; Ps. 89.24, 29, 38; Isa. 11.5; 16.5; 42.3; Pss. Sol. 17.34, 39–40; Odes Sol. 4.3, 5; 8.10; 39.5, 13; 1 Enoch 39.6; 83.8; cf. Eccles. R. III.9.1 (on Eccles. 3.9); Tg. Isa. on 11.4.

atoning, as people of faith may have proved formative for the apostle.[255] 4 Maccabees is of particular significance here in that the Maccabean martyrs are linked with previous Jewish exemplars on the basis of a common faith (τὴν αὐτὴν πίστιν).[256] There is also the influence of the Akedah tradition,[257] which celebrates Abraham's faith seen in his willingness to obey God's command to kill Isaac, his only son and heir of the promise, and God's reciprocating covenantal faithfulness in providing an alternative sacrifice. Although the parallel here is not exact, for in the end no human life is sacrificed and it is Abraham's and not Isaac's faith which is stressed,[258] the similarities with Paul's notion of God's covenantal faithfulness being revealed in Christ's faith-in-obedience on the cross are significant. And, finally, given the nature of Paul's initial encounter with the risen Lord, he must have reflected upon the origin of his own faith and, on the basis of his total dependence upon Christ, may have traced this back to him as well.

255 E.g. 4 Macc. 5.16, 25; 7.10, 16–19, 21–2; 15.24; 16.18–23; 17.1–2, 20–2. There are two aspects here which are noteworthy: firstly, the depiction of martyrs as men or women of faith and, secondly, the soteriological significance of their deaths. As we shall see, both these elements are taken up in later Christian reflection upon Christ's faith; less clear is whether there was already a Jewish precedent in this respect. See the discussions of van Henten, 'Background', 101–28, and Swetnam, *Jesus*, 23–75.

256 4 Macc. 16.18–23, discussed in Section 3.2; also de Jonge, 'Jesus' Death', 142–51; cf. 4 Macc. 7.11–14; 13.12; 16.18–20; 18.11.

257 Most of the relevant texts can be found in Daly, 'Significance', 45–75; see Childs, *Biblical Theology*, 325–36, for relevant bibliography and review of recent discussion.

258 As Christ is the 'victim' for Paul, this would need to be reflected in Akedah traditions with emphasis upon Isaac's faith; although this may be implied in certain cases, it is Abraham's faith which tends to be mentioned explicitly.

4

JESUS' FAITH IN THE DEUTERO-PAULINE AND PASTORAL EPISTLES

1 Deutero-Pauline Epistles: Ephesians

The deutero-Pauline epistles contain only one occurrence of a construction which resembles Paul's πίστις Χριστοῦ and this is significantly different (i.e. διὰ τῆς πίστεως αὐτοῦ, Eph. 3.12). For one thing, πίστις is followed by the personal pronoun αὐτοῦ, referring back to Christ in verse 11, and not Χριστοῦ or some other designation; πίστις is also qualified by the definite article.[1] No other πιστεύω cognate is attested in the immediate context with the result that, if διὰ τῆς πίστεως αὐτοῦ relates to Christ's faith, the faith of believers is either excluded or must be accommodated within the same phrase. And finally, the presence of πίστιν ἐν τῷ κυρίῳ Ἰησοῦ in 1.15 (cf. καὶ πιστοῖς ἐν Χριστῷ Ἰησοῦ, 1.1) demonstrates that the author was familiar with the construction 'πίστις ἐν plus the dative' and could have used it in 3.12; had this occurred, the uncertainty over how to relate faith and Christ would have been greatly reduced.[2]

A review of the nature and function of faith in Ephesians[3] reveals a complex structure and one which is perhaps best understood in terms of different perspectives. From one stance, the place of faith within the salvation process is clear: belief either follows from or is consecutive with hearing the gospel; and, on coming to faith, a believer is sealed with the Holy Spirit (1.13). Yet the entire salvation

[1] One of the reasons why J. D. G. Dunn rejects the subjective genitive interpretation for πίστις Χριστοῦ in Romans, Galatians and Philippians is because the article is missing; he is, therefore, open to the possibility that Eph. 3.12 refers to the faith of Christ ('Once More', 733).

[2] Πίστις ἐν, however, is not without ambiguity for the phrase may refer to the location rather than the object of faith.

[3] Occurrences of the πιστεύω group in Ephesians can be summarised as follows: πιστεύω (2): 1.13, 19; πίστις (8): 1.15; 2.8; 3.12, 17; 4.5, 13; 6.16, 23; πιστός (2): 1.1; 6.21.

process is embraced by the grace of God communicated through Christ and, viewed from this perspective, even hearing and believing are a function of being in Christ (cf. ἐν ᾧ, 1.13). Great emphasis is placed upon personal election in Christ as a reality which precedes human response (e.g. 1.4–5, 11–12, 18; 2.10) and, whilst the importance of faith can be underlined (e.g. 1.15), it is clear that even this disposition originates in and is enabled by God's all-encompassing graciousness in Christ.[4]

Further, on a number of occasions faith is spoken of as a gift from God. For example, in Ephesians 2.8 the author claims that τῇ γὰρ χάριτί ἐστε σεσῳσμένοι διὰ πίστεως· καὶ τοῦτο οὐκ ἐξ ὑμῶν, θεοῦ τὸ δῶρον. This verse comes towards the end of a section exploring the all-pervasiveness of Christ's salvation (2.1–10):[5] when humankind was caught up in transgression, death and wilful disobedience, Christ made them alive with him (συνεζωοποίησεν τῷ Χριστῷ, v. 5); he raised them up from death and seated them with him in the heavenly places (συνήγειρεν καὶ συνεκάθισεν, v. 6). We note here how the completeness of God's work in Christ extends beyond dying to sin and encompasses resurrection and exaltation. For the author, therefore, Christ not only brings the possibility of life, but also seals that life prior to human response: χάριτί ἐστε σεσῳσμένοι (v. 5).[6] The refrain is repeated in verse 8, but qualified on this occasion with διὰ πίστεως. Taken in isolation, this looks like an acknowledgement of the contribution made by the believer to salvation, but the following καὶ τοῦτο οὐκ ἐξ ὑμῶν, θεοῦ τὸ δῶρον indicates that even faith originates in God and is given by him as a gift of grace.[7]

4 Faith, therefore, is portrayed as just one of many blessings secured through Christ; see also: redemption and forgiveness 1.7–8; life 2.1, 5; resurrection 2.6; reconciliation 2.11–17; 3.5–6; access to God 2.18; 3.12; membership 2.19–22; 3.6; grace 1.6, 7; 2.7; wisdom and knowledge 1.9, 17–23; 3.18–19; Holy Spirit 1.13–14; 3.16; gifts 4.11–12; armour of God 6.10–17.

5 Lincoln, *Ephesians*, 83–121, and Schnackenburg, *Ephesians*, 86–101.

6 The perfect tense stresses the ongoing nature of salvation in Christ.

7 C. L. Mitton suggests that the author had two aspects of faith in mind at this point: a passive willingness to receive God's gifts of salvation and an active readiness to follow where God's grace leads (*Ephesians*, 96). He also maintains that whilst the former can be understood as a gift from God, the latter cannot. There is, however, little in the text to suggest this distinction which, in any case, fails to grasp the scope of Christ for salvation; that is, his function within not only the gift of salvation, but also the response to that gift. In contrast, R. Schnackenburg's comment seems to be on the right lines: 'Δῶρον (only here in Eph.) appears to have been chosen deliberately to denote the grace of their calling which simultaneously brings the

Although the author may well be describing the whole salvation process – and not simply faith – as a gift from God, the latter is certainly included.[8] Moreover, the way in which οὐκ ἐξ ὑμῶν is echoed by the following οὐκ ἐξ ἔργων indicates that the focus at this juncture is upon the place of human response within salvation. There is little in Ephesians to favour a narrow interpretation for ἔργων in terms of works of the law and a more appropriate rendering would be along the lines of human endeavour leading to confidence in self (cf. ἵνα μή τις καυχήσηται, 2.9).[9] Clearly, faith itself could be viewed in this way, were it not interpreted as an expression of God's grace given freely and without merit. Thus, it seems that even the coming to or demonstration of faith must be located within God's predilection in Christ (cf. 1.4–6; 2.10).

The conviction that faith is a gift from God may also be evident in Ephesians 6.16.[10] The shield of faith (τὸν θυρεὸν τῆς πίστεως) represents part of God's armour which the Ephesian Christians are exhorted to embrace (ἐνδύσασθε, 6.11; ἀναλάβετε, 6.13; cf. 6.16) so that they will be able to stand firm in the face of spiritual opposition. Of the six components mentioned, five manifestly originate in God (e.g. truth, righteousness, gospel of peace, salvation and Spirit), suggesting that πίστις comes from the same source.[11] Attention

faith which is bestowed on all Christians in contrast to special graces (cf. δωρέα in 3.7; 4.7).' (*Ephesians*, 98)

[8] 'The neuter pronoun "this" may refer to one of three things: the "grace," the verb "saved," the noun "faith." It is Augustine's merit to have pointed out that the *gratia gratis data* includes the gift of "faith" to man. Faith is not a contribution of man to salvation, least of all a meritorious contribution. A true believer will never boast that his coming to faith, his solid stance in faith, and his (ethical) demonstration of faith are of his own doing . . . Still, the pronoun "this" in Eph. 2.8 need not have the restricted (anti-Pelagian) meaning. It may also refer to the eternal election by grace and the "outpouring" of grace mentioned in 1.4–8, and to the preaching of the "true word, the message that saves" (1.13).' (M. Barth, *Ephesians*, vol. 1, 225; also Ernst, *Philipper*, 309, and Schnackenburg, *Ephesians*, 98).

[9] 'But here in Ephesians, it is simply the term "works," not "works of the law," that is employed . . . "Works" now stands for human effort in general. Salvation is not achieved by human performance or any attempt to earn God's approval.' (Lincoln, *Ephesians*, 112) Ἔργον occurs four times in Ephesians (2.9–10; 4.12; 5.11) and is never associated with νόμος.

[10] Mitton, *Ephesians*, 226; Schnackenburg, *Ephesians*, 278–9; see also how M. Barth relates God's faithfulness to humanity's faith (*Ephesians*, vol. 2, 772–3).

[11] The Old Testament and, in particular, the Psalms contain many references to Yahweh in person or to one of his qualities as a shield (e.g. Gen. 15.1; 2 Sam. 22.3, 31, 36; Pss. 3.3; 5.12; 7.10; 18.2, 30; 28.7; 33.20; 59.11; 84.9, 11; 91.4; 115.10; 144.2; Prov. 2.7; 30.5; cf. Pss. 47.9; 89.19). On occasion, Yahweh's shieldlike protection is the basis for trust (e.g. Pss. 28.7; 33.20–21; 84.11–12; 115.10), and in Ps. 91.4 his faithfulness is likened to a shield.

should also be drawn to the benediction in Ephesians 6.23, where peace, love and faith are brought together. The precise relationship between these elements is uncertain, but there can be little doubt that all three are ἀπὸ θεοῦ πατρὸς καὶ κυρίου Ἰησοῦ Χριστοῦ. It may well be, therefore, that Ephesians supports a number of references to faith as a gift from God (2.8; 6.16, 23), although it is not clear at this stage in what sense πίστις should be understood as a divine attribute or prerogative.

With these observations in mind, we return to διὰ τῆς πίστεως in Ephesians 3.12. This verse forms part of a larger presentation in which the author's and the church's responsibilities in evangelism are encompassed within God's predetermined salvific purposes made known through Jesus Christ. From this perspective, it is Christ who constitutes the grounds (ἐν ᾧ) for τὴν παρρησίαν καὶ προσαγωγὴν ἐν πεποιθήσει.[12] But how should διὰ τῆς πίστεως αὐτοῦ be understood? Αὐτοῦ refers back to ἐν τῷ Χριστῷ Ἰησοῦ τῷ κυρίῳ ἡμῶν in the previous verse, inviting comparison with similar genitival constructions including Christ. Most of these require a possessive or subjective interpretation, although others are more ambiguous or must be rendered differently.[13] Moreover, διά followed by a reference to Christ in the genitive is frequently used in Ephesians to describe the means by which God's salvation is secured.[14] Ephesians 2.18 is particularly significant here in that it also talks about access (προσαγωγή) to God through Christ. Indeed, when considered in conjunction with other διά-constructions, the correspondence between 3.12 and 2.18 militates against interpreting διὰ τῆς πίστεως αὐτοῦ as an objective genitive (i.e. faith in him) and favours a reference to Christ's own faith (e.g. '...

[12] The context does not make it clear whether these qualities relate to the sphere of discipleship and mission or, more specifically, to the Christian's standing before God. Προσαγωγή occurs only three times in the New Testament and its usage here is reminiscent of Eph. 2.18 (cf. Rom. 5.2), where the means of salvation is in focus; see M. Barth, *Ephesians*, vol. 1, 347; Mitton, *Ephesians*, 128; Schnackenburg, *Ephesians*, 143.

[13] E.g. Παῦλος ἀπόστολος Χριστοῦ Ἰησοῦ (1.1); ἐν τῷ αἵματι τοῦ Χριστοῦ (2.13); τὸ ἀνεξιχνίαστον πλοῦτος τοῦ Χριστοῦ (3.8); τὴν ὑπερβάλλουσαν τῆς γνώσεως ἀγάπην τοῦ Χριστοῦ (3.19); κατὰ τὸ μέτρον τῆς δωρεᾶς τοῦ Χριστοῦ (4.7); εἰς οἰκοδομὴν τοῦ σώματος τοῦ Χριστοῦ (4.12); εἰς μέτρον ἡλικίας τοῦ πληρώματος τοῦ Χριστοῦ (4.13); ἐν ὀνόματι τοῦ κυρίου ἡμῶν Ἰησοῦ Χριστοῦ (5.20); ὡς δοῦλοι Χριστοῦ (6.6); cf. ὁ δέσμιος τοῦ Χριστοῦ (3.1); ἐν τῷ μυστηρίῳ τοῦ Χριστοῦ (3.4); ὑποτασσόμενοι ἀλλήλοις ἐν φόβῳ Χριστοῦ (5.21).

[14] E.g. adoption (1.5); redemption (1.7); reconciliation (2.16); access to God (2.18); spiritual strength (3.16); also, salvation (2.8); fellow-heirs (3.6); indwelling of Christ (3.17); cf. 1.1; 2.4; 3.10.

in whom [i.e. Jesus Christ] we have boldness and confidence of access [to God] through his [i.e. Christ's] faith [in which we share] . . .').[15]

Christ's faith may also be implied later on in the chapter, where the author prays that the Ephesian Christians will be resourced, according to God's riches in glory, to know the extent of Christ's love and God's fulness (3.14–21). At least two dimensions of this resourcing are specified and they reflect a similar structure (3.16–17):[16]

to be strengthened in/with power	διὰ τοῦ πνεύματος αὐτοῦ	εἰς τὸν ἔσω ἄνθρωπον
for Christ to inhabit	διὰ τῆς πίστεως	ἐν ταῖς καρδίαις ὑμῶν

If, in the first case, Christ's Spirit is the agent or means by which believers are strengthened, then, in the second, the author may be claiming that the indwelling presence of Christ is secured by Christ's faith.

It is possible, therefore, that reference to Christ's faith should be identified in διὰ τῆς πίστεως αὐτοῦ of 3.12 and διὰ τῆς πίστεως of 3.17; what remains unclear is what the author meant by this. Unlike the πίστις Χριστοῦ constructions in Romans, Galatians and Philippians, there is little indication from the immediate context as to the content of Christ's faith. The link between 3.12 and 2.18,[17] however, provides a way forward in that the latter verse comes towards the end of a section relating how God's reconciliation is established through the death of Christ. In fact, Ephesians 2.1–18 constitutes the only detailed examination of the 'mechanics' of salvation in Ephesians (cf. Eph. 1.7, 20)[18] and although it is by no means as comprehensive or nuanced as those found in the Pauline epistles, it does appear to undergird much of what the author goes on to say about the 'outworkings' of salvation. Consequently, unless Ephesians 2.1–18 is understood as the central reference point providing significance to and authority for the ramifications of God's grace through Christ discussed else-

[15] M. Barth renders Eph. 3.12 thus: 'In him and because of his faithfulness, confidently we make use of our free access [to God].' (*Ephesians*, vol. 1, 326) In support of this translation, he goes on to comment: 'Since in 2.18, in the closest parallel to 3.12, Christ alone is described as the mediator of the Jews' and Gentiles' access to God, and since (except in 1.1, 15, 19; 2.8) the faith of the believing church members has not yet been explicitly mentioned, it is unlikely that Paul should suddenly attribute to "their" faith alone a mediating function.' (*Ephesians*, vol. 1, 347; also Mitton, *Ephesians*, 128, and D. W. B. Robinson, 'Faith', 75)

[16] Gnilka, *Epheserbrief*, 182–5, and Lincoln, *Ephesians*, 206–7.

[17] M. Barth, *Ephesians*, vol. 1, 347, and Schnackenburg, *Ephesians*, 142.

[18] On the importance of this section, see Lincoln, *Ephesians*, xci-xcii and *loc cit*.

where in the letter, a comparable exposition would need to be assumed.

In the light of this, it seems reasonable to expect that the meaning of Christ's faith in 3.12 and 3.17 would be informed by 2.1–18[19] and, in particular, by Christ's death through which reconciliation was secured for all people (2.13–17). A more general interpretation of Christ's faith in terms of God's faithfulness is possibly implied,[20] but the stress is clearly upon the soteriological significance of the cross; in this respect, the author's understanding is similar to that expounded in Romans, Galatians and Philippians. It should also be noted that the exemplary function of Christ's faith is not explored, although his faith does provide the basis for the faith of believers. This observation, however, requires further clarification.

We have already mentioned that the author can speak unambiguously about the importance of the faith of believers (e.g. 1.13–15),[21] whilst also affirming that faith belongs within the dispensation of grace and must ultimately be seen as a gift from God (e.g. 2.8; 6.16, 23). Faith, then, is part of God's salvific provision which gains definition in relation to the person of Christ and, ostensibly, to his death; the author may even envisage the communication of divine love as an expression of faith (cf. 6.23). In Ephesians, faith both originates in and, to a certain extent, is given substance by Christ; but more than that, there is a sense in which all faith is grounded in him, for it is he who encompasses every aspect of God's salvation. This intimate relationship between Christ and the believer could explain why on occasion the faith of believers appears to be ignored. In contrast to the πίστις Χριστοῦ formulations, where reference to Christ's faith is associated with a separate reference to the faith of believers, there is only a single occurrence of the πιστεύω group in 3.12 and the surrounding verses.[22] Further, we have indicated why this is unlikely to refer primarily to faith in Christ, an assessment which resonates with the emphasis elsewhere

[19] Christ's faith is not the only phenomenon which needs to be understood in relation to the soteriological core of the letter; a similar approach is needed for Christ's mystery (3.4), riches (3.8), love (3.19), gift (4.7), knowledge (4.13) and fulness (4.13).

[20] For example, M. Barth's assessment of πίστις in 2.8 where he identifies three elements: God's faithfulness, Christ's faith(fulness) and human faith (*Ephesians*, vol. 1, 224–5).

[21] 'As regards acceptance of the Christian gospel, believing can be seen to be the vital link between hearing the word and receiving the Spirit.' (Lincoln, *Ephesians*, 39; also Gnilka, *Epheserbrief*, 85).

[22] We have already noted that Eph. 3.17 may well refer to Christ's faith.

in the chapter upon God's initiative.[23] However, whilst the faith of believers is unlikely to be the primary referent for πίστις in 3.12, it may be encompassed within the author's understanding of the inclusive nature of Christ's faith. That is to say, as with other aspects of salvation, the faith of believers is embraced within God's gracious provision in Christ.

If this assessment is accepted, a natural but none the less significant development in the relationship between the faith of Christ and that of the believer can be discerned in Ephesians. We noted in the case of Romans, Galatians and Philippians, that faith should be understood within the context of what it means to participate in Christ and that Christ's faith, epitomised in his suffering obedience on the cross, provides the grounds and context for all faith. Within this scenario, a distinction between the different expressions of faith is maintained. The evidence from Ephesians, however, suggests that the intimacy of the relationship between Christ and believers is so profound that the faith of the latter can be spoken of almost exclusively in terms of the faith of Christ – his response encompasses all human response. We may conclude, therefore, that for the author of Ephesians, faith has become a part of God's preordained purposes and pre-election in Christ.[24]

Pastoral Epistles: 1 and 2 Timothy

The absence of πίστις Χριστοῦ constructions from the Pastoral epistles necessitates a revised approach to our investigations into the faith of Christ.[25] This omission may simply be a matter of style, although we shall indicate possible theological grounds at a later

[23] E.g. God's grace and its expressions are given (3.2, 8, 9, 16–19), made known (3.3) and revealed (3.3, 5); further, God's eternal purposes are realised in Christ (3.11).

[24] See R. C. Tannehill's comments on Christ as the inclusive and representative man in Ephesians and Colossians (*Dying*, 47–54). In the light of the author's understanding of God's salvation fully realised in Christ, it does seem that the objective genitive interpretation for διὰ τῆς πίστεως αὐτοῦ in 3.12 is problematic. Rudolf Schnackenburg, for example, considers that the 'phrase "faith in him (Jesus Christ)" reminds us of the basic requirement for the achievement of salvation (2.8) and the constant basis of Christian existence (cf. 4.5; 6.16)' (*Ephesians*, 142); however, during his discussion of Eph. 2.8, he stresses that faith is a gift from God in Christ (98). If faith is a gift from God, it is not at all clear in what sense it can also be a 'requirement for the achievement of salvation'.

[25] The πιστεύω word group is well represented in the Pastorals: *1 Timothy* – πιστεύω (3): 1.11, 16; 3.16; πίστις (19): 1.2, 4, 5, 14, 19[x2]; 2.7, 15; 3.9, 13; 4.1, 6, 12; 5.8, 12; 6.10, 11, 12, 21; πιστός (11): 1.12, 15; 3.1, 11; 4.3, 9, 10, 12; 5.16; 6.2[x2]; ἀπιστία (1): 1.13; ἄπιστος (1): 5.8; *2 Timothy* – πιστεύω (1): 1.12; πίστις (8): 1.5, 13; 2.18, 22; 3.8, 10, 15; 4.7; πιστός (3): 2.2, 11, 13; πιστόω (1): 3.14; ἀπιστέω (1): 2.13; Titus

stage. For the present, however, let us turn our attention to a number of similar formulations in which an anarthrous occurrence of πίστις is qualified by an attributive prepositional phrase including Χριστῷ Ἰησοῦ:

1 Tim. 1.14	ἡ χάρις τοῦ κυρίου ἡμῶν μετὰ πίστεως καὶ ἀγάπης τῆς ἐν Χριστῷ Ἰησοῦ
1 Tim. 3.13	καὶ πολλὴν παρρησίαν ἐν πίστει τῇ ἐν Χριστῷ Ἰησοῦ
2 Tim. 1.13	ὧν παρ' ἐμοῦ ἤκουσας ἐν πίστει καὶ ἀγάπῃ τῇ ἐν Χριστῷ Ἰησοῦ
2 Tim. 3.15	εἰς σωτηρίαν διὰ πίστεως τῆς ἐν Χριστῷ Ἰησοῦ

The placement of the article after πίστις and not before[26] underlines the qualificatory nature of what follows and cautions against an interpretation along the lines of 'faith in Christ Jesus'. A review of similar constructions in the Pastorals suggests that the dative qualifier denotes the context and/or the content of that which is qualified.[27] Of particular interest here are 2 Timothy 1.1 (κατ' ἐπαγγελίαν ζωῆς τῆς ἐν Χριστῷ Ἰησοῦ) and 2.10 (καὶ αὐτοὶ σωτηρίας τύχωσιν τῆς ἐν Χριστῷ Ἰησοῦ), where the 'promise of life' and 'salvation' are intimately associated with being in Christ. It is possible, therefore, that a similar sense is intended for the πίστις constructions under review.

Further insight into the meaning of these phrases is afforded by context. 1 Timothy 1.14 is set within an autobiographical section describing how Paul[28] came to faith (1.12–17). The emphasis throughout is upon divine initiative in the face of human opposition as the grace of Christ superabounds μετὰ πίστεως καὶ ἀγάπης τῆς ἐν Χριστῷ Ἰησοῦ (1.14). Given that πίστις and ἀγάπη are spoken about here within a situation of human alienation (ἀπιστίᾳ, 1.13), they probably constitute the outworkings of grace and not responses to it.[29] These same expressions of the Lord's graciousness

– πιστεύω (2): 1.3; 3.8; πίστις (6): 1.1, 4, 13; 2.2, 10; 3.15; πιστός (3): 1.6, 9; 3.8; ἄπιστος (1): 1.15. On the meaning of faith in the Pastorals, see: Bultmann, 'πιστεύω', esp. 213–14; Kretschmar, 'Glaube', 115–40; von Lips, *Glaube*, 25–93; Towner, *Goal*, 121–47; S. G. Wilson, *Luke*, 28–31; Wolter, *Pastoralbriefe*, esp. 38–40.

26 Or, indeed, both before and after (cf. ἐν τῇ χάριτι τῇ ἐν Χριστῷ Ἰησοῦ; 2 Tim. 2.1).

27 E.g. ἢ οἰκονομίαν θεοῦ τὴν ἐν πίστει (1 Tim. 1.4); καὶ πάντων τῶν ἐν ὑπεροχῇ ὄντων (1 Tim. 2.2); πρὸς παιδείαν τὴν ἐν δικαιοσύνῃ (2 Tim. 3.16); οὐκ ἐξ ἔργων τῶν ἐν δικαιοσύνῃ (Tit 3.5); cf. μὴ ἀμέλει τοῦ ἐν σοὶ χαρίσματος (1 Tim. 4.14); ὑπόμνησιν λαβὼν τῆς ἐν σοὶ ἀνυποκρίτου πίστεως (2 Tim. 1.5).

28 Although the Pastorals may not have been written by Paul, the biographical sections are framed in terms of his life and, as such, he is at least the implied author.

29 Dibelius and Conzelmann, *Pastoral Epistles*, 28, and Roloff, *Timotheus*, 95. In some ways, this distinction is artificial as faith and love may be the outworkings of grace seen in human response to God; a response which is itself enabled by that

in Paul's ministry may result in others coming to faith, but only because of Christ working through him (1.16). It is, then, the initiative of Christ within Paul's life which is the basis for his relationship with God and discipleship:[30] Christ Jesus demonstrated mercy (ἠλεήθην, 1.13, 16), considered[31] him faithful for service (πιστόν, 1.12) and entrusted him with the gospel (ἐπιστεύθην, 1.11). It seems likely, therefore, that πίστεως καὶ ἀγάπης represent characteristics of Christ and his enabling presence within the life of the Christian, rather than human responses to God's grace in Christ.[32] As we shall see, this neither implies possession against the will of the believer, nor that faith and love cannot be spoken of as human qualities; but it does underline the author's conviction that they are fundamentally linked with the person of Christ.[33] For him, faith and love belong to Christ and their meaning is intimately tied up with his soteriological significance.

The notion of Christ as the one giving faith definition and substance is also present in 1 Timothy 3.13, where it is pointed out that conscientious deacons gain in standing and confidence ἐν πίστει τῇ ἐν Χριστῷ 'Ιησοῦ. As the context makes clear, this confidence (παρρησία) is not based upon believing in Christ or in the right things about him, but on practising a particular mode of existence which is defined by Christ.[34] This correspondence alerts us to the

grace. The point we wish to make, however, is that faith and love stem from divine rather than human initiative.

30 Hasler, *Timotheus*, 14–15, and Kelly, *Pastoral Epistles*, 51–6.

31 The verb ἡγέομαι in 1 Tim. 1.12 does not necessarily imply a value judgement concerning the appropriateness of the one who is considered πιστός; it may simply denote the prerogative of the subject. This appears to be the force of the verb in the only other occurrence in the Pastorals, where slaves are to regard (ἡγείσθωσαν) their masters as worthy of honour for the sake of the gospel and not because they are necessarily deserving of it (1 Tim. 6.1).

32 'By saying that ἀγάπη and πίστις are ἐν Χριστῷ 'Ιησοῦ, Paul indicates that their sources are in Christ because of his being in Christ.' (Knight, *Pastoral Epistles*, 99; also Brox, *Pastoralbriefe*, 110–11, and Roloff, *Timotheus*, 95).

33 'The *faith* and *love* are characterized as *in Christ Jesus* (cf. 2 Tim. 1.13), a phrase which, as the translation attempts to bring out, is much more than a periphrasis for "Christian". Those who limit its meaning argue that where "in Christ" has the full mystical sense usual in Paul it is used of persons, not qualities. But faith and love are not qualities hanging in the air but always belong to persons; even if he remains unmentioned, their personal possessor is always implied. It is here suggested that they are the visible expression of the Christian's living relationship with his Saviour.' (Kelly, *Pastoral Epistles*, 53–4; *contra* Dibelius and Conzelmann, *Pastoral Epistles*, 28, who understand faith and love here and elsewhere in terms of Christian virtues)

34 See the comments of C. Spicq, who notes that the phrase ἐν πίστει τῇ ἐν Χριστῷ 'Ιησοῦ may be intended as a corrective against a misplaced confidence on the part

emphasis within the Pastorals upon the definition of faith[35] and concurs with the commonly held view that the author is concerned with faith as *fides quae creditur*.[36] It is crucial, however, that the parameters of faith's definition are correctly understood. Great emphasis is placed throughout the epistles upon the importance of sound instruction,[37] and on a number of occasions πίστις is spoken of in these terms (e.g. 1 Tim. 3.9; 4.6; 6.21; Tit. 1.13).[38] And yet in other passages where the content of faith is under review, the focus rests equally on teaching and conduct (e.g. 1 Tim. 4.1; 6.10, 12; 2 Tim. 4.7) or simply on conduct (e.g. 1 Tim. 5.8). All this suggests that the author was equally concerned to explore both the doctrinal and practical dimensions of faith. And in order to accommodate these elements, he does not formulate or make reference to a particular body of teaching about Christ, but rather takes Christ himself as the canon for both orthodoxy and orthopraxy.[39]

For this reason, the standing of deacons in 1 Timothy 3.8–16 is not simply based on whether they possess qualities and beliefs appropriate for that office,[40] but on whether they exhibit a confidence which is rooted in the conviction that by adopting a par-

of believers; he concludes: 'Dans ce contexte, la *pistis* serait plutôt la *foi-charisme* qui opère des miracles au service du Royaume de Dieu (Lc. 17.5–6; 1 Cor. 12.9; 13.2; cf. Jo. 14.12).' (*Épîtres Pastorales*, vol. 1, 463)

35 See the thorough and nuanced discussions of Towner, *Goal*, esp. 145–68, and von Lips, *Glaube*, 25–93.

36 Bultmann, 'πιστεύω', 213–4, and S. G. Wilson, *Luke*, 30. References to πίστις as *fides quae creditur* include 1 Tim. 3.9; 4.1, 6; 5.8; 6.10, 12, 21; 2 Tim. 4.7; Tit 1.13. It is probable that at least some of the following occurrences of πίστις without the article should also be interpreted in this way: 1 Tim. 1.2, 4, 14; 3.13; 2 Tim. 1.13; 3.15; Tit 1.1, 4; 3.15.

37 Ὑγιαίνω occurs eight times (1 Tim. 1.10; 6.3; 2 Tim. 1.13; 4.3; Tit 1.9, 13; 2.1, 2) and ὑγιής once (Tit 2.8); they qualify διδασκαλία (1 Tim. 1.10; 2 Tim. 4.3; Tit 1.9; 2.1; cf. 1 Tim. 4.6), λόγος (1 Tim. 6.3; 2 Tim. 1.13; Tit 2.8) or πίστις (Tit 1.13; 2.2). On the meaning of ὑγιαίνω and ὑγιής in the Pastorals, see Dibelius and Conzelmann, *Pastoral Epistles*, 24–5.

38 Also πιστὸς ὁ λόγος (1 Tim. 1.15; 3.1; 4.9; 2 Tim. 2.11; Tit 3.8; cf. Tit 1.9).

39 In this way, the author ensures that the dynamic and relational dimensions are accommodated within the definition of faith: 'Generally, *pistis* expresses the proper alignment of the individual with Christ and the message about him.' (Towner, *Goal*, 146; also Guthrie, *Pastoral Epistles*, 86). This point has been missed by many exegetes with the result that the definition of faith is perceived in static categories which are detached from – rather than informed by – existential encounter with Christ (e.g. G. Barth, 'πίστις', 230; Bultmann, 'πιστεύω', 213; S. G. Wilson, *Luke*, 30).

40 The ethical dimensions of the diaconate are spelt out in 1 Tim. 3.8, 10–12; the correspondence between τὸ μυστήριον τῆς πίστεως in 1 Tim. 3.9 and the exposition of τὸ τῆς εὐσεβείας μυστήριον in 1 Tim. 3.16 may indicate something of the theological content.

ticular way of life they participate in a faith which originates in Christ Jesus himself.[41] Furthermore, Christ is not simply conceived of as the object of or stimulus for this faith, but as the one who gives faith its theological and ethical content. For this reason, the Pastorals contain many references to Christ's personal qualities: he demonstrates τὴν ἅπασαν μακροθυμίαν (1 Tim. 1.16), his testimony before Pontius Pilate makes τὴν καλὴν ὁμολογίαν (1 Tim. 6.13; also 2 Tim. 1.8), his ὑγιαίνοντες λόγοι constitute the norm against which other teaching must be assessed (1 Tim. 6.3; also 2 Tim. 1.13) and he is the source of ἀγάπη, πίστις and χάρις.[42]

It also seems to be the case that as faith finds its definition in Christ, so it may also be spoken of as a gift from him. Consider, for example, 2 Timothy 1.13 where Timothy is exhorted to adhere to a pattern of sound words (ὑποτύπωσιν ἔχε ὑγιαινόντων λόγων). The relationship between the following ἐν πίστει καὶ ἀγάπῃ τῇ ἐν Χριστῷ Ἰησοῦ and the rest of the verse is ambiguous for at least two reasons: firstly, it is not clear whether faith and love are the result of or the means for continuing in an orthodox manner; and, secondly, faith and love can be understood as either Christian virtues or gifts from God.[43] As we shall see, the resolution of the first dichotomy is related to the second and, from our perspective, more significant one.

The author reminds Timothy that the gospel for which they suffer and bear witness concerns God's saving action in Jesus Christ (2 Tim. 1.8–11). He then goes on to explain that their ability to continue in the tasks entrusted to them is not based upon their resolve, but upon God's enabling and sustaining presence.[44] It is God who, in the form of the Holy Spirit, guards what has been entrusted to them and provides inspiration for its practical expression (1.12, 14). The same Spirit also bestows power, love and self-control (1.7), whilst grace is given ἐν Χριστῷ Ἰησοῦ (1.9). Thus, it seems probable that when Timothy is exhorted to maintain a particular pattern of teaching (1.13), the means for doing so will

41 Brox, *Pastoralbriefe*, 155, and Roloff, *Timotheus*, 168.

42 E.g. ἀγάπη (2 Tim. 1.13), πίστις (1 Tim. 1.14; 3.13; 2 Tim. 1.13; 3.15) and χάρις (2 Tim. 1.9; 2.1; Tit 1.4; cf. 2 Tim. 4.22).

43 On these options see: Brox, *Pastoralbriefe*, 235; Dibelius and Conzelmann, *Pastoral Epistles*, 97, 105; Guthrie, *Pastoral Epistles*, 133; Kelly, *Pastoral Epistles*, 166–7; Spicq, *Épîtres Pastorales*, vol. 2, 721.

44 Παραθήκη (2 Tim. 1.12, 14) should probably be equated with the vocations of the author and Timothy in relation to the gospel (2 Tim. 1.6, 9, 11); von Lips, *Glaube*, 268–70, and Towner, *Goal*, 124–6.

resemble those already mentioned in relation to his salvation and vocation, namely, that God will provide the necessary 'activation energy'. That is to say, Timothy will be able to remain steadfast in sound teaching because of a faith and love which originate in Christ Jesus himself.

In order to grasp the author's understanding of faith and the overall nexus of human response in 2 Timothy 1.8–14, therefore, it is necessary to distinguish between three perspectives: firstly, God's gift of salvation in Christ (1.9–10); secondly, humanity's inability to secure salvation for itself (οὐ κατὰ τὰ ἔργα ἡμῶν, 1.9); and, thirdly, response to God's salvific initiative in Christ which is itself empowered by God (1.12–14). The difference between the second and third perspectives is critical and whilst it is clear in the present context,[45] this is not the case elsewhere. For instance, what is the significance of the author's emphasis throughout the Pastorals upon human endeavour in relation to following the faith?

The author encourages Christians to embrace the faith wholeheartedly using language which speaks of personal achievement as much as of commitment.[46] He spells out the necessity for dedication in terms indicative of desert and reward (2 Tim. 2.3–6, 15). Discussions of the requisite qualities of bishops, deacons and elders, together with servants, the wealthy, widows, women and believers in general are presented.[47] Great stress is placed upon the need for good deeds to abound[48] and for conduct to be such that opponents are not given grounds for criticism (Tit. 2.8). Sound doctrine and training must be adhered to,[49] and false or unwholesome teaching rebuked or shunned.[50] On top of this, many traditional Christian qualities are spoken of as goals in their own right: 'So shun youthful passions and aim (δίωκε) at righteousness, faith, love and peace, along with those who call upon the name of the Lord with a pure

45 Although not articulated in these terms, this distinction is recognised by: Hasler, *Timotheus*, 57–60; Kelly, *Pastoral Epistles*, 160–7; Spicq, *Épîtres Pastorales*, vol. 2, 714–21; *contra* Dibelius and Conzelmann, *Pastoral Epistles*, 99–105.

46 E.g. γυμνάζω (1 Tim. 4.7), κοπιάω (1 Tim. 4.9), ἀγωνίζομαι (1 Tim. 4.9; 6.12), φυλάσσω (1 Tim. 5.21), διώκω (1 Tim. 6.11; 2 Tim. 2.22), φεύγω (1 Tim. 6.11; 2 Tim. 2.22), λατρεύω (e.g. 2 Tim. 1.3), συγκακοπαθέω (2 Tim. 1.8; 2.3; cf. 2 Tim. 4.5), ὑπομένω (2 Tim. 2.12), ἐκκαθαίρω (2 Tim. 2.21), and σπένδω (2 Tim. 4.6).

47 Bishops (1 Tim. 3.1–7; Tit 1.7–9), deacons (1 Tim. 3.8–13), elders (1 Tim. 5.17–24; Tit 1.5–6), servants (1 Tim. 6.1–2), the wealthy (1 Tim. 6.9–10, 17–19), widows (1 Tim. 5.1–16), women (1 Tim. 2.8–15), and believers in general (Tit 2.2–10; 3.1–2).

48 1 Tim. 2.10; 5.10, 25; 2 Tim. 3.16; Tit 2.7; 3.8.

49 1 Tim. 4.6–8, 11–16; 5.21; 2 Tim. 1.13–14; 3.14–17; Tit 2.1.

50 1 Tim. 1.4–7; 4.1–3, 7; 6.3–5, 20–1; 2 Tim. 2.14–3.9; 4.3–4; Tit 1.10–16; 3.9.

heart.'[51] In this passage, Timothy is encouraged to acquire by personal efforts not simply faith and love, but also righteousness and peace. This stress upon self-attainment is reflected elsewhere in terms of the relation between a believer's conduct and the attainment of God's blessings. Indeed, on occasion, it is so pronounced that the author appears to be propounding a form of self-righteousness vehemently opposed in Romans, Galatians and Philippians:

> For I am already on the point of being sacrificed; the time of my departure has come. I have fought the good fight, I have finished the race, I have kept the faith. Henceforth there is laid up for me the crown of righteousness, which the Lord, the righteous judge, will award to me on that Day, and not only to me but also to all who have loved his appearing. (2 Tim. 4.6–8; also 1 Tim. 2.3, 15; 4.8–16; 6.18–19; 2 Tim. 2.3–6)

It was inevitable that the delay of the Parousia would require church leaders sooner or later to focus not simply on the means of salvation, but also on the content of the saved life or, expressed differently, on how believers should behave.[52] The ethical outworkings of salvation are clearly foremost in the mind of our author when, for example, the appropriate characteristics and responsibilities for Christians following different vocations are defined. And yet the freedom to speak about the nature and content of the Christian life so fully and in such causal terms without espousing self-justification is only possible because it is undergirded by an adequate understanding of God's salvation in Christ Jesus, which forms the basis for all human response and initiative.[53] And this is what we find in the Pastorals.

The epithet σωτήρ is used frequently by the author[54] and God's

[51] 2 Tim. 2.22; also 1 Tim. 4.8–12; 6.11; 2 Tim. 3.10–17. Qualities spoken of in this way include: ἀγάπη (1 Tim. 2.15; 4.12; 6.11; 2 Tim. 2.22), ἁγιασμός (1 Tim. 2.15), ἁγνεία (1 Tim. 4.12), δικαιοσύνη (1 Tim. 6.11; 2 Tim. 2.22), εἰρήνη (2 Tim. 2.22), εὐσέβεια (1 Tim. 6.3, 6, 11), πίστις (1 Tim. 1.5, 19; 2.15; 4.12; 6.11; 2 Tim. 2.22; cf. 1 Tim. 1.12), πραϋπαθία (1 Tim. 6.11), συνείδησις (1 Tim. 1.5, 19; 2 Tim. 1.3), and ὑπομονή (1 Tim. 6.11).

[52] Especially, Towner, *Goal*, 9–16.

[53] Substantial discussions of salvation in the Pastoral epistles can be found in: Dibelius and Conzelmann, *Pastoral Epistles*, 100–3; von Lips, *Glaube*, 87–93; Spicq, *Épîtres Pastorales*, vol. 1, 257–62; Wolter, *Pastoralbriefe*, 64–95. P. H. Towner refers to salvation as 'the centerpoint of the message' in the Pastorals (*Goal*, 75–119).

[54] God: 1 Tim. 1.1; 2.3; 4.10; Tit 1.3; 2.10; 3.4. Christ: 2 Tim. 1.10; Tit 1.4; 2.13; 3.6.

desire for humanity to be saved is stressed on a number of occasions, sometimes with pronounced universalist implications.[55] Christ is presented as the one true mediator (1 Tim. 2.5) whose death and resurrection secure salvation (e.g. 1 Tim. 1.6; 2 Tim. 2.8; Tit. 2.14), and pass judgement upon all human attempts to secure standing before God (e.g. 2 Tim. 1.9–10; Tit. 3.4–7). God also freely bestows gifts of grace, love, mercy, peace, power, self-control and strength.[56]

At first glance, the author's emphasis upon both the efficacy of God's work in Christ and the significance of human endeavour appears to be contradictory or, at least, inconsistent. However, in terms of the three perspectives outlined above (i.e. God's gift of salvation in Christ – human impotence – divinely inspired response to the gift of salvation), this is only sustainable if the human dimension is divorced from the divine and not enabled by it. But, in the Pastorals, God's salvific initiatives in Christ encompass not only the divine–human movement, as the possibility of salvation is established, but also the human–divine movement, as individuals are enabled to respond. Furthermore, as Christ informs and enables the latter as much as the former, the substance of the Christian life can be discussed in detail and given a high profile without fear of it being misunderstood in terms of self-justification.

In consequence, when the author exhorts Timothy to pursue, amongst other things, faith and love (e.g. 1 Tim. 6.11; 2 Tim. 2.22), it is on the basis that these qualities originate in God's salvific provision and can neither be engendered by the individual in isolation nor acquired as a reward for human endeavour. Rather, they are mediated through Christ and can only be experienced in relation to him.[57] Further, it is this dual perspective in which response to God can be viewed from divine and human angles which is captured in the phrase ἐν πίστει καὶ ἀγάπῃ τῇ ἐν Χριστῷ Ἰησοῦ (2 Tim. 1.13) and its variants. As Timothy is exhorted to guard what has been entrusted to him διὰ πνεύματος ἁγίου τοῦ ἐνοικοῦντος ἐν ἡμῖν (2 Tim. 1.14), so he should also adopt a pattern of sound

[55] 1 Tim. 2.4; 4.10; Tit 2.11; also 1 Tim. 1.15; 6.13; 2 Tim. 4.18 (see S. G. Wilson, *Luke*, 23).

[56] Χάρις (1 Tim. 1.2, 14; 2 Tim. 1.9; 2.1; 4.22; Tit 1.4), ἀγάπη (2 Tim. 1.7; cf. 1 Tim. 1.14; 2 Tim. 1.13), ἔλεος (1 Tim. 1.2), εἰρήνη (1 Tim. 1.2; Tit 1.4), δύναμις (2 Tim. 1.7), σωφρονισμός (2 Tim. 1.7), and ἐνδυναμόω (1 Tim. 1.12; 2 Tim. 4.17).

[57] Fee, *1 and 2 Timothy*, 113; Kelly, *Pastoral Epistles*, 140–1; Knight, *Pastoral Epistles*, 381.

teaching by a faith and love which originate in and are defined by Christ Jesus.[58]

This dual perspective is also evident in 2 Timothy 3.15, where our construction forms part of the larger clause, εἰς σωτηρίαν διὰ πίστεως τῆς ἐν Χριστῷ Ἰησοῦ, qualifying τὰ (i.e. [τὰ] ἱερὰ γράμματα) δυνάμενά σε σοφίσαι. Both purposive and teleological senses are possible for εἰς,[59] although, as sacred writings make Timothy wise εἰς σωτηρίαν διὰ πίστεως, the stress falls on human response. This suggests that the content of the saved life, in contrast to the means of salvation, is in view. Verse 16 supports this interpretation with the significance of πᾶσα γραφή expounded in ethical terms. But how does faith relate to the moderation of the saved life? On the basis of other occurrences of διά with the genitive, a good case can be made for rendering διὰ πίστεως here as 'by means of faith',[60] where faith constitutes the disposition by which salvation becomes and remains a reality for the believer.[61] In this way, the author emphasises the importance of human response, whilst also indicating that faith is not simply in Christ, but πίστεως τῆς ἐν Χριστῷ Ἰησοῦ. Once again, Christ cannot be abstracted from faith and considered the object of belief; rather, the faith which appropriates salvation is one which has its source and substance in the faith of Christ Jesus himself. Timothy, therefore, is encouraged to live out the faith of the one who first believed and, like Christ himself, the scriptures provide a sound resource for its exposition.[62]

58 'Paul is saying very plainly that the attitudes and actions of "faith" and "love" found in Christ are essential to one who is to preserve the apostolic standard.' (Knight, *Pastoral Epistles*, 98–9, 381)

59 The following schedule should be taken as a rough indication of interpretative trends. Εἰς with a predominantly teleological sense: 1 Tim. 1.3, 6, 12, 15, 17; 2.4; 3.6, 7; 5.24; 6.9; 2 Tim. 1.12; 3.6, 7; 4.10, 12, 18; Tit 3.12. Εἰς with a predominantly purposive sense: 1 Tim. 1.16; 2.7; 4.3, 10; 6.12, 17, 19; 2 Tim. 1.11; 2.20, 21, 26; 4.11; Tit 3.14.

60 Knight, *Pastoral Epistles*, 444; διά with the genitive has a similar force in the following verses: 1 Tim. 4.5, 14; 2 Tim. 1.1, 6, 10, 14; 2.2; 4.17; Tit 3.5, 6. The emphasis upon the human dimension in salvation is probably most pronounced in 1 Tim. 2.15: 'Yet women will be saved through bearing children (διὰ τῆς τεκνογονίας).'

61 Most commentators translate διὰ πίστεως τῆς ἐν Χριστῷ Ἰησοῦ along the lines of 'through faith in Christ Jesus' without explaining the force of διά, the presence of τῆς or how faith relates to the ongoing nature of salvation.

62 A similar understanding of human response empowered by divine initiative may be present in the author's conviction that, whilst πᾶσα γραφή has been written down by human agency, it is at the same time θεόπνευστος (2 Tim. 3.16); see also 2 Tim. 3.12, καὶ πάντες δὲ οἱ θέλοντες εὐσεβῶς ζῆν ἐν Χριστῷ Ἰησοῦ διωχθήσονται.

We have now discussed the four cases of πίστις qualified by an attributive prepositional phrase including Χριστῷ Ἰησοῦ and, in doing so, have considered the principal evidence from the Pastorals suggestive of Christ's faith. Our investigations lead us to conclude that the author does refer to the faith of Christ Jesus, but in a different way to Paul and one which can be explained, at least in part, by the different purposes and subject matter of the various letters. In the case of Romans, Galatians, Philippians and, to a lesser extent, Ephesians, the faith of Christ is understood in relation to how God's salvation is disclosed and made available through the cross. It is intimately linked with Christ's obedience, which is in turn identified with his suffering, shedding of blood and death. By this demonstration of faith, God's righteousness or covenantal faithfulness reaches out to embrace all people, Gentile and Jew alike. Furthermore, owing to the representative and inclusive nature of Christ's humanity, the faith of believers is enabled by and encompassed within Christ's own faith. As we have seen, whilst there is a participatory dimension to Paul's thinking here, Christ's faith neither replaces nor can be equated with the believers' faith.

In the Pastoral epistles, however, the emphasis – as their modern title betrays – is upon the content of the saved life and the need to prescribe appropriate responses to God's gifts of salvation and calling. Within this context, Christ's faith is not explicitly linked with his death nor the means by which salvation is wrought, but with the definition of faith itself, both in terms of orthodoxy and orthopraxy. As a result, it is not so much a matter of Christ's faith securing the possibility of faith for others, but of faith which has Christ as its source, content and object. We noted previously with reference to Ephesians that the distinction between Christ's faith and that of the believer begins to disappear; a further development takes place in the Pastorals, where the author does not speak of Christ's faith and the faith of Christians, but only of faith which can in no sense be divorced from the person of Christ and must make reference to him at every stage. Faith, therefore, is not only a personal or subjective quality, but also something – or almost someone – to be explored and lived out. To a certain extent it can be quantified in terms of doctrine and given ethical substance in terms of appropriate conduct, but the person of Christ always remains its canon. Finally, one implication of this emphasis upon the definition of faith is that, whilst Christ remains central, his personal life of faith becomes absorbed within a broader reality of faith. In this way, as the various expressions of Jesus' ministry provide guidance for but do not exhaust the parameters of discipleship, so πίστις ἡ ἐν Χριστῷ Ἰησοῦ necessarily transcends his life of faith and encompasses faith as it finds expression in the relationship between the believer and the risen Christ.

5

JESUS' FAITH IN HEBREWS AND REVELATION

1 The Epistle to the Hebrews

The Letter to the Hebrews furnishes us with the most explicit references to Jesus' faith in the New Testament. Pride of place goes to the description of Jesus as τὸν τῆς πίστεως ἀρχηγὸν καὶ τελειωτήν in Hebrews 12.2, which is supported by mention of him as πιστὸς ἀρχιερεύς in 2.17 and, as we shall see, 3.2 and 6. We shall attempt to examine these passages in relation to key lines of christological and soteriological thinking developed by the author in response to the pastoral situation addressed by the letter.[1]

1.1 Jesus as Πιστός (Hebrews 2.17, 3.2 and 6)

The comparison between Jesus and the angels at the outset of the epistle (1.4–14) is followed by one involving Jesus and humanity (2.10–3.6); whereas the former establishes Jesus' ultimate superiority, the latter stresses his total identification with mortal flesh through incarnation.[2] Almost from the beginning, therefore, the author underlines the importance of Jesus' earthly existence and, as we shall see, this dimension is of central importance for much of

[1] Although no consensus over the situation addressed by Hebrews has been reached as yet (see Guthrie, *Introduction*, 698–711; and, more recently: Attridge, *Hebrews*, 9–13; Lane, *Hebrews*, vol. 1, li-lxvi; Lindars, *Theology*, 1–21), there can be little doubt that the effects of some form of external challenge, possibly including persecution (cf. 10.32–9; 12.1–11), together with an ostensible lack of commitment on the part of believers (cf. 2.1–4; 4.14–16; 6.1–12; 10.19–31) were determining factors.

[2] Incarnation is taken to be the significance of the repeated reference to Jesus becoming subordinated (ἐλαττόω) to the angels for a period (2.7, 9); see also 2.11, 14; 10.5. Attridge, *Hebrews*, 79–82; P. E. Hughes, *Hebrews*, 87–94; Westcott, *Hebrews*, 45.

what follows.[3] Jesus' humanity is taken up first of all in relation to his high-priestly function. Through his incarnate life, he shares in the common lot of all (2.11, 14, 17). He experiences suffering (2.10, 18) and temptation (2.18; 4.15). He learns obedience and, through these things, becomes perfect (2.10; 5.8–9). Whilst he was God's son before creation (1.2, 5–6; 5.5), Jesus has to become a high priest (2.17; 5.7–10).[4] And although the primary locus for his high-priestly ministry is heaven (7.23–6; 8.1–6; 9.11–14), the author probably understood Jesus' death as his inauguration into this role. It was the offering of himself and spilling of his blood which constitute the effective, atoning sacrifice for the sins of all (2.9–10; 10.10–21).[5] Without this death, there could be no re-establishment of covenantal relationship between humanity and God, represented by Jesus' subsequent ascension and perfection.[6]

One interpretative difficulty concerns whether or not the author understood Jesus' earthly life of obedience as a part of his high-priestly ministry.[7] Although the exact moment is not defined, the nature of atoning sacrifice encompassing both the sacrificial act of sin offering and subsequent entry of the priest into the holiest place (cf. Lev. 16.15), together with the stress upon the heavenly session for his duties, supports the view that Jesus' death marks his assumption to this role.[8] Within this scenario, his earthly tour becomes the essential prerequisite to his fulfilling this function as, in terms of the definition of high-priesthood provided in Hebrews 5.1–2, it is the locus for his perfecting and, consequently, for his eligibility to offer a pure sacrifice for the sins of all (5.8–10; 9.11–14). Moreover,

[3] On the humanity of Jesus in the theology of Hebrews, see: Anderson, *Jesus*, 280–8; Grässer, 'Jesus', 63–91; G. Hughes, *Hebrews*, esp. 75–100; Luck, 'Geschehen', 192–215; Pollard, *Humanity*, 73–87; Rissi, *Theologie*, 28–45; Terveen, Jesus, esp. 266–83.

[4] On the high-priestly function of the son of God and the relationship between these two designations, see: Attridge, *Hebrews*, 146–7; Lane, *Hebrews*, vol. 1, esp. cxxxix-cxliv; Loader, *Sohn*, esp. 251–60; Milligan, *Theology*, 101–33. Although it remains unclear whether the author also considered Jesus' high-priesthood in ontological terms, the emphasis does seem to fall on the functional dimension. As we shall note during the discussion of Heb. 3.1–5, it is possible that sonship and high-priesthood relate to Jesus as ontological and functional categories.

[5] Loader, *Sohn*, 161–202, and Rissi, *Theologie*, 70–8.

[6] Lindars, *Theology*, 71–101, and Peterson, *Hebrews*, 119, 129, 143. For detailed examinations of the covenant theme in Hebrews, see: Dunnill, *Covenant*, esp. part III; J. J. Hughes, 'Hebrews 9.15ff', 28–66; Lehne, *Covenant*, esp. 93–124.

[7] This is the view of those identifying the incarnation as the occasion when Jesus becomes high priest (Montefiore, *Hebrews*, 125–6, and Spicq, *Hébreux*, vol. 2, 111, 193).

[8] Käsemann, *Wandering*, 228; Peterson, *Hebrews*, 191–5; Schrenk, 'ἱερός', 276.

because he has travelled the journey before each believer, Jesus is capable of performing his continuing sacerdotal ministry of intercession and provision of help in heaven (4.15–16; 7.25).[9]

The emphasis upon heaven, however, does not mean that the author considered Jesus' high-priesthood to constitute an expression of his divinity. On the contrary, it is clear that Jesus is able to maintain this role because of his continuing solidarity with humanity.[10] In contrast to other priests whose ministries are curtailed by death (7.23–8), Jesus is able to perpetuate his mediatory function in the heavenly sanctuary as one from the order of Melchizedek (7.11–22) who now serves in an exalted and perfected state. Thus, access to God through Jesus is not simply a function of his death, but of his continuing representation of humanity (10.19–25). And whilst the author distinguishes between these two dimensions, they are in effect part of the same sacerdotal function: Jesus' perpetual intercession is a direct implication of his sacrificial death, followed by exaltation, and has no independent salvific efficacy apart from it.[11]

It is this high-priestly office which provides the framework within which Jesus is considered as πιστός in Hebrews 2.17, 3.2 and, by implication, 3.6.[12] Jesus' oneness with humanity through the incarnation and his life of suffering and temptation are developed in Hebrews 2.9–18. This solidarity is not presented as an end in itself, but as the prerequisite to his becoming a mediator.[13] That is to say, Jesus is not simply one with all people, but one with them so that he

[9] The crux for our own investigation is not so much the moment when Jesus became high priest, as the recognition that his earthly tour was essential for this ministry.

[10] P. E. Hughes, *Hebrews*, 349–54, and Peterson, *Hebrews*, 104–25.

[11] Lane, *Hebrews*, vol. 1, 189–91, and Peterson, *Hebrews*, 114–17. Jesus' heavenly ministry may, therefore, be likened to the presence of the high priest within the Holy of Holies on the Day of Atonement and understood to represent the continuing reality of communion with God.

[12] The occurrences of the πιστεύω group in Hebrews can be summarised as follows: πιστεύω (2): 4.3; 11.6; πίστις (32): 4.2; 6.1, 12; 10.22, 38, 39; 11.1, 3, 4, 5, 6, 7[x2], 8, 9, 11, 13, 17, 20, 21, 22, 23, 24, 27, 28, 29, 30, 31, 33, 39; 12.2; 13.7; πιστός (5): 2.17; 3.2, 5; 10.23; 11.11; ἀπιστία (2): 3.12, 19. The significance of faith in the epistle has received considerable scholarly attention; see, for example: Attridge, *Hebrews*, 311–14; O. Betz, 'Firmness', 92–113; Braun, *Hebräer*, 106–8; Crosby, *Composition*, 25–40; Dautzenberg, 'Hebräerbrief', 161–77; Grässer, *Glaube*; Hamm, 'Faith', 270–91; G. Hughes, *Hebrews*, esp. 75–136; Käsemann, *Wandering*, esp. 37–48; Lane, *Hebrews*, vol. 2, esp. 312–430; Lindars, *Theology*, esp. 101–8; Lührmann, *Glaube*, 70–7; 'Glaube', 75–7; Rusche, 'Glauben', 94–104; Schlatter, *Glaube*, 520–36; Schoonhoven, 'Analogy', 92–110; Spicq, *Hébreux*, vol. 2, 371–81 (cites further bibliography); Williamson, *Philo*, 309–85.

[13] Bruce, *Hebrews*, 53, and Rissi, *Theologie*, 59–61.

can perform on their behalf what they are unable to accomplish for themselves; in this sense, he is τὸν ἀρχηγὸν τῆς σωτηρίας αὐτῶν (2.10).[14] Further, whilst πιστός could relate to Jesus' earthly life, it is more likely that the author intended this epithet to describe his continuing high-priestly ministry.[15] In Hebrews 2.17, the consequential relation between Jesus' earthly life and his sacerdotal function is made clear: it is as a result of the former 'that he might become a merciful and faithful high priest in the service of God (ἵνα ἐλεήμων γένηται καὶ πιστὸς ἀρχιερεὺς τὰ πρὸς τὸν θεόν)'. Ἐλεήμων and πιστός, therefore, qualify ἀρχιερεύς and are not specifically applied to Jesus' earthly existence. Context does not permit over-precision, but it seems probable that πιστός communicates here both the sense of Christ as a trustworthy or reliable high priest and one who is faithful to God.[16]

Discussion of Jesus' high-priestly office continues in chapter 3 in the form of a comparison between Jesus and Moses.[17] Both figures are depicted as πιστός, although in the first instance the former is faithful to God and the latter τῷ οἴκῳ αὐτοῦ. Whilst it is possible that τῷ ποιήσαντι αὐτόν (3.2) relates to God's begetting of Jesus, the context favours the occasion of his appointment to the priesthood.[18] The nature of the comparison is difficult to assess for, on the one hand, it is presented to further consideration of Jesus τὸν ἀπόστολον καὶ ἀρχιερέα τῆς ὁμολογίας ἡμῶν and yet, on the other, it is worked out in terms of his ontological (i.e. υἱός, 3.6) – rather than functional (i.e. high priest) – status. One can only assume that the author wishes to discuss Jesus' high-priestly session in terms of his fundamental relationship with God. The comparison itself finds scriptural foundation in Numbers 12.7, where Moses is

14 We follow D. Peterson in recognising the idea of 'originator/initiator' as well as 'leader/pioneer' in the usage of ἀρχηγός here (*Hebrews*, 55–63). On the dynamic force of ἀρχηγός, see Terveen, Jesus, 223.

15 Grässer, *Glaube*, 21–2; P. E. Hughes, *Hebrews*, 120; Westcott, *Hebrews*, 57; *contra* Moffatt, *Hebrews*, 37, and Montefiore, *Hebrews*, 67. Some scholars maintain that πιστός relates to both Jesus' earthly and heavenly ministries, yet within the context of his high-priesthood; obviously, the occasion when Jesus becomes high priest is significant here.

16 Bruce, *Hebrews*, 52, and Spicq, *Hébreux*, vol. 2, 48; *contra* Braun, *Hebräer*, 70, and Vanhoye, 'Jesus', 291–305. There is little to support H. W. Attridge's view that Christ's πιστός in 2.17 performs an exemplary function (*Hebrews*, 95).

17 See commentaries *ad loc*, plus D'Angelo, *Moses*, 65–93; Käsemann, *Wandering*, 122–66; Vanhoye, *Hébreux*, 291–305.

18 Moffatt, *Hebrews*, 42, and R. M. Wilson, *Hebrews*, 69. On the importance of this verse and, in particular, τῷ ποιήσαντι αὐτόν for later christological development, see Greer, *Captain*.

described by the Lord as a servant who *bᵉkol bêṯî neʾᵉmān hûʾ* or, as rendered by the Septuagint, ἐν ὅλῳ τῷ οἴκῳ μου πιστός ἐστιν.[19] Three key words are taken up. Whereas reference to Moses as the Lord's servant (ὁ θεράπων) in Numbers 12.7 is indicative of his superiority over Aaron and Miriam, in Hebrews 3.5 it demonstrates his subordination to Jesus, who is God's son. This distinction is illustrated with reference to God's house (οἶκος),[20] where Moses fulfilled a preparatory role for Christ, who now presides over the community of believers ὡς υἱός (3.6).[21]

The third link word adopted from Numbers 12.7 is πιστός, which occurs twice in Hebrews 3.1–6 and describes the conduct of Jesus and Moses in relation to God. It is unlikely that any comparison is intended here in the sense that Jesus was more faithful than Moses;[22] on the contrary, πιστός provides a point of contact and is exercised by each within the context of their vocation. The notion of Moses as a faithful servant with respect to his responsibilities in God's house is readily understood, but greater ambiguity surrounds what is meant by Jesus being faithful as God's son (ὡς υἱός, 3.6). However, qualification of his sonship by ἐπὶ τὸν οἶκον αὐτοῦ, where the believing community is intended, together with Jesus' depiction as πιστός with respect to his sacerdotal appointment (τῷ ποιήσαντι), favours the conclusion that his faithfulness relates principally to his continuing high-priestly function.[23] We may conclude,

19 W. L. Lane considers that the primary allusion here is to 1 Chron. 17.14 (LXX), καὶ πιστώσω αὐτὸν ἐν οἴκῳ μου (*Hebrews*, vol. 1, 76).

20 The equation of οἶκος with the community of faith is suggested by οὗ οἶκός ἐσμεν ἡμεῖς in Heb. 3.6. There is little to suggest that οἶκος is used in a qualitatively different sense when applied to Moses; Heb. 11.23–8 indicates that the author considered the patriarch a part of the household of faith. See Attridge, *Hebrews*, 109–12, for other views.

21 The household image is utilised again in Heb. 10.21, where Jesus is described as ἱερέα μέγαν ἐπὶ τὸν οἶκον τοῦ θεοῦ.

22 'Moses and Christ were alike "faithful" (v 2), but their perfect fidelity was exercised in different respects.' (Westcott, *Hebrews*, 78; *contra* Spicq, *Hébreux*, vol. 2, 63)

23 See also Heb. 2.17; the introduction of the functional title χριστός for the first time in 3.6 may support this conclusion. The comparison here between Jesus and Moses can readily be misconceived; for example, the author does not believe that Jesus – like Moses – has completed his responsibilities in relation to the household of faith (e.g. RSV: 'He was (ὄντα!) faithful to him who appointed him ... but Christ was faithful over God's house as a son.'). This option is difficult to substantiate linguistically and is at variance with the author's theological intention: believers may have confidence and hope in God's salvation not simply because of what Jesus accomplished on the cross, but also on the basis of his continuing sacerdotal ministry (3.6).

therefore, that reference to Christ as πιστός in Hebrews 3.2 and 3.6 should be interpreted within the context of God's faithfulness to his promises (10.23; 11.11): as a faithful and trustworthy mediator,[24] he makes salvation available and, in this way, provides the context for human response to God.[25]

1.2 Jesus' Πίστις (Hebrews 12.2)

The high-priesthood of Jesus receives further attention later on in the letter, where the focus falls upon the nature and completeness of his sacrifice (7.1–18), together with the way in which God's covenant is thereby established forever (8.1–10.18). This detailed exposition of God's provision in Jesus then provides the foundation and impetus for human response:[26]

> Therefore, brethren, since we have confidence to enter the sanctuary by the blood of Jesus, by the new and living way which he opened for us through the curtain, that is, through his flesh, and since we have a great priest over the house of God, let us draw near (προσερχώμεθα) with a true heart in full assurance of faith (ἐν πληροφορίᾳ πίστεως), with our hearts sprinkled clean from an evil conscience and our bodies washed with pure water. Let us hold fast (κατέχωμεν) the confession of our hope without wavering, for he who promised is faithful (πιστὸς γὰρ ὁ ἐπαγγειλάμενος); and let us consider (κατανοῶμεν) how to stir up one another to love and good works, not neglecting to meet together, as is the habit of some, but encouraging one

24 Hamm, 'Faith', 282. Whilst the author recognises both the theological (i.e. the means for God's salvation) and the anthropological (i.e. the means for human response to God's salvation) dimensions of Christ's high-priesthood, it is unlikely that his depiction of him as πιστός in chapters 2 and 3 serves any emulative function (*contra* Grässer, *Glaube*, 22). For one thing, the adjective relates primarily to Christ's heavenly session. For another, unlike Heb. 12.2, Jesus is not presented here as an example for the life of faith; rather, the author emphasises how Jesus continues to minister before God on behalf of humanity in a way that humanity is unable to do for itself. We are nearer to the author's intention, therefore, if we conceive of Jesus' πιστός as the basis for human faith and not as an example of it.

25 We should note the correlation between the establishing of Christ as πιστός in 2.17; 3.2, 6 and τὴν παρρησίαν καὶ τὸ καύχημα τῆς ἐλπίδος of believers in 3.6; Christ's faithfulness is the basis of their confidence and boast.

26 On the significance of the transition, see Attridge, *Hebrews*, 283–91, and Lindars, *Theology*, 101–6.

another, and all the more as you see the Day drawing near (βλέπετε ἐγγίζουσαν τὴν ἡμέραν). (Heb. 10.19–25)

Within this passage God is described as πιστός; and we have seen how the author considers that Jesus' faithful and trustworthy high-priestly ministry (cf. πιστός in 2.17; 3.2, 6) provides the definitive expression of this divine characteristic and creates the opportunity for faith (πίστις) in others.[27] The possibilities of life within the promises of God are then developed further in terms of confidence in approaching God (προσερχώμεθα κτλ), personal commitment (κατέχωμεν κτλ) and corporate responsibilities (κατανοῶμεν κτλ). The eschatological tone stressed at the conclusion of this section (βλέπετε ἐγγίζουσαν τὴν ἡμέραν) leads into a candid discussion of the perils facing those who do not stand firm (10.26–31). No doubt, these verses are intended to shock believers into action on the basis of fear of judgement; in more general terms, however, they also underline the necessity of human response if God's benefits are to be fully enjoyed.[28]

The exhortation next strikes a more encouraging note as the author reflects on how the recipients of the letter fared in the time following their conversion (cf. φωτισθέντες, 10.32). The addressees' discipleship during that period not only demonstrates their ability to cope when faced with hardships, but also provides a basis for perseverance in the present: 'Therefore do not throw away your confidence (τὴν παρρησίαν), which has a great reward. For you have need of endurance, so that you may do the will of God and receive what is promised' (10.35–6). Scriptural support for the paraenesis is then supplied in the form of Habakkuk 2.3–4,[29] which focuses attention once more upon faith (ὁ δὲ δίκαιός μου ἐκ πίστεως ζήσεται). Finally, having outlined the alternatives in relation to God's salvation, the readers are encouraged to see themselves as those πίστεως εἰς περιποίησιν ψυχῆς (10.39).

[27] Michel, *Hebräer*, 347–8, and Westcott, *Hebrews*, 78.

[28] P. E. Hughes, *Hebrews*, 414–17; Montefiore, *Hebrews*, 176; R. M. Wilson, *Hebrews*, 193.

[29] The quotation follows the wording of the Septuagint quite closely, although not always its order (see Braun, *Hebräer*, 333–4, and Grässer, *Glaube*, 43–4); μικρὸν ὅσον ὅσον comes from Isa. 26.20 (LXX). The qualification of δίκαιος with the personal pronoun μοῦ (also LXX, MSS A and C; cf. ὁ δὲ δίκαιος ἐκ πίστεως ζήσεται in Rom. 1.17 and Gal. 3.11) is interesting. Ὁ δίκαιός μου probably applies not only to the recipients of the letter, but also to the cloud of witnesses of chapter 11, culminating with Jesus himself; see the detailed discussion of Lane, *Hebrews*, vol. 2, 303–11.

We may note from this overview, how the author's train of thought in this section flows from the certainty of God's salvation established in the high-priestly ministry of Jesus to the need for a continuing and committed response on the part of Christians. Further, whilst this latter requirement is explored from a number of angles, it is faith which has the last word. However, rather than simply emphasising the need for this disposition, the writer furnishes a working definition and then lists a host of exemplars who give substance to that definition and, by doing so, provide inspiration and, possibly, paradigms for others who must also travel the way of faith.

The definition of faith in Hebrews 11.1 (ἔστιν δὲ πίστις ἐλπιζομένων ὑπόστασις, πραγμάτων ἔλεγχος οὐ βλεπομένων) is problematic for a number of reasons and no shortage of interpretations have been forthcoming.[30] It is apparent from the nature of the verse and its immediate context that it constitutes neither an abstract nor an exhaustive exposition.[31] The perspective is forward-looking, if not teleological, and should be understood in terms, firstly, of the situation faced by the recipients of the epistle (cf. 10.19–39)[32] and, secondly, the interpretation placed upon the following list of exemplars.[33] The call for endurance (ὑπομονῆς, v. 36) and the charge not to abandon the kind of boldness demonstrated during previous oppression (μὴ ἀποβάλητε οὖν τὴν παρρησίαν, v. 35) suggest that the letter was written to a group facing hardship and, quite possibly, persecution. Past experience alluded to in Hebrews 10.34b illustrates that survival in conditions of austerity and deprivation is facilitated by recognising the superior and permanent possession (κρείττονα ὕπαρξιν καὶ μένουσαν) which, presumably, should be identified with the future reception of God's promise (v. 36) and περιποίησιν ψυχῆς (v. 39). In this way, the

30 The extent of the definition also remains a matter of debate; on this and a review of interpretations: Attridge, *Hebrews*, 305–16; Crosby, *Composition*, 25–40; Spicq, *Hébreux*, vol. 2, 336–40.

31 Moffatt, *Hebrews*, 160, and Westcott, *Hebrews*, 349–50.

32 'In the case of Hebrews 11, however, the author does not build his entire argument on his definition of faith. Functionally, the definition is formulated to validate the exhortation delivered in 10.19–39, and its validity is illustrated in the numerous examples that follow in 11.3–38.' (Crosby, *Composition*, 29)

33 Given that the author attributes faith to many figures who are not explicitly associated with this disposition in Jewish traditions, it is necessary to pay special attention to the summary statements in which the nature of their faith is defined (e.g. 11.1–3, 13–16, 39).

immediate, transitory context of life is transcended by recognition of and relation to the hidden and permanent reality.

A similar perspective may also provide the organising principle for the champions of faith mentioned in chapter 11. The author is clearly convinced that, irrespective of differing situations, expressions and outcomes, all those listed demonstrated πίστις in one way or another. Whatever the circumstances surrounding their faith, however, Hebrews 11.13–16 suggests that each embraced the present in terms of God's promise (μὴ λαβόντες τὰς ἐπαγγελίας, ἀλλὰ πόρρωθεν αὐτὰς ἰδόντες καὶ ἀσπασάμενοι, κτλ). That is to say, they related to the immediate as those whose investment was in a future, heavenly reality tied up with the promise of God; as such, their outlook and conduct were determined by unseen factors (cf. 11.10, 26, 35). In certain cases, fulfilment of God's promises within the present, temporal framework accompanied faith; in others, faith was met by hardship, persecution and death (11.35b-8).[34] For all, death came without the full realisation of God's ultimate purposes, although their faith received attestation (11.13, 39).

The phrase μαρτυρηθέντες διὰ τῆς πίστεως at the conclusion of chapter 11 is similar to the one introducing the *exempla fidei* in Hebrews 11.2 (ἐν ταύτῃ γὰρ ἐμαρτυρήθησαν οἱ πρεσβύτεροι) and invites consideration of the relation between faith and attestation. On a number of occasions in the letter, μαρτυρέω denotes divine authentication of some form and this may be the sense here.[35] Support for this is provided by those *exempla* alluded to in the encomium whose faith failed to yield any material or tangible effect. It is true that in other cases, miracles or other means of attestation accompany faith, but these are unlikely to equate with the author's understanding of μαρτυρέω in Hebrews 11.2 and 39. For one thing, it would be strange if a faith which relates the exponent to the

[34] The importance of hope and steadfastness within the author's understanding of faith is stressed by: Dautzenberg, 'Hebräerbrief', 163–71; Grässer, *Glaube*, 45–63; Schlatter, *Glaube*, 523–33.

[35] 'Here tithes are received by mortal men; there, by one of whom it is testified (μαρτυρούμενος) that he lives.' (7.8); 'For it is witnessed (μαρτυρεῖται) of him, "Thou art a priest for ever, after the order of Melchizedek."' (7.17); 'And the Holy Spirit also bears witness (μαρτυρεῖ) to us . . .' (10.15); 'By faith Abel offered to God a more acceptable sacrifice than Cain, through which he received approval (ἐμαρτυρήθη) as righteous, God bearing witness (μαρτυροῦντος) by accepting his gifts; he died, but through his faith he is still speaking. By faith Enoch was taken up so that he should not see death; and he was not found, because God had taken him. Now before he was taken he was attested (μεμαρτύρηται) as having pleased God.' (11.4–5).

eternal purposes of God gained confirmation from the finite order it transcended. For another, many of those listed in chapter 11 do not receive any such confirmation, but are subjected to greater hardships as a result of their faith. It seems more likely, therefore, that the attestation of faith in Hebrews 11.2 and 39 relates to God's promise of eternal salvation, realised in Christ, in which the believer participates πίστει.[36]

This brings us back to the definition of faith in Hebrews 11.1. Initially, faith is spoken of in relation to hope (ἐλπιζομένων) and, in the light of what has been said already, hope's referent should be equated with God's promise of an eternal, heavenly inheritance (10.36; 11.13–16, 39; cf. 9.11–28).[37] This is reminiscent of the dual perspective adopted by the author throughout Hebrews: the recipients of the letter, like many of the exemplars mentioned in chapter 11, are challenged to live by faith in the face of oppression, temporality and other manifestations of hopelessness; but in living by faith, they are able to transcend these difficulties through participating in God's eternal, ever-hopeful reality. These perspectives are not chronologically sequential or mutually exclusive; rather, in the opinion of the author, Christians can only survive in the former by participating in the latter.

A number of translations for ὑπόστασις in Hebrews 11.1 are possible.[38] Subjective interpretations equate ὑπόστασις with a disposition of the believer, such as assurance, confidence, expectation or resolve; objective options relate it to a reality discrete from the believer and giving substance to faith, such as a foundation, guarantee, creative power or even God and the gift of heavenly salvation. The case for rendering ὑπόστασις in terms of a condition or conviction possessed by believers must be weakened in the light of the situation addressed by the letter; otherwise, faith would have no referent outside of those exhibiting hope and, as a result, could provide little basis for perseverance in times of despondency or opposition. In any case, the burden of chapter 11 is that, in the face of overwhelming circumstances, the champions of faith survive by relating through faith to something beyond their predicaments. It seems more likely, therefore, that ὑπόστασις denotes an indepen-

36 P. E. Hughes, *Hebrews*, 441; cf. Trites, *Witness*, 221.

37 Especially, Michel, *Hebräer*, 373–97.

38 See the discussions in: Attridge, *Hebrews*, 307–10; Crosby, *Composition*, 34–40; Grässer, *Glaube*, 46–54; Harder, 'ὑπόστασις', 710–14; Köster, 'ὑπόστασις', 585–8; Spicq, *Hébreux*, vol. 2, 336–9.

dent reality which is apprehended through faith[39] and only, by implication, the effects of that apprehension.[40] Further, given that the author exhorts his readers to faith in order that they may participate in God's transcendent realm, renderings along the lines of 'objective power' or 'creative potential' can also be dismissed; faith does not create reality, but relates the believer to God's eternal reality. And yet, by living in relation to the being and promises of God, the believer substantiates them in the sense that there is no other way in which they can be apprehended this side of death.[41]

The structure of Hebrews 11.1 favours the view that the second part of the definition of faith should be understood as complementary to the first. This suggests that some degree of correlation between ὑπόστασις and ἔλεγχος is intended.[42] Renderings for ἔλεγχος along the lines of personal 'conviction' or 'commitment' have been proposed,[43] although, given that ὑπόστασις denotes God's transcendent reality, a more consistent translation would be 'proof'.[44] But in what sense can faith be equated with the proof of unseen realities (πραγμάτων ἔλεγχος οὐ βλεπομένων)?[45] The answer is provided by the first part of the verse where, as we have noted, the demonstration of faith substantiates the horizon of hope by relating the believer to the eternal provision of God. Yet, in doing so, it also constitutes proof of that imperceptible reality as the

39 Attridge, *Hebrews*, 309–10; Braun, *Hebräer*, 338; Hamm, 'Faith', 278–9; Köster, 'ὑπόστασις', 587–8; Lane, *Hebrews*, vol. 2, 328–9.

40 R. M. Wilson cautions against taking objective and subjective interpretations for ὑπόστασις as mutually exclusive; he quotes Marcus Dods in support: 'Substantially the words mean that faith gives to things future, which as yet are only hoped for, all the reality of actual present existence; and irresistibly convinces us of the reality of unseen things and brings us into their presence.' (*Hebrews*, *ad loc*)

41 The proposed understanding for ὑπόστασις in terms of transcendent reality concurs with the usage of the noun in Heb. 1.3 (cf. 3.14). H. Köster draws attention to the correspondence between the presentation of, on the one hand, Jesus as ὑπόστασις of God who demonstrates divinity through suffering humanity and, on the other, faith as ὑπόστασις which demonstrates the reality of God through situations of difficulty and hardship ('ὑπόστασις', 587).

42 Buchanan, *Hebrews*, 182; Link, 'ἐλέγχω', 142; Michel, *Hebräer*, 374–5.

43 Bruce, *Hebrews*, 278–9; P. E. Hughes, *Hebrews*, 440; Moffatt, *Hebrews*, 159. There appears to be scant lexiographical support for this interpretation (see Attridge, *Hebrews*, 310, and Büschel, 'ἐλέγχω', 476).

44 Büschel, 'ἐλέγχω', 476; Grässer, *Glaube*, 51–3, 126–8; Käsemann, *Wandering*, 41–4; Westcott, *Hebrews*, 350.

45 Πίστις cannot simply be equated with its well-attested Classical meaning of 'proof'; it is true that the objective basis for πίστις is stressed, but not in the sense that it can be isolated from the subjective apprehension of that reality. Perhaps a deliberate polyvalence is intended here; see the comments of Lane, *Hebrews*, vol. 2, 328–30.

believer participates in it. Thus, a dialectical relationship involving the two halves of Hebrews 11.1 can be discerned: faith substantiates the transcendent reality which is the focus of hope and, in doing so, provides proof of that reality.[46]

As we have already noted, the *exempla fidei* follow on from the definition of faith presented in verse 1. The author clearly believes that the figures mentioned from Israel's past elucidate the virtue of faith,[47] although it is apparent from 11.13 and 39 that they failed to realise faith's goal as defined at the beginning of the chapter. This outcome, however, does not amount to a judgement upon their faith, but rather points towards the fulfilment of God's promises in the on-going, high-priestly ministry of Jesus.[48] In this way, although the recipients of the letter are surrounded by a cloud of witnesses whose faith attests the transcendent reality encapsulated within God's promises (12.1), they are none the less encouraged to focus upon (ἀφορῶντες)[49] the one who is τὸν τῆς πίστεως ἀρχηγὸν καὶ τελειωτὴν (12.2).[50]

There are principally two contexts in which Jesus can be considered as τὸν τῆς πίστεως ἀρχηγὸν καὶ τελειωτὴν:[51] firstly, in relation to the goal of faith and, secondly, in relation to its performance.[52] Given the anticipatory or proleptic perspective of Hebrews 11.1, together with the way in which the endeavours of the νέφος μαρτύρων are necessarily frustrated (11.13, 39), it seems probable

[46] '*Pistis* as a concrete experience is, though it may sound paradoxical, (a participation in) the reality of what is hoped for and a demonstration (*elenchos*) of what is not seen with the eye.' (Hamm, 'Faith', 297)

[47] On the composition of chapter 11 and its relation to other catalogues of *exempla virtutis*, see: Attridge, *Hebrews*, 306; Crosby, *Composition*, esp. 17–24; Lane, *Hebrews*, vol. 2, 314–23.

[48] Although it is difficult to determine the timetable precisely, there can be little doubt that the author considers the perfecting of all believers, including those before the incarnation, to be determined by God's salvific and perfecting work in Christ (Heb. 11.40; 12.22–4). On this, see Peterson, *Hebrews*, 163–6.

[49] F. F. Bruce observes how the Maccabean martyrs are described in 4 Macc. 17.9 as those who keep their eyes fixed on God (εἰς θεὸν ἀφορῶντες) in the midst of persecution and death (*Hebrews*, 350). We have already noted that faith is attributed to these Jewish heroes within the same book.

[50] '... the author of Hebrews clearly understands Jesus as part of the faith community of Hb. 11 and of contemporary Christians, those with whom Jesus says: ἐγὼ ἔσομαι πεποίθως ἐπ' αὐτῷ (Hb. 2.13a).' (Terveen, Jesus, 245)

[51] We understand πίστις to be qualified here equally by τελειωτής and ἀρχηγός; Lane, *Hebrews*, vol. 2. 410–11, and Müller, *ΧΡΙΣΤΟΣ*, 308–9.

[52] P. J. DuPlessis describes these as the 'soteriological' and 'pedagogical' positions respectively (*ΤΕΛΕΙΟΣ*, 222–3), whilst E. Grässer speaks of the 'soteriologisch' and 'praktisch' dimensions (*Glaube*, 59–62).

that Jesus' unique contribution to faith is intended.[53] This is consistent with the strong emphasis throughout the epistle upon Jesus' exclusive mediatory role within the fulfilment of God's salvific intentions. Further, although without biblical precedent, a rendering for τελειωτής along the lines 'perfecter, completor or fulfiller of faith' has found general support.[54] Jesus is, thus, the first to reach faith's heavenly goal and, as a result of the way in which this was accomplished, has enabled others to follow in his footsteps.[55] Within this framework of τελειωτής, Jesus can also be described as ἀρχηγός in that, by initiating its fulfilment, he has become the source of faith for others.[56]

However, we cannot ignore that reference to Jesus as τὸν τῆς πίστεως ἀρχηγὸν καὶ τελειωτὴν occurs at the conclusion of a list of *exempla fidei* and within an exhortatory framework in which the recipients of the letter are encouraged to keep faith.[57] The testimony of past sojourners provides the basis for a fresh call to perseverance (δι' ὑπομονῆς), which is couched in athletic imagery (12.1).[58] Fellow competitors in the ἀγών of faith should fix their attention (ἀφορῶντες) upon Jesus and, with the emphasis throughout the previous verses upon the need to exercise faith, the rationale for this commendation must reside in the conviction that he has already completed the course and received the prize.[59] From this perspec-

53 Anderson, *Jesus*, 287–8; DuPlessis, *ΤΕΛΕΙΟΣ*, 223–7; Lane, *Hebrews*, vol. 2, 412.

54 Delling, 'τέλος', 86–7; Müller, *ΧΡΙΣΤΟΣ*, 310; Peterson, *Hebrews*, 171–3; τελειωτής is only attested here in the New Testament and Septuagint.

55 P. E. Hughes draws attention to the importance of Jesus' continuing mediatory role in maintaining the possibility of faith for others (*Hebrews*, 522).

56 Cf. Jesus as αἴτιος σωτηρίας αἰωνίου in Heb. 5.9. There is still considerable debate concerning whether ἀρχηγός should be understood in the sense of the 'source' (e.g. author, originator, initiator) or 'pioneer' (e.g. leader, forerunner, pathfinder) of faith. As we shall see, there is reason to believe that both aspects are intended by the author. A similar *double entendre* may also be present in Heb. 2.10: the phrase πολλοὺς υἱοὺς εἰς δόξαν ἀγαγόντα τὸν ἀρχηγόν suggests the latter, whilst the broader context in which Jesus' unique salvific function is explored (2.10–17) favours the former.

57 The emphasis here, as in much of Hebrews, is upon the disposition of faith rather than upon its content (e.g. 'believing faithfulness'; G. Hughes, *Hebrews*, 79); so Lindars, *Theology*, 108–12, and Müller, *ΧΡΙΣΤΟΣ*, 309. This does not mean, however, that faith is void of christological significance (see section 1.3).

58 J. L. Terveen and others have explored this motif in relation to the Greek 'Agon' (Jesus, 216–22); P.-G. Müller stresses the eschatological perspective of the 'Glaubenskampf' (*ΧΡΙΣΤΟΣ*, 303–4).

59 D. Hamm, citing E. B. Horning's analysis of Heb. 12.1–2's chiastic structure ('Chiasmus', 41) in support of the author's presentation of Jesus as an exemplar of faith, goes on to comment: 'The structure of the parallel members of the chiasm

tive, therefore, it is the exemplary function of Jesus' life of faith which is in view.[60] He is the one who has gone before (cf. πρόδρομος, 6.20) and provides not only inspiration, but also a focus for others to emulate; in a very real sense, he is faith incarnate. Jesus constitutes the ultimate exemplar (τελειωτής) of faith and, as such, is its leader or forerunner (ἀρχηγός) as well as its source.

Confirmation that Jesus' life of faith is implicated within Hebrews 12.2 comes from the second part of the verse where his enduring (ὑπέμεινεν) the cross is considered in the light of the previous definition (11.1). Jesus faces his passion as one who by faith relates to God's eschatological promises (ὃς ἀντὶ τῆς προκειμένης αὐτῷ χαρᾶς) and who, through suffering, inherits them (ἐν δεξιᾷ τε τοῦ θρόνου τοῦ θεοῦ κεκάθικεν). Reference to his suffering here as a fellow human is suggestive of the fuller exploration of this theme in Hebrews 5.7–10,[61] where it provides the basis for his perfecting (τελειωθεὶς) and ability to fulfil a high-priestly function. The endurance (ὑπομεμενηκότα) shown by Jesus is taken up again in 12.3 and, on this occasion, in relation to oppression from others. It is possible that this focus upon Jesus' approach to adversity reflects the difficulties faced by the readers (cf. 10.32–6); in the face of their own problems, they should consider the example set by Jesus who endured greater hardship than they have encountered to date (12.4).[62]

In the light of this discussion, we may conclude that both contexts proposed for τὸν τῆς πίστεως ἀρχηγὸν καὶ τελειωτὴν were in the author's mind.[63] On the one hand, as a result of his appointment to the highly-priestly office through death and subsequent heavenly enthronement, Jesus stands in a unique and unrepeatable relation to faith as its source and perfector. On the other hand, his eligibility for this position was determined by a life of faith epitomised by obedience and endurance in the face of suffering and, ultimately, death.

highlights the parallel content between the faith-race of Jesus and the faith-race of disciples.' ('Faith', 280)

60 G. Hughes, *Hebrews*, 78–86; Peterson, *Hebrews*, 171–3; Terveen, Jesus, 222–8.

61 'In Heb. 5.7–8, then, when our author describes Jesus' disposition vis-à-vis God as *eulabeia*, he is using a quality that elsewhere in Hebrews is paralleled with *pistis* (11.7 and 12.28). Moreover, *eulabeia* is an obedience that models the obedience to which Christians are called.' (Hamm, 'Faith', 284)

62 In this respect, note the way in which ὑπομένω is used of both Jesus (12.2–3) and the addressees (10.32; 12.7) in this section of the letter. On the literary support for this correspondence, Vanhoye, *Hébreux*, 196–204.

63 Attridge, *Hebrews*, 354–9; G. Hughes, *Hebrews*, 78–90; Lindars, *Theology*, 112–14; Terveen, Jesus, 222–44.

In this sense, as believer amongst other believers, he provides the perfect example of faith-in-practice: the one who has not only completed the worldly race, but also inherited the eternal prize.

1.3 Concluding remarks

Our investigations have isolated two distinct ways in which the author of Hebrews relates the πιστεύω group to Jesus. In the first place, πιστός characterises Jesus' continuing high-priestly function by which God's heavenly inheritance, promised of old, is made available. It is not applied in general terms to his incarnate life, although it is dependent upon his continuing solidarity with humanity; rather, it relates specifically to his soteriological significance as perpetual mediator between God and humankind, a role which he assumed on the occasion of his crucifixion. This depiction of Jesus as a faithful high priest who is the locus for access to God and fulfilment of the divine promises appears, therefore, to be an expression of or vehicle for God's covenantal faithfulness.[64] Through Jesus' death, enthronement and continuing intercession, God has established an eternal means of salvation for all.

Secondly, Jesus is also described as τὸν τῆς πίστεως ἀρχηγὸν καὶ τελειωτήν. In this case, it is his life of faith as a believer amongst believers which is intended. Although his incarnate existence, characterised by obedience and suffering as expressions of identification with humanity, was an essential prerequisite to his sacerdotal role and, as such, underlines his uniqueness within the dispensation of salvation, the primary significance of his characterisation as one who exhibited πίστις rests elsewhere. Coming at the apex of a list of faith's exemplars, Jesus is portrayed as the believer *par excellence*. He is the first one to have completed the earthly sojourn in faith and inherited God's promises. Thus, his earthly existence is not only necessary in order to become the source of God's salvation as high priest, but also so that he might exemplify human response to God. His life of faith, evident in learning obedience, suffering and death, incarnates faith and constitutes a focus for inspiration and emulation.

Whilst Hebrews demonstrates interest in Jesus as one who lived

[64] In this manner, the author of Hebrews develops a similar line of thinking to that identified in Romans 3. However, whereas Paul focuses upon Jesus' faith-in-obedience in the face of suffering and death as a vehicle for God's faithfulness, the present writer stresses the faithfulness of Jesus' ongoing high-priestly ministry.

by πίστις and who remains πιστός, the motivation for this is not primarily biographical.[65] On the contrary, rather than representing signs of an historicising tendency to record details of Jesus' life for their own sake, they reflect an attempt to relate post-resurrection belief to the person and ministry of Jesus. In the case of πιστός, this results from a process of reflection upon Jesus' significance within God's dispensation of salvation. As one who is known within the community of faith to mediate God's promises, he can be described as a faithful and trustworthy high priest. With πίστις, however, the dynamic is different, for here it is the faith of Jesus, who completes the same earthly journey of discipleship and relates to God as others are called to do, which is in view. In consequence, Jesus' πίστις cannot be so readily understood as a product of theological evaluation, but is consistent with a level of existential comparison between Jesus and fellow-believers grounded upon a shared understanding of situation and vocation.[66]

Although this correlation may represent the fruit of a deductive process in which faith is projected onto the earthly figure of Jesus in order to provide the community with an ἀρχηγὸν καὶ τελειωτήν, this seems an unnecessary and unmerited complication. Rather, recognition that Jesus possessed faith is more likely to have arisen from reflection upon his earthly life by those called to complete a similar journey. It is Jesus' πίστις which makes faith possible for others; his example not only provides the basis for his faithful high-priestly ministry, but also gives definition to and inspiration for discipleship in faith. Thus, without Jesus, supported in certain respects by the cloud of witnesses, the author's call to faith in times of difficulty would lack historical foundation, precedent and legitimation.

Before bringing our discussion of Hebrews to a close, a number of

[65] Terveen, Jesus, 266, 271; on the other hand, we would not wish to follow E. Grässer in claiming that all interest in Jesus' life originates in theological reflection ('Jesus', 271).

[66] On faith as the primary hermeneutic for linking those Christians addressed in Hebrews with the life of Jesus, see G. Hughes, *Hebrews*, esp. 75–100, 114–36. The parallels between the process indicated here and that adopted by exponents of the so-called 'New Quest' for the historical Jesus, whereby the event of the resurrection is bridged by a common understanding of experience on the part of Jesus and the early church, are significant (e.g. Braun, 'Meaning', 89–127; E. Fuchs, *Studies*, 11–31; also Cook, 'Call', 679–700; Ebeling, *Word*, 201–46; Keck, *Future*, 47–99; Mackey, 'Historical Jesus', 155–74; Marxsen, *Beginnings*, 57–68, 77–85). In this respect, it is strange how rarely Hebrews is used within such discussions; but see Anderson, *Jesus*, 281–8, and Terveen, Jesus, esp. 266–82.

observations concerning the relationship between faith and christology are pertinent. We have noted how Jesus is presented as an exemplar of πίστις and how his understanding of faith is informed by moments of personal struggle and conflict from his life. In this way, the author explores what it means to live by faith in an alien and hostile environment. This has led some scholars to conclude that the notion of faith in Hebrews lacks substantial christological content.[67] It is questionable, however, whether this deduction can be sustained for it not only conflicts with the centrality of Jesus for salvation in the epistle, but also seems to be based upon a perceived incompatibility between assessments of Jesus as an exponent of faith and one who in some sense provides its content.

Our investigations do not support this dichotomy, but suggest a broader appraisal of how Jesus defines faith and one which is developed within the presentation of him as high priest. From one perspective, Jesus' atoning death and continuing sacerdotal ministry underline his uniqueness and centrality for the salvation of all; from another, his high-priestly function is based upon sharing fully in humanity, including the life of faith.[68] Within this framework, Jesus' faith constitutes a prerequisite for his becoming the focus or channel for faith in God and the realisation of God's promises. It seems, therefore, that faith possesses a profoundly christological dimension in Hebrews and one which is firmly rooted in the person of Jesus and his continuing salvific ministrations, rather than in more detached theological reflection upon his life, death and exaltation. What is more, it is an understanding of faith in which the person of Jesus mediates not only God's initiative of salvation, but also human response to that initiative. In a very real sense, Jesus is τὸν τῆς πίστεως ἀρχηγὸν καὶ τελειωτήν.

2 The Revelation to John

The Revelation to John constitutes another document addressed to Christians experiencing serious difficulties, including internal prob-

[67] So Dautzenberg, 'Hebräerbrief', 171, and Grässer, *Glaube*, 79.

[68] J. L. Terveen recognises what he calls a duality in christology, which frames Jesus both as (i) a part of the faith community who exemplifies the life of faith, and (ii) the focus of faith's confession who is the source of salvation (Jesus, 272–82; also Hamm, 'Faith', 270–91; G. Hughes, *Hebrews*, esp. 75–100; Lane, *Hebrews*, vol. 1, esp. cxxxv-cxliv).

lems (cf. 2.6, 14–21) and persecution from outside sources.[69] In the opening chapters, pastoral situations relating to the churches in Asia Minor are addressed and, in each case, the author attempts to motivate his readers to keep the faith by interpreting their conduct within an eschatological framework.[70] Those who stand firm can look forward to future blessings (2.7, 10–11, 17, 26–8; 3.4–5, 12), but those who fall away will be judged accordingly (2.5, 16, 22–3; 3.1). Both options are described graphically as this teleological perspective is reiterated throughout the book and, in this way, is used as a vehicle for investing the present with theological significance.[71]

The person of Jesus Christ features prominently within this scenario as the one who makes salvation available in the first place (1.5; 5.9; 7.14; 12.11) and will be its final arbiter (1.7; 3.11; 22.7, 12–13, 20). Further, during the period between his sacrificial death and future return, Jesus performs an ongoing heavenly ministry,[72] which is linked to his earthly existence and eschatological responsibilities by repeated reference to him as the Lamb (ἀρνίον).[73] By characterising Jesus in this way, the Apocalypse underlines the continuity between the earthly Jesus who suffered and the exalted Christ who now reigns and will judge all people.[74] In addition to his unique responsibilities as saviour and judge, the author also presents Jesus as a source of inspiration and, perhaps, emulation for Christians called to bear witness to the faith in a hostile environment. It is this theme which is of particular interest to us here and we shall explore it by examining how πιστός and πίστις are used in relation to Jesus.

69 Rev. 1.9; 2.2–3, 9–10, 13; 6.9–11; 7.14; 12.17; 13.7; 18.24; 20.4; cf. Rev. 2.19, 25; 3.10. On the situation addressed by Revelation: Boring, *Revelation*, 5–23; Rowland, *Open Heaven*, 403–13; Sweet, *Revelation*, 27–35.

70 Aune, *Prophecy*, 274–9, and Beasley-Murray, *Revelation*, 72.

71 E.g. Rev. 6.10, 12–17; 9.3–6, 18; 14.9–11, 13, 19–20; 15.2–4; 16–18, 21. It should be pointed out that not all those addressed were facing persecution for their faith; others had already compromised and needed to re-commit themselves (see Bauckham, *Theology*, esp. 12–17).

72 Cf. Rev. 1.5, 16; 2.5, 16; 3.20; 7.17. It is possible that these allusions to Jesus' interim ministry belong to his return, but this seems unlikely. Consider, for example, 3.20 where a continuing beckoning (κρούω) by Jesus is in view. On the priestly nature of Jesus' ongoing heavenly ministry, see Charles, *Revelation*, vol. 1, cxiii-cxiv.

73 Rev. 5.6, 8, 12, 13; 6.1, 16; 7.9, 10, 14, 17; 12.11; 13.8, 11; 14.1, 4[x2], 10; 15.3; 17.14 [x2]; 19.7, 9; 21.9, 14, 22, 23, 27; 22.1, 3.

74 Ford, *Revelation*, 13–16, and Guthrie, *Theology*, 227; also Swete, *Apocalypse*, clviii-clix. Little has been written on the role of Jesus' humanity in Revelation, but see the brief comments of Anderson, *Jesus*, 288–91.

2.1 Jesus as Πιστός (Revelation 1.5, 3.14 and 19.11)

On three occasions the epithet πιστός is attributed to Jesus. The first occurs at the beginning of the book, where the author extends grace and peace to his readers 'from him who is and who was and is to come ... and from Jesus Christ the faithful witness (ὁ μάρτυς ὁ πιστός), the first-born of the dead, and the ruler of kings on earth' (1.4–5).[75] The contents of this salutation, when considered in relation to the situations addressed by the Apocalypse, suggest that it is not simply a piece of epistolary protocol,[76] but an attempt to establish the pedigree of the one to whom Christians are called to bear witness and, if necessary, suffer for:[77] Jesus Christ, who now sits exalted over them and who administers judgement as well as blessing, is also the one whose love led him to the cross and death to secure salvation (1.6). From the outset, therefore, reference to Jesus' humanity and, in particular, his passion supplies not only legitimation of Jesus, but also a point of identification between the one who has suffered and those who must now suffer.[78]

Review of the other references to μάρτυς in Revelation indicates that its association with Jesus' death in the present context is significant. Although it is unlikely to be a *terminus technicus* for martyrdom at this stage, a strong link between μάρτυς and death is already apparent.[79] For example, Antipas, Jesus' witness and faithful one (ὁ μάρτυς μου ὁ πιστός μου), was executed for refusing to deny Christ's faith (καὶ οὐκ ἠρνήσω τὴν πίστιν μου, 2.13); and again, when Jesus' two witnesses (τοῖς δυσὶν μάρτυσίν μου) have completed τὴν μαρτυρίαν αὐτῶν, they too will meet their end

[75] It is possible that ὁ μάρτυς ὁ πιστός can be traced back to Ps. 89 (cf. καὶ ὁ μάρτυς ἐν οὐρανῷ πιστός, Ps. 88.38 [LXX]). This would be interesting not only because the psalm speaks of a Davidic deliverer, but also because that figure is a channel for divine covenantal faithfulness (see section 1.3 above; also Bauckham, *Theology*, 73).

[76] Cf. '... in Rev. 1.5–6 John quotes a traditional baptismal formula which stresses that by his blood Christ has freed the baptized from their sins, has installed them to kingship, and has made them priests for God.' (Fiorenza, *Revelation*, 76)

[77] Caird, *Revelation*, 16, and Krodel, *Revelation*, 81–6.

[78] Boring, *Revelation*, 75–9, and Mounce, *Revelation*, 71.

[79] A. A. Trites, who identifies a five-stage development in the meaning of μάρτυς and other cognates from 'a witness in a court of law with no expectation of death' to an absolute use denoting martyrdom without the idea of witness, associates μάρτυς in Revelation with stage 4: 'Μάρτυς becomes equivalent to "martyr". Here the idea of death is uppermost, though the idea of witness is not entirely lacking.' ('Μάρτυς', esp. 77–80)

(11.1–14).[80] Finally, the political authorities[81] responsible for persecuting Christians are described in chapter 17 as a great harlot who has become 'drunk with the blood of the saints καὶ ἐκ τοῦ αἵματος τῶν μαρτύρων Ἰησοῦ' (17.6).

The qualification of μάρτυς by πιστός in Revelation 1.5,[82] however, suggests that the idea of bearing testimony is still denoted by the former in that the faithfulness of a martyr is self-evident. Πιστός is used elsewhere to underline the reliability or trustworthiness of the seer's prophetic words (21.5; 22.6),[83] but it can also characterise those disciples remaining faithful to the point of death. We have already noted the case of Antipas, ὁ μάρτυς μου ὁ πιστός μου (2.13), and the Christians at Smyrna are similarly exhorted to γίνου πιστὸς ἄχρι θανάτου so that they might receive the crown of life (2.10). Further, although far from certain, the κλητοὶ καὶ ἐκλεκτοὶ καὶ πιστοί (17.14), who accompany the Lamb in his conquests, may be the same people as die for their witness in 17.6.[84]

Thus, although μάρτυς in isolation may not convey the idea of martyrdom, the Apocalypse clearly illustrates how giving testimony for one's faith can result in death. In this respect, the ultimate test of a witness' faithfulness and, by implication, trustworthiness and reliability is a willingness to face death. A faithful witness (ὁ μάρτυς ὁ πιστός) within the framework of Revelation, therefore, can be equated with a martyr;[85] consequently, when Jesus is described in 1.5 as ὁ μάρτυς ὁ πιστός, it is likely that this designation should be understood in similar terms.[86] Confirmation of this is supplied by

80 A. A. Trites maintains that the parallel between Rev. 11.1–11 and Zech. 4.1–13 favours an understanding of the two witnesses in terms of the kingly and priestly functions of the redeemed community recognised by the Seer elsewhere (e.g. 1.5–6; 5.10; 20.4–6). More specifically, he thinks that Rev. 11.7 demonstrates that Christian martyrs were particularly in view (*Witness*, 164–70).

81 The depiction of the Lamb's opponents in chapter 17 is often the basis for linking the Apocalypse with the persecution of Christians under Roman rule; see Rowland, *Open Heaven*, 403–13.

82 Μάρτυς and πιστός are linked together in the Septuagint. They can be used to underline the importance of trustworthy and truthful testimony (Prov. 14.5, 25; Isa. 8.2), and on one occasion the Lord is appealed to εἰς μάρτυρα δίκαιον καὶ πιστόν (Jer. 49.5).

83 E.g. οὗτοι οἱ λόγοι πιστοὶ καὶ ἀληθινοί, 21.5; 22.6; cf. οἱ λόγοι ἀληθινοὶ τοῦ θεοῦ, 19.9. A similar usage of πιστός is common in the Pastorals (πιστὸς ὁ λόγος, 1 Tim. 1.15; 3.1; 4.9; 2 Tim. 2.11; Tit 3.8).

84 Cf. Caird, *Revelation*, 220.

85 Strathmann, 'μάρτυς', 495–6, and Trites, 'Μάρτυς', 79–80.

86 P. E. Hughes, *Revelation*, 18; Krodel, *Revelation*, 83; Satake, *Gemeindeordnung*, 114.

the same verse, where Jesus is spoken of as ὁ πρωτότοκος τῶν νεκρῶν and the one λύσαντι ἡμᾶς ἐκ τῶν ἁμαρτιῶν ἡμῶν ἐν τῷ αἵματι αὐτοῦ.[87]

Although more ambiguous, the second reference to Jesus as a faithful witness (ὁ ἀμήν, ὁ μάρτυς ὁ πιστὸς καὶ ἀληθινός, 3.14) probably relates to his martyrdom as well.[88] The Christians at Laodicea are admonished to repent and seek the Lord in earnest so that they might be victorious in their struggle and share Christ's glory: ὁ νικῶν δώσω αὐτῷ καθίσαι μετ' ἐμοῦ εὐ τῷ θρόνῳ μου, ὡς κἀγὼ ἐνίκησα καὶ ἐκάθισα μετὰ τοῦ πατρός μου ἐν τῷ θρόνῳ αὐτοῦ (3.21). The implication is that Jesus provides a precedent for others to follow and one which entails witness to the point of death. Πιστός, therefore, does not simply mean reliable or true (cf. ἀμήν),[89] but embraces Jesus' keeping faith in the midst of suffering and death (1.5); it is this which constitutes his pedigree.

The third occurrence of πιστός applied to Jesus takes the form of a title: πιστὸς καὶ ἀληθινός (19.11).[90] Unlike the previous references, it does not qualify μάρτυς[91] and is used here absolutely. The relationship between this form of address and Jesus' overcoming of opposition in the following verses (19.11–21) or, indeed, any of his achievements narrated in Revelation is difficult to determine. On two occasions God's judgements are described as ἀληθινός,[92] and this might be reflected here in the sense that the rider who executes judgement upon the beast and the false prophet is called πιστὸς καὶ

[87] A number of scholars maintain that the three titles attributed to Jesus in 1.5 correspond to the three phases of his ministry: 'the faithful witness' – death; 'the first-born of the dead' – resurrection; 'the ruler of kings of earth' – ascension/second coming (see Beasley-Murray, *Revelation*, 56–7, and Lohmeyer, *Offenbarung*, 10).

[88] Caird, *Revelation*, 57, and Trites, 'Μάρτυς', 80. Contrary to the view of a number of scholars (e.g. Charles, *Revelation*, vol. 1, 14, and Satake, *Gemeindeordnung*, 115), it is not simply that the exalted Christ is a μάρτυς to the promise of salvation, but that he himself remained πιστός to the point of death and, having been raised from the dead and exalted to take his place in the heavenly session, now stands as a μάρτυς to that which he knows first-hand.

[89] *Contra* Ford, *Revelation*, 418, and Rissi, *Future*, 21, who claim that ὁ μάρτυς ὁ πιστὸς καὶ ἀληθινός is simply a translation of ἀμήν.

[90] On the pedigree of καλούμενος, see Metzger, *Commentary*, 760–1.

[91] The designation is, however, similar to that of 3.14, ὁ μάρτυς ὁ πιστὸς καὶ ἀληθινός.

[92] Cf. ἀληθιναὶ καὶ δίκαιαι αἱ κρίσεις σου, 16.7; ἀληθιναὶ καὶ δίκαιαι αἱ κρίσεις αὐτοῦ, 19.2; cf. δίκαιαι καὶ ἀληθιναὶ αἱ ὁδοί σου, 15.3; ὁ ἀληθινός, 3.7; ὁ ἅγιος καὶ ἀληθινός, 6.10.

ἀληθινός.[93] Further, if the blood spilt upon the rider's robe is that of Jesus himself,[94] πιστός may imply his martyrdom; however, given the strong allusions to Isaiah 63.1–6, where the blood of God's opponents is in view,[95] this remains more tentative. In consequence, as the context does not permit precision, it seems safest to interpret the title πιστὸς καὶ ἀληθινός in terms of Jesus' ministry or witness in general, with the possibility that the author wished his readers to recall those particular incidents where Jesus is described as πιστὸς καὶ ἀληθινός.[96]

From what we have said to date, it is apparent that πιστός is used of Jesus in relation to his earthly existence and, in particular, to his testimony resulting in death: he kept faith to the end. In this way, the Apocalypse depicts Jesus as the first faithful witness;[97] but unlike those aspects of his ministry which are exclusive to his vocation, this is one characteristic which believers are called to emulate. As Antipas and others have already followed Jesus in keeping a faithful witness to the point of death,[98] so others are now exhorted to do the same (cf. 14.12–13).[99]

2.2 Jesus' Πίστις (Revelation 2.13 and 14.12)

There are two occurrences in Revelation of genitival constructions involving πίστις and Jesus' name (τὴν πίστιν Ἰησοῦ, 14.12) or a

93 The portrayal of Jesus as the conquering messiah depicted in 19.11–21 is consistent with Jewish expectation encapsulated in Pss. Sol. 17.24–7 (Charles, *Revelation*, vol. 2, 131–2, and Lohmeyer, *Offenbarung*, 158). As we have already noted, the πιστεύω group is used of the messiah in that context as well (ἐν πίστει καὶ δικαιοσύνῃ, Pss. Sol. 17.40)

94 Boring, *Revelation*, 196; P. E. Hughes, *Revelation*, 204 ; Sweet, *Revelation*, 283.

95 Beasley-Murray, *Revelation*, 280, and Mounce, *Revelation*, 345; other alternatives include the blood of the Parthian kings (Charles, *Revelation*, vol. 2, 133) and the blood of the martyrs (Caird, *Revelation*, 243).

96 'In turning warrior he has not deserted his original function of witness-bearing, on which all his other achievements are founded ... This is not some supernatural figure from the fantasies of Jewish apocalytic, but the Jesus of history, whose final victory in the battle to come serves only to make plain to the world the victory seen by faith from the beginning in the Cross.' (Caird, *Revelation*, 240)

97 This interpretation conflicts with the view that Jesus as μάρτυς is restricted to his post-resurrection activities (e.g. Holtz, *Christologie*, 57–8, and Rissi, *Future*, 21–2). Such a restriction not only distances Jesus' words from the offering of his life which gives them authority, but also fails to accommodate the exemplary function of Jesus in relation to bearing witness and martyrdom.

98 Rev. 2.13; 12.11; 16.6; 17.6; 18.24; 19.2; 20.4. A similar phrase is applied to Antipas in 2.13 (ὁ μάρτυς μου ὁ πιστός μου) as to Jesus in 1.5 and 3.14 (ὁ μάρτυς ὁ πιστός).

99 'With respect to his past, he is the "faithful witness", who has completed his witness on behalf of God by his death on the cross. Our witness to Christ,

personal pronoun referring to him (τὴν πίστιν μου, 2.13). The latter is one of two expressions used to describe the Christians at Pergamum who remain steadfast in the face of opposition: κρατεῖς τὸ ὄνομά μου and οὐκ ἠρνήσω τὴν πίστιν μου. Reference here to Jesus' name is suggestive of profession (cf. 2.3; 3.8) and, given the turbulent situation addressed by the letter, testimony before hostile authorities may be intended.[100] It is usually assumed without comment that τὴν πίστιν μου constitutes an objective genitive (i.e. the faith in Jesus),[101] although there is little support for this interpretation. For one thing, with the possible exception of the texts under review, the πιστεύω group is not used to denote the content of belief in the Apocalypse. The verbal form πιστεύω is not attested at all[102] and the remaining occurrences of πίστις are more consistent with the disposition rather than the object of faith:[103] in 2.19, πίστις occurs within a list of personal qualities or modes of service exhibited by the Christians at Thyatira (οἶδά σου τὰ ἔργα καὶ τὴν ἀγάπην καὶ τὴν πίστιν καὶ τὴν διακονίαν καὶ τὴν ὑπομονήν σου) and in 13.10, the challenge for the saints to demonstrate ἡ ὑπομονὴ καὶ ἡ πίστις is unlikely to be about belief in Jesus, but the quality of life which is characterised by endurance and faithfulness.

As we noted in chapter 3, there are no unambiguous cases of πίστις with the objective genitive in the New Testament, and the present context is no exception.[104] Indeed, it is unlikely that believers would be congratulated for the substance of their Christian affirmation (i.e. 'the faith in me') only to be criticised in the

therefore, must be determined by Jesus' own uncompromising faithfulness, a faithfulness that may include suffering obedience (cf. 2.13).' (Krodel, *Revelation*, 83; also Boring's '"shared" christology', *Revelation*, 76–7).

100 Bousset, *Offenbarung*, 212, and P. E. Hughes, *Revelation*, 44.

101 Beasley-Murray, *Revelation*, 84; Charles, *Revelation*, vol. 1, 61; Ford, *Revelation*, 397; Lohmeyer, *Offenbarung*, 25; Swete, *Apocalypse*, 34.

102 The πιστεύω group is not well represented in Revelation – πίστις (4): 2.13, 19; 13.10; 14.12; πιστός (8): 1.5; 2.10, 13; 3.14; 17.14; 19.11; 21.5; 22.6; ἄπιστος (1): 21.8.

103 Bousset, *Offenbarung*, 365, and Michel, 'πίστις', 603.

104 T. Holtz claims that οὐκ ἠρνήσω τὴν πίστιν μου and indeed the equivalent in Rev. 14.12 must be taken as objective genitives because the former construction 'im synthetischen Parallelismus zu κρατεῖς τὸ ὄνομά μου steht'. (*Christologie*, 23) He does not develop what is intended by 'synthetischen Parallelismus' and its meaning is not self-evident. There can be no question of τὸ ὄνομά μου being an objective genitive and whilst the phrase καὶ οὐκ ἠρνήσω τὸ ὄνομά μου in 3.8 may favour understanding οὐκ ἠρνήσω τὴν πίστιν μου in terms of confessing the faith in the narrow sense of verbal testimony, this is not the only option. For example, the call for Christians to exhibit πίστις in the face of persecution is not so narrowly conceived in 2.19 and 13.10, where the life of faith is intended.

following verses for embracing false teaching (τὴν διδαχὴν Βαλαάμ and τὴν διδαχὴν [τῶν] Νικολαϊτῶν, 2.14–15). In addition, the presence of the definite article qualifying πίστις in both 2.13 and 14.12 is problematic for the objective genitive interpretation in that it suggests a particular definition of faith. Whereas the arthrous form of πίστις used absolutely can denote the content of belief,[105] the qualification by a personal pronoun or name suggests that the faith of a particular individual is in view.

Further, we have already observed that Jesus and Antipas are both described, against the background of their martyrdoms, as ὁ μάρτυς (μου) ὁ πιστός (μου).[106] This suggest that, with respect to matters of discipleship, the author considered them as fellow witnesses who remained faithful to the end. Thus, when the Pergamum Christians are exhorted not to deny τὴν πίστιν μου, it seems more likely that they are being challenged to hold fast to the testimony of faith which links all faithful witnesses together and which originates in its greatest exponent, Jesus Christ.[107]

Revelation 14.12 contains the second πίστις construction for consideration. The preceding verses describe in graphic detail the punishments awaiting those who do not remain faithful to the Lamb and lead into an exhortation for endurance (ἡ ὑπομονή) on behalf of the saints: οἱ τηροῦντες τὰς ἐντολὰς τοῦ θεοῦ καὶ τὴν πίστιν Ἰησοῦ. The meaning of this phrase is not immediately apparent and requires clarification. Although τὰς ἐντολὰς τοῦ θεοῦ is manifestly a subjective genitive ('the commandments of God'), τὴν πίστιν Ἰησοῦ could be either subjective ('the faith of Jesus') or objective ('the faith in Jesus').[108] The use of Ἰησοῦς in isolation may indicate an emphasis upon Jesus' earthly ministry,[109] and a comparison with similar phrases in Revelation provides additional help:

105 BAGD, 664; Bultmann, 'πιστεύω', 213–14; Lampe, *Lexicon*, 1086–7.

106 The personal pronoun μοῦ may reflect a degree of dependency, but it could also reflect continuity between martyrs.

107 'To be approved as "my witness, my faithful one" is to be accepted as essentially Christlike, for Christ himself is supremely "the faithful witness" (1.5).' (P. E. Hughes, *Revelation*, 44; cf. Charles, *Revelation*, vol. 1, 61) It is worth reiterating that both πίστις and πιστός can convey an active (e.g. trust/trusting) and/or passive (e.g. faithful) sense; they are different parts of speech and are not necessarily semantically discrete.

108 As in 2.13, the objective genitive receives greater support: Bousset, *Offenbarung*, 386; Caird, *Revelation*, 188; Mounce, *Revelation*, 277; Swete, *Revelation*, 183.

109 Bauckham, *Theology*, 66, and Vos, *Synoptic Traditions*, 207–8. Ἰησοῦς occurs fourteen times in Revelation: three times with Χριστός (1.1, 2, 5), two times with

14.12	τὰς ἐντολὰς τοῦ θεοῦ καὶ		τὴν πίστιν	Ἰησοῦ
12.17	τὰς ἐντολὰς τοῦ θεοῦ καὶ	.....	τὴν μαρτυρίαν	Ἰησοῦ
1.2	τὸν λόγον τοῦ θεοῦ καὶ		τὴν μαρτυρίαν	Ἰησοῦ Χριστοῦ
1.9	τὸν λόγον τοῦ θεοῦ καὶ		τὴν μαρτυρίαν	Ἰησοῦ
6.9	τὸν λόγον τοῦ θεοῦ καὶ	διὰ	τὴν μαρτυρίαν	ἣν εἶχον
19.10			τὴν μαρτυρίαν	Ἰησοῦ
20.4	τὴν μαρτυρίαν Ἰησοῦ καὶ	διὰ	τὸν λόγον	τοῦ θεοῦ

This table suggests that certain phrases are used interchangeably by the author and are semantically equivalent. More specifically, it appears that, on the one hand, τὰς ἐντολὰς τοῦ θεοῦ and τὸν λόγον τοῦ θεοῦ and, on the other, τὴν πίστιν Ἰησοῦ and τὴν μαρτυρίαν Ἰησοῦ are utilised in this way.[110] The situation, however, is more complex and ambiguous. At the beginning of the Apocalypse, both τὸν λόγον τοῦ θεοῦ and τὴν μαρτυρίαν Ἰησοῦ Χριστοῦ are identified with the ἀποκάλυψις Ἰησοῦ Χριστοῦ given to John and contained in the following work. In the next verse, this same entity is referred to as τοὺς λόγους τῆς προφητείας (1.3), a form which is echoed repeatedly in the final chapter.[111] Particular sections within the book are also highlighted as οὗτοι οἱ λόγοι ἀληθινοὶ τοῦ θεοῦ (19.9; cf. 17.17) or οὗτοι οἱ λόγοι πιστοὶ καὶ ἀληθινοί (21.5; 22.6) and in 19.13 the rider of the white horse, who must be identified with the Lamb, is himself called ὁ λόγος τοῦ θεοῦ.

Although a number of these expressions can be equated with the Book of Revelation itself, reference to Jesus as ὁ λόγος τοῦ θεοῦ alerts us to the probability that, in certain cases, a broader and more dynamic understanding of God's word is intended.[112] This may be reflected in the association of τὴν μαρτυρίαν/τὴν πίστιν Ἰησοῦ with τὸν λόγον/τὰς ἐντολὰς τοῦ θεοῦ and is almost certainly in view when the testimony of Jesus is identified with τὸ πνεῦμα τῆς

κύριος (22.20, 21) and nine times alone (1.9[x2]; 12.17; 14.12; 17.6; 19.10[x2]; 20.4; 22.16). We discuss the construction τὴν μαρτυρίαν Ἰησοῦ (Χριστοῦ) below, but the use of Ἰησοῦς in 1.9 (συγκοινωνὸς ἐν τῇ θλίψει καὶ βασιλείᾳ καὶ ὑπομονῇ ἐν Ἰησοῦ) and 17.6 (ἐκ τοῦ αἵματος τῶν μαρτύρων Ἰησοῦ) indicate Jesus' solidarity with those called to share in suffering, in 20.4 it stands in contrast to the exalted Christ and in 22.16 Ἰησοῦς denotes one who is ἡ ῥίζα καὶ τὸ γένος Δαυίδ.

110 Cf. D. Hill ('Revelation', 411–14) and L. A. Vos (*Synoptic Traditions*, 197–214), who both discuss the meaning of τὴν μαρτυρίαν Ἰησοῦ (Χριστοῦ) in detail and yet fail to consider τὴν πίστιν Ἰησοῦ.

111 E.g. τοὺς λόγους τῆς προφητείας τοῦ βιβλίου τούτου, 22.7; τοὺς λόγους τῆς προφητείας τοῦ βιβλίου τούτου, 22.10; τοὺς λόγους τῆς προφητείας τοῦ βιβλίου τούτου, 22.18; τῶν λόγων τοῦ βιβλίου τῆς προφητείας ταύτης, 22.19; cf. τῶν προφητῶν καὶ τῶν τηρούντων τοὺς λόγους τοῦ βιβλίου τούτου, 22.9.

112 Vos, *Synoptic Traditions*, 196–207; also Satake, *Gemeindeordnung*, 98–107.

προφητείας (19.10). Further evidence of this broader conception is provided by those martyrs who died διὰ τὴν μαρτυρίαν Ἰησοῦ καὶ διὰ τὸν λόγον τοῦ θεοῦ (20.4) or as a result of their witness to the same;[113] they manifestly did not possess the Apocalypse. And again, Revelation 1.9 informs us that John is on Patmos διὰ τὸν λόγον τοῦ θεοῦ καὶ τὴν μαρτυρίαν Ἰησοῦ; it is possible that his presence on the island is voluntary and reflects a desire to communicate with God, but his description as συγκοινωνὸς ἐν τῇ θλίψει καὶ βασιλείᾳ καὶ ὑπομονῇ ἐν Ἰησοῦ suggests that he was exiled as a result of his discipleship.[114]

This survey is far from exhaustive, but it does indicate at least two things: firstly, the interrelatedness of phrases such as τὸν λόγον τοῦ θεοῦ, τὰς ἐντολὰς τοῦ θεοῦ, τὴν μαρτυρίαν Ἰησοῦ and τὴν πίστιν Ἰησοῦ; and, secondly, that their meaning cannot simply be equated with the Apocalypse, but must embrace other dimensions of early Christian witness to God's work in Christ. This is borne out elsewhere in the New Testament where the phrase ὁ λόγος τοῦ θεοῦ is used to describe Jesus' ministry, death and resurrection.[115] The Johannine writings are especially interesting here not only because λόγος and ἐντολή are used to denote Jesus' utterances,[116] but also because the meaning of μαρτυρία is always linked with the person of Jesus and not simply the kerygma about him.[117] This is particularly striking in 1 John 5 where ὁ πιστεύων εἰς τὸν υἱὸν τοῦ θεοῦ possesses not only τὴν μαρτυρίαν (5.10), but also τὸν υἱόν (5.12).

113 E.g. τὰς ψυχὰς τῶν ἐσφαγμένων διὰ τὸν λόγον τοῦ θεοῦ καὶ διὰ τὴν μαρτυρίαν ἣν εἶχον (6.9); καὶ αὐτοὶ ἐνίκησαν αὐτὸν διὰ τὸ αἷμα τοῦ ἀρνίου καὶ διὰ τὸν λόγον τῆς μαρτυρίας αὐτῶν (12.11); cf. 3.8, 10.

114 Mounce, *Revelation*, 75, and Vos, *Synoptic Traditions*, 198–201.

115 E.g. Luke 8.11; Acts 4.31; 6.2; 8.14; 11.1; 13.5, 7, 46; etc.; 1 Cor. 14.36; 2 Cor. 2.17; 4.2. Luke defines the contents of God's word in passages such as Acts 2.22–36; 3.12–26; 10.36–41; 13.16b-39; 17.22–31. See Kittel, 'λέγω', 114–19, and with special reference to Luke, Taeger, *Mensch*, esp. 123–6, 163–76.

116 '... for in the Johannine writings "the commandments of God" are synonymous with the message which Jesus brought to the world. The words of Jesus constitute the commandments of God (John 12.49), and the commandments of God are those which the early Christians received from Jesus (I John 3.23, 4.21).' (Vos, *Synoptic Traditions*, 203) Compare John 14.15, 21 with 14.23–4, John 15.10 with 15.20 and 1 John 2.4 with 1 John 2.5. See also the discussion of G. Schrenk ('ἐντέλλομαι', esp. 553–6), who observes that the correlation between λόγος and ἐντολή is made in the Synoptics as well (e.g. Matt. 15.3–6; Mark 7.9–13).

117 The key figures who give witness are: John the Baptist (John 1.7, 19; 5.32), John the Evangelist (John 19.35; 21.24), God (John 5.34, 36; 1 John 5.9[x2], 10, 11), Jesus (John 3.11, 32, 33; 5.31; 8.13, 14); also John 8.17; 1 John 5.9, 10; 3 John 12; cf. Acts 22.18.

This intimate association between μαρτυρία and Jesus suggests that τὴν μαρτυρίαν Ἰησοῦ (Χριστοῦ) should be taken as a subjective genitive denoting the witness which originates in the earthly figure of Jesus.[118] The linking of τὴν μαρτυρίαν Ἰησοῦ with other subjective genitives (τὸν λόγον τοῦ θεοῦ and τὰς ἐντολὰς τοῦ θεοῦ) lends support to this interpretation. For example, τὴν μαρτυρίαν Ἰησοῦ occurs with τὸν λόγον τοῦ θεοῦ in 1.2, where both expressions refer to the ἀποκάλυψις given to John. Although the revelation may be about God and Jesus, the point being made here is that it originates from them and has their authority (cf. 22.18–20).[119] Further, reference to Jesus as a μαρτύς (1.5; 3.14) and the way in which his μαρτυρία (1.9; 12.17; 19.10; 20.4) is described in comparable terms to those of other believers (6.9; 11.7; 12.11) adds force to the subjective genitive option. And finally, the identification of Jesus' witness with τὸ πνεῦμα τῆς προφητείας in 19.10 is striking, and is reminiscent of the relationship between Jesus and the Paraclete in John 14–16: Jesus' testimony is continued by the Spirit, who bears witness to Jesus (John 14.26; 15.26; 16.13–14); in a similar way, the Seer speaks of the testimony of Jesus, which is mediated by the Spirit and comes from Jesus himself.

The testimony of Jesus within the Apocalypse, therefore, originates in the earthly life of Jesus and, in particular, with his witness to God in the face of suffering and death. Even though the relationship between τὸν λόγον/τὰς ἐντολὰς τοῦ θεοῦ and τὴν μαρτυρίαν Ἰησοῦ remains problematic, a distinction can be discerned and one which is best articulated in terms of the relation between 'theory' and 'practice': once the word and commandments of God have been received by revelation, they must be borne witness to in the face of oppression.[120] Moreover, as on one occasion τὴν πίστιν Ἰησοῦ

[118] Especially, Sweet, 'Maintaining', 103–9; also Caird, *Revelation*, 237, and Hill, 'Revelation', 411–14. D. Hill points out that the use of the verb ἔχω favours the subjective genitive option.

[119] 'The expression in Rev. 1.2 is also revealing in another respect, and that is for the proper interpretation of the genitives θεοῦ and Ἰησοῦ in the expression "the word of God and the testimony of Jesus (Christ)." The apocalypse of which John bore witness (Rev. 1.2) is not the word *about* God (objective genitive). Rather, it is the word, the revelation, *from* God (subjective genitive): "das von God gesprochene Wort." Similarly, the parallel construction "μαρτυρία Ἰησοῦ Χριστοῦ" in Rev. 1.2 is not the testimony *about* Jesus Christ, but as the following words, ὅσα εἶδεν, indicate, it is the testimony *from* Jesus Christ: "das von Jesus abgelegte Zeugnis."' (Vos, *Synoptic Traditions*, 198)

[120] On this approach, Caird, *Revelation*, 237–8; Sweet, 'Maintaining', 106; Swete, *Apocalypse*, 3.

(14.12) replaces the usual τὴν μαρτυρίαν Ἰησοῦ in the construction exhibiting either τὸν λόγον τοῦ θεοῦ or τὰς ἐντολὰς τοῦ θεοῦ, it seems likely that this should also be similarly interpreted. That is to say, as a subjective genitive[121] denoting Jesus' life of faith, lived in response to God's word and in the midst of persecution.

For persecuted Christians to keep τὰς ἐντολὰς τοῦ θεοῦ καὶ τὴν πίστιν Ἰησοῦ or, indeed to suffer for τὴν μαρτυρίαν Ἰησοῦ and τὸν λόγον τοῦ θεοῦ, they must stand in a similar relation to the commandments of God as Jesus did. They are called to bear witness to God; and, to do this, they must keep faith as Jesus, the source of that witness, kept faith[122] – the same faith that was shared by Antipas (cf. 2.13) and other martyrs (cf. ὧδέ ἐστιν ἡ ὑπομονὴ καὶ ἡ πίστις τῶν ἁγίων, 13.10).[123] For the author of the Apocalypse, the challenge of persecution requires disciples to stand firm, but not in the sense of standing alone: rather, they are exhorted to keep the faith or witness of Jesus. The repeated use of τηρέω in this context is significant[124] for it implies the possession of something which is discrete from the exponent, yet is apprehended when allowed to find expression in the life of discipleship.[125] To keep τὴν πίστιν Ἰησοῦ, then, is to participate in a continuum reaching back to Jesus himself; it is to become a part of the tradition of Jesus.[126]

121 M. Barth, 'Faith', 364; Dunn, 'Once More', 732–3; cf. P. E. Hughes, *Revelation*, 164, and Krodel, *Revelation*, 270.

122 Cf. 1 Tim. 6.13, 'In the presence of God who gives life to all things, and of Christ Jesus who in his testimony before Pontius Pilate made the good confession (καὶ Χριστοῦ Ἰησοῦ τοῦ μαρτυρήσαντος ἐπὶ Ποντίου Πιλάτου τὴν καλὴν ὁμολογίαν).'

123 'In this imagery Christ is not only the church's Lord but also its elder brother whose life, death, and vindication/exaltation is the paradigm for the Christian's life. They are characterised (13.10) as those who have *hypomone* (steadfast endurance), faithfulness: faith in the sovereignty of God as the hidden Actor in the whole drama . . .' (Boring, *Revelation*, 153; also Bauckham, *Theology*, 73–80; Sweet, 'Maintaining', 103–9)

124 Cf. οἱ ἀκούοντες τοὺς λόγους τῆς προφητείας καὶ τηροῦντες τὰ ἐν αὐτῇ γεγραμμένα (1.3); ἐτήρησάς μου τὸν λόγον καὶ οὐκ ἠρνήσω τὸ ὄνομά μου (3.8); ὅτι ἐτήρησὰς τὸν λόγον τῆς ὑπομονῆς (3.10); τῶν τηρούντων τὰς ἐντολὰς τοῦ θεοῦ καὶ ἐχόντων τὴν μαρτυρίαν Ἰησοῦ (12.17); μακάριος ὁ τηρῶν τοὺς λόγους τῆς προφητείας τοῦ βιβλίου τούτου (22.7); τῶν προφητῶν καὶ τῶν τηρούντων τοὺς λόγους τοῦ βιβλίου τούτου (22.9; cf. 3.26).

125 Vos, *Synoptic Traditions*, 202.

126 Once again, a similar perspective is evident in the Pastorals: 'I have fought the good fight, I have finished the race, I have kept the faith (τὴν πίστιν τετήρηκα).' (2 Tim. 4.7)

2.3 Concluding remarks

Our investigations into the Apocalypse have led us to conclude that both πιστός and πίστις are used by the author with reference to Jesus' earthly ministry. The qualification of μάρτυς with πιστός in the phrase 'faithful witness' (1.5; 3.14) indicates the nature of his testimony and, by implication, the outcome: Jesus is ὁ μάρτυς ὁ πιστός because he bears faithful witness to God's message of salvation to the point of death. And even when πιστός is used absolutely (19.11), the reader is reminded of those occasions where it qualifies μάρτυς. But if πιστός describes the character of Jesus as a witness, πίστις denotes the substance of his testimony. The faith of Jesus (2.13; 14.12), therefore, cannot be equated with the kerygma about him, abstracted from the earthly figure, but must be understood in terms of his life of faith and, in particular, his testimony to God in the midst of suffering and persecution. In this way, Jesus' faith fulfils both an inspirational and an emulative function as fellow believers are challenged to share his testimony and martyrdom (cf. 2.13; 13.10; 14.12).

Before drawing this chapter to a close, we should note the strong similarities between the ways in which πίστις and to a lesser extent πιστός are used in relation to Jesus within Hebrews and the Apocalypse.[127] This is perhaps not surprising in that both works were written to encourage perseverance amongst believers facing oppression. Although the authors attempt to secure this goal in part by stressing the reality of future punishment,[128] it is significant that Jesus is portrayed within these documents not simply as the one who secures salvation for those remaining faithful to the end, but also as the one who provides a model for others to emulate. As one who shared in humanity, he also had to live, suffer and face death by faith; and this recognition appears to have stimulated interest in Jesus' life, especially in his passion, as well as in what that life achieved. As a result, Jesus is understood by these authors to be the source of faith in a comprehensive sense, embracing both the possibility of belief through his atoning death and subsequent exaltation,

[127] There are, of course, differences as well. Both authors use πίστις in a similar way, referring to Jesus' life of faith in the face of persecution and death. Πιστός in Hebrews, however, describes Jesus' continuing heavenly high-priestly ministry; in Revelation, it relates principally to his witness to God on earth.

[128] E.g. Heb. 3.12–19; 6.1–8; 10.26–31; Rev. 2.5, 16, 22–3; 3.1; 6.10, 12–17; 9.3–6, 18; 14.9–11, 19–20; 16.1–21; 18.1–24.

and the substance of belief in the form of a life lived for God. He becomes, so to speak, the place where opposites meet: where God's salvation is mediated to humanity through the faith of one who suffered death on behalf of others, and where humanity's response to God is incarnated in that very same life of faith.[129]

[129] If this assessment is an accurate representation of the authors' concerns, we have reason to call into question the view that, within the early church, faith had become divorced from the person of Jesus in the sense that it consisted primarily of theological interpretation upon his life and death from a post-resurrection perspective – a kerygma which had to be believed in and lived out. It is true that within this conception, Jesus remains the content of faith as one who opens up new possibilities of relationship with God; however, the evidence of Hebrews and Revelation requires a broader understanding and one which accommodates the exemplary function of his life of faith as well. That is to say, if the work of Christ is the basis for and object of belief, the faith of Jesus gives substance to the life of faith.

6

JESUS' FAITH IN EXTRA-BIBLICAL SOURCES

1 Preliminary considerations

Our review of the New Testament is now largely complete and in this chapter we shall extend our investigation to other early Christian sources. Before proceeding in this way, however, we need to explain why the evidence from the Letter of James has been excluded from our biblical survey. At the beginning of chapter 2, James points out that practising favouritism (προσωπολημψίαις) is incompatible with τὴν πίστιν τοῦ κυρίου ἡμῶν Ἰησοῦ Χριστοῦ τῆς δόξης (2.1). In the light of what has been said about πίστις Χριστοῦ in Paul and similar formulations in Ephesians and Revelation, this appears to be another occurrence of the subjective genitive denoting the faith of Christ.[1] No doubt, this is a viable interpretation and one which is favoured by similar constructions elsewhere in the letter,[2] together with the rare reference here to the person of Jesus (cf. 1.1). Yet these factors must be weighed against others. For instance, although much of the teaching and exhortation in James is reminiscent of the Synoptics,[3] Jesus is never cited as a paradigm for the essentially practical understanding of faith espoused by the letter; rather, Abraham and Rahab are the exemplars of faith (2.21–5), Job and the prophets of suffering (5.10–11), and Elijah of prayer (5.17–18). There is, then, nothing in the letter which gives meaning or substance to the faith of Christ, if alluded to in 2.1. Further, although the designation Ἰησοῦ Χριστοῦ suggests that the earthly figure of Jesus is in view, its qualification by τοῦ κυρίου

[1] Dunn, 'Once More', 732.

[2] Other subjective genitives include: τὰ ὦτα κυρίου Σαβαώθ (5.4); τῆς παρουσίας τοῦ κυρίου; (5.7; also 5.8); ἐν τῷ ὀνόματι κυρίου (5.10); τὸ τέλος κυρίου (5.11).

[3] See Adamson, *James*, 169–74; Davids, 'James', 63–84; Martin, *James*, 56–75. This correspondence also includes the understanding of faith; for example, Jas. 1.6–8 seems to be informed by Jesus' teaching in Matt. 21.21–2 and Mark 11.23–4.

ἡμῶν and τῆς δόξης shifts the focus back to the heavenly session of the exalted Christ.[4] On balance, therefore, although τὴν πίστιν τοῦ κυρίου ἡμῶν Ἰησοῦ Χριστοῦ τῆς δόξης may be a subjective genitive, the absence of corroborative evidence means that the content of Christ's faith remains undefined and its significance for the rest of the letter unspecified. In consequence, it adds little to our understanding of why Christians were interested in the faith of Christ.

We move on, then, to consider the extra-biblical sources. It is not within the compass of the present study to offer a comprehensive survey of patristic literature or, indeed, to attempt exhaustive assessments of those authors discussed; rather, we must limit ourselves to considering the trajectories of interest in Jesus' faith isolated in the biblical sources and examine what became of them in subsequent Christian writings. Most of the literature to be considered comes from the first three centuries, but we shall conclude by suggesting that the Arian controversy may explain why talk of Jesus' faith ultimately became untenable within the context of christological reflection.

Before proceeding, however, a number of more general observations about the significance and meaning of faith in this formative period of church history are in order. Even a cursory overview of Christian thought during this period reveals a remarkable development in the understanding of faith.[5] This can be highlighted by comparing the largely 'incarnational' approach which we isolated in certain strands of early Judaism and Christianity, where the response of people such as Abraham, Moses and Jesus to God defined faith, with the highly sophisticated and precise formulations encapsulated in, for instance, the Nicene Creed.

Clearly, this development was a gradual one and its progress can be charted via more modest credal affirmations from the New Testament canon onwards.[6] Furthermore, the course followed was

[4] Κύριος denotes both God (1.7; 3.9; 4.10, 15; 5.5, 10[?], 11[x2], 14, 15) and Christ (1.1; 2.1; 5.7, 8, 10[?]); in 5.7–8, it clearly refers to Christ's exalted status. It is unclear how τῆς δόξης relates to the rest of the construction; see: Adamson, *James*, 272–5; Davids, *James*, 106–7; Dibelius, *James*, 127–8; Martin, *James*, 59–60.

[5] For more detailed discussions, see, Hatch, *Christian Literature*, 72–144, and Lührmann, 'Glaube', 79–119.

[6] Most of the relevant texts can be found in R. P. C. Hanson, *Tradition*, 85–94, and Kelly, *Creeds*, 13–23. It is noteworthy that the substantial development in the understanding of faith was accommodated within the semantics of the one Greek root, πιστεύω (cf. *fides* and *credo* in Latin).

by no means arbitrary, but was shaped by a number of factors, including: (i) the continuing theological reflection upon the significance of Jesus; (ii) the establishment of the church's catholic and apostolic basis; and (iii) the dialogue between Christianity and culture.[7] These influences affected the meaning of faith in different ways. For example, belief in the full divinity of Christ as articulated in the great ecumenical creeds was the culmination of the church's attempt to evaluate Jesus' significance in relation to knowledge of God and salvation – a pursuit which eventually yielded what came to be accepted as the central core of the Christian faith.[8] Secondly, the proliferation of christologies[9] in the early centuries eventually had to be controlled by defining Jesus' relationship to faith more precisely. Here the notion of apostolicity was determinative for supplying a platform upon which faith could be prescribed so as to provide a touchstone for competing christological assessments and a basis for church unity.[10] Thirdly, the dialogue between Christianity and cultures alien to the Judaeo-Christian world-view resulted in the articulation of faith in categories drawn from alternative philosophical outlooks.[11]

One consequence of these and other processes was the growing concentration upon the propositional content of faith (*fides quae creditur*), in contrast to the dispositional (*fides qua creditur*). In this respect, the formulations of belief leading up to the Nicene Creed bear witness to a concerted attempt to evaluate faith by abstracting it from the experience of the same: that is to say, to define faith in such a way as to provide a concrete basis for the Christian encounter with God which would permit the church to perform its didactic, apologetic and polemical functions.[12] The intention here was not so much to divorce the propositional from the dispositional dimension

[7] On the development of 'rules of faith' and creeds in the early centuries, see: Flesseman-van Leer, *Tradition*; Hägglund, 'Bedeutung', 1–44; R. P. C. Hanson, *Tradition*, 75–129; Kelly, *Creeds*; Mitros, 'Norm', 444–71; T. F. Torrance, 'Deposit', 1–28; Young, *Creeds*, esp. 1–15.

[8] T. F. Torrance, *Reconciliation*, 215–66, and *Trinitarian Faith*, esp. 146–90.

[9] See the surveys of Grillmeier, *Christ*, and Kelly, *Doctrines*, 138–62, 280–343.

[10] Flesseman-van Leer, *Tradition*, 186–97, and Mitros, 'Norm', 455–65.

[11] Lührmann, *Glaube*, 85–99, and Stead, *Divine Substance*.

[12] These seem to represent the main thrusts which contributed to the definition of faith in the early Christian centuries; for example, catechesis and baptism undoubtedly provided the context for many of the early declaratory statements of faith, whilst the debate with philosophies such as Platonism significantly modified the language and categories used. Further, controversies with gnosticism, Arianism and other 'heresies' contributed to the precision and comprehensiveness of later credal formulations.

of faith, as to establish the means by which the former could regulate and substantiate the latter. Thus, whilst a number of the church fathers supply 'rules of faith' in one shape or another, they also underline the centrality of the church as the context where such articulations find significance and, so to speak, come to life within the dynamic continuum of divine–human encounter which reaches back to Jesus himself.[13] In this way, a link between *fides quae* and *fides qua creditur* could be maintained at the same time as supporting a critical or reflective perspective on faith.[14]

However, the relationship between the disposition and the content of faith is a complex one and can readily be misunderstood.[15] For example, the articulation of faith in credal form permits intellectual evaluation of belief in a way that can be divorced from experience of the phenomenon described. Whilst this permits a degree of objectivity, it runs the danger of severing propositional belief from its historical basis in personal encounter with God. As we have indicated, the emphasis upon apostolicity and the worshipping community provided controls for 'in-house' theology, although they had little force in the sphere of apologetics. What is more, it is clear that the tendency to drive a wedge between *fides quae* and *fides qua creditur*, where none exists, is a very real danger for all critical investigations – including the present study.

During our discussion of the New Testament, we considered a number of ways in which Jesus and faith were associated. Our conclusions in relation to interest in the faith of Jesus will be summarised shortly, but more generally we observed how Jesus was thought to inform both the act (*fides qua*) and the content of faith (*fides quae creditur*). We also noted that, although representing assessments of Jesus from different perspectives, they were not necessarily thought to be incompatible. Further, we recognised that all such discussions of faith were based upon and informed by personal encounter with Jesus Christ. Thus, as we continue our inquiry beyond the New Testament, we must be careful not to

[13] E.g. Irenaeus, *Haer*. IV.26 and V.20; Tertullian, *Haer*. 19–29; on this, especially, T. F. Torrance, *Mediation*, 1–11, and *Trinitarian Faith*, 252–301.

[14] This dynamic between 'rules of faith' or creeds and the church is, in fact, part of a broader perspective which is rooted in the relation between scripture and the church (Flesseman-van Leer, *Tradition*; R. P. C. Hanson, *Bible*, 3–7; Mitros, 'Norm', 444–5).

[15] On how this relates to patristic literature, see T. F. Torrance, *Trinitarian Faith*, 13–46; for more general discussions: Niebuhr, *Faith*; Smith, *Faith*; Swinburne, *Faith*.

prejudge or oversimplify the relation between Jesus Christ and faith. For example, we cannot assume that Jesus was considered solely as one who provided information about God and his offer of salvation (i.e. the object of belief). Moreover, discussions which appear to equate Christ with the substance or content of faith may in fact be a good deal more complicated; that is, if faith is grounded upon the apostolic witness to Jesus Christ and personal encounter with the risen Lord in the worshipping community, then it becomes so intimately linked with Christ himself as to be inseparable from him and, in this way, comes to be defined by him in every respect.[16]

It is hoped that these brief comments will help us to locate and evaluate the trajectories concerning interest in Jesus' faith within the broader contours of the development of the phenomenon in the first Christian centuries and so alert us to some of the factors which are likely to have shaped their progress and determined their fate. However, before we continue our investigations, it will be helpful to summarise our findings to date. To this end, the evidence for the faith of Jesus in the New Testament can be accommodated within three categories of interest: paradigmatic, theological and canonic. As we shall see, the first two readily split into sub-divisions and it should be pointed out that, whilst these groupings identify basic emphases, they are not intended to be mutually exclusive. The proposed classification can be represented by the following schema:

paradigmatic function
Jesus' faith and discipleship, especially miracle-working
(Matthew and Mark)
Jesus' faith and discipleship, especially suffering and martyrdom
(Hebrews and Revelation)

theological function
Jesus' faith and the faithfulness/righteousness of God
(Romans, Galatians and Philippians)
Jesus the faithful high priest
(Hebrews)

canonic function
Jesus as the source, object and substance of faith
(Ephesians and Pastorals)

[16] It may follow from this, as we remarked in the case of Paul, that constructions such as πίστις Χριστοῦ are used precisely because they are ambiguous and, therefore, can more adequately embrace the full extent of the relationship between Christ and faith.

With respect to the paradigmatic function, we noted how certain traditions in Matthew and Mark reflect a correspondence between Jesus' conduct and that required of his followers. This is particularly apparent from the way in which Jesus is portrayed as one who performs miracles by faith and who calls his disciples to follow suit. We also recognised that in Hebrews and Revelation, the emulative function of Jesus' faith comes to expression in relation to persecution and martyrdom. The determinative insight here is the recognition that Jesus' faith informs his attitude to and experience of suffering and death. In these ways, Christians identified in Jesus one whose life of faith epitomised different facets of human response to God.

Interest in Jesus' faith was not limited to discipleship, however, but could also inform the understanding of God's offer of salvation in Christ. In particular, we noticed how Paul speaks of Jesus' faith as a vehicle for communicating God's righteousness: Jesus' faith-inspired obedience, which endured suffering and the cross, is the channel both for God's covenantal faithfulness and for human response. Further, the author of Hebrews uses the adjective πιστός to describe Jesus' on-going, heavenly, high-priestly function, as he continues to minister on behalf of all.

Finally, we recognised that the deutero-Pauline and, especially, the Pastoral epistles demonstrate a growing desire to formalise the revelation and provisions of God in Christ, together with their implications for response to God, in doctrinal terms which could inform and to a certain extent regulate the outworkings of faith. Within this trend, the emphasis upon and distinguishing of Jesus' own faith fade as the focus becomes increasingly trained onto the theological interpretation of his life, death and resurrection, and their implications for the faith of others. However, Ephesians and the Pastorals bear witness to a stage in which Jesus' faith has not become totally divorced or excluded from this process; on the contrary, it finds its place within a christology which sees Jesus Christ as the canon of faith, defining its source, object and substance.

With this overview in mind, we shift our attention to the extra-biblical sources in order to assess how these patterns of thought fared in other Christian traditions.[17]

[17] Although much of the material to be discussed was written after the majority of New Testament books, some of it (e.g. Barnabas; 1 Clement; Didache; Ignatius) may well predate or be contemporaneous with the later contributions.

2 The paradigmatic function of Jesus' faith

Following the lead of certain New Testament traditions,[18] we find that the miracles of Jesus are often interpreted, especially amongst the church fathers, as indications of his special significance or divinity.[19] Even in the New Testament Apocrypha, where the emphasis tends to be on the miracles currently performed by the disciples rather than those of their Lord, it is still Jesus who is considered to be working through them.[20] That is to say, rather than the disciples following Jesus' example, they become channels for his on-going ministry as miracles continue to be performed in his name, by his presence, power or authority.[21] Further, although faith is occasionally a prerequisite,[22] we more frequently encounter cases where miracles lead to belief in and commitment to Jesus.[23] Within this scenario, it is apparent that the healings, exorcisms and natural wonders of Jesus have become elevated to a superhuman plane where they reveal something about him, rather than the content of discipleship *per se*. This does not deny that miracles were still thought to characterise the early church,[24] but it does demonstrate that the dynamics by which they take place were conceived in fundamentally different terms from those operative in Jesus' minis-

[18] Cf. Matt. 11.2–6/Luke 7.18–23; Matt. 12.28/Luke 11.20; John 5.1–21; Acts 2.22; 10.38; 14.3.

[19] Arnobius, *Adv. Nat.* I.42–3; Athanasius, *De Inc.* 15; 18; Eusebius, *Hist. Eccl.* I.13; II.3; Gregory of Nyssa, *Or. Catech.* 23; 34; Irenaeus, *Haer.* II.32; Justin Martyr, *Dial.* 69; *Apol.* I.30–1; Origen, *Contra Celsum* I.38; II.48; Tertullian, *Apol.* 23; cf. Exod. 4.5, 8, 9, 31; 14.31; 19.9; Num. 14.11. See: Brown, *Miracles*, 3–11; Lampe, 'Miracles', 205–18; van der Loos, *Miracles*, 240–3; Wiles, 'Miracles', esp. 231.

[20] Lampe, 'Miracles', 214–15; the New Testament Apocrypha, however, does narrate many miracle stories relating to the infancy of Jesus; see Achtemeier, 'Miracle Workers', 161–2.

[21] The main emphasis is upon the name of Jesus, especially in exorcism: Act. John 83; Act. Pet. 11; Act. Thom. 33; 41; 53; 75; Irenaeus, *Haer.* II.32; Justin Martyr, *Dial.* 33; *Apol.* II.6; Origen, *Contra Celsum* I.67; II.33; III.24, 28; Tertullian, *Apol.* 23. For alternative expressions, see: Act. John 22; Act. Pet. 15; 16; 26; Act. Thom. 59; 141; Eusebius, *Hist. Eccl.* II.3; cf. Mark 16.17–20; John 14.12–13; Acts 4.9–12; 16.18.

[22] E.g. 'And when the apostle [i.e. Thomas] heard this from the captain he was greatly grieved for him: "Dost thou believe that Jesus will heal them [i.e. his demon-possessed wife and daughter]?" And the captain said: "Yes." And the apostle: "Commit thyself then to Jesus, and he will heal them and bring them help."' (Act. Thom. 65; also Act. Thom. 150; Act. John 23)

[23] Act. John 33; 39; 93; Act. Pet. 2; 4; 11; 17; 23–4; Act. Paul 37–43; Act. Thom 36–8; 59; Origen, *Contra Celsum* III.28; *Comm. in Joh.* X.44; cf. John 2.11, 23; 4.35; 7.31; 20.30–1; Acts 9.36–43; 13.12; 16.25–34; 19.11–20; Gal. 3.5.

[24] On the place of healing in the ante-Nicene church, see, Frost, *Christian Healing*.

try: whilst Jesus' miracles are a function of his divinity, those of the disciples are also expressions of his sovereignty and, as such, are executed by him through his servants. In consequence, the way in which Jesus' thaumaturgic activities are presented in much early Christian literature indicates that this aspect of his ministry was not, strictly speaking, thought to be emulative.[25]

There are indications, however, that other assessments of his wonder-working abilities were considered and that, in certain cases, these attributed faith to Jesus. Two strands are worthy of comment. Firstly, there are instances where Jesus' miraculous activity is in view and faith is either explicitly mentioned or implied as a determining factor for his success. For example, in book eight of the Sibylline Oracles, the miracles of Christ are spoken of within the context of his humanity. He is linked with Moses, who similarly fulfils his God-given vocation πίστει,[26] and his incarnation is described in kenotic terms. Although no parallels are explicitly drawn between his own discipleship and that of Christian believers, they are implied; further it is clear that Christ's assuming of human form is the source of faith for others:

> Moses prefigured him [i.e. Christ], stretching out his holy arms, conquering Amalek by faith (νικῶν τὸν 'Αμαλὴκ πίστει) so that the people might know that he is elect and precious with God his father, the staff of David and the stone he promised. The one who has believed in him will have eternal life (εἰς ὃν ὁ πιστεύσας ζωὴν αἰώνιον ἕξει). For he will come to creation not in glory, but as a man, pitiable, without honor or form, so that he might give hope to the pitiable. He will give form to perishable flesh and

25 There are, of course, exceptions. For example, whilst it is emphasised that the apostle Thomas is not Jesus (cf. 'I am not Jesus, but a servant of Jesus. I am not Christ, but a minister of Christ. I am not the Son of God . . .'; Act. Thom. 160), there are places where he is described in terms remarkably similar to those used in the canonical gospels of his Lord. In the following extract, the friends of king Gundaphorus of India offer their opinion on the apostle: '. . . but he goes about the towns and villages, and if he has anything he gives it all to the poor, and he teaches a new God <.> and heals the sick and drives out demons and does many other wonderful things; and we think he is a magician. But his works of compassion, and the healings which are wrought by him without reward, and moreover his simplicity and kindness and the quality of his faith, show that he is righteous or an apostle of the new God whom he preaches.' (Act. Thom. 20)

26 Cf. Heb. 3.1–6, where both Moses and Jesus are considered to be πιστός in God's house. This theme is also taken up by other early Christian authors (Athanasius, *contra Arianos* II.1–10; 1 Clem. 43).

> heavenly faith to the faithless (ἵν' οἰκτροῖς ἐλπίδα δώσει· καὶ φθαρτῇ σαρκὶ μορφὴν καὶ πίστιν ἀπίστοις οὐράνιον δώσει) . . . He will stop the winds with a word. He will calm the raging sea by walking on it with feet of peace and with faith (τοὺς ἀνέμους παύσειε λόγῳ, στορέσει δὲ θάλασσαν μαινομένην ποσὶν εἰρήνης πίστει τε πατήσας). (Sib. Or. 8.251–9, 273–8 [*OrS* 157–61])

A less explicit reference to Jesus' faith is discernible in Origen's commentary on Matthew's Gospel and, in particular, his handling of the healing of the epileptic boy pericope (cf. Matt. 17.14–21). The discussion is too extensive to quote in full, but as the following extracts indicate, one implication of his exegesis is that Jesus performed the deliverance – at least in part – by faith:[27]

> But since our present object is not to make inquiry about every case, but about the passage before us, let us, adopting a figurative interpretation, consider . . . that he could not be healed by the disciples but by Jesus Himself . . . We have already, then, spoken in part of the words, 'If ye have faith as a grain of mustard seed, ye shall say unto this mountain,' etc.; but nevertheless also we shall speak in this place the things that appear to us fitted to increase perspicuity . . . Whenever, then, any one has all faith so that he no longer disbelieves in any things which are contained in the Holy Scriptures, and has faith such as was that of Abraham, who believed in God to such a degree that his faith was counted for righteousness, he has all faith as a grain of mustard seed; then will such an one say to this mountain – I mean, the dumb and deaf spirit in him who is called lunatic, – 'Remove hence,' clearly, from the man who is suffering, perhaps to the abyss, and it shall remove. And the Apostle, taking, I think, his starting-point from this place, says with apostolic authority, 'If I have all faith so as to remove mountains,' for not one mountain merely, but also several analogous to it, he removes who has all faith which is as a grain of mustard seed; and nothing shall be impossible to him who has so great faith. (Origen, *Comm. in Matt.* XIII.3–7; trans. ANF 10.477–81)

[27] The conversation between Jesus and his disciples recorded on a fragment which is thought to constitute part of the Acts of Paul may reflect a similar understanding (quoted in *NTA* 2.383).

Although Origen employs a discursive or 'figurative' interpretation of the story in order to demonstrate its pertinence for contemporary situations, he does not ignore the internal structure of the narrative. For instance, he starts by drawing attention to questions raised by the text, including why Jesus was able to heal the boy when others were unsuccessful. Much of the subsequent discussion relates the passage to Christian discipleship and, although the significance of mountain-moving faith (cf. Matt. 17.20) is explored primarily in relation to the faith of Abraham (cf. Gen. 15.6) and the teaching of Paul (cf. 1 Cor. 13.2), he does suggest that the healing of the paralytic was due to the power of faith (cf. '... then will such an one say to this mountain – I mean, the dumb and deaf spirit in him who is called lunatic, – "Remove hence," ...'). In this way, Jesus' faith is implied by Origen; he almost seems to take it for granted – presumably, it was not a contentious issue for him.

In addition to enabling his own mighty acts, Jesus' faith was also conceived of as something to be shared by others performing or experiencing miracles and answers to prayer.[28] For instance, the readers of the Shepherd of Hermas are exhorted to shun double-mindedness (δίψυχος) and to put on a faith (ἔνδυσαι δὲ τὴν πίστιν) which comes from the Lord above (ὅτι ἡ πίστις ἄνωθέν ἐστι παρὰ τοῦ κυρίου).[29] Such faith is full of power (τὴν πίστιν τὴν ἰσχυρὰν καὶ δυνατήν ... καὶ ἔχει δύναμιν μεγάλην) and those who possess it will have their petitions answered by God (ἔνδυσαι δὲ τὴν πίστιν, ὅτι ἰσχυρά ἐστι, καὶ πίστευε τῷ θεῷ ὅτι πάντα τὰ αἰτήματά σου ἃ αἰτεῖς λήψῃ ... ἡ γὰρ πίστις πάντα ἐπαγγέλλεται, πάντα τελειοῖ; *Man.* 9.6–12 [GCS 48.37]) . Although no examples from Jesus' ministry are given in support, the strong allusions to his teaching on faith recorded in the Synoptics,[30] together with the way in which he is spoken of as the one who gives faith, indicate that the author's thinking here is rooted in and informed by Jesus' ministry. Christians are called to share his faith; not only to believe in the one who

[28] It is possible that this understanding is reflected in the problematic Acts 3.16. Could it be that ἡ πίστις ἡ δι' αὐτοῦ refers to faith which originates in Jesus? For other interpretations, see Neirynck, 'Miracle Stories', 205–13.

[29] Κύριος is a regular title for Jesus in Hermas; see Quasten, *Patrology*, vol. 1, 99.

[30] For example, the notion of faith being free from doubt (Matt. 21.21/Mark 11.23; Mark 5.36/Luke 8.50; Matt. 8.13; Mark 4.40) and able to tap into God's omnipotence (Matt. 21.21/Mark 11.23; Luke 17.6; Matt. 17.20; Mark 9.23; Mark 5.34). Linguistically, there are similarities as well (e.g. διὰ τοῦτο λέγω ὑμῖν, *πάντα* ὅσα προσεύχεσθε καὶ *αἰτεῖσθε*, πιστεύετε ὅτι *ἐλάβετε*, καὶ ἔσται ὑμῖν (Mark 11.24; cf. Matt. 21.22).

is able to perform miracles on their behalf, but also to be clothed with that faith which comes from above and communicates miracle-working power.[31]

The paradigmatic function of Jesus' faith in relation to believers facing suffering, persecution and martyrdom is also taken up by Christian authors outside of the New Testament. A number of different emphases and applications can be discerned, ranging from interpretations of Jesus' own passion to the appropriation of his faith by others who share the way of suffering. For example, the Gospel of Truth records how 'Jesus, the merciful and faithful (πιστός), patiently accepted the endurance of suffering . . .'[32] Origen reflects a similar outlook in *Exhortatio ad martyrium*, when he describes how Jesus hoped in God when facing his passion (ἤλπιζε δὲ καὶ ἐπὶ θεῷ πεπληρωμένη ἱερῶν δογμάτων αὐτοῦ καρδία; *Mart.* 29 [GCS 2.25]). It is true that ἐλπίζω is used here rather than πιστεύω,[33] but the idea of a trusting and believing relationship with God is clearly implied. The same root is used by Origen elsewhere in relation to the mother of the Maccabean martyrs (*Mart.* 27; cf. 4 Macc. 15.24; 17.1–2) and, again, at the beginning of his exhortation, where ἡ ἐπ' ἐλπίδι ἐλπίς is given to those who persevere (*Mart.* 2 [GCS 2.3]).

It is also significant how Origen presents Jesus as an exemplar for those called to give up their lives for the faith.[34] Although he does

[31] Elsewhere, the author actually speaks about putting on (ἐνδύω) the faith of the Lord (e.g. *Vis.* 4.1.8; *Man.* 9.1.7; *Sim.* 6.1.2); these texts will be discussed later. A similar understanding may be present in the Acts of Peter: the apostle, having cured a woman of blindness, is asked to perform further healings; he responds by inquiring whether they possess the faith that is in Christ (*Si est in uobis fides, quae est in Christo*; Act. Pet. 21). *Fides quae est in Christo* suggests more than simply believing in Christ, but sharing the faith which Christ shared. See the discussion of 1 Tim. 1.14, 3.13, 2 Tim. 1.13 and 3.15 in chapter 4, section 2; the Vulgate translates ἐν πίστει τῇ ἐν Χριστῷ Ἰησοῦ (1 Tim. 3.13) as *fide quae est in Christo Jesu* (similarly 1 Tim. 1.14 and 2 Tim. 3.15; cf. 2 Tim. 1.13).

[32] G.Tr. 20.10–14 [*EV* 10–11]. Although this work only survives in Coptic translations, it is believed that the original was written in Greek; hence the editors' conjecture concerning the Vorlage (i.e. πιστός). On the link with Heb. 2.17–18, see J. A. Williams, *Gospel of Truth*, 44–6.

[33] Origen's choice of ἐλπίζω here is determined by the quotation from Ps. 26.1–3 (LXX); he can, however, use the πιστεύω group in relation to Jesus (e.g. *Comm. in Joh.* X.44).

[34] E.g. *Mart.* 37; 42. The correspondence between Jesus and other martyrs even leads Origen to explore the soteriological significance of their deaths: 'Perhaps also just as we have been redeemed by the precious blood of Jesus, Jesus who has received the name that is above every name, so also some are redeemed by the precious blood of the martyrs.' (*Mart.* 50; trans. LCC 2.429)

not say explicitly that martyrs must exhibit the same πίστις as Jesus demonstrated, the deduction is obvious. As Jesus gives a pattern to follow in matters of prayer[35] and obedience,[36] so it seems probable that Origen also recognised the exemplary nature of his relation to God in times of suffering.[37] Certainly, he acknowledged the need for believers to share the mind of Christ[38] and, following St Paul's confession in Galatians 2.20, to know his presence.[39]

A more explicit reference to Jesus' faith can be found in the work of Clement of Alexandria where, during an extended discussion on martyrdom in which he draws heavily on the Epistle to the Hebrews, he cites with approval Hebrews 12.1–2, the implication being that Jesus should be counted amongst the martyrs of faith (*Strom.* IV.16). Cyprian also speaks of Jesus' faith in the context of his prayers in Gethsemane and obedience to God's will in the crucifixion: 'Now that is the will of God which Christ both did and taught. Humility in conversation; stedfastness in faith (*stabilitas in fide*) . . . to love God with all one's heart; to love Him in that He is a Father; to fear him in that He is God . . .' (*De dom. or.* 15 [PL 4.529]; trans. ANCL 8.408). The emulative significance of Christ's passion is developed in *Ad Fortunatum de exhortatione martyrii*, where faith is repeatedly mentioned as a key characteristic of those Christians

35 'Now if Jesus prays, and does not pray in vain, obtaining through prayer what he asks for (and perhaps he would not have received it without prayer), which of us may neglect prayer?' (*De oratione* 13.1; trans. LCC 2.262); reference to Jesus' earthly ministry is confirmed by quotations from the gospels (i.e. Mark 1.35; Luke 11.1; 6.12, John 17.1; 11.42).

36 'Hence the only begotten Son of God, who was the Word and Wisdom of God, though he was "with the Father in the glory, which he had before the world was," "abased himself and taking the form of a servant was obedient unto death" that he might teach obedience unto those who could not achieve salvation save through obedience.' (*De prin.* III.5; trans. *ECF* 213)

37 Origen was by no means alone in recognising this intimate relationship between Jesus and fellow martyrs; consider, for example, Mart. Poly. 1.2; 2.2–3; 6.2; 7.2; 14.2–3; 17.3; 19.1.

38 'And if sometimes you feel anguish in your soul, may the mind of Christ within us (ὁ ἐν ἡμῖν Χριστοῦ νοῦς) speak to the soul, even though desire does everything possible to confuse even the mind of Christ . . .' (*Mart.* 4 [GCS 2.5]; trans. LCC 2.395)

39 'Long ago we ought to have denied ourselves, saying, "It is no longer I who live." Now it is revealed whether or not we have taken up our cross and followed Jesus. This will have happened if Christ is living within us. If we wish to save our soul, so that we may receive it back as better than a soul, let us lose it even by martyrdom.' (*Mart.* 12; trans. LCC 2.401); also, 'For Christ is found in every saint, and so from the one Christ there come to be many Christs, imitators of Him and formed after Him who is the image of God.' (*Comm. in Joh.* VI.6; trans. ANF 10.353; cf. John 1.19)

who stand firm and are 'honoured by Christ among the martyrs'.[40] Christ is presented as the martyr *par excellence*[41] and although his faith is not specifically mentioned, it is assumed that he also faced suffering and death by faith; it is this shared humanity, which forms the bridge between the passion of Jesus and the sufferings of his church.

The exemplary function of Jesus' faith may have been in mind when Polycarp encourages his readers to 'follow the example of the Lord (*et domini exemplar sequimini*), being firm in faith (*firmi in fide*) and immovable, in love of the brotherhood kindly affectioned one to another, partners with the truth, forestalling one another in the gentleness of the Lord, despising no man' (*Phil.* 10.1 [*ApV* 118]; trans.* *AF* 180). And a similar line of thought is captured in the Acts of Thomas, when the apostle, having been imprisoned for his witness to the gospel, offers the following prayer: 'I praise you, Jesus, that you have made me worthy not only of your faith, but also of suffering much for your sake (ὅτι οὐ μόνον τῆς πίστεώς σου ἄξιόν με ἐποίησας).' (Acts. Thom. 107; trans.*)

The author of the Shepherd of Hermas develops further the idea of sharing or partaking in the Lord's faith with reference to Christian discipleship. In the *Fourth Vision*, an allegory unfolds in which the Shepherd confronts a stampeding beast, representing the tribulations coming upon the church. He is able to stand firm by shunning double-mindedness (Μὴ διψυχήσεις) and putting on the faith of the Lord and calling to mind his mighty works (ἐνδυσάμενος οὖν, ἀδελφοί, τὴν πίστιν τοῦ κυρίου καὶ μνησθεὶς ὧν ἐδίδαξέν με μεγαλείων; *Vis.* 4.1.1–2.5 [GCS 48.19–21]; trans. *AF* 419–20).[42] The identity of the Lord's μεγαλεία is not specified, although it seems probable that Jesus' miracles are intended (cf. τὰ μεγαλεῖα τοῦ θεοῦ, Acts 2.11). As we noted before, the efficacy of faith in the

[40] *Ad Fort.* 12; trans. ANCL 13.76; cf. 'So many martyrdoms of the righteous have, in fact, often been celebrated; so many examples of faith and virtue have been set forth to future generations.' (*Ad Fort.* 11; trans. ANCL 13.68)

[41] E.g. 'since He [i.e. Christ], when He came, not only exhorted us with words, but with deeds also, but after all wrongs and contumelies, suffered also, and was crucified, that He might teach us to suffer and to die by His example . . .' (*Ad Fort.* 5; trans. ANCL 13.59–60) A similar understanding is reflected in *De laude martyrii*, which may also have been written by Cyprian.

[42] The approach here is similar to the one noted previously in relation to answered prayer and the performance of miracles.

absence of doubt and double-mindedness[43] is reminiscent of Jesus' teaching in the Synoptic Gospels (e.g. Matt. 21.21–2/Mark 11.23–4; cf. Mark 5.36/Luke 8.50) and the whole passage invites readers to allow their faith to be defined by Christ's. The idea here is not so much of being a fellow exponent of faith with Jesus, but of sharing Jesus' faith. Jesus is still considered an exponent of faith; but, in addition, he is also its source. This insight is repeated a little further on in relation to the Shepherd's ability to keep the commandments of the Lord:[44] 'Doubt not at all; but clothe thyself in the faith of the Lord (ὅλως μηδὲν διψυχήσῃς· ἀλλ' ἔνδυσαι τὴν πίστιν τοῦ κυρίου), and thou shalt walk in them. For I will strengthen thee in them.' (*Sim.* 6.1.2 [GCS 48.58–9]; trans. *AF* 448; also *Sim.* 6.3.6 and 9.16.5)

At the beginning of Ignatius' *Letter to the Ephesians*, we find the following appreciation of his reader's Christian standing:

> Having received in God (ἐν θεῷ) your much loved name, which you possess by a just nature according to faith and love in Christ Jesus, our Savior – being imitators of God, enkindled by the blood of God (ὃ κέκτησθε φύσει δικαίᾳ κατὰ πίστιν καὶ ἀγάπην ἐν Χριστῷ Ἰησοῦ, τῷ σωτῆρι ἡμῶν· μιμηταὶ ὄντες θεοῦ, ἀναζωπυρήσαντες ἐν αἵματι θεοῦ), you accomplished perfectly the task suited to you ... (*Eph.* 1.1 [*ApV* 82]; trans. Schoedel, *Ignatius*, 40; cf. *Eph.* 5.1–2)

The emphasis throughout is upon the salvation wrought by God in Christ: their name is received ἐν θεῷ, they have been enkindled ἐν αἵματι θεοῦ; but the basis for their φύσις δικαία is more ambiguous. The ἐν constructions just mentioned caution against rendering κατὰ πίστιν καὶ ἀγάπην ἐν Χριστῷ Ἰησοῦ simply in terms of their faith in and love for Jesus. Further, recognition that the Ephesian believers can be considered imitators of God (μιμηταὶ ὄντες θεοῦ)[45] suggests that the love and faith spoken of here may originate in the life of

43 Double-mindedness (διψυχέω κτλ) is frequently identified in Hermas as the cause of ineffectual discipleship; cf. the use of δίψυχος in Jas. 1.8; 4.8 (Seitz, 'Antecedents', 131–40)

44 The close proximity of ἐντολή and πίστις is reminiscent of Rev. 14.12 (τὰς ἐντολὰς τοῦ θεοῦ καὶ τὴν πίστιν Ἰησοῦ); as with Revelation, the emphasis for πίστις falls upon the practical outworkings of the commandments.

45 For Ignatius, imitation of God is defined by Christ; see Schoedel, *Ignatius*, 29–31, 41.

Jesus, being mediated through his death (cf. ἐν αἵματι θεοῦ) and, perhaps, commemorations of this in the Eucharist.[46]

The notion of sharing Jesus' faith as a characterisation of discipleship may also be present in the Odes of Solomon. In Ode 39, Jesus is portrayed as the trail-blazer who has crossed the rivers of adversity, namely, the way of discipleship, and established a pattern for others to emulate. In the light of this, Christians are exhorted to follow in his footsteps and, as his journey was characterised by faith, so disciples are required to share in that way of faith which has its origin and substance in the person and works of Jesus:

> Therefore, put on (*lbsw*) the name of the Most High and know Him,
> And you shall cross without danger;
> Because rivers shall be obedient to you [cf. Luke 17.6] ...
> And the Way has been appointed for those who cross over after Him,
> And for those who adhere to the path of His faith (*dhymnwth*);
> And who adore His name.
> Hallelujah. (Odes Sol. 39.8, 13 [*OSol* 135–6])

Finally, from a slightly different perspective, we note that Tertullian articulates the continuity between Jesus and the believer in terms of a continuum of faith which has its origin in Jesus' ministry (*Haer.* 20 [CCL I.201–2]). In a discussion on the place of scripture within matters of church discipline, he highlights that it is not sufficient simply to cite supporting texts; rather, one's theology must be grounded in Christ, to whom the scriptures refer. He alone is the authentic canon of faith and the authority of the church is located in the tradition of faith (*traducem fidei*) which not only has Christ as its object, but is also anchored in the life of Jesus himself, who was the first witness to that faith. In this way, it seems that Tertullian depicts Jesus as the teacher of the faith which has himself as its content (cf. *cuiuscumque fidei praeceptor*).

[46] Cf. 'I glorify Jesus Christ, the God who made you so wise; for I perceived that you are settled in immovable faith (ἐν ἀκινήτῳ πίστει), having been nailed, as it were, on the cross of our Lord Jesus Christ both in flesh and spirit, and established in love by the blood of Christ (καὶ ἡδρασμένους ἐν ἀγάπῃ ἐν τῷ αἵματι Χριστοῦ) ...' (*Smyrn.* 1.1 [*ApV* 106]; trans. Schoedel, *Ignatius*, 220); also, 'But for me the archives are Jesus Christ, the inviolable archives are his cross and death and his resurrection and faith which is through him (καὶ ἡ πίστις ἡ δι' αὐτοῦ).' (*Philad.* 8.2 [*ApV* 104]; trans.* Schoedel, 207)

Before drawing this section to a close, a number of general observations can be made. Firstly, whereas some of the evidence depicts Jesus as a believer amongst others, most of it bears witness to a broader conception in which he is both the exemplar and the source of faith. That is to say, he is conceived of as the one who incarnates the life of faith and engenders that faith in others so that they are also able to follow his example. Secondly, a broader review of the sources quoted would reveal that Jesus was also considered to be in some sense the object of faith; as we have noted already, this conviction is not necessarily incompatible with his paradigmatic function, but may reflect a different perspective or concern. For instance, if 'Jesus the believer' informs what it means to live by faith in God, then 'belief in Jesus' explains his place within God's salvific initiatives. Thirdly, most of the passages discussed in this section are concerned with matters of discipleship; although this is what one would expect, it does suggest that the implications of affirming Jesus as an exemplar of faith for broader theological assessments of his significance remained largely unexamined.

3 The theological function of Jesus' faith

Later on in this chapter we shall examine how the paradigmatic function of Jesus' faith fared when christological reflection became increasingly concerned with defining the nature of the relationship between Christ and God. Before then, however, we need to consider whether Jesus' faith continued to play a part in the early church's understanding of how God's gift of salvation was mediated through Christ.

We start with Ignatius of Antioch, who appears to follow Paul in understanding the crucifixion as a demonstration of Jesus' faith. In the *Letter to the Ephesians* he explains that those false teachers who corrupt 'faith in God for which Jesus Christ was crucified' (ἐὰν πίστιν θεοῦ ἐν κακῇ διδασκαλίᾳ φθείρῃ, ὑπὲρ ἧς Ἰησοῦς Χριστὸς ἐσταυρώθη) will not inherit the kingdom of God (*Eph.* 16.1–2 [*ApV* 87]; trans. Schoedel, *Ignatius*, 79). The genitive πίστιν θεοῦ is clearly objective and, although the relation between Jesus and faith in God is not spelt out, the implication is that the latter was the cause (ὑπὲρ ἧς) of his execution: Jesus died because of his faith in God. A similar understanding is reflected at the end of the letter when he indicates that an additional correspondence will be required in order to explain the dispensation relating to 'the new human being, Jesus Christ, having to do with his faith and his love, with his suffering and resurrection' (εἰς τὸν καινὸν ἄνθρωπον Ἰησοῦν Χριστόν, ἐν τῇ αὐτοῦ πίστει καὶ ἐν τῇ αὐτοῦ ἀγάπῃ, ἐν πάθει αὐτοῦ καὶ ἀναστάσει; *Eph.* 20.1 [*ApV* 88]; trans.* Schoedel, *Ignatius*, 95). Having covered the incarnation (cf. 19.1–3), Jesus' crucifixion and resurrection are to provide the subject matter for the next instalment. Further, as Ignatius' exposition revolves around τὸν καινὸν ἄνθρωπον Ἰησοῦν Χριστόν and, in particular, his death and resurrection, ἐν τῇ αὐτοῦ πίστει and ἐν τῇ αὐτοῦ ἀγάπῃ are best taken as subjective genitives referring to Jesus' faith and love.[47]

This intimate association between Jesus' faith and the crucifixion is reflected in his *Letter to the Trallians*. In this case, the context has strong eucharistic overtones as Ignatius exhorts his readers on behalf of the love of Jesus Christ (ἀλλ' ἀγάπη Ἰησοῦ Χριστοῦ; *Trall.* 6.1) to show discernment in their eating habits so that the devil is not given opportunity. He then draws attention to the true source of sustenance: 'You, then, take up gentleness and renew yourselves in faith – which is the flesh of the Lord – and in love – which is the blood of Jesus Christ' (ὑμεις οὖν τὴν πραϋπάθειαν ἀναλαβόντες ἀνακτίσασθε ἑαυτοὺς ἐν πίστει, ὅ ἐστιν σὰρξ τοῦ κυρίου, καὶ ἐν ἀγάπῃ, ὅ ἐστιν αἷμα Ἰησοῦ Χριστοῦ; *Trall.* 8.1 [*ApV* 94]; trans. Schoedel, *Ignatius*, 149). Faith and love are often used together by Ignatius to characterise Christian response to God and this sense may be present here;[48] however, their identification in this case with the body and blood of Christ suggests that Jesus' sacrificial death on the cross was considered by the author to be the event through which faith and love find their ultimate expression.[49]

The causative link between Christ and faith is expressed differ-

[47] W. R. Schoedel admits this possibility, but is swayed by his contention that 'elsewhere in Ignatius faith and love are always the religious affections of people' (*Ignatius*, 96). Not only is the objective interpretation of ἐν τῇ αὐτοῦ πίστει καὶ ἐν τῇ αὐτοῦ ἀγάπῃ questionable contextually (Schoedel claims that the ἐν must 'indicate vaguely the major themes associated with Christ and salvation in Ignatius' mind'), but it is also debatable whether faith and love are the sole prerogative of believers elsewhere in Ignatius' letters (e.g. *Rom.* Inscr.).

[48] See Schoedel, *Ignatius*, 24–6, for a summary.

[49] Cf. 'Ignatius ... to the church beloved and enlightened by the will of him who willed all things that are, according to the faith and love of Jesus Christ our God (καὶ πεφωτισμένῃ ἐν θελήματι τοῦ θελήσαντος τὰ πάντα, ἅ ἔστιν, κατὰ πίστιν καὶ ἀγάπην Ἰησοῦ Χριστοῦ, τοῦ θεοῦ ἡμῶν) ...' (*Rom.* Inscr. [*ApV* 96–7]; trans.* Schoedel, *Ignatius*, 165) 'But as for me, my charter is Jesus Christ, the inviolable charter is His cross and His death and His resurrection, and faith which is through Him (καὶ ἡ πίστις ἡ δι' αὐτοῦ).' (*Philad.* 8.2 [*ApV* 104]; trans.* *AF* 155; also *Magn.* 1.1–2)

ently by Clement of Alexandria. *Paedagogus* contains a rich and nuanced exposition of belief in which faith is described as 'the one universal salvation of humanity' (μία καθολικὴ τῆς ἀνθρωπότητος σωτηρία ἡ πίστις; *Paed.* I.6 [GCS 12.108]). He supports this claim by quoting Galatians 3.23–8, where the coming of faith and ensuing justification of all people is equated with the coming of Christ. Although Clement recognises the importance of response to God, his conception of πίστις is this passage is more comprehensive and resembles Paul's disposition of faith inaugurated for both Jew and Gentile through Christ's πίστις. The form of the quotation from Galatians lends support to this and, in particular, his rendering of verse 26 as πάντες γὰρ υἱοί ἐστε διὰ πίστεως θεοῦ ἐν Χριστῷ Ἰησοῦ ('for you are all sons through faith in/of God [which is] in Christ Jesus'). The positioning of θεοῦ after διὰ πίστεως suggests that the divine origin of faith, rather than the believer's response, is in focus; a faith that is revealed in Christ Jesus.[50]

During our discussion of Romans 3, we noted how Paul interprets Jesus' faith as a vehicle for the revelation of God's righteousness or covenantal faithfulness. This line of thinking is picked up by Clement during a defence of God's justice and goodness in which he quotes from verses 21, 22 and 26 of Romans 3 (*Paed.* I.8 [GCS 12.132–3]). Although it is possible that διὰ πίστεως Ἰησοῦ Χριστοῦ and τὸν ἐκ πίστεως Ἰησοῦν refer primarily to the faith of believers, it seems improbable that Clement would hinge his vindication of God's salvific initiatives towards humanity around the response of Christians. As with Paul, it is much more likely that he conceives of God's justice and goodness being mediated through the faith of Christ, manifested on the cross, as God's covenantal faithfulness is established eternally and universally.

In addition to the theological significance of Jesus' faith developed in relation to his obedience in the face of death, we also noted how the author of Hebrews describes Jesus as a πιστός high priest who continues to minister on behalf of others. The title ἀρχιερεύς is employed by certain early fathers,[51] but they do not develop Jesus' characterisation as πιστός. There are, however, indications that this

50 Cf. 26th Nestle-Aland text, πάντες γὰρ υἱοὶ θεοῦ ἐστε διὰ τῆς πίστεως ἐν Χριστῷ Ἰησοῦ. Whether Clement cites the text as he received it or changes it, he clearly believes that the passage from Galatians supports his case.

51 Cf. Clement, *Prot.* 12; 1 Clem. 36.1; 61.3; Ignatius, *Philad.* 9.1; Mart. Poly. 14.1–2; Origen, *De oratione* 10; 15; Tertullian, *Adv. Marc.* IV.35. On Jesus as high priest in post-biblical literature, see Greer, *Captain* and Schrenk, 'ἱερός', esp. 283.

epithet was thought appropriate for at least certain aspects of Jesus' ongoing, post-resurrection ministry. Consider, for instance, the following extract from the Acts of Peter. The apostle is addressed by one Ariston concerning the damage caused to the Christian community at Rome by Simon Magus, who had managed to lead many astray. Ariston affirms his conviction that Jesus is able to put things right: 'Now therefore I believe in my Lord that he is rebuilding his ministry, for all deception shall be uprooted from among his servants. For our Lord Jesus Christ is faithful (*fidelis est enim dominus noster Iesus Christus*), who can restore our minds.' (Act. Pet. 6)[52]

Finally, a significant development in the soteriological understanding of Christ's faith is reflected in Tertullian's *De carne Christi*. This tractate is concerned with defending the incarnation and full humanity of Christ against various docetic tendencies and speculations. At one point Tertullian refutes the claim that Christ's flesh is of a different, more spiritual, nature than normal human flesh or even that it should be equated with his soul. He explains that it was necessary for salvation that Christ should become human, sharing fully in the flesh and possessing an incorporeal soul like all other people: 'Christ, however, could not have appeared among men except as a man. Restore, therefore, to Christ His faith (*Redde igitur Christo fidem suam*); [believe] that He willed to walk the earth as man exhibited even a soul of a thoroughly human condition, not making it of flesh, but clothing it with flesh.' (*De carne Christi* 11.6 [SC 216/1.260]; trans. ANCL 15.189) It appears that Tertullian considered faith to be a key characteristic of human being and, in consequence, one which Christ needed to exercise if he was to secure salvation for all people through his incarnation and resurrection (cf. *De resurrectione carnis*).

Before drawing this section to a close, we should perhaps underline the distinction between the function of Jesus' faith evident in the material presented here and that embraced by the paradigmatic category discussed previously. In section 2, we noted how Jesus was perceived as an exemplar of faith and, in many cases, as its source as well. The notion of Jesus as the source of faith, however, is ambigu-

[52] Cf. 'But if you repent of your action, he [i.e. God] is faithful (*fidelis est*), so that he can wipe away your sins (and) deliver you from this sin.' (Act. Pet. 2; cf. 1 John 1.9); 'My spirit [i.e. Ignatius'] is offered up for you, not only now, but also when I shall attain unto God. For I am still in peril; but the Father is faithful in Jesus Christ (ἀλλὰ πιστὸς ὁ πατὴρ ἐν Ἰησοῦ Χριστῷ) to fulfil my petition and yours.' (*Trall.* 13.2–3 [*ApV* 96]; trans. *AF* 149)

ous and requires further clarification. Within the context of the literature surveyed in the previous section, source relates primarily to matters of definition and focus. That is to say, certain stories about Jesus and, especially, about his miracle-working ability and passion, were considered to incarnate what it means to live (and die) by faith. The faith of his followers, therefore, gains definition from examples of his faith and, as a result, his faith becomes a focus for others to emulate. But because the setting for such comparisons is discipleship, where faith is seen in relation to particular aspects of following Jesus, the more fundamental soteriological issue of the possibility of faith remains largely unexplored: Christians may share Jesus' faith as they face challenges which he faced, they may consider him to be the ultimate exemplar of that faith; but such considerations presuppose, rather than establish, the opportunity for relationship with God.

In the present section, however, we have seen how Jesus' faith occupies much more of a soteriological, rather than a paradigmatic, perspective in which the possibility of others sharing his faith is based not so much upon what he exhibits of the life of faith as upon what his faith achieved. Most if not all the passages discussed demonstrate an intimate association between Jesus' faith and his death, the latter being interpreted in terms of God's salvific purposes and provision. As a result, because Jesus' faith is epitomised in the circumstances surrounding a death which mediates God's salvation, he becomes the source of faith for others. Because of what he achieved on behalf of all, others may now share his faith and its benefits. In this way, we can discern how Jesus' life of faith is gradually absorbed within interpretations of the salvation event by which God's offer of life is made available through faith. In the next section, we see how this process reaches a point where it becomes almost impossible to identify his own contribution within a broader conception of faith, but in the present this element can still be recognised. Even here, however, it is not so much a question of Jesus' faith and a believer's, but of a shared faith which has its source in Jesus. Not simply in the sense that he is its first exponent, supplier or object, but that Jesus himself embodies all that faith is and his faith makes faith possible for others.

4 Jesus as canon for faith

The previous two sections can, broadly speaking, be mapped onto different interests pursued by the early church. The paradigmatic explores Jesus' faith from the perspective of human response to God and how it relates to discipleship; the theological explores Jesus' faith from the perspective of God's salvific provision and, as such, is concerned with Christ's theological status. In the following pages we shall attempt to show how the tendency, recognised in relation to theological concerns, for focus to shift away from the contribution made by Jesus' personal faith within the salvation process to a broader and more comprehensive understanding of how he informs Christian faith reaches a point where the former can no longer be identified with any degree of certainty.

An interesting point of departure is the Epistle of Barnabas, where the author likens the earthly manifestion of Jesus to his presence in the lives of believers.[53] Christians are encouraged to see themselves as temples needing to be occupied by Christ himself[54] and, to facilitate this, belief or hope must be directed Godwards (πιστεῦσαι τῷ θεῷ);[55] yet these very responses originate in Jesus and find definition in relation to him:

> The word of His faith [or 'His word of faith'] (ὁ λόγος αὐτοῦ τῆς πίστεως), the calling of His promise, the wisdom of the ordinances, the commandments of the teaching, He Himself prophesying in us, He Himself dwelling in us ... For he that desireth to be saved looketh not to the man, but to Him that dwelleth and speaketh in him ... (Barn. 16.6–10 [*ApV* 30–1]; trans. *AF* 284–5)[56]

Clement of Alexandria also comes close to equating faith with the person of Christ and not simply with belief in him or belief about what God has done through him. For example, in a passage cited

[53] 'Forasmuch then as He was about to be manifested in the flesh and to suffer, His suffering was manifested beforehand ... Set your hope on Him who is about to be manifested to you in the flesh, even Jesus ... for He Himself was to be manifested in the flesh and to dwell in us.' (Barn. 6.7, 9, 14; trans.*]; trans.* *AF* 273–6; also Barn. 1.4)

[54] 'For a holy temple unto the Lord, my brethren, is the abode of our heart.' (Barn. 6.15 (Barn. 6.15; trans.); trans. *AF* 275; also Barn. 16.1–2; cf. 1 Cor. 6.19)

[55] Both the πιστεύω (e.g. 7.2; 9.4; 11.11; 12.7; 13.7; 16.7) and ἐλπίζω (e.g. 6.9; 8.5; 11.8; 12.2–3; 19.7) groups are well represented and, on occasion, are used synonymously (e.g. Καὶ ὁ πιστεύων εἰς αὐτὸν ζήσεται εἰς τὸν αἰῶνα and καὶ ὅτι οἱ ἐλπίζοντες ἐπ' αὐτὸν ζήσονται εἰς τὸν αἰῶνα; Barn. 6.3; 8.5 [*ApV* 16; 20]).

[56] Also '... that the covenant of the beloved Jesus might be sealed unto our hearts in the hope which springeth from His faith (ἐγκατασφαγισθῇ εἰς τὴν καρδίαν ἡμῶν ἐν ἐλπίδι τῆς πίστεως αὐτοῦ).' (Barn. 4.8 [*ApV* 13]; trans.* *AF* 271–2; cf. Barn. 6.17)

earlier, he defines faith as 'the one universal salvation of humanity (ὅτι γε μία καθολικὴ τῆς ἀνθρωπότητος σωτηρία ἡ πίστις)' and then identifies this with the coming of Christ described in terms of Galatians 3.23–6 (*Paed.* I.6 [GCS 12.108]; trans. ANCL 4.135). In response to those who consider themselves to be 'perfect and gnostics', his description of perfection includes the idea of 'regeneration into the faith of the only perfect One (καὶ εἰς πίστιν τοῦ μόνου τελείου ἀναγεγεννῆσθαι)' (*Paed.* I.6 [GCS 12.121]; trans. ANCL 4.148). Of equal interest is an exhortation in which 'Jesus, who is eternal, the one great High Priest of the one God' expresses his desire that others should participate in the grace of God and fulness of humanity communicated through himself: 'I desire to restore you according to the original model, that you may become also like me. I anoint you with the unguent of faith (χρίσω ὑμᾶς τῷ πίστεως ἀλείμματι), by which you throw off corruption, and show you the naked form of righteousness by which you ascend to God.' (*Prot.* 12 [GCS 12.85]; trans. ANCL 4.108) Although Clement can speak openly about faith as a personal disposition of the believer or as a body of teaching, the overarching sense here and elsewhere is that of a dynamic entity which is anchored in Christ.[57]

The question of whether faith should be considered as an essentially human prerogative by which God's gift of salvation in Christ is appropriated came to a head in the controversy between Augustine and Pelagius.[58] It was, however, anticipated before then with widely different views being expressed. For example, Irenaeus could maintain that faith epitomises human freedom in relation to God's offer of salvation:

> ... but also in faith, has God preserved the will of man free and under his own control, saying, 'According to thy faith be it unto thee'; thus showing that there is a faith specially

[57] E.g. 'Learning, then, is also obedience to the commandments, which is faith in God (ὅ ἐστι πιστεύειν τῷ θεῷ). And faith is a power of God (καὶ ἡ πίστις δύναμίς τις τοῦ θεοῦ), being the strength of the truth. For example, it is said, "If ye have faith as a grain of mustard, ye shall remove the mountain (ἐὰν ἔχητε πίστιν ὡς κόκκον σινάπεως, μεταστήσετε τὸ ὄρος)." And again, "According to thy faith let it be to thee (κατὰ τὴν πίστιν σου γενηθήτω σοι)." And one is cured, receiving healing by faith (τῇ πίστει τὴν ἴασιν); and the dead is raised up in consequence of the power of one believing that he would be raised (ὁ δὲ νεκρὸς ἀνίσταται διὰ τὴν τοῦ πιστεύσαντος ὅτι ἀναστήσεται ἰσχύν).' (*Strom.* II.11 [GCS 15.138]; trans. ANCL 12.30–1; cf. Matt. 17.20; 9.29) It is interesting to note that elsewhere Clement likens Christ to a κόκκῳ νάπυος (e.g. *Paed.* I.11).

[58] See the discussion in McGrath, *Iustitia Dei*, vol. 1, 17–36.

> belonging to man, since he had an opinion specially his own ... Now all such expressions [i.e. Matt. 8.13; Mark 9.23] demonstrate that man is in his own power with respect to faith. (*Haer.* IV.37.5; trans. ANCL 9.39)

In contrast, Origen draws on Paul's teaching about the body of Christ in 1 Corinthians to explain that faith must in certain respects be understood as a gift of the Spirit (esp. 1 Cor. 12.9);[59] he claims 'that the faith which comes from man cannot be perfect, unless it has added to it the faith which comes from God ... That very faith by which we seem to believe in God is confirmed in us by the gift of grace.' (*Comm. in Rom.* IV.5 (Rom. IV.5; trans.); trans. *ECF* 201)[60] We can discern here the intimate relation between Christ and faith in Origen's thinking. Elsewhere, he almost seems to equate them: in the *Excerpta*, he equates the rock mentioned in Ps. 39.4 (LXX, καὶ ἔστησεν ἐπὶ πέτραν τοὺς πόδας μου) with Christ ('Επεὶ πέτρα ἦν ὁ Χριστός, *Exc. in Ps.* 23 [PG 17.113]) and in the *Selecta* with the faith of Christ (Πέτρα ἐστὶ πίστις Χριστοῦ, *Sel. in Ps.* 39 [PG 12.1409]).

Clement of Rome can also bring Christ and faith into close association. In a passage reminiscent of Romans 3, he explains how human response is rendered impotent in the light of God's salvific initiatives fulfilled in Christ;[61] he goes on to say that 'we, having been called through His will in Christ Jesus, are not justified through ourselves or through our own wisdom or understanding or piety or works which we wrought in holiness of heart, but through faith (ἀλλὰ διὰ τῆς πίστεως) whereby the Almighty God justified all men that have been from the beginning ...' (1 Clem. 32.3–4 [*ApV* 52]; trans. *AF* 70) Clement contrasts faith with all forms of human response to God and associates it intimately with God's salvific

[59] Other fathers considered that Paul was referring here to a different kind of faith; for instance, Cyril of Jerusalem would distinguish between dogmatic faith, which is the prerogative of believers, and superhuman faith, which is a gift of grace (*Catech.* V.10–11).

[60] The text used here is the free Latin version of Rufinus; only fragments of the Greek have survived. Also: 'Celsus' next remark must now be considered, where he says that faith has prejudiced "our souls and makes us hold this belief about Jesus." It is true that faith makes us hold this belief; but consider whether faith does not of itself prove that it is laudable. For we entrust ourselves to the supreme God, confessing our gratitude to him who guided us to this faith and saying that without God's power we could not have ventured upon or accomplished so great an undertaking.' (*Contra Celsum* III.39; trans.* *CC* 155)

[61] The centrality of Jesus for salvation is stressed throughout the letter (e.g. Inscr.; 7.4–6; 16.1–3; 21.6; 24.1; 36.1–3; 38.1; 42.1–3; 58.2).

provision in Christ; and whilst some may choose to ignore the divine graciousness in Christ,[62] others will receive it as a gift from God.[63] Further, in chapter 27, he exhorts his readers, on the basis of God's faithfulness, not so much to believe in God as to allow his faith to take seed in them: 'With this hope therefore let our souls be bound unto Him that is faithful to His promises (τῷ πιστῷ ἐν ταῖς ἐπαγγελίαις) and that is righteous in His judgements ... Therefore let His faith be kindled within us (ἀναζωπυρησάτω οὖν ἡ πίστις αὐτοῦ ἐν ἡμῖν), and let us understand that all things are nigh unto Him.' (1 Clem. 27.1–3 [*ApV* 50]; trans.* *AF* 69)

A number of other sources are worthy of mention at this juncture. Although the relation between Jesus and faith is not often developed, the intimate way in which they are associated is indicative of the early church's tendency to 'canonise' faith in terms of Christ. For example, Jesus is described as ἡ ζωὴ τῆς πίστεως in 4 Baruch (9.15 [*PJer* 45]) and in the Apocryphon of James, Christ responds to the challenge of Peter and James concerning his graciousness in the following way: 'I have given you (the) faith (πίστις) many times. And moreover I have revealed myself to you.' (Apoc. Jas. 13.32–9 [*EIA* 127]) In the Martyrdom of Peter, the apostle, having received a revelation from Christ concerning his imminent death, encourages his fellow Christians by reminding them that, amongst other things, the Lord is able to establish them in his faith (cf. ὑμᾶς δὲ ὁ κύριος στηρίξαι δυνατός ἐστιν εἰς τὴν πίστιν αὐτοῦ) so that they will be able to persevere to the last (Mart. Pet. 7). A doxology from the Didache is also significant here in that it gives God praise 'for the knowledge and faith and immortality, which Thou hast made known through Thy Son Jesus (καὶ ὑπὲρ τῆς γνώσεως καὶ πίστεως καὶ ἀθανασίας, ἧς ἐγνώρισας ἡμῖν διὰ Ἰησοῦ τοῦ παιδός σου)' (Did. 10.2 [*ApV* 6]; trans. *AF* 232–3). And, finally, the following passage from the Apostolic Constitutions is interesting in that it reflects a tendency to define faith in terms of Jesus' earthly life; once again the context is liturgical:

> We give thanks to you, O God and Father of Jesus our Savior, on behalf of your holy name which you caused to encamp among us, and on behalf of the knowledge and

[62] 'For this cause righteousness and peace stand aloof, while each man hath forsaken the fear of the Lord and become purblind in the faith of Him (ἐν τῇ πίστει αὐτοῦ) ...' (1 Clem 3.4 [*ApV* 36–7]; trans. *AF* 58)

[63] 'How blessed and marvellous are the gifts of God (τὰ δῶρα τοῦ θεοῦ), dearly beloved! Life in immortality, splendour in righteousness, truth in boldness, faith in

> faith and love and immortality which you gave to us through Jesus your Son (καὶ ὑπὲρ τῆς γνώσεως καὶ πίστεως καὶ ἀγάπης καὶ ἀθανασίας ἧς ἔδωκας ἡμῖν διὰ Ἰησοῦ τοῦ Παιδός σου). O Master Almighty, the God of the universe, you created the world and what is in it through him; and you planted deeply in our souls a law; and you prepared for men the things (necessary) for communion; (you are) the God of the holy and blameless ones, our fathers Abraham and Isaac and Jacob, your faithful servants (τῶν πιστῶν δούλων σου); the powerful God, the faithful and true One (ὁ πιστὸς καὶ ἀληθινὸς), without falsehood in your promises; the One who sent forth upon earth Jesus your Christ, to live together with men as a man, being divine Word and Man, and radically to destroy error. (Apost. Const. VII.26.1–3 [SC 336.54–6]; trans. *OTP* 2.677)[64]

We have attempted in this section to demonstrate how the person of Jesus Christ, rather than proclamation or teaching about him, could remain intimately linked with the substance of faith within a context where consideration of his own life of faith no longer made a discrete contribution.[65] Jesus' relationship to faith could, of course, have been explored from a different angle, such as, the formation of creeds or rules of faith;[66] however, without establishing a hard and fast chronology or progression in thought, our selection of material does seem to illustrate how interest in Jesus' personal faith could be absorbed within a broader understanding embracing the believer's faith, the theological content of belief and the relationship of Christ to these elements. This development is most discernible in the transition from what we have called the 'theological' function of Jesus' faith to the 'canonic'. For example,

confidence (πίστις ἐν πεποιθήσει), temperance in sanctification!' (1 Clem 35.1–2 [*ApV* 54]; trans. *AF* 71–2)

[64] The possible Arian pedigree of this work (R. P. C. Hanson, *Search*, 100–1) is significant in the light of Athanasius' response to the question of whether Heb. 3.2 indicates that the incarnate Son demonstrated faith (see section 5).

[65] This observation is also made by T. F. Torrance in his examination of early christological reflection (esp. Irenaeus): 'In the last analysis "the Deposit of Faith", as it came to be called, is to be understood as the whole living Fact of Christ and his saving Acts in the indivisible unity of his Person, Word and Life, as through the Resurrection and Pentecost he fulfilled and unfolded the content of his self-revelation as Saviour and Lord within his Church.' ('Deposit', 2)

[66] If this approach had been adopted, for example, much more attention would have been paid to figures such as Irenaeus and Tertullian; cf. Kelly, *Creeds*, 62–99.

one can envisage how focus on Jesus, whose faith to the point of death initiated new opportunities for others, would, after sustained theological experience and reflection, lead to a more comprehensive understanding of the initial and continuing significance of the person of Christ for faith.[67]

Whether it is possible to locate the 'paradigmatic' function of Jesus' faith within such a development is less clear.[68] For one thing, it is unlikely that the two principal trajectories evolved in the same way. As we have seen, discussion of Jesus' faith with respect to mediating or accomplishing God's salvific will tends to be informed by factors such as God's faithfulness to the covenant, the expectation that God's messiah would be a man of faith and the recognition that Jewish martyrs exhibited faith as they approached death. In contrast, interest in Jesus' faith in relation to discipleship is rooted in reflection upon his ministry by those seeking to share the life of faith; here it is what Jesus shares in common with other believers which is central. Although, Jesus' crucifixion was clearly important for both perspectives, it is improbable that either trajectory can adequately account for the other.

One implication of recognising the existence of two trajectories which originated and developed independently is that, whilst we have managed so far to suggest how the theological one became absorbed within a broader understanding of Jesus' significance for faith, we have not as yet been able to account for the paradigmatic one. In this respect, we have to explain why our investigations to date have produced little evidence of interest in Jesus' faith *per se* beyond the end of the third century. On the basis that this phenomenon may well reveal what became of the paradigmatic function, we turn our attention to it in the final section.

5 What became of Jesus' faith?

So far in this chapter we have traced the trajectories relating to the faith of Jesus through the first three Christian centuries. Owing to

67 This is not to deny that the soteriological significance of Christ's faith would still, on occasion, be referred to by later writers. For example, in a similar way to Paul in Romans 3.35, Epiphanius Constantiensis describes how righteousness is mediated through Christ's faith (δικαιοσύνη μὲν, διὰ πίστεως αὐτοῦ ἁμαρτίαν λύσας, *Anc.* 65 [GCS 25.79]; quoted by van Henten, 'Background', fn. 15).

68 It is possible that the idea of Jesus as the giver of faith which we encountered earlier provides a way forward here (e.g. Apoc. Jas. 13.32–9; Apost. Const. VII.26.1–3; 1 Clem 27.1–3; Clem, *Paed.* I.6; Hermas, *Vis.* 4.1.1–4; 6.1.2; Origen,

the scale of this undertaking, we have not been able to set our survey within a detailed examination of early christology, although we have indicated the theological issues associated with our theme. And yet any interest in the faith of Jesus during this period will have been influenced by broader assessments of his significance. Whilst the process of formulating an adequate interpretation of Jesus started before the resurrection,[69] it was considerably later that the implications and shortcomings of proposed alternative christologies could be evaluated and, where necessary, modified.[70] In this respect, the fourth century proved a watershed as, in the midst of controversy, the business of creed-making gained momentum[71] and with it the desire to articulate and, thereby, delimit the orthodox faith.

The figure of Jesus, therefore, soon became the focus for questions concerning knowledge of God and experience of salvation. Furthermore, this theologically motivated perspective is from a very early stage the principal hermeneutic for interpreting his life, death and resurrection. That is to say, assessments of Jesus focus primarily upon what he reveals of God, rather than what he reveals about humanity in relation to God. One implication of this is that every aspect of his ministry is accounted for theologically. We have already come across an example of this in the way in which his miracles are taken to furnish proof of his divinity. But what about more human elements and, specifically, faith? Could Jesus still be considered to exhibit faith? Or expressed in explicitly christological

Comm. in Rom. IV.5; Sib. Or. 8.258). It may be that Jesus was thought of not only as the one who makes faith possible and is the focus for that faith, but also as the one who exemplifies the life of faith. We shall return to this possibility in the final chapter.

69 E.g. Gunton, *Yesterday*, esp. 56–85; Hengel, *Son of God*, 57–83; Marxsen, 'Kerygmata', 42–64; Moule, *Origin*; Trocmé, *Jesus*.

70 For general information on early christology, the works of A. Grillmeier (*Christ*), J. N. D. Kelly (*Doctrines*), G. W. H. Lampe ('Christian Theology') and T. E. Pollard (*Johannine Christology*) have been used.

71 J. N. D. Kelly (*Creeds*) and F. M. Young (*Making*) provide convenient introductions to the development of the credal form from the local and liturgically motivated expressions to the more ecumenical and polemically directed constructions; on the Niceno-Constantinopolitan creed, see T. F. Torrance, *Trinitarian Faith*. This movement towards orthodoxy is also reflected in the formalisation of liturgy in the fourth century; *see* especially, Dix, *Shape*. Attention should also be drawn to the work of J. A. Jungmann, who examines the effects of christology on liturgical prayer; particularly significant are his observations concerning the way in which prayer increasingly becomes addressed 'to' – rather than 'through' – Christ (*Place*, esp. 213–38).

language, in what sense could faith be considered a characteristic of God the Son in the incarnate life of Jesus?

Athanasius' refutation of the Arian position[72] addresses this issue in what is probably the only substantial discussion of Jesus' faith to have survived from the early Christian centuries. It is generally recognised that the Arian controversy revolves around the nature of the divinity of the incarnate Son.[73] From what we can gather, Arius and those who adopted a similar approach, did not deny the Son's divinity *per se* or, indeed, the incarnation and suffering of God for that matter.[74] On the contrary, largely out of a desire to affirm these data, together with the inscrutable being of God the Father,[75] they thought it necessary to interpret the Son as the first and unique generation of God by which all other creations, including the Holy Spirit, would come into being. The Son's generation was unlike all future creations, but none the less he was not coeternal with or of the same substance as God the Father; he was a creature.[76]

Scriptural support for the Arian position revolved around a number of key texts, including Hebrews 3.1–2.[77] Athanasius, who recognised the soteriological implications of affirming a reduced view of the divinity of the incarnate Son,[78] vehemently attacked this position in a number of works, the most substantial being the

72 It is questionable how far it is legitimate to speak about followers of Arius or an Arian school of thought. 'Arian' is used in the present work as a convenient description for the view, which came into focus during the third and fourth centuries, that the Son, whilst being divine, was not consubstantial or coeternal with the Father, but was in the last count a creature.

73 Dragas, *Athanasiana*, 37–73, and Heron, 'HOMOOUSIOS', 58–87.

74 Esp. Gregg and Groh, *Early Arianism*, 1–42. This work pays special attention to Arianism as a soteriological system.

75 Broadly speaking, Arianism is philosophically associated with Middle Platonism. This is particularly apparent in the complete otherness of God and the need for a mediator (i.e. Demiurge) in the creation process. For a detailed assessment of the philosophical issues, see R. Williams, *Arius*, 181–232.

76 The Arian position has received considerable attention in recent years. The following works are amongst the best treatments and introduce the characters as well as the issues: Gregg and Groh, *Early Arianism*, esp. 1–129; R. P. C. Hanson, *Search*, esp. 3–128, 557–638; R. Williams, *Arius*, esp. 95–116 (this work also contains a useful collection of sources in an appendix); Young, *Nicea*, esp. 57–83. T. E. Pollard offers a convenient summary of the Arian position (*Johannine Christology*, 187–8).

77 Numerous proof texts must have been used; if the amount of attention paid by Athanasius is any guide, the following were the most important: Prov. 8.22, John 1.14, Acts 2.36; Heb. 3.2.

78 Dragas, *Athanasiana*, 145–55; Greer, *Captain*, esp. 88–92; T. F. Torrance, *Reconciliation*, esp. 224–66.

Orationes contra Arianos,[79] in which he devotes considerable space to reinterpreting the relevant scriptures.[80] At the beginning of the second book, focus shifts to Hebrews 3.2 (πιστὸν ὄντα τῷ ποιήσαντι αὐτὸν) and, in particular, two deductions drawn from this text are challenged. Firstly, as with κτίζω in Proverbs 8.22 (cf. LXX, κύριος ἔκτισέν με ἀρχὴν ὁδῶν αὐτοῦ εἰς ἔργα αὐτοῦ) and γίνομαι in John 1.14, ποιέω was taken by the Arian camp to indicate the generation of the Son; Athanasius refutes this, however, by demonstrating that it cannot be understood in this way and should be equated with the incarnation instead or, in terms of the Epistle to the Hebrews, with the point when the Son became high priest.[81] Because, Athanasius argues, ποιέω refers to the incarnation, it in no way suggests the generation and, hence, creatureliness of the Son. Rather, through this act of becoming, the Son, whilst losing nothing of his consubstantiality and coeternity with the Father, assumes the nature of fallen humanity for the sake of the salvation of all.[82]

The second point arising from Hebrews 3.2 addressed by Athanasius concerns the depiction of the Son as πιστός; evidently, the Arians thought this furnished further proof that he was a ποίημα, presumably, on the basis that faith constitutes a creaturely response which is incompatible with the creator.[83] Athanasius replies, however, by distinguishing between two different meanings for πιστός and the πιστεύω group in general:

> Further, if the expression, 'Who was faithful,' is a difficulty to them, from the thought that 'faithful' is used of Him as of others, as if He exercises faith and so receives the reward of faith (Εἰ δ', ὅτι γέγραπται, 'πιστὸν ὄντα,' πάλιν ταράττει αὐτοὺς νομίζοντας ὡς ἐπὶ πάντων λέγεσθαι καὶ ἐπ'

79 On the contents of and christological issues addressed in the *Orationes contra Arianos*, see Dragas, *Contra Apollinarem*, 444–513. The Athanasian provenance of the fourth book is generally rejected (R. P. C. Hanson, *Search*, 418).

80 A good introduction to Athanasius' approach to scripture and, in particular, to its place within his theology is provided by T. F. Torrance in a series of four articles ('Hermeneutics', 89–106, 237–49, 446–68, 133–49).

81 Greer, *Captain*, 95. Athanasius maintained that Jesus became high priest through the incarnation and not, as we observed in Hebrews (a view probably shared by Arians as well), through his death and heavenly ascension. For the bishop, the incarnation was the supreme act of God's identification with humanity.

82 Athanasius, *contra Arianos* II.8; this basic line of argument is repeated time and time again in relation to different proof texts (e.g. *contra Arianos* II.1; cf. John 1.14; Acts 2.36; Prov. 8.22; Heb. 1.4; Phil. 2.7; Heb. 3.1–2)

83 Gregg and Groh, *Early Arianism*, 11, 57.

> αὐτοῦ τὸ 'πιστὸν,' ὅτι πιστεύων ἐκδέχεται τῆς πίστεως τὸν μισθόν), they must proceed at this rate to find fault with Moses for saying, 'God faithful and true ('Ὁ Θεὸς πιστὸς καὶ ἀληθινός),' and with St Paul for writing, 'God is faithful (Πιστὸς ὁ Θεὸς), who will not suffer you to be tempted above what ye are able.' But when the saints spoke thus, they were not thinking of God in a human way (οὐκ ἀνθρώπινα), but they acknowledged two senses of the word 'faithful' in Scripture, first 'believing,' then 'trustworthy,' of which the former belongs to man, the latter to God (ἀλλ' ἐγίνωσκον διπλοῦν εἶναι τὸν νοῦν ἐν τῇ Γραφῇ περὶ 'τοῦ πιστοῦ·' τὸ μὲν ὡς πιστεύον, τὸ δὲ, ὡς ἀξιόπιστον· καὶ τὸ μὲν ἐπ' ἀνθρώπων, τὸ δὲ ἐπὶ Θεοῦ ἁρμόζειν) ... Accordingly the words, 'Who is faithful (Πιστὸν) to Him that made Him,' implies no parallel with others, nor means that by having faith (πιστεύων) He became well-pleasing; but that, being Son of the True God, He too is faithful (πιστός), and ought to be believed (πιστεύεσθαι) in all He says and does, Himself remaining unalterable and not changed in His human Economy and fleshly presence (αὐτὸς ἄτρεπτος μένων, καὶ μὴ ἀλλοιούμενος ἐν τῇ ἀνθρωπίνῃ οἰκονομίᾳ καὶ τῇ ἐνσάρκῳ παρουσίᾳ). (*contra Arianos* II.6 [*OrAth* 74]; trans. NPNF/II 4.351)

Athanasius' defence here is interesting in that, although the context for the Son's description as πιστός is the incarnation, he chooses to interpret this epithet theologically and not anthropologically.[84] That is, rather than placing faith alongside other characteristics of the Son's assumption of human flesh and limitation, he takes it as indicative of the incarnate Son's full divinity. For the Son, as for the Father, πιστός is appropriate for he too is trustworthy (ἀξιόπιστος) and unchanging (αὐτὸς ἄτρεπτος μένων, καὶ μὴ ἀλλοιούμενος κτλ); as a result, the Son is also a suitable focus for human faith and veneration. A little later on, however, the bishop offers a somewhat different assessment of the Son's description as πιστός:

> ... for when was Christ 'made,' when became He 'Apostle,' except when, like us, He 'took part in flesh and blood?' And when became He 'a merciful and faithful High Priest,'

[84] Dragas, *Contra Apollinarem*, 463–4, and T. F. Torrance, 'Hermeneutics', 141.

> except when 'in all things He was made like unto His brethren?' And then was He 'made like' when He became man, having put upon Him our flesh. Wherefore Paul was writing concerning the Word's human Economy, when he said, 'Who was faithful to Him that made Him,' and not concerning His Essence. Have not therefore any more the madness to say that the Word of God is a work; whereas He is Son by nature Only-begotten, and then had 'brethren,' when He took on Him flesh like ours; which moreover; by Himself offering Himself, He was named and became 'merciful and faithful,' – merciful, because in mercy to us He offered Himself for us, and faithful, not as sharing faith with us, nor as having faith in any one as we have, but as deserving to receive faith in all He says and does, and as offering a faithful sacrifice, one which remains and does not come to nought (πιστὸς δὲ, οὐ πίστεως μετέχων, οὐδὲ εἴς τινα πιστεύων ὥσπερ ἡμεῖς, ἀλλὰ πιστεύεσθαι ὀφείλων περὶ ὧν ἐὰν λέγῃ καὶ ποιῇ, καὶ ὅτι πιστὴν θυσίαν προσφέρει τὴν μένουσαν καὶ μὴ διαπίπτουσαν) ... For He is faithful as not changing, but abiding ever, and rendering what He has promised (πιστὸς γάρ ἐστιν, οὐκ ἀλλασσόμενος, ἀλλ' ἀεὶ διαμένων, καὶ ἀποδιδοὺς ἃ ἐπηγγείλατο). (*contra Arianos* II.9 [*OrAth* 77–8]; trans. NPNF/II 4.353)

In contrast to the previous exposition, Athanasius starts off by asserting that πιστὸν ὄντα τῷ ποιήσαντι αὐτόν relates to the Son's ἄνθρωπον οἰκονομίας (e.g. '... writing concerning the Word's human Economy ... and not concerning His Essence'.), but then – exploiting the semantics of πιστός (i.e. faithful: trustworthy, reliable) – he changes tack and proceeds to explain that the adjective qualifies the Son as high priest, whose being and sacrificial ministry are of eternal significance.[85] Πιστός may, therefore, be applied to

[85] Both G. D. Dragas (*Contra Apollinarem*, 463–4) and R. A. Greer (*Captain*, 94–7) claim that there is no inconsistency at this juncture as Athanasius is simply interpreting πιστός in terms of the unchangeability of the eternal Son in his incarnate being. But, as Athanasius has already noted, Heb. 3.2 is about the incarnation and, specifically, the Son's appointment as high priest, which is not eternal; rather, he maintains that, although it has eternal implications, it is intimately associated with the Son's identification with humanity and, as such, with that which was accomplished by this assumption of temporality and finitude. To then take πιστός as an attribute of the eternal Son in incarnate form and not as a characteristic of the relationship between the incarnate Son and God, is to undermine the salvific significance of the incarnation which requires the Son's

the Son in the same way as to God the Father, namely, that he is eternal, unchanging and trustworthy in relation to his promises.[86]

Athanasius' reluctance to attribute faith to the human nature of the incarnate Son is even more puzzling in the light of *contra Arianos*, book three, where in the second half of the work he deals with those scriptures used by the Arians to suggest that the Son was not omniscient, but exhibited human limitations.[87] In this case, he maintains that such traits are evidence of the Son's identification with humanity and, as such, characterise his incarnate – rather than his eternal – being, which in no way undermine his divinity.[88] For example, commenting on the scriptural references to Jesus' weeping and fear, he says: '. . . these affections were not proper to the nature of the Word, as far as He was Word; but in the flesh which was thus affected was the Word . . . For He said not all this prior to the flesh; but when the "Word became flesh," and has become man, then is it written that He said this, that is, humanly.' (*contra Arianos* III.55; trans. NPNF/II 4.423) If Athanasius was prepared to maintain that these and other signs of human frailty were indicative of the incarnate Son, why did he not also include faith as a characteristic of that dispensation? Further, if he recognised the salvific necessity for the Son to enter fully through his incarnate life into humanity so that he might redeem all and bear all to the Father, surely the Son would need to share the human response of faith? It seems that by applying πιστός to the eternal Son in Hebrews 3.2, Athanasius declined a golden opportunity to underline the completeness of the incarnation.

identification with humanity: on the one hand, the Son had to become the high priest through the incarnation; on the other hand, his high-priesthood is a function of his divine and not of his incarnate being.

86 Athanasius' train of thought at this juncture now seems strained. It is clear that he wishes to establish the continuing presence of the eternal Son during the incarnation; it is also apparent that he considers certain elements of Jesus' life and ministry to be characteristic of the eternal Son and others of the incarnate Son (Dragas, *Contra Apollinarem*, 464). What is less obvious, however, is that πιστός can shift from the former to the latter without any explanation. Further, given his linking of ποιέω in Heb. 3.2 with the incarnation, together with the observation that πιστός in that verse qualifies the relationship between the one who becomes high priest and the one appointing him (cf. πιστὸν ὄντα τῷ ποιήσαντι αὐτόν), it is stretching credulity to the limit to then claim that πιστός in fact relates to the eternal Son.

87 See Dragas' summary in *Contra Apollinarem*, 492–513.

88 See A. Pettersen, who attempts to show that Athanasius considered the emotions of fear and courage to be legitimate characteristics of the incarnate Son ('Christ's Fear', 327–40; 'Courage of Christ', 363–77; cf. Hilary, *De Trin.* X.44–5).

In all probability, part of the reason why he steered clear of imputing faith to the human nature of the incarnate Son resides in his understanding of the incarnation itself. There is still considerable debate over whether Athanasius, especially in his earlier writings,[89] envisaged the Son's identification with humanity to extend beyond an enfleshment to include the assumption of a human soul.[90] It is not possible to rehearse the arguments here, but the issue is significant.[91] For instance, if the incarnation involves no more than an enfleshment, Athanasius would not be able to attribute to the Son a human disposition like faith, which involves volition; on the other hand, if the Son enters into humanity more fully through the incarnation, one would expect the bishop to attribute faith to his assumed human nature. However, before we assume that his silence here reflects a Λόγος-σάρξ christology, we must not overlook the polemical intention of *contra Arianos* and the implications for Athanasius' defence of attributing faith to Jesus within a context where he attempts to establish that the Son is not a creature.

89 The Council of Alexandria (362) has been identified as the turning-point when Athanasius was forced to recognise the need to attribute a human soul to Christ (R. P. C. Hanson, *Search*, 450–8); certainly, it is in his later works that the more substantial evidence is found (e.g. *Ep. Epict.*; *Tom.*).

90 The view that Athanasius' understanding of the incarnation belongs within the Alexandrian λόγος-σάρξ (cf. Antiochene λόγος-ἄνθρωπος) stereotype is defended by many (e.g. Grillmeier, *Christ*, 308–28; R. P. C. Hanson, *Search*, 446–58; Kelly, *Doctrines*, 284–9); a number of scholars, however, maintain that this conception is too narrow and fails to do justice to his soteriologically motivated christology (e.g. Dragas, ''Ενανθρώπησις', 281–94; Pettersen, 'Christ's Fear', 327–40; 'Courage of Christ', 363–77; T. F. Torrance, *Trinitarian Faith*, 146–90). A survey and critique of the major contributions can be found in Dragas, *Contra Apollinarem*, 289–399. In certain respects, Dragas' own position represents something of a compromise: 'What is crystal clear however, in the light of the above reviews, is that Athanasius would readily accept the presence of a soul in Christ provided that this implied a physical (objective) as opposed to a personal (subject) factor ... To argue for the presence of a human soul in Christ in a personalistic individualistic sense, as many modern critics would have liked, would have led to a Samosatean Christ of whom Athanasius thoroughly and decisively disapproved ... The only condition that we have laid down for the acceptability and use of such language by Athanasius was that the soul would have an objective, as opposed to subjective, ontological status, because it will have to be coordinated with the uncompromising Athanasian intuition that the only subject active in Christ is the Logos – albeit, the Logos of God as man – but not as a mere or particular man.' (*Contra Apollinarem*, 389–90)

91 In terms of future christological developments, it is whether Athanasius expounds an implicit Apollinarianism or is a precursor to the full humanity of Christ – body and soul – affirmed by the Cappadocian Fathers (cf. Τὸ γὰρ ἀπρόσληπτον ἀθεράπευτον, Gregory Nazianzus, *Ep.* 101).

The passages from *contra Arianos*, book two, quoted above indicate that he was aware of the dangers in this sphere. For instance, when he maintains that πιστός in Hebrews 3.2 does not mean that the Son 'exercises faith and so receives the reward of faith (ὅτι πιστεύων ἐκδέχεται τῆς πίστεως τὸν μισθόν)' nor implies his 'sharing faith with us, nor as having faith in any one as we have (πιστὸς δὲ, οὐ πίστεως μετέχων, οὐδὲ εἴς τινα πιστεύων ὥσπερ ἡμεῖς)', he is clearly not attempting to establish the Son's identification with humanity; on the contrary, he is doing precisely the opposite. For to claim that the incarnate Son exhibited faith in God and so received the reward of faith implies something about the nature of the relationship between God and the incarnate being of the Son which he could not affirm without undermining the full divinity of the latter.[92] Whether he conceptualised the incarnation in narrow terms of enfleshment or in broader categories encompassing the assumption of a human soul,[93] Athanasius does not maintain that the incarnate Son is only a human being; rather, he is the eternal Son or Logos incarnated in order that through his solidarity with humanity he might redeem it.[94]

From Athanasius' perspective, therefore, it was impossible for the incarnate Son to have faith in God and, in this way, to share in the human predicament; in his eyes, this would imply the Son's creatureliness and thus a diminishment of his divinity. Faith in God is clearly not a divine prerogative and for the incarnate Son's relationship with God to be mediated by faith implies that it is external, transitory and open to change.[95] As Athanasius maintained that the incarnate Son is also the eternal Son, his relationship to God must be intrinsic, eternal and consubstantial. In consequence, faith cannot be considered an appropriate disposition within such a dynamic and cannot, therefore, have been embraced

92 Gregg and Groh, *Early Arianism*, 57. In this respect, it is interesting that Athanasius never really answers the Arian observation that scriptures such as Matt. 26.39, Mark 15.34 and John 12.27 suggest that the Son prayed to the Father (cf. *contra Arianos* III.26, 54–8). Perhaps he thought that, like faith, prayer suggests an external relationship between Son and Father.

93 Even if Athanasius attributed a human soul to the incarnate Son in the objective sense suggested by G. D. Dragas, he would still not be able to speak of the Son's faith; for this would assume the presence of an active 'subject' within the Son, who was not divine and who would need to relate to God externally.

94 For Athanasius, the divinity of the eternal Son or Logos is not diminished or impaired by the incarnation (e.g. *contra Arianos* III.57).

95 We must not forget that for Athanasius the active 'subject' in the person of Jesus was God the Son, the incarnate Logos.

at the incarnation. Hence, πιστός in Hebrews 3.2 is interpreted in terms of the eternal and not the incarnate Son even though, as we have seen, Athanasius asserts that the rest of the verse relates to the incarnation!

It is difficult to assess whether Athanasius would have viewed the matter of the incarnate Son's faith differently had he addressed it in a less polemical context. Certainly, there are places in his writings where the incarnate Son is not simply the object of faith, but also its source and substance (e.g. *De Inc.* 29–31; 50; 55–6; *Syn.* 39; *V. Anton.* 78–80; 89).[96] However, inference is little match for the explicit evidence from *contra Arianos* propounding the opposite view; here, the dangers of attributing faith to Jesus within a climate characterised by those wishing to undermine the full divinity of the incarnate Son proved determinative. Had Athanasius not been responding to what he considered a misinterpretation of Hebrews 3.2, but instead had been able to address the issue of faith within the context of the Son's identification with humanity, the outcome might have been different. As it was, the attribution of faith to the human nature of the incarnate Son became flagged as problematic for maintaining his continuing divinity in the face of claims that the Son or Logos was a creature.

It is interesting to note, however, that Hilary of Poitiers, a contemporary of Athanasius who shared his commitment to defending the full divinity of the Son against Arianism, does seem to attribute faith to the human nature of the incarnate Son. For example, in *De Trinitate* he speaks of the Son as the only faithful witness to the Father (*qui solus testis fidelis est*; *De Trin.* II.6 [PL 10.56]) and as the one who is simultaneously the author and witness of true faith in God ('sure that for us the one true faith concerning God is that of which He is at once the Author and the Witness [*as quod de se credendum ipse sibi nobiscum et testis et auctor exsistat*]; *De Trin.* III.26 [PL 10.95]; trans. NPNF II/9.70). It is the Lord who 'enunciated the faith of the Gospel in the simplest words that could be found' (*Quanta potuit enim Dominus verborum simplicitate evangelicam fidem locutus est, De Trin.* IX.40 [PL 10.312]; trans. NPNF II/9.168; also *De Trin.* IX.44; XI.7) and his 'soul, warned by the happy glow of its own heavenly faith and hope (*quae ubi coelestis spei ac fidei suae beato calore*), soars above its own origin in the beginnings of an earthly body, and raises that body to union with

96 T. F. Torrance, 'Hermeneutics', 458–63.

itself in thought and spirit, so that it ceases to feel the suffering of that which, all the while, it suffers.' (*De Trin.* X.44 [PL 10.378]; trans. NPNF II/9.193–4) Further, those who are called to follow him in the way of the cross are able to draw on that faith which originates in and is exemplified by the incarnate Son:

> The Apostles rejoiced in suffering and death for the Name of Christ ... The consciousness of faith takes away the weakness of nature, transforms the bodily senses that they feel no pain, and so the body is strengthened by the fixed purpose of the soul, and feels nothing except the impulse of its enthusiasm ... But Jesus Christ the Lord of glory ... dare we think of His pierced body in that pain and weakness, from which the spirit of faith in Him rescued the glorious and blessed Martyrs? (*et truncus aure non truncus est, in ea infirmitate compuncti ac dolentis corporis deputabitur, in qua gloriosos ac beatos viros fidei suae spiritus non reliquit?*) (*De Trin.* X.46 [PL 10.380]; trans. NPNF II/9.194)

And yet the silence of those who followed in Athanasius' footsteps and developed his understanding of the soteriological importance of the incarnation, concerning whether the Son's assumption of human nature embraced faith, is striking. For instance, Gregory of Nazianzus, in a defence of the incarnate Son's complete identification with humanity, alludes to almost every human attribute of Jesus apart from faith:

> But, in opposition to all these, do you reckon up for me the expressions which make for your ignorant arrogance, such as 'My God and your God,' or 'greater,' or 'created,' or 'made,' or 'sanctified;' add, if you like, 'servant' and 'obedient' and 'gave' and 'learned,' and 'was commanded,' 'was sent,' 'can do nothing of himself,' either say, or judge, or give, or will. And further, these – his 'ignorance,' 'subjection,' 'prayer,' 'asking,' 'increase,' 'being made perfect.' And, if you like, even more humble than these: such as speak of his sleeping, hungering, being in agony, and fearing; or perhaps you would make even his cross and death a matter of reproach to him. (*Orationes* XXIX.18; trans. *LCC* 3.172–3)[97]

[97] We cannot explain this state of affairs by maintaining that all the characteristics mentioned here have scriptural precedent; what about Heb. 3.2, 12.2, etc.? See also *Orationes* XXIX.19–20; XXX.16.

Further, when Gregory of Nyssa, who elsewhere anchors the substance of the Christian faith firmly within the person of Jesus,[98] follows Athanasius in maintaining that Hebrews 3.2 refers to the incarnation and the occasion of the Son becoming high priest, he makes no attempt to interpret the significance of πιστός:[99]

> Moreover, in the Epistle to the Hebrews we may learn the same truth from Paul, when he says that Jesus was made an Apostle and High Priest by God, 'being faithful to him that made Him so (πιστὸν ὄντα τῷ ποιήσαντι αὐτόν).' For in that passage too, in giving the name of High Priest to Him Who made with His own Blood the priestly propitiation for our sins, he does not by the word 'made' declare the first existence of the Only-begotten, he says 'made' with the intention of representing the grace which is commonly spoken of in connection with the appointment of priests. (*Eun.* VI.2 [PG 45.717]; trans. NPNF/II 5.184)[100]

Finally, even Augustine, who through the Pelagian controversy was forced to revise his position concerning the origins of saving faith and to locate it firmly within the graciousness of God,[101] could

98 'The Christian Faith, which in accordance with the command of our Lord has been preached to all nations by His disciples, is neither of men, nor by men, but by our Lord Jesus Christ Himself, Who being the Word, the Life, the Light, the Truth, and God, and Wisdom, and all else that He is by nature, for this cause above all was made in the likeness of man, and shared our nature, becoming like us in all things, yet without sin. He was like us in all things, in that He took upon Him manhood in its entirety with soul and body, so that our salvation was accomplished by means of both ... We believe, then, even as the Lord set forth the Faith to His Disciples, when He said, "Go, teach all nations, baptizing them in the name of the Father, and of the Son, and of the Holy Ghost."' (*Eun.* II.1; trans. NPNF/II 5.101)

99 It is interesting to note that elsewhere Gregory summarises the position of his Arian opponent Eunomius in this way: 'And concerning the Father he [i.e. Eunomius] says, that He is faithful in words and faithful in works, while of the Son he does not assert faithfulness in word and deed, but only obedience and not faithfulness, so that his profanity extends impartially through all his statements.' (*Eun.* II.11; trans. NPNF/II 5.121)

100 Faith is also omitted from Gregory's characterisation of the incarnate Son (e.g. *Eun.* V.5).

101 E.g. 'And lest men should arrogate to themselves the merit of their own faith at least, not understanding that this too is the gift of God, this same apostle, who says in another place that he had "obtained mercy of the Lord to be faithful," here also adds: "and that not of yourselves; it is the gift of God: not of works, lest any man should boast."' (*Enchiridon* 31; trans. NPNF/I 3.247–8; also *De Praed. Sanct.* 3–7)

still interpret Hebrews 12.2 in terms of Christ as the source and goal of faith, but not its exemplar:

> Thus also our being born again of water and the Spirit is not recompensed to us for any merit, but freely given; and if faith has brought us to the laver of regeneration, we ought not therefore to suppose that we have first given anything, so that the regeneration of salvation should be recompensed to us again; because He made us to believe in Christ, who made for us a Christ on whom we believe. He makes in men the beginning and the completion of the faith in Jesus who made the man Jesus the beginner and finisher of faith (*ille quippe nos fecit credere in Christum, qui nobis fecit in quem credimus Christum; ille facit in hominibus principium fidei et perfectionem in Jesum, qui fecit hominem principem fidei et perfectorem Jesum*); for thus, as you know, He is called in the epistle which is addressed to the Hebrews. (*De Praed. Sanct.* 31 [PL 44.983]; trans. NPNF/I 5.513)[102]

It seems, therefore, that the paradigmatic significance of Jesus' faith – of the way in which his life and passion inform the practice of faith – was a casualty of the movement towards establishing Christ's divinity. As we shall suggest in the final chapter, it is questionable whether this development was either inevitable or prudent; certainly, it was one made in the midst of heated theological controversy, but its implications for the church's understanding of the relationship between *fides quae* and *fides qua creditur*, and of the nature and function of Christ's humanity, have not been insignificant.

102 A similar point is made in *De Patientia*, where as part of his exposition of God's prevenient salvific initiatives in Christ, Augustine claims that even faith is preceded and enabled by grace. He goes on to explain that faith originates in Christ and can only be received as a gift from him (*De Pat.* 17–18).

7

CONCLUDING REMARKS

At the beginning of this investigation we defined our task as to assess whether early Christian traditions bear witness to interest in the faith of Jesus Christ. During the course of the study, a large stock of ancient literature has been surveyed, firstly, to understand the currency and language of faith at the disposal of nascent Christianity and, secondly, in pursuit of our goal. Such an approach inevitably results in uneven coverage of sources, but we have attempted to provide sufficient detailed exegesis to establish our case for particular texts, whilst also mapping out a broader context within which talk of Jesus' faith becomes meaningful. In this latter respect, the notion of trajectory has been helpful in that it has provided us with a means of correlating material so as to draw attention to a particular perspective or trend in early Christian reflection.

As we intimated at the beginning of chapter 6, two principal trajectories concerned with Jesus' faith can be isolated. One of these, the paradigmatic, revolves around assessments of how Jesus of Nazareth informs the life of faith. In the Synoptic Gospels, we discussed a number of miracle traditions which imply that Jesus' faith was considered a contributory factor. Additional support for this assessment emerged from a comparison between the faith logia attributed to Jesus and the means by which he was recorded as performing miracles. Particularly striking here were a shared eschatological context, an emphasis upon the disposition of faith rather than its object and, finally, a focus on the potential or performatory nature of faith. In more general terms, we noted how the synoptic portrayal of Jesus is congruent with the life of faith as depicted in Jewish sources (e.g. trust in God, prayerfulness, faithfulness to the Torah, etc.) and exhibits sufficient areas of correspondence with the Old Testament picture of king David to suggest that this archetype – coming from the stock of Israel's great men of faith – may have been a formative influence for one or more of the evangelists.

Much of the evidence gleaned from the first three Gospels predates the evangelists and, in certain cases, we were able to assess their attitude towards Jesus' faith; in general terms, Matthew was found to be favourable, Mark ambivalent if not antagonistic and Luke ambiguous, owing to the lack of relevant data. We also observed that the correlation between Jesus' faith and miracles can be traced through sources such as Origen, the Shepherd of Hermas and the Sibylline Oracles into the first half of the third century. It should also be noted, that although much of the relevant material here revolves around 'the miraculous', the intention was probably not so much to link Jesus' faith with wonder-working in a narrow sense as with the broader phenomenon of announcing the proximity of the kingdom of God – a kingdom which in Jewish expectation would be characterised by miracles and even by the gift of faith.

If our researches into the Synoptic Gospels revealed interest in Jesus' faith in relation to the performance of miracles or the demonstration of the kingdom's immediacy, then our analysis of texts from Hebrews and Revelation (e.g. Heb. 12.2; Rev. 1.5; 2.13; 3.14; 14.12 and 19.11) uncovered another strand to the paradigmatic trajectory concerned, in this instance, with Jesus' faith viewed from the perspective of his approach to suffering and death. We noted that both these works exhibit a strong hortatory component and were written to Christians undergoing or shortly to undergo persecution or hardship of one sort or another for their faith. It is striking, therefore, how Jesus is presented not only in terms of what he has secured for those who remain faithful to the end, but also as one who himself approached suffering and death with faith. Thus, whilst his death and resurrection inform the basis for and content of belief, his approach to suffering and death exemplify and inspire the way of faith. Further, as one who has already concluded faith's journey, his exalted status now substantiates its goal and, in this way, fuels the hopes of those still 'in transit'.

Once again we found signs of this approach beyond the biblical canon and were able to distinguish two emphases. Firstly, as with Hebrews and Revelation, Clement of Alexandria, Cyprian, Origen and others encourage Christians to persevere in faith by drawing attention to Jesus as a fellow-believer who kept faith in the face of persecution and death. Secondly, in the Shepherd of Hermas and the works of Ignatius of Antioch, the distinction between Jesus' and the believer's faith gives way to a common faith; that is to say, Christians are not encouraged to believe as Jesus believed, but to share or put on his faith. We meet this converging tendency again in the next trajectory, but here the emphasis is firmly upon the disposition or practical outworkings of faith: it is as if Jesus' life of faith was thought to be lived out through his followers. Finally, we also noted how the Odes of Solomon and Tertullian maintain in more general terms a continuity of faith linking Jesus with his church.

It should be recognised that these distinctions between perspectives on Jesus' faith within the paradigmatic trajectory may well owe more to our method of investigation than anything else. And it is crucial that we do not lose sight of what they share in common, namely, the conviction that certain aspects of Jesus' life and passion were thought to inform the disposition of faith. Such interest is primarily motivated by what Jesus reveals about the believer's response to God, rather than about God's initiative or offer of salvation. In this respect, therefore, it seems that Jesus was considered as one – perhaps the greatest – of Israel's exemplars of faith. This is certainly the case in the Epistle to the Hebrews where he epitomises the νέφος μαρτύρων (Heb. 12.1), but it is also inferred by the way that most of the traditions suggestive of Jesus' faith are concerned with matters of discipleship and demonstrate a conscious correspondence between Jesus and his followers: as Abraham, Moses and many others incarnate the life of faith, providing inspiration and example, so Jesus was also appreciated as one whose approach to life and death eloquently inform the *fides qua creditur*.

What is more, this link with discipleship is likely to indicate the provenance and purpose of the paradigmatically motivated interest in Jesus' faith. Rather than representing a historicising tendency (*pace* R. Bultmann *et al.*), it is rooted in the conviction that Jesus incarnates the life of faith and as such provides a valuable example for others to emulate and a fruitful context for the church's teaching on this subject. It may not be going too far to claim that Jesus' faith was thought to be the basis of his encounter with God and, by implication, of other people's encounters as well. Further, whilst it is possible that such an interpretation represents a projection by the post-resurrection community upon the ministry of Jesus, it is much more likely to have originated in the first disciples' assessment of their master; for whatever other categories they may have entertained for him, they must surely have been impressed by and attracted to the profundity of his relationship with God – a relationship which when interpreted from the perspective of Judaism would be understood as one of faith.

An additional reason why this interest in Jesus' faith is unlikely to be a post-Easter creation is the recognition that the resurrection transcended attempts to assess his significance in terms of human categories and demanded that he be understood from the perspective of what he reveals of God and his salvific provisions. Whilst this christological process started prior to his death, it unquestionably assumed a new impetus after the first Easter when Jesus Christ was increasingly interpreted as one who modified the content of faith in God. In the light of this initiative, fresh attempts to frame Jesus as a believer amongst believers must be considered improbable. Indeed, as the controversy between Athanasius and Arius indicates, a conflict which may well betray earlier concerns, the exemplary function of Jesus' faith could be seen as a barrier to exploring his theological significance. Certainly, it appears to have been a perceived incompatibility between affirming, on the one hand, that Jesus was the incarnate Son of God whilst, on the other, that he was also a man of faith which seems to have put paid to the paradigmatic trajectory outlined above.

The second trajectory relating to Jesus' faith which we identified is concerned more overtly with theological matters. If the paradigmatic trajectory revolves around how Jesus' faith informs the life of faith, the theological trajectory focuses upon how Jesus' faith is instrumental within the structure of God's salvific initiatives. Once again, we discerned two strands here and the first one finds its most eloquent exponent in St Paul. In Romans, Galatians and Philippians we noted a convergence between the revelation of God's righteousness or covenantal faithfulness and the faith of Jesus Christ, in the sense that the latter was the vehicle for the former. In the apostle's thinking, Christ's faith is epitomised in his obedience to God's will which led him to the cross; and through that death, God's love reaches out to all people – both Jews and Gentiles – and so fulfils the covenantal promise made to Abraham, the father of all believers. It is important that we do not confuse Jesus Christ's faith with God's faithfulness; Paul considers Christ's faith to be a function of his humanity – of his solidarity with fallen humankind – and thus the response that he alone could make on their behalf so that God's covenantal faithfulness can be encountered by all and perhaps especially by the Gentiles. His faith-in-obedience on the cross, therefore, is the channel for God's faithfulness; one is known through the other as God's initiative becomes real in one 'representative' man's response.

We also noted that although Paul conceives of Jesus' faith in terms of his humanity, he does not consciously attribute to it any paradigmatic function; he does, however, explore its significance for the faith of others. As the cross is the centre of God's redeeming activity and as his covenantal faithfulness is revealed there through Christ's faith, so the latter becomes the basis for and the grounds of all faith: others may believe because of Christ's faith, which both makes faith possible and legitimates it. But more than that, owing to Paul's understanding of the inclusive nature of Christ's humanity, faith must be conceived not so much as a matter of believing in Christ or what God has accomplished through him, but of finding oneself in the faith of Christ and so of being located within his corporate response to God. In this sense, Paul conceives of faith as part of God's grace mediated through Christ.

Although we found evidence that a similar association between Christ's faith, his death on the cross and God's salvation was made by Ignatius of Antioch and Clement of Alexandria, their understanding is by no means as comprehensive or nuanced as Paul's. In addition, it is much more likely that the burden of the apostle's theological reflection in this sphere fed into what we described in chapter 6 as the canonic function of Christ's faith. From this perspective, the distinction between the faith of Christ and that of believers largely disappears as faith becomes intimately defined by Christ. As we have indicated, the rudiments for this development are present in Paul himself and it is not difficult to envisage how his understanding of Christ's faith as the vehicle for God's righteousness and, as such, as the grounds, context and legitimation for all faith should lead to a situation where, from the perspective of knowledge of God and of his salvific blessings, Christ and faith become to all intents and purposes equivalent. And we were able to demonstrate this process within Ephesians, 1 and 2 Timothy and then beyond the New Testament in the Epistle of Barnabas and the thought of Clement of Alexandria, Clement of Rome, Origen and others.

In contrast to the paradigmatic trajectory, Paul's theological interpretation of Christ's faith is unlikely to have originated in reflection upon how the earthly Jesus was considered to inform the life of faith; we would have expected the exemplary function to be more in evidence if this had been the case. On the contrary, the apostle's own extraordinary experience of the risen Christ, together with his Jewish background, seem more fruitful sources. For example, the unmerited and unanticipated context for Christ's revelation of himself to Paul must have profoundly influenced not only his understanding of God's grace, but also the source and substance of faith. Further, in the process of bringing that faith to articulation, he was able to draw upon a tradition which attributed great significance to the faith of Abraham, which expected that the long-awaited messiah would be a man of faith and which celebrated the faith of martyrs whose deaths were imbued with sacrificial and atoning efficacy. Nor should we overlook the possible influence of the Akedah, in which God's covenantal faithfulness in providing an alternative sacrifice comes to expression through the faith-in-obedience of Abraham as he prepares to offer the only heir to the promise. Although the parallel here is not exact, the similarities with Paul's notion of God's covenantal faithfulness being revealed in Christ's faith-in-obedience are significant.

In addition to expounding the exemplary function of Jesus' faith, we also noted how the Epistle to the Hebrews bears witness to a second strand within our theological trajectory: here, Jesus is portrayed as faithfully continuing his high-priestly ministries in heaven. Once again this provides a channel for God's salvific blessings, although not in the sense of Jesus' faith mediating God's covenantal faithfulness as we saw in Paul; but of how, by his continuing intercession on their behalf, he remains faithful to his sacerdotal functions in mediating between God and humankind. Although Jesus' identification with humanity is considered an essential prerequisite for this ministry, his description as πιστός probably owes more to reflection upon his priestly office in the light of the Old Testament (Num. 12.7 and Heb. 3.1–5; cf. ἱερέα πιστόν, 1 Sam. 2.35) than to interpretation upon his life of faith. Further, apart from Hebrews, we discovered little interest in this strand of the theological trajectory before Athanasius, who makes much of Hebrews 3.2 and the epithet for Christ in particular. As we noted, however, whilst the author of Hebrews uses πιστός in chapters 2 and 3 to underline Jesus' continuing identification with humanity, the bishop of Alexandria – drawing attention to the way in which God's faithfulness demonstrates his praiseworthiness – takes it as evidence of the incarnate Son's divinity. Finally, we noted how in contrast to Athanasius a century or so later, Tertullian affirms the importance of Christ's faith for the full incarnation of the Son or Logos.

In brief, then, these are the fruits of our investigations: that two trajectories of interest in Jesus' faith can be identified in early Christian traditions. The first is the paradigmatic trajectory, originating in pre-Easter reflection upon Jesus' significance for the disposition of faith in God, which came to expression in relation to matters of discipleship and which proved problematic for, if not incompatible with, establishing Jesus' divinity. And the second is the theological trajectory, a post-resurrection phenomenon, which attempted to articulate how Jesus of Nazareth and, in particular, his death could be the channel for God's grace and which gradually became subsumed within a more comprehensive understanding of how Jesus informed Christian belief.

It should be apparent from these conclusions why it was necessary to adopt a fairly loose definition of faith at the outset, for without doing this we would have been in danger not only of excluding relevant data concerning Jesus' faith, but also of misconstruing its relation to the faith of believers and God's faithfulness. Further, by locating our investigations within the heritage of faith found in Judaism and elsewhere, we have hopefully been able to demonstrate that consideration of Jesus as a man of faith would have been a meaningful exercise within the process of assessing his significance as a mediator of God's salvation. Finally, although we have not been concerned directly with conceptions of Jesus Christ in terms of *fides quae creditur*, it has been interesting to observe how recognition of Jesus' faith fed into broader explorations of his importance for the content of belief.

Before drawing this study to a close, we should perhaps indicate some of the ramifications of the disappearance of Jesus' faith from christological discourse. Firstly, we noted how Athanasius was not prepared – at least in his refutation of Arianism – to attribute faith to Jesus as this would, in his opinion, undermine the divinity of the incarnate Son and could not, therefore, have been a necessary implication of his becoming human. It is questionable, however, whether even from the perspective of Nicean or Chalcedonian orthodoxy this assessment is in fact the case. Clearly, the incarnation involved a voluntary kenosis on the part of the Son which, as Athanasius himself admitted, can be demonstrated from scripture in terms of Jesus' need to pray, his ignorance of the Father's will and so forth; but surely these characteristics attest an external relating to the Father no less than faith and it is difficult to see how the incarnation can be taken seriously in terms of the Son's assumption of humanity if such a distinctively human trait is ignored. Further, there is the whole issue of the relationship between the incarnation and salvation: if the unassumed remains the unhealed, then surely the Son must have assumed humanity to the extent of living by faith? But more directly, as we saw in Paul, Jesus' faith is not only the context for God's offer of renewed relationship, but also the context for response to that offer: people may believe because their faith is a function of being found in Christ and so of being a part of Christ's response of faith to the Father. In consequence, if the faith of believers is divorced from Christ's faith, we seem to end up with yet another permutation of humanity pulling itself up by its own bootstraps.

Secondly, we noted in relation to the theological trajectory how interest in Jesus' faith was absorbed within a broader understanding of faith. To start with, this development was of little significance because faith remained intimately linked, through the apostolic witness and through his risen presence in the worshipping community, with the person of Jesus Christ. However, the movement towards formalising Christian belief had the effect of distancing the articulation of faith from the phenomenon which it purported to embrace. In consequence, it became possible to affirm a set of propositions about Christ without encountering the person to whom they referred. What is more, this tendency has the effect of severing faith from its historical roots. As we have seen, reflection upon Jesus' πίστις may well have been the start of christological reflection in that it was the profundity of his faith which revealed the graciousness of God in his performance of 'kingdom miracles' and in his obedience to the point of death. In addition, as Paul maintains, it is Christ's πίστις or, expressed in terms of orthodox patristic christology, the fullness of the incarnate Son's humanity which is the vehicle for God's salvation. This is, so to speak, where opposites meet; it is here that God's covenantal faithfulness and humanity's response of faith intersect in the one person. In Christ we find both God's gift of salvation and our response to that gift – for he conveys the things of God to humanity and the things of humanity to God.

In consequence, it may be that any incompatibility between maintaining, on the one hand, that Jesus informs *fides qua creditur* and, on the other, that he constitutes the content of *fides quae creditur* is more apparent than real; these perspectives simply represent different evaluations of Jesus' significance, firstly, from the paradigmatic or anthropological and, secondly, from the theological or, more commonly, christological. What is more, these two approaches map onto and can adequately be accommodated within what became formalised through the Council of Chalcedon, as the doctrine of the two natures of Christ. Further, from a historical basis, these two perspectives need not be incompatible in the sense that they inevitably lead to the conclusion that Jesus of Nazareth must have believed in himself; such a proposal would be anachronistic for, as we have seen, consideration of Jesus' πίστις probably originated in a pre-Easter situation where his response would have been interpreted as faith in God. The process concerned with how Jesus modified the content of belief in God was essentially a post-resurrection initiative which, in affirming both the full humanity and the divinity of the Son, developed a framework which could accommodate the faith of Jesus Christ.

It is the conviction of the present author that interest in Jesus' faith was an unfortunate and unnecessary casualty of early christological controversy, in which its significance was determined more in terms of what it conceded to rival positions rather than of what it contributed to our knowledge of God and humanity in Jesus Christ. There are signs, however, that this assessment is being reconsidered both by those wishing to reaffirm Jesus' significance in terms of patristic orthodoxy and those exploring other approaches.[1] Certainly, Jesus' faith does seem to provide a point of departure for christology which is rooted in common human experience and which explores his theological significance through reflection upon his human being in relation to God. It is hoped that our investigations will help towards establishing a historical and exegetical basis upon which more overtly theological explorations can draw.

[1] E.g. T. A. Hart and D. P. Thimell, *Christ*; Mackey, *Jesus*, esp. 205–47; Macquarrie, Jesus Christ, esp. 359–414; Moltmann, *Way*, esp. Part III; Schillebeeckx, *Jesus*, esp. Part II; Sobrino, *Christology*, esp. 79–145; J. B. Torrance, 'Humanity', 127–47; T. F. Torrance, *Mediation*, esp. 83–108.

SELECT BIBLIOGRAPHY

Primary sources

Editions of primary sources and translations are cited wherever possible by series rather than by individual volume. Where details of sources do not accompany references, the following editions have been used:

Old Testament, Apocrypha and Pseudepigrapha

Biblia Hebraica Stuttgartensia, edited by K. Elliger and W. Rudolf (Stuttgart: Deutsche Bibelstiftung, 1977).

Septuaginta, edited by A. Ralphs, 2 vols. (Stuttgart: Deutsche Bibelstiftung, 1935).

Revised Standard Version (Division of Christian Education of the National Council of the Churches of Christ in the USA, 1952 [OT], 1957 [Apocrypha]).

Old Testament Pseudepigrapha, edited by J. H. Charlesworth, 2 vols. (London: Darton, Longman & Todd, 1983 and 1985).

New Testament and Apocrypha

Novum Testamentum Graece, edited by K. Aland, M. Black, C. M. Martini, B. M. Metzger and A. Wikgren (Stuttgart: Deutsche Bibelstiftung, 1979).

Acta Apostolorum Apocrypha, edited by R. A. Lipsius and M. Bonnet, 3 vols. (Hildesheim: Georg Olms, 1959).

Revised Standard Version (Division of Christian Education of the National Council of the Churches of Christ in the USA, 1971).

New Testament Apocrypha, edited by E. Hennecke and W. Schneemelcher. 2 vols. trans. R. McL. Wilson (London: Lutterworth, 1963 and 1965).

Other Jewish literature

The Aramaic Bible: The Targums, edited by K. Cathcart, M. Maher and M. McNamara, many vols. (Edinburgh: T. & T. Clark, 1987–).

The Babylonian Talmud: Translated into English with Notes, Glossary and Indices, edited by I. Epstein, many vols. (London: Soncino, 1935–52).

The Dead Sea Scrolls in English, edited by G. Vermes, 2nd edn. (Harmondsworth: Penguin, 1975).
Mekilta de Rabbi Ishmael, edited by J. Z. Lauterbach, 3 vols. (Philadelphia: Jewish Publication Society of America, 1933).
The Midrash on Psalms, edited by W. G. Braude, 2 vols. (New Haven: Yale University Press, 1959).
Midrash Rabbah, edited by H. Freedman and M. Simon, 10 vols. (London: Soncino, 1939).
The Mishnah: Translated from the Hebrew with Introduction and Brief Explanatory Notes, edited by H. Danby (Oxford: Oxford University Press, 1933).
Die Texte aus Qumran, edited by E. Lohse (München: Kösel, 1964).

Secondary literature

Achtemeier, P. J. 'Person and Deed: Jesus and the Storm-Tossed Sea', *Interpretation* 16 (1962), 169–76.
'Miracles and the Historical Jesus: A Study of Mark 9:14–29', *CBQ* 37 (1975), 471–91.
Mark, Proclamation Commentaries (Philadelphia: Fortress Press, 1975).
'Jesus and the Disciples as Miracle Workers in the Apocryphal New Testament', in E. S. Fiorenza (ed.), *Aspects of Religious Propaganda in Judaism and Early Christianity* (Notre Dame: Notre Dame University Press, 1976), 149–86.
Adamson, J. B. *James: The Man and His Message* (Grand Rapids: Eerdmans, 1989).
Aichinger, H. 'Zur Traditionsgeschichte der Epileptiker-Perikope Mk 9,14–29 par Mt 17,14–21 par Lk 9,37–43a', in A. Fuchs (ed.), *Probleme der Forschung*, SNTU A/3 (München: Herold Wien, 1978), 114–43.
Anderson, H. *Jesus and Christian Origins: A Commentary on Modern Viewpoints* (Oxford: Oxford University Press, 1964).
The Gospel of Mark, New Century Bible (London: Marshall, Morgan & Scott, 1976).
Aquinas, T. *St Thomas Aquinas' Summa Theologiae, Volume 49: The Grace of Christ* (London: Eyre & Spottiswoode, 1974).
Attridge, H. W. *The Epistle to the Hebrews: A Commentary on the Epistle to the Hebrews*, Hermeneia (Philadelphia: Fortress Press, 1989).
Aune, D. E. *Prophecy in Early Christianity and the Ancient Mediterranean World* (Grand Rapids: Eerdmans, 1983).
Baillie, D. M. *Faith in God and its Christian Consummation* (London: Faber, 1964).
Barclay, J. M. G. 'Paul and the law: observations on some recent debates', *Themelios* 12 (1986), 5–15.
Obeying the Truth: A Study of Paul's Ethics in Galatians, SNTW (Edinburgh: T. & T. Clark, 1988).
Barr, J. *The Semantics of Biblical Language* (Oxford: Oxford University Press, 1961).

Barrett, C. K. *The Epistle to the Romans*, BNTC, rev. edn. (London: A. & C. Black, 1962).

From First Adam to Last: A Study in Pauline Theology (London: A. & C. Black, 1962).

Freedom and Obligation: A Study of the Epistle to the Galatians (London: SPCK, 1985).

Barth, G. 'Glaube und Zweifel in der synoptischen Evangelien', *ZTK* 72 (1975), 269–92.

Der Brief an die Philipper, Züricher Bibelkommentare (Zürich: Theologischer Verlag, 1979).

'Pistis in hellenistischer Religiosität', *ZNW* 73 (1982), 110–26.

'πίστις κτλ', *EWNT*, vol. 3, 216–31.

Barth, K. *The Epistle to the Romans*, trans. E. C. Hoskyns (Oxford: Oxford University Press, 1933).

Barth, M. 'Jews and Gentiles: The Social Character of Justification in Paul', trans. N. Adams, *Journal of Ecumenical Studies* 5 (1968), 241–67.

'The Faith of the Messiah', *HeyJ* 10 (1969), 363–70.

Justification: Pauline Texts Interpreted in the Light of the Old and New Testaments, trans. A. M. Woodruff (Grand Rapids: Eerdmans, 1971).

Ephesians: Introduction, Translation, and Commentary, The Anchor Bible, 2 vols. (New York: Doubleday, 1974).

Bauckham, R. *The Theology of the Book of Revelation*, New Testament Theology (Cambridge: Cambridge University Press, 1993).

Beare, F. W. *The Gospel According to Matthew* (Oxford: Blackwell, 1981).

Beasley-Murray, G. R. *The Book of Revelation*, New Century Bible, rev. edn. (London: Oliphants, 1978).

Jesus and the Kingdom of God (Exeter: Paternoster, 1986).

Beker, J. C. *Paul the Apostle: The Triumph of God in Life and Thought* (Philadelphia: Fortress Press, 1980).

Benoît, A. *Biblia Patristica*, 2 vols. (Paris: Centre Nàtional de la Recherche Scientifique, 1975 and 1977).

Berger, K. 'Die königlichen Messiastraditionen des Neuen Testaments', *NTS* 20 (1973), 1–44.

Best, E. 'Discipleship in Mark: Mark 8:22–10:52', *SJT* 23 (1970), 323–37.

'The Role of the Disciples in Mark', *NTS* 23 (1976), 377–401.

Following Jesus: Discipleship in the Gospel of Mark, JSNTSS 4 (Sheffield: JSOT, 1981).

Betz, H. D. *Galatians: A Commentary on Paul's Letter to the Churches in Galatia*, Hermeneia (Philadelphia: Fortress Press, 1979).

Betz, O. 'Firmness in Faith: Hebrews 11:1 and Isaiah 28:16', in B. P. Thompson (ed.), *Scripture, Meaning and Method: Essays Presented to Anthony Tyrell Hanson* (Hull: Hull University Press, 1987), 92–113.

Binder, H. *Der Glaube bei Paulus* (Berlin: Evangelische, 1968).

Black, C. C. *The Disciples According to Mark: Markan Redaction in Current Debate*, JSNTSS 27 (Sheffield: JSOT, 1989).

Bligh, J. 'Did Jesus Live by Faith?', *HeyJ* 9 (1968), 414–19.

Bogdan, R. J. (ed.), *Belief: Form, Content and Function* (Oxford: Clarendon Press, 1986).

Boring, M. E. *Revelation*, Interpretation (Louisville: John Knox Press, 1989).

Bornkamm, G. *Jesus of Nazareth*, trans. I. and F. McLuskey with J. M. Robinson (London: Hodder & Stoughton, 1960).

'End-Expectation and Church in Matthew', in G. Bornkamm, G. Barth and H. J. Held (eds.), *Tradition and Interpretation in Matthew*, NTL, trans. P. Scott (Philadelphia: Westminster, 1963), 15–51.

'The Stilling of the Storm in Matthew', in G. Bornkamm, G. Barth and H. J. Held (eds.), *Tradition and Interpretation in Matthew*, NTL, trans. P. Scott (Philadelphia: Westminster, 1963), 52–7.

Early Christian Experience, NTL, trans. P. L. Hammer (London: SCM Press, 1969).

'The Revelation of Christ to Paul on the Damascus Road and Paul's Doctrine of Justification and Reconciliation: A Study of Galatians 1', trans. J. M. Owen, in R. J. Banks (ed.), *Reconciliation and Hope: New Testament Essays on Atonement and Eschatology Presented to L. L. Morris on his 60th Birthday* (Grand Rapids: Eerdmans, 1974), 90–103.

Borse, U. *Der Brief an die Galater*, Regensburger Neues Testament (Regensburg: Friedrich Pustet, 1984).

Bousset, W. *Die Offenbarung Johannis*, KEK, rev. edn. (Göttingen: Vandenhoeck & Ruprecht, 1906).

Bowker, J. *The Targums and Rabbinic Literature: An Introduction to Jewish Interpretations of Scripture* (Cambridge: Cambridge University Press, 1969).

Braun, H. 'The Meaning of New Testament Christology', trans. P. J. Achtemeier, *Journal of Theology and Church*, 5 (1968), 89–127.

An die Hebräer, HNT 14 (Tübingen: J. C. B. Mohr [Paul Siebeck], 1984).

Brown, C. *Miracles and the Critical Mind* (Grand Rapids: Eerdmans, 1984).

Brox, N. *Die Pastoralbriefe*, Regensburger Neues Testament, 4th edn. (Regensburg: F. Pustet, 1969).

Bruce, F. F. *The Epistle to the Hebrews: The English Text with Introduction, Exposition and Notes*, NICNT (London: Marshall, Morgan & Scott, 1964).

'Galatian Problems 3: The "Other" Gospel', *BJRL* 53 (1970), 253–71.

The Epistle to the Galatians: A Commentary on the Greek Text, NIGTC (Exeter: Paternoster, 1982).

Brueggemann, W. 'David and his Theologian', *CBQ* 30 (1968), 156–81.

'From Dust to Kingship', *ZAW* 84 (1972), 1–18.

In Man We Trust: The Neglected Side of Biblical Faith (Atlanta: John Knox Press, 1972).

Hope within History (Atlanta: John Knox Press, 1987).

Buber, M. *Two Types of Faith*, trans. N. P. Goldhawk (London: Routledge & Kegan Paul, 1951).

Buchanan, G. W. *To the Hebrews: Translation, Comment and Conclusions*, The Anchor Bible (New York: Doubleday, 1972).

Bultmann, R. *Theology of the New Testament*, 2 vols., trans. K. Grobel (London: SCM Press, 1952 and 1955).

Jesus and the Word, trans. L. P. Smith and E. H. Lantero (New York: Charles Scribner's Sons, 1958).

'The Primitive Christian Kerygma and the Historical Jesus', in C. E. Braaten and R. A. Harrisville (eds. and trans.), *The Historical Jesus and the Kerygmatic Christ* (New York: Abingdon, 1964), 15–42.

Bultmann, R. and Weiser, A. 'πιστεύω κτλ', *TDNT*, vol. 6, 174–228.

Burridge, R. A. *What are the Gospels? a comparison with Graeco-Roman biography*, SNTSMS 70 (Cambridge: Cambridge University Press, 1992).

Burton, E. de W. *A Critical and Exegetical Commentary on the Epistle to the Galatians*, ICC (Edinburgh: T. & T. Clark, 1921).

Büschel, F. 'ἐλέγχω κτλ', *TDNT*, vol. 2, 473–6.

Busse, U. *Die Wunder des Propheten Jesus: Die Rezeption, Komposition und Interpretation der Wundertradition im Evangelium des Lukas*, Forschung zur Bibel, 2nd edn. (Stuttgart: Katholisches Bibelwerk, 1979).

Caird, G. B. *A Commentary on the Revelation of St John the Divine*, BNTC (London: A. & C. Black, 1966).

Cairns, D. S. *The Faith that Rebels: A Re-examination of the Miracles of Jesus*, 5th edn. (London: SCM Press, 1933).

Campbell, D. A. *The Rhetoric of Righteousness in Romans 3.21–26*, JSNTSS 65 (Sheffield: JSOT, 1992).

'The Meaning of ΠΙΣΤΙΣ and ΝΟΜΟΣ in Paul: A Linguistic and Structural Perspective', *JBL* 111 (1992), 91–103.

Charles, R. H. *A Critical and Exegetical Commentary on the Revelation of St John*, ICC, 2 vols. (Edinburgh: T. & T. Clark, 1920).

Childs, B. S. *Biblical Theology of the Old and New Testaments: Theological Reflection on the Christian Bible* (London: SCM Press, 1992).

Clements, R. E. *Abraham and David: Genesis 15 and its Meaning for Israelite Tradition*, SBT 2/2 (London: SCM Press, 1974).

Coats, G. W. 'Abraham's Sacrifice of Faith: A Form-Critical Study of Genesis 22', *Interpretation* 27 (1973), 389–400.

Collange, J.-F. *The Epistle of Saint Paul to the Philippians*, trans. A. W. Heathcote (London: Epworth, 1979).

Cook, M. L. 'The Call to Faith of the Historical Jesus: Questions for the Christian Understanding of Faith', *Theological Studies* 39 (1978), 679–700.

Coutts, J. 'The Authority of Jesus and of the Twelve in St Mark's Gospel', *JTS* (ns) 8 (1957), 111–18.

Cranfield, C. E. B. 'St Mark 9.14–29', *SJT* 3 (1950), 57–67.

The Gospel According to Saint Mark, CGNT, rev. edn. (Cambridge: Cambridge University Press, 1972).

A Critical and Exegetical Commentary on The Epistle to the Romans, I*CC*, 2 vols. (Edinburgh: T. & T. Clark, 1975 and 1979).

Crosby, M. R. *The Rhetorical Composition and Function of Hebrews 11* (Macon: Mercer University Press, 1988).

Dahl, N. A. 'The Parables of Growth', *Studia Theologica* 5 (1952), 132–66.

Daly, R. J. 'The Soteriological Significance of the Sacrifice of Isaac', *CBQ* 39 (1977), 45–75.

D'Angelo, M. R. *Moses in the Letter to the Hebrews*, SBLDS 42 (Missoula, MT: Scholars Press, 1979).

Dautzenberg, G. 'Der Glaube im Hebräerbrief', *Biblische Zeitschrift* (nf) 17 (1973), 161–77.
'Der Glaube in der Jesusüberlieferung', in G. Jendorff and G. Schmalenberg (eds.), *Anwalt des Menschen: Beiträge aus Theologie und Religionspädagogik. Feschrift für Ferdinand Hahn* (Giessen: Selbstverlag des Fachbereichs, 1983), 41–62.
Davids, P. H. *The Epistle of James: A Commentary on the Greek Text*, NIGTC (Exeter: Paternoster, 1982).
'James and Jesus', in D. Wenham (ed.), *Gospel Perspectives: Volume 5 – The Jesus Tradition Outside of the Gospels* (Sheffield: JSOT, 1985), 63–84.
Davies, G. N. *Faith and Obedience in Romans: A Study of Romans 1–4*, JSNTSS 39 (Sheffield: JSOT, 1990).
Davies, P. R. and Chilton, B. D. 'The Aqedah: A Revised Tradition History', *CBQ* 40 (1978), 514–46.
Davies, W. D. *The Setting of the Sermon on the Mount* (Cambridge: Cambridge University Press, 1963).
Paul and Rabbinic Judaism: Some Rabbinic Elements in Pauline Theology, 3rd edn. (London: SPCK, 1970).
Davies, W. D. and Allison, D. C. Jr. *A Critical and Exegetical Commentary on the Gospel According to Saint Matthew*, ICC, vol. 2 (Edinburgh: T. & T. Clark, 1991).
Deissmann, A. *Paul: A Study in Social and Religious History*, trans. W. E. Wilson (New York: Harper & Row, 1957).
Delling, G. 'Das Verständnis des Wunders im Neuen Testament', *ZST* 24 (1955), 265–80.
'The Significance of the Resurrection of Jesus for Faith in Jesus Christ', in C. F. D. Moule (ed.), *The Significance of the Message of the Resurrection for Faith in Jesus Christ*, trans. R. A. Wilson (London: SCM Press, 1968), 77–104.
'τέλος κτλ', *TDNT*, vol. 2, 49–87.
Derrett, J. D. M. 'Figtrees in the New Testament', *HeyJ* 14 (1973), 249–65.
'Moving Mountains and Uprooting Trees (Mk 11:22; Mt 17:20, 21:21; Lk 17:6)', *Bibbia e Oriente* 30 (1988), 231–44.
Dewey, J. *Markan Public Debate: Literary Technique, Concentric Structure, and Theology in Mark 2:1–3:6*, SBLDS 48 (Chicago: Scholars Press, 1980).
Dibelius, M. *From Tradition to Gospel*, trans. B. L. Woolf (Cambridge: James Clarke, 1971).
James: A Commentary on the Epistle of James, Hermeneia, rev. H. Greeven, trans. M. A. Williams (Philadelphia: Fortress Press, 1976).
Dibelius, M. and Conzelmann, H. *The Pastoral Epistles: A Commentary on the Pastoral Epistles*, Hermeneia, trans. P. Buttolph and A. Yarbro (Philadelphia: Fortress Press, 1972).
Dix, G. *The Shape of the Liturgy*, 2nd edn. (London: A. & C. Black, 1945).
Dobschütz, E. von. 'Zur Erzählerkunst des Markus', *ZNW* 27 (1928), 193–8.

Donahue, J. R. 'Temple, Trial, and Royal Christology', in W. H. Kelber (ed.) *The Passion in Mark* (Philadelphia: Fortress Press, 1976), 61–79.

Donaldson, T. L. *Jesus on the Mountain: A Study in Matthean Theology*, JSNTSS 8 (Sheffield: JSOT, 1985).

'The "Curse of the Law" and the Inclusion of the Gentiles: Galatians 3.13–14', *NTS* 32 (1986), 94–112.

Doughty, D. J. 'The Priority of ΧΑΡΙΣ', *NTS* 19 (1972), 163–80.

Dragas, G. D. *Athanasiana: Essays in the Theology of St Athanasius*, vol. 1 (London: no publisher, 1980)

St Athanasius Contra Apollinarem (Athens: no publisher, 1985).

''Ενανθρώπησις, or ἐγένετο ἄνθρωπος: A neglected aspect of Athanasius' Christology', *Studia Patristica*, 16 (1985), 281–94.

Drane, J. W. *Paul: Libertine or Legalist? A Study in the Theology of the Major Pauline Epistles* (London: SPCK, 1975).

Duling, D. C. 'The Therapeutic Son of David: An Element in Matthew's Christological Apologetic', *NTS* 24 (1977), 392–410.

Dungan, D. L. *The Sayings of Jesus in the Churches of Paul: The Use of the Synoptic Tradition in the Regulation of Early Church Life* (Oxford: Blackwell, 1971).

Dunn, J. D. G. *Baptism in the Holy Spirit: A Re-examination of the New Testament Teaching on the Gift of the Spirit in relation to Pentecostalism today*, SBT 2/15 (London: SCM Press, 1970).

'Paul's Understanding of the Death of Jesus', in R. J. Banks (ed.), *Reconciliation and Hope: New Testament Essays on Atonement and Eschatology Presented to L. L. Morris on his 60th Birthday* (Grand Rapids: Eerdmans, 1974), 125–41.

Jesus and the Spirit: A Study of the Religious and Charismatic Experience of Jesus and the First Christians as Reflected in the New Testament, NTL (London: SCM Press, 1975).

Unity and Diversity in the New Testament: An Inquiry into the Character of Earliest Christianity (London: SCM Press, 1977).

'The Birth of a Metaphor – Baptized in Spirit (Part 2)', *ExpT* 89 (1978), 173–5.

Christology in the Making: A New Testament Inquiry into the Origins of the Doctrine of the Incarnation (London: SCM Press, 1980).

Romans, WBC 38, 2 vols. (Dallas, Texas: Word Books, 1988).

Jesus, Paul and the Law: Studies in Mark and Galatians (London: SPCK, 1990).

'"A Light to the Gentiles", or "The End of the Law"? The Significance of the Damascus Road Christophany for Paul', in *Jesus, Paul and the Law*, 89–107 [cf. revision of *The Glory of Christ in the New Testament*, L. D. Hurst and N. T. Wright (eds.) (Oxford: Clarendon Press, 1987), 251–66].

'The New Perspective on Paul', in *Jesus, Paul and the Law*, 183–214 [cf. revision of *BJRL* 65 (1983), 95–122].

'Works of the Law and the Curse of the Law (Gal. 3.10–14)', in *Jesus, Paul and the Law*, 215–41 [cf. revision of *NTS* 31 (1985), 523–42].

'The Theology of Galatians', in *Jesus, Paul and the Law*, 242–64 [cf.

revision of *SBL 1988 Seminar Papers* (Atlanta: Scholars Press, 1988), 1–16].
'Once More, ΠΙΣΤΙΣ ΧΡΙΣΤΟΥ', in E. H. Lovering, Jr. (ed.), *Society of Biblical Literature 1991 Seminar Papers*, E. J. Lull (ed.) (Atlanta, Georgia: Scholars Press, 1991), 730–44.
A Commentary on The Epistle to the Galatians, BNTC (London: A. & C. Black, 1993).
Dunnill, J. *Covenant and sacrifice in the Letter to the Hebrews*, SNTSMS 75 (Cambridge: Cambridge University Press, 1992).
DuPlessis P. J. *ΤΕΛΕΙΟΣ: The Idea of Perfection in the New Testament* (Kampen: J. H. Kok, 1959).
Dupont, J. 'The Conversion of Paul, and its Influence on his Understanding of Salvation by Faith', trans. R. P. Martin, in W. W. Gasque and R. P. Martin (eds.), *Apostolic History and the Gospel* (Exeter: Paternoster, 1970), 176–94.
Ebeling, G. *The Nature of Faith*, trans. R. G. Smith (London: Collins, 1961).
Word and Faith, trans. J. W. Leitch (London: SCM Press, 1963).
The Truth of the Gospel: An Exposition of Galatians, trans. D. Green (Philadelphia: Fortress Press, 1985).
Edelstein, L. and E. J. *Asclepius: a collection and interpretation of testimonies*, Institute of the History of Medicine Publications, 2 vols. (Baltimore: John Hopkins Press, 1945).
Eichrodt, W. *Theology of the Old Testament*, OTL, 2 vols., trans. J. Baker (London: SCM Press, 1961 and 1967).
Ellis, P. F. *Matthew: his Mind and his Message* (Collegeville: Liturgical Press, 1974).
Ernst, J. *Die Briefe an die Philipper, an Philemon, an die Kolosser, an die Epheser*, Regensburger Neues Testament (Regensburg: Friedrich Pustet, 1974).
Evans, D. 'Faith and Belief', *Religious Studies* 10 (1974), 1–19 and 199–212.
Fee, G. D. *1 and 2 Timothy, Titus* (San Francisco: Harper & Row, 1984).
Fiorenza, E. S. *The Book of Revelation – Justice and Judgement* (Philadelphia: Fortress Press, 1985).
Fitzmyer, J. A. *The Gospel According to Luke*, The Anchor Bible, 2 vols. (New York: Doubleday, 1981 and 1985).
Flesseman-van Leer, E. *Tradition and Scripture in the Early Church* (Assen: van Gorcum, 1954).
Foerster, W. 'ὄρος', *TDNT*, vol. 5, 475–87.
Ford, J. M. *Revelation: Introduction, Translation and Commentary*, The Anchor Bible (New York: Doubleday, 1975).
Fowl, S. E. *The Story of Christ in the Ethics of Paul: An Analysis of the Function of the Hymnic Material in the Pauline Corpus*, JSNTSS 36 (Sheffield: JSOT, 1990).
Franklin, E. *Christ the Lord: A Study in the Purpose and Theology of Luke-Acts* (London: SPCK, 1975).
Friedrich, G. 'εὐαγγελίζομαι κτλ', *TDNT*, vol. 2, 707–37.
'Glaube und Verkündigung bei Paulus', in F. Hahn and H. Klein (eds.), *Glaube*, 93–113.

Frost, E. *Christian Healing: A Consideration of the Place of Spiritual Healing in the Church of To-day in the Light of the Doctrine and Practice of the Ante-Nicene Church*, 3rd edn. (London: A. R. Mowbray & Co., 1954).
Fuchs, A. *Sprachliche Untersuchungen zum Matthäus und Lukas: Ein Bietrag zum Quellenkritik*, Analecta biblica 49 (Rome: Pontifical Institute, 1971).
Fuchs, E. *Studies in the Historical Jesus*, SBT 1/42, trans. A. Scobie (London: SCM Press, 1964).
Fuller, R. H. *The Mission and Achievement of Jesus: An Examination of the Presuppositions of New Testament Theology*, SBT 1/12 (London: SCM Press, 1954).
Interpreting the Miracles (London: SCM Press, 1963).
Furnish, V. P. *Theology and Ethics in Paul* (Nashville: Abingdon, 1968).
Gadamer, H.-G. *Truth and Method*, trans. W. Glen-Doepel (London: Sheed & Ward, 1975).
Gaston, L. *Paul and the Torah* (Vancouver: University of British Columbia, 1987).
'Abraham and the Righteousness of God', in *Paul*, 45–63 [cf. revision of *Horizons in Biblical Theology* 2 (1980), 39–68].
'For *All* the Believers: The Inclusion of Gentiles as the Ultimate Goal of Torah in Romans', in *Paul*, 116–34.
'Paul and the Law in Galatians 2 and 3', in *Paul*, 64–79 [cf. revision of *Anti-Judaism in Early Christianity: Vol. 1 – Paul and the Gospels*, P. Richardson and D. Granskou (eds.) (Waterloo: Wilfred Laurier University Press, 1986), 37–57].
'Paul and the Torah', in *Paul*, 15–34 [cf. revision of *Anti-Semitism and the Foundations of Christianity*, A. T. Davies (ed.) (New York: Paulist Press, 1979), 48–71].
Gatzweiler, K. 'Les Récits de Miracles dans L'Évangile selon Saint Matthieu', in M. Didier (ed.), *L'Évangile selon Matthieu: Rédaction et Théologie*, BETL 29 (Gembloux: J. Duculot, 1972), 209–20.
Gaventa, B. R. *From Darkness to Light: Aspects of Conversion in the New Testament*, Overtures to Biblical Theology 20 (Philadelphia: Fortress Press, 1986).
Gerhardsson, B. *The Mighty Acts of Jesus According to Matthew*, trans. R. Dewsnap (Lund: Gleerup, 1979).
The Origins of the Gospel Traditions (London: SCM Press, 1979).
Gibbs, J. M. 'Purpose and Pattern in Matthew's Use of the Title "Son of David"', *NTS* 10 (1963), 446–64.
Gnilka, J. *Der Philipperbrief*, HTKNT 10/3 (Freiburg: Herder, 1968).
Der Epheserbrief, HTKNT 10/2, 2nd edn. (Freiburg: Herder, 1977).
Das Evangelium nach Markus, EKKNT 2/1–2, 2 vols. (Köln/Neukirchen: Benziger/Neukirchener, 1978 and 1979).
Gogarten, F. *Christ the Crisis*, Library of Philosophy and Theology, trans. R. A. Wilson (London: SCM Press, 1970).
Goodenough, E. R. (completed by A. T. Kraabel), 'Paul and the Hellenization of Christianity', in J. Neusner (ed.), *Religions in Antiquity. Essays in Memory of Erwin Ramsdell Goodenough* (Leiden: E. J. Brill, 1968), 23–68.

Goppelt, L. *Theology of the New Testament*, 2 vols., trans. J. Alsup (Grand Rapids: Eerdmans, 1981 and 1982).

Typos: The Typological Interpretation of the Old Testament in the New, trans. D. H. Madvig (Grand Rapids: Eerdmans, 1981).

Grant, R. M. 'The Coming of the Kingdom', *JBL* 67 (1948), 297–303.

Grässer, E. *Der Glaube im Hebräerbrief*, Marburger theologische Studien 2 (Marburg: N. G. Elwert, 1965).

'Der historische Jesus im Hebräerbrief', *ZNW* 56 (1965), 63–91.

Greer, R. A. *The Captain of our Salvation: A Study in Patristic Exegesis of Hebrews*, BGBE 15 (Tübingen: J. C. B. Mohr [Paul Siebeck], 1973).

Greeven, H. 'Die Heilung des Gelähmten nach Matthäus', *Wort und Dienst* 4 (1955), 65–78.

Gregg, R. C. and Groh, D. E. *Early Arianism – A View of Salvation* (London: SCM Press, 1981).

Grillmeier, A. *Christ in Christian Tradition – Volume 1: From the Apostolic Age to Chalcedon (AD 451)*, rev. edn., trans. J. Bowden (London: Mowbrays, 1975).

Grundmann, W. 'The Teacher of Righteousness of Qumran and the Question of Justification by Faith in the Theology of the Apostle Paul', in J. Murphy-O'Connor (ed.), *Paul and Qumran: Studies in New Testament Exegesis* (London: Geoffrey Chapman, 1968), 85–114.

Guelich, R. A. *Mark*, WBC 34, vol. 1 (Dallas, Texas: Word Books, 1989).

Gundry, R. H. *Matthew: A Commentary on his Literary and Theological Art* (Grand Rapids: Eerdmans, 1982).

'Grace, Works and Staying Saved in Paul', *Biblica* 66 (1985), 1–38.

Gunton, C. E. *Yesterday and Today: A Study of Continuities in Christology* (London: Darton, Longman & Todd, 1983).

Guthrie, D. *The Pastoral Epistles: An Introduction and Commentary*, TNTC (Leicester: Inter-Varsity Press, 1957).

New Testament Introduction, 3rd edn. (Leicester: Inter-Varsity Press, 1970).

Galatians, New Century Bible, rev. edn. (London: Oliphants, 1974).

New Testament Theology (Leicester: Inter-Varsity Press, 1981).

Hägglund, B. 'Die Bedeutung der "regula fidei" als Grundlage theologischer Aussagen', *Studia Theologica* 12 (1958), 1–44.

Hahn, F. 'Genesis 15:6 im Neuen Testament', in H. W. Wolff (ed.), *Probleme biblischer Theologie: Gerhard von Rad zum 70 Geburtstag* (München: Kaiser, 1971), 90–107.

'Das Verständnis des Glaubens im Markusevangelium', in F. Hahn and H. Klein (eds.), *Glaube*, 43–67.

'Jesu Wort vom bergeversetzenden Glauben', *ZNW* 76 (1985), 149–69.

Hahn, F. and Klein, H. (eds.) *Glaube im Neuen Testament: Studien zu Ehren von Herman Binder anlässlich seines 70 Geburtstags*, Biblisch-Theologische Studien 7 (Neukirchen-Vluyn: Neukirchener, 1982).

Hamm, D. 'Faith in the Epistle to the Hebrews: The Jesus Factor', *CBQ* 52 (1990), 270–91.

Hansen, G. H. *Abraham in Galatians: Epistolary and Rhetorical Contexts*, JSNTSS 29 (Sheffield: JSOT, 1989).

Hanson, A. T. *Studies in Paul's Technique and Theology* (London: SPCK, 1974).

Hanson, R. P. C. *Tradition in the Early Church*, Library of History and Doctrine (London: SCM Press, 1962).

The Bible as the Norm of Faith (Durham: Durham University Press, 1963).

The Search for the Christian Doctrine of God: The Arian Controversy 318–381 (Edinburgh: T. & T. Clark, 1988).

Harder, G. 'ὑπόστασις', *NIDNTT*, vol. 1, 710–15.

Hart, T. A. and Thimell, D. P. (eds.) *Christ in our Place: The Humanity of God in Christ for the Reconciliation of the World* (Exeter: Paternoster, 1989).

Harvey, A. E. *Jesus and the Constraints of History: The Bampton Lectures, 1980* (London: Duckworth, 1982).

Hasler, V. *Die Briefe an Timotheus und Titus*, Züricher Bibelkommentare (Zürich: Theologischer Verlag, 1978).

Hatch, W. H. P. *The Pauline Idea of Faith in its Relation to Jewish and Hellenistic Religion* (Cambridge, Mass.: Harvard University Press, 1917).

The Idea of Faith in Christian Literature from the Death of St Paul to the Close of the Second Century (Cambridge, Mass.: Harvard University Press, 1926).

Haussleiter, J. 'Der Glaube Jesu Christi und der christliche Glaube', *NKZ* 2 (1891), 109–45 and 205–30.

Hawthorne, G. F. *Philippians*, WBC 43 (Waco, Texas: Word Books, 1983).

Hay, D. M. 'Pistis as "Ground for Faith" in Hellenized Judaism and Paul', *JBL* 108 (1989), 461–76.

Hays, R. B. 'Psalm 143 and the logic of Romans 3', *JBL* 99 (1980), 107–15.

The Faith of Jesus Christ: An Investigation of the Narrative Substructure of Galatians 3:1–4:11, SBLDS 56 (Chicago: Scholars Press, 1983).

'"Have we found Abraham to be our Forefather according to the Flesh?" A Consideration of Rom. 4:1', *NovT* 27 (1985), 76–98.

Echoes of Scripture in the Letters of Paul (New Haven: Yale University Press, 1989).

'"The Righteous One" as Eschatological Deliverer: A Case Study in Paul's Apocalyptic Hermeneutics', in J. Marcus and M. L. Soards (eds.), *Apocalyptic and the New Testament: Essays in Honour of J. Louis Martyn*, JSNTSS 24 (Sheffield: JSOT, 1989), 191–215.

'ΠΙΣΤΙΣ and Pauline Christology: What Is at Stake?, in E. H. Lovering, Jr. (ed.), *Society of Biblical Literature 1991 Seminar Papers* (Atlanta, Georgia: Scholars Press, 1991), 714–29.

Hebert, G. '"Faithfulness" and "Faith"', *Theology* 58 (1955), 373–9.

Heidland, H. W. 'λογίζομαι κτλ', *TDNT*, vol. 4, 284–92.

Held, H. J. 'Matthew as Interpreter of the Miracle Stories', in G. Bornkamm, G. Barth and H. J. Held (eds.) *Tradition and Interpretation in Matthew*, NTL, trans. P. Scott (Philadelphia: Westminster, 1963), 165–299.

Hengel, M. *The Son of God: The Origin of Christology and the History of Jewish-Hellenistic Religion*, trans. J. Bowden (London: SCM Press, 1976).

The Charismatic Leader and his Followers, SNTW, trans. J. C. G. Greig (Edinburgh: T. & T. Clark, 1981).
Henten, J. W. van (ed.) *Die Entstehung der Jüdischen Martyrologie*, Studia Post-Biblica (Leiden: E. J. Brill, 1989).
'The Tradition-Historical Background of Rom. 3.25: A Search for Pagan and Jewish Parallels', in M. C. De Boer (ed.), *From Jesus to John: Essays on Jesus and New Testament Christology in Honour of Marinus de Jonge*, JSNTSS 84 (Sheffield: JSOT, 1993), 101–28.
Hermisson, H.-J. and Lohse, E. *Faith*, Biblical Encounters, trans. D. W. Stott (Nashville: Abingdon, 1981).
Heron, A. I. C. 'HOMOOUSIOS with the Father', in T. F. Torrance (ed.), *The Incarnation: Ecumenical Studies in the Nicene-Constantinopolitan Creed A. D. 381* (Edinburgh: Handsel, 1981), 58–87.
Hester, J. D. *Paul's Concept of Inheritance: A Contribution to the Understanding of Heilsgeschichte*, Scottish Journal of Theology Occasional Papers 14 (Edinburgh: Oliver & Boyd, 1968).
Hick, J. *Faith and Knowledge*, 2nd edn. (London: Collins, 1966).
Hiers, R. H. '"Not the Season for Figs"', *JBL* 87 (1968), 394–400.
Hill, D. *Greek Words and Hebrew Meanings: Studies in the Semantics of Soteriological Terms*, SNTSMS 5 (Cambridge: Cambridge University Press, 1967).
'Prophecy and Prophets in the Revelation of St John', *NTS* 18 (1971), 401–18.
The Gospel of Matthew, New Century Bible (London: Marshall, Morgan & Scott, 1972).
'False Prophets and Charismatics: Structure and Interpretation in Matthew 7:15–23', *Biblica* 57 (1976), 327–48.
New Testament Prophecy, Marshalls Theological Library (London: Marshall, Morgan & Scott, 1979).
Holladay, C. H. *THEIOΣ ANEP IN HELLENISTIC-JUDAISM: A Critique of the Use of This Category in New Testament Christology*, SBLDS 40 (Missoula: Scholars Press, 1977).
Holtz, T. *Die Christologie der Apokalypse des Johannes*, TU, 2nd edn. (Berlin: Akademie, 1971).
Hooker, M. D. 'Interchange in Christ', *JTS* (ns) 22 (1971), 349–61.
'Interchange and Atonement', *BJRL* 60 (1977), 462–81.
'ΠΙΣΤΙΣ ΧΡΙΣΤΟΥ', *NTS* 35 (1989), 321–42.
A Commentary on The Gospel According to Mark, BNTC (London: A & C Black, 1991).
Horning, E. B. 'Chiasmus, Creedal Structure and Christology', *Biblical Research* 23 (1978), 37–48.
Howard, G. 'On the "Faith of Christ"', *HTR* 60 (1967), 459–84.
'Christ the End of the Law: The Meaning of Romans 10:4ff', *JBL* 88 (1969), 331–7.
'Romans 3:21–31 and the Inclusion of the Gentiles', *HTR* 63 (1970), 223–33.
'The "Faith of Christ"', *ExpT* 85 (1974), 212–15.
'Phil. 2:6–11 and the Human Christ', *CBQ* 40 (1978), 368–87.

Paul: Crisis in Galatia. A Study in Early Christian Theology, SNTSMS 35 (Cambridge: Cambridge University Press, 1979).
Hübner, H. *Law in Paul's Thought: A Contribution to the Development of Pauline Theology*, SNTW, trans. J. C. G. Greig (Edinburgh: T. & T. Clark, 1984).
Hughes, G. *Hebrews and Hermeneutics: The Epistle to the Hebrews as a New Testament Example of Biblical Interpretation*, SNTSMS 36 (Cambridge: Cambridge University Press, 1979).
Hughes, J. J. 'Hebrews 9:15ff and Galatians 3:15ff', *NovT* 21 (1979), 27–96.
Hughes, P. E. *A Commentary on the Epistle to the Hebrews* (Grand Rapids: Eerdmans, 1977).
The Book of Revelation: A Commentary (Leicester: Inter-Varsity Press, 1990).
Hull, J. M. *Hellenistic Magic and the Synoptic Tradition*, SBT 2/28 (London: SCM Press, 1974).
Hultgren, A. J. 'The PISTIS CHRISTOU Formulation in Paul', *NovT* 22 (1980), 248–63.
Inge, W. R. *Faith and its Psychology* (London: Duckworth, 1919).
Jepsen, A. 'אָמַן *et al.*', *TDOT*, vol. 1, 292–323.
Jeremias, J. ''Aβραάμ', *TDNT*, vol. 1, 8–9.
The Prayers of Jesus, trans. J. Bowden and C. Burchard (London: SCM Press, 1967).
New Testament Theology – Volume 1: The Proclamation of Jesus, NTL, trans. J. Bowden (London: SCM Press, 1971).
Johnson, L. T. 'Rom. 3:21–26 and the Faith of Jesus', *CBQ* 44 (1982), 77–90.
Jonge, M. de, 'Jesus' death for others and the death of the Maccabean martyrs', in T. Baarda, A. Hilhorst, G. P. Luttikhuizen and A. S. van der Woude (eds.), *Text and Testimony: Essays on New Testament and Apocryphal Literature in Honour of A. F. J. Klijn* (Kampen: J. H. Kok, 1988).
Juel, D. *Messianic Exegesis: Christological Interpretation of the Old Testament in Early Christianity* (Philadelphia: Fortress Press, 1988).
Jungmann, J. A. *The Place of Christ in Liturgical Prayer*, 2nd edn. (London: Geoffrey Chapman, 1989).
Käsemann, E. *New Testament Questions of Today*, trans. W. J. Montague (London: SCM Press, 1969).
Perspectives on Paul, trans. M. Kohl (London: SCM Press, 1971).
Commentary on Romans, trans. G. W. Bromiley (London: SCM Press, 1980).
The Wandering People of God: An Investigation of the Letter to the Hebrews, trans. R. A. Harrisville and I. L. Sandberg (Minneapolis: Augsburg, 1984).
Keck, L. E. *A Future for the Historical Jesus: The Place of Jesus in Preaching and Theology* (London: SCM Press, 1980).
'"Jesus" in Romans', *JBL* 108 (1989), 443–60.
Kee, H. C. *Community of the New Age: Studies in Mark's Gospel*, NTL (London: SCM Press, 1977).

Miracle in the Early Christian World: A Study in Sociohistorical Method (New Haven: Yale University Press, 1983).
Medicine, Miracle and Magic in New Testament Times, SNTSMS 55 (Cambridge: Cambridge University Press, 1986).
Kelly, J. N. D. *A Commentary on the Pastoral Epistles*, BNTC (London: A. & C. Black, 1963).
Early Christian Creeds, 3rd edn. (Harlow: Longman, 1972).
Early Christian Doctrines, rev. edn. (New York: Harper & Row, 1978).
Kertelge, K. *'Rechtfertigung' bei Paulus: Studien zur Struktur und zum Bedeutungsgehalt des paulinischen Rechtfertigungsbegriffes*, Neutestamentliche Abhandlungen 3 (Münster: Aschendorff, 1967).
Die Wunder Jesu im Markusevangelium: Eine redaktionsgeschichtliche Untersuchung, SANT 23 (München: Kösel, 1970).
Kim, S. *The Origin of Paul's Gospel*, WUNT 2/4 (Tübingen: J. C. B. Mohr [Paul Siebeck], 1981).
Kingsbury, J. D. 'The Title "Kyrios" in Matthew's Gospel', *JBL* 94 (1975), 246–55.
'The Title "Son of David" in Matthew's Gospel', *JBL* 95 (1976), 591–602.
'Observations on the "Miracle Chapters" of Matthew 8–9', *CBQ* 40 (1978), 559–73.
Kittel, G. 'Πίστις Ἰησοῦ Χριστοῦ bei Paulus', *TSK* 79 (1906), 419–36.
'λέγω κτλ (NT Section)', *TDNT*, vol. 4, 100–43.
Klein, H. 'Das Glaubensverständnis im Matthäusevangelium', in F. Hahn and H. Klein (eds.), *Glaube*, 29–42.
Klopperborg, J. S. *The Formation of Q: Trajectories in ancient wisdom collections*, Studies in antiquity and Christianity (Philadelphia: Fortress Press, 1987).
Knight, G. W. III, *The Pastoral Epistles: A Commentary on the Greek Text*, NIGTC (Eerdmans: Grand Rapids, 1992).
Koch, D.-A. *Die Bedeutung der Wundererzählungen für die Christologie des Markusevangeliums*, BZNW 42 (Berlin: Walter de Gruyter, 1975).
'Der Text von Hab. 2.4b in der Septuaginta und im Neuen Testament,' *ZNW* 76 (1985), 68–85.
Köster, H. 'ὑπόστασις', *TDNT*, vol. 8, 572–89.
Introduction to the New Testament, 2 vols, trans. by H. Köster (Philadelphia and Berlin: Fortress Press and Walter de Gruyter, 1982).
Kretschmar, G. 'Der paulinische Glaube in den Pastoralbriefen', in F. Hahn and H. Klein (eds.), *Glaube*, 115–40.
Krodel, G. A. *Revelation*, Augsburg Commentary on the New Testament (Minneapolis, Minnesota: Augsburg, 1989).
Künzel, G. *Studien zum Gemeindeverständnis des Matthäus-Evangeliums*, Calwer theologische Monographien 10 (Stuttgart: Calwer, 1978).
Kurz, W. S. 'Kenotic Imitation of Paul and of Christ in Philippians 2 and 3', in F. F. Segovia (ed.), *Discipleship in the New Testament* (Philadelphia: Fortress Press, 1985), 103–26.
Lampe, G. W. H. *A Patristic Greek Lexicon* (Oxford: Clarendon Press, 1961).
'Miracles and Early Christian Apologetic', in C. F. D. Moule (ed.),

Miracles: Cambridge Studies in their Philosophy and History (London: Mowbray, 1965), 205–18.

'Christian Theology in the Patristic Period', in H. Cunliffe-Jones (ed.), *A History of Christian Doctrine* (Edinburgh: T. & T. Clark, 1978), 21–180.

Lane, W. L. *The Gospel According to Mark*, NICNT (Grand Rapids: Eerdmans, 1974).

Hebrews, WBC 47, 2 vols. (Dallas, Texas: Word Books, 1991).

Lehne, S. *The New Covenant in Hebrews*, JSNTSS 44 (Sheffield: JSOT, 1990).

Lightfoot, J. B. *St Paul's Epistle to the Galatians*, 10th edn. (London: Macmillan, 1890).

St Paul's Epistle to the Philippians, 12th edn. (London: Macmillan, 1913).

Lincoln, A. T. *Ephesians*, WBC 42 (Dallas: Word Books, 1990).

Lindars, B. 'The Rhetorical Structure of Hebrews', *NTS* 35 (1989), 382–406.

The Theology of the Letter to the Hebrews, New Testament Theology (Cambridge: Cambridge University Press, 1991).

Lindsay, D. R. *Josephus and Faith: Πίστις and Πιστεύειν as Faith Terminology in the Writings of Flavius Josephus and in the New Testament*, AGJU 19 (Leiden: E. J. Brill, 1993).

Link, H.-J. 'ἐλέγχω', *NIDNTT*, vol. 2, 140–42.

Lips, H. von. *Glaube – Gemeinde – Amt*, FRLANT 122 (Göttingen: Vandenhoeck & Ruprecht, 1979).

Ljungman, H. *Pistis: A Study of its Presuppositions and its Meaning in Pauline Use* (Lund: Gleerup, 1964).

Loader, W. R. G. *Sohn und Hoherpriester: Eine traditionsgeschichtliche Untersuchung zur Christologie des Hebräerbriefes*, WMANT 53 (Neukirchen: Neukirchener, 1981).

Lohmeyer, E. *Die Offenbarung des Johannes*, HNT, 2nd edn. (Tübingen: J. C .B. Mohr, 1953).

Das Evangelium des Markus, KEK, 17th edn. (Göttingen: Vandenhoeck & Ruprecht, 1967).

(with the assistance of W. Schmauch) *Das Evangelium des Matthäus*, KEK, 4th edn. (Göttingen: Vandenhoeck & Ruprecht, 1967).

Lohse, E. 'Emuna und Pistis – Jüdisches und urchristliches Verständnis des Glaubens', *ZNW* 68 (1977), 147–63.

'Glaube und Wunder: Ein Beitrag zur theologia crucis in den synoptischen Evangelien', in C. Andresen and G. Klein (eds.), *Theologia Crucis – Signum Crucis: Festschrift für Erich Dinkler zum 70 Geburtstag* (Tübingen: J. C. B. Mohr [Paul Siebeck], 1979), 335–50.

Longenecker, B. W. 'ΠΙΣΤΙΣ in Romans 3.25: Neglected Evidence for the "Faithfulness of Christ"?', *NTS* 39 (1993), 478–80.

Longenecker, R. N. *Paul, Apostle of Liberty: The Origin and Nature of Paul's Christianity* (New York: Harper & Row, 1964).

'The Obedience of Christ in the Theology of the Early Church', in R. J. Banks (ed.), *Reconciliation and Hope: New Testament Essays on Atonement and Eschatology Presented to L. L. Morris on his 60th Birthday* (Grand Rapids: Eerdmans, 1974), 142–52.

Galatians, WBC 41 (Dallas, Texas: Word Books, 1990).
Loos, H. van der. *The Miracles of Jesus*, NovTSup 9 (Leiden: E. J. Brill, 1968).
Luck, U. 'Himmlisches und irdisches Geschehen im Hebräerbrief', *NovT* 6 (1963), 192–215.
Lührmann, D. 'Pistis in Judentum', *ZNW* 64 (1973), 19–38.
Glaube in frühen Christentum (Gütersloh: G. Mohn, 1976).
'Glaube', *RAC*, vol. 9, 48–122.
Luz, U. 'The Disciples in the Gospel According to Matthew', trans. R. Morgan, in G. N. Stanton (ed.), *The Interpretation of Matthew*, Issues in Religion and Theology 3 (London: SPCK, 1983), 98–128.
McGrath, A. E. *Iustitia Dei: A History of the Christian Doctrine of Justification*, 2 vols. (Cambridge: Cambridge University Press, 1986).
Mackey, J. P. 'The Theology of Faith: A Bibliographical Survey (and More)', *Horizons* 2 (1975), 207–37.
'The Faith of the Historical Jesus', *Horizons* 3 (1976), 155–74.
Jesus: the Man and the Myth – A Contemporary Christology (London: SCM Press, 1979).
Macquarrie, J. *Jesus Christ in Modern Thought* (London: SCM Press, 1990).
Manson, T. W. *The Sayings of Jesus – As Recorded in the Gospels According to St Matthew and St Luke Arranged with Introduction and Commentary* (London: SCM Press, 1949).
Marmorstein, A. *The Doctrine of Merits in Old Rabbinical Literature* (New York: KTAV, 1968 [= 1920 edn.]).
Marshall, C. D. *Faith as a theme in Mark's narrative*, SNTSMS 64 (Cambridge: Cambridge University Press, 1989).
Marshall, I. H. *The Gospel of Luke. A Commentary on the Greek Text*, NIGTC (Exeter: Paternoster, 1978).
Martin R. P. *Philippians: An Introduction and Commentary*, TNTC (Leicester: Inter-Varsity Press, 1959).
Mark: Evangelist and Theologian (Exeter: Paternoster, 1972).
Philippians, New Century Bible (London: Marshall, Morgan & Scott, 1976).
Mark, Knox Preaching Guides (Atlanta: John Knox Press, 1981).
Reconciliation: A Study in Paul's Theology, Marshall's Theological Library (London: Marshall, Morgan & Scott, 1981).
James, WBC 48 (Waco, Texas: Word Books, 1988).
Marxsen, W. 'Die urchristlichen Kerygmata und das Ereignis Jesus von Nazareth', *ZTK* 73 (1976), 42–64.
The Beginnings of Christology together with the Lord's Supper as a Christological Problem, trans. P. J. Achtemeier and L. Nieting (Philadelphia: Fortress Press, 1979).
Metzger, B. M. *A Textual Commentary on the Greek New Testament*, rev. edn. (London-New York: United Bible Societies, 1975).
Meyer, A. *Das Rätsel des Jacobusbriefes* (Giessen: Töpelmann, 1930).
Meyer, B. F. *The Aims of Jesus* (London: SCM Press, 1979).
Michel, O. *Der Brief an die Hebräer: Ubersetzt und erklärt*, KEK, 12th edn. (Göttingen: Vandenhoeck & Ruprecht, 1966).

Der Brief an die Römer, KEK, 4th edn. (Göttingen: Vandenhoeck & Ruprecht, 1966).
'πίστις', *NIDNTT*, vol. 1, 593–606.
Miller, M. H. The Character of the Miracles in Luke-Acts, unpublished Th.D. thesis (Graduate Theological Union, California, 1971).
Milligan, G. *The Theology of the Epistle to the Hebrews with a Critical Introduction* (Edinburgh: T. & T. Clark, 1899).
Minear, P. S. 'The Disciples and the Crowds in the Gospel of Matthew', *Anglican Theological Review Supplementary Series* 3 (1974), 28–44.
Mitros, J. F. 'The Norm of Faith in the Patristic Age', *Theological Studies* 29 (1968), 444–71.
Mitton, C. L. *Ephesians*, New Century Bible (London: Marshall, Morgan & Scott, 1976).
Moltmann, J. *The Way of Jesus Christ: Christology in messianic dimensions*, trans. M. Kohl (London: SCM Press, 1990).
Montefiore, H. W. *The Epistle to the Hebrews*, BNTC (London: A. & C. Black, 1964).
Moffatt, J. *A Critical and Exegetical Commentary on the Epistle to the Hebrews*, ICC (Edinburgh: T. & T. Clark, 1924).
Moo, D. 'Paul and the Law in the Last Ten Years', *SJT* 40 (1987), 287–307.
Moule, C. F. D. 'The Biblical Concept of "Faith"', *ExpT* 68 (1956), 157 and 222.
The Origin of Christology (Cambridge: Cambridge University Press, 1977).
Mounce, R. H. *The Book of Revelation*, NICNT (London: Marshall, Morgan & Scott, 1977).
Müller, P.-G. *ΧΡΙΣΤΟΣ ΑΡΧΗΓΟΣ: Der religionsgeschichtliche und theologische Hintergrund einer neutestamentlichen Christusprädikation*, Europäische Hochschulschriften 23/28 (Frankfurt: Lang, 1973).
Mundle, W. *Der Glaubensbegriff des Paulus: Eine Untersuchung zur Dogmengeschichte des altesten Christentums* (Leipzig: M. Heinsius, 1932).
Murphy-O'Connor, J. 'Christological Anthropology in Phil. 2, 6–11', *Revue biblique* 83 (1976), 25–50.
Murray, J. *The Epistle to the Romans*, NICNT, 2 vols. (Grand Rapids: Eerdmans, 1959 and 1965).
Mussner, F. *The Miracles of Jesus*, trans. A. Wimmer (Shannan: Ecclesia, 1970).
Der Galaterbrief, HTKNT 9, 2nd edn. (Freiburg: Herder, 1977).
Neirynck, F. 'The Miracle Stories in the Acts of the Apostles', in J. Kremer (ed.), *Les Acts des Apôtres: Traditions, rédaction, théologie*, BETL 48 (Gembloux: Leuven University, 1979), 169–213.
Duality in Mark: Contributions to the Study of the Markan Redaction, BETL 31, rev. edn. (Leuven: University Press, 1988).
Neugebauer, F. *In Christus: Eine Untersuchung zum Paulinischen Glaubensverständnis* (Göttingen: Vandenhoeck & Ruprecht, 1961).
Niebuhr, R. H. *Faith on Earth* (New Haven: Yale University Press, 1989).
Nineham, D. E. *The Gospel of St Mark*, Pelican New Testament Commentaries, rev. edn. (Harmondsworth: Penguin, 1969).
Nixon, R. E. 'Faith, Faithfulness', in M. C. Tenney (ed.), *The Zondervan*

Pictoral Encyclopedia of the Bible, vol. 2 (Grand Rapids: Zondervan, 1975), 479–91.

Nolan, A. *Jesus before Christianity: The Gospel of Liberation* (London: Darton, Longman & Todd, 1980).

Nygren, A. *Commentary on Romans*, trans. C. Rasmussen (Philadelphia: Fortress Press, 1949).

O'Brien, P. T. *The Epistle to the Philippians: A Commentary on the Greek Text*, NIGTC (Grand Rapids: Eerdmans, 1991).

O'Connor, E. D. *Faith in the Synoptic Gospels: A problem in the correlation of Scripture and Theology* (Notre Dame: Notre Dame University Press, 1961).

Oepke, A. *Der Brief des Paulus an die Galater*, THKNT 9, 3rd edn. (Berlin: Evangelische, 1964).

'δύω κτλ', *TDNT*, vol. 2, 318–21.

Oesterreicher, J. M. *The Unfinished Dialogue: Martin Buber and the Christian Way* (Secaucus: Citadel, 1987).

Panikkar, R. 'Faith – A Constitutive Dimension of Man', *JES* 8 (1971), 223–54.

Peisker, M. Der Glaubensbegriff bei Philon, unpublished Ph.D. thesis (Breslau, 1936).

Peloni, A. 'Faith as a Grain of Mustard Seed', *The Expositor* 8 (1884), 207–15.

Perels, O. *Die Wunderüberlieferung der Synoptiker in Ihrem Verhältnis zur Wortüberlieferung* (Stuttgart: W. Kohlhammer, 1934).

Perkins, P. *Resurrection: New Testament Witness and Contemporary Reflection* (London: Geoffrey Chapman, 1984).

Perrin, N. *Rediscovering the Teaching of Jesus*, NTL (London: SCM Press, 1967).

Perry, E. 'The Meaning of *'emuna* in the Old Testament', *JBR* 21 (1953), 252–6.

Pesch, R. *Das Markusevangelium*, HTKNT 2/1–2; 2 vols. 4th edn. & 3rd edn. (Freiburg: Herder, 1984).

Peterson, D. *Hebrews and Perfection: An Examination of the Concept of Perfection in the 'Epistle to the Hebrews'*, SNTSMS 47 (Cambridge: Cambridge University Press, 1982).

Pettersen, A. 'Did Athanasius Deny Christ's Fear?' *SJT* 39 (1986), 327–40.

'The Courage of Christ in the Theology of Athanasius', *SJT* 40 (1987), 363–77.

Pobee, J. S. *Persecution and Martyrdom in the Theology of Paul*, JSNTSS 6 (Sheffield: JSOT, 1985).

Polhill, J. B. 'Perspectives on the Miracle Stories', *Review and Expositor* 74 (1977), 389–99.

Pollard, T. E. *Johannine Christology and the Early Church*, SNTSMS 13 (Cambridge: Cambridge University Press, 1970).

Fullness of Humanity: Christ's Humanness and Ours, The Croall Lectures, 1980 (Sheffield: Almond Press, 1982).

Quasten, J. *Patrology*, 3 vols. (Utrecht: Spectrum, 1950).

Rad, G. von. *The Problem of the Hexateuch and other Essays*, trans. E. W. Trueman Dicken (Edinburgh: Oliver & Boyd, 1966).

Räisänen, H. *Paul and the Law*, WUNT 29 (Tübingen: J. C. B. Mohr [Paul Siebeck], 1983).

Jesus, Paul and Torah: Collected Essays, JSNTSS 43, trans. D. E. Orton (Sheffield: JSOT, 1992).

Reitzenstein, R. *Hellenistic Mystery-Religions: Their Basic Ideas and Significance*, The Pittsburgh Theological Monograph Series, trans. J. E. Steely (Pittsburgh: Pickwick, 1978).

Reploh, K.-G. *Markus – Lehrer der Gemeinde: Eine redaktionsgeschichtliche Studie zu den Jüngerperikopen des Markusevangeliums*, Stuttgarter biblische Monographien 9 (Stuttgart: Katholisches Bibelwerk, 1969).

Richardson, A. *The Miracle-Stories of the Gospels* (London: SCM Press, 1941).

Richardson, P. *Israel in the Apostolic Church*, SNTSMS 10 (Cambridge: Cambridge University Press, 1969).

Richardson, P. and Gooch, P. 'Logia of Jesus in 1 Corinthians', in D. Wenham (ed.), *Gospel Perspectives – Volume 5: The Jesus Tradition Outside the Gospels* (Sheffield: JSOT, 1984), 39–62.

Riesner, R. *Jesus als Lehrer: Eine Untersuchung zum Ursprung der Evangelien-Überlieferung*, WUNT 2/7, 2nd edn. (Tübingen: J. C. B. Mohr [Paul Siebeck], 1984).

Rissi, M. 'Die Menschlichkeit Jesu nach Hebr 5, 7–8', *Theologische Zeitschrift* 11 (1955), 28–45.

The Future of the World: An Exegetical Study of Revelation 19.11–22.15, SBT 2/23 (London: SCM Press, 1972).

Die Theologie des Hebräerbriefs, WUNT 41 (Tübingen: J. C. B. Mohr [Paul Siebeck], 1987).

Robbins, V. K. *Jesus the Teacher: A Socio-Rhetorical Interpretation of Mark* (Philadelphia: Fortress Press, 1984).

Robinson, D. W. B. '"Faith of Jesus Christ": a New Testament Debate', *RTR* 29 (1970), 71–81.

'Towards a Definition of Baptism', *RTR* 34 (1975), 1–15.

Robinson, J. A. *St Paul's Epistle to the Ephesians: A Revised Text and Translation with Exposition and Notes*, 2nd edn. (London: Macmillan, 1928).

Robinson, J. A. T. *The Body: A Study in Pauline Theology*, SBT 1/5 (London: SCM Press, 1952).

'The One Baptism', *SJT* 6 (1953), 257–74.

Robinson, J. M. and Köster, H. *Trajectories through Early Christianity* (Philadelphia: Fortress Press, 1971).

Roloff, J. *Das Kerygma und der irdische Jesus: Historische Motive in den Jesuserzählungen der Evangelien* (Göttingen: Vandenhoeck & Ruprecht, 1970).

Der erste Brief an Timotheus, EKKNT 15 (Neukirchen-Vluyn; Benziger/Neukirchener, 1988).

Rowland, C. *The Open Heaven: A Study of Apocalyptic in Judaism and Early Christianity* (London: SPCK, 1982).

Rhyne, C. T. *Faith Establishes the Law*, SBLDS 55 (Chicago: Scholars Press, 1981).

Rusche, H. 'Glauben und Leben nach dem Hebräerbrief: Einführende Bemerkungen', *Bibel und Leben* 12 (1971), 94–104.

Sabourin, L. *The Divine Miracles Discussed and Defended* (Rome: Catholic Book Agency, 1977).

Sanday, W. and Headlam, A. C. *A Critical and Exegetical Commentary on the Epistle to the Romans*, ICC (Edinburgh: T. & T. Clark, 1902).

Sanders, E. P. *Paul and Palestinian Judaism: A Comparison of Patterns of Religion* (London: SCM Press, 1977).

'On the Question of Fulfilling the Law in Paul and Rabbinic Judaism', in E. Bammel, C. K. Barrett and W. D. Davies (eds.), *Donum Gentilicium: New Testament Studies in Honour of David Daube* (Oxford: Clarendon Press, 1978), 103–26.

Paul, the Law and the Jewish People (Philadelphia: Fortress Press, 1983).

Jesus and Judaism (London: SCM Press, 1985).

Satake, A. *Die Gemeindeordnung in der Johannesapokalypse*, WMANT 21 (Neukirchen: Neukirchener, 1966).

Schläger, G. 'Bemerkungen zu πίστις Ἰησοῦ Χριστοῦ', *ZNW* 7 (1906), 356–8.

Schenk, W. 'Die Gerechtigkeit Gottes und der Glaube Christi', *Theologische Literaturzeitung* 97 (1972), 161–74.

Die Philipperbriefe des Paulus (Stuttgart: W. Kohlhammer, 1984).

Schenke, L. *Die Wundererzählungen des Markusevangeliums*, Stuttgarter Biblische Beiträge (Stuttgart: Katholisches Bibelwerk, 1974).

Schillebeeckx, E. *Jesus: An Experiment in Christology*, trans. H. Hoskins (London: Collins, 1979).

Schlatter, A. *Der Glaube im Neuen Testament*, 6th edn. with introduction by P. Stuhlmacher (Stuttgart: Calwer, 1982).

Schlier, H. *Der Brief an die Galater*, KEK, 5th edn. (Göttingen: Vandenhoeck & Ruprecht, 1971).

Der Römerbrief, HTKNT (Freiburg: Herder, 1977).

Schmidt, H. W. *Der Brief des Paulus an die Römer*, THKNT (Berlin: Evangelische, 1966).

Schmithals, W. 'Die Heilung des Epileptischen (Mk. 9, 14–29). Ein Beitrag zur notwendigen Revision der Formgeschichte', *Theologia Viatorum* 13 (1975), 211–33.

Das Evangelium nach Markus, ÖTNT; 2nd edn. 2 vols. (Gütersloh: Gerd Mohn, 1986).

Schnackenburg, R. *Baptism in the Thought of St Paul: A Study in Pauline Theology*, trans. G. R. Beasley-Murray (Oxford: Blackwell, 1964).

The Epistle to the Ephesians: A Commentary, trans. H. Heron (Edinburgh: T & T Clark, 1991).

Schoedel, W. R. *Ignatius of Antioch: A Commentary on the Letters of Ignatius of Antioch*, Hermeneia (Philadelphia: Fortress Press, 1985).

Schoeps, H. J. *Paul: The Theology of the Apostle in the Light of Jewish Religious History*, trans. H. Knight (Philadelphia: Westminster, 1961).

Schoonenberg, P. *The Christ*, trans. D. Couling (London: Sheed & Ward, 1972).

Schoonhoven, C. R. 'The "Analogy of Faith" and the Intent of Hebrews', in W. W. Gasque & W. S. LaSor (eds.), *Scripture, Tradition and*

Interpretation: Essays Presented to Everett F. Harrison by His Students and Colleagues in Honor of His Seventy-fifth Birthday (Grand Rapids: Eerdmans, 1978), 91–110.

Schreiber, J. *Theologie des Vertrauens: Eine redaktionseschichtliche Untersuchung des Markusevangeliums* (Hamburg: Furche, 1967).

Schrenk, G. 'ἐντέλλομαι, ἐντολή', *TDNT*, vol. 2, 544–56.

'ἱερός κτλ', *TDNT*, vol. 3, 221–83.

Schürmann, H. 'Die vorösterlichen Anfänge der Logientradition', in H. Ristow and K. Matthiae (eds.), *Der historische Jesus und der kerygmatische Christus: Beiträge zum Christusverständnis in Forschung und Verkündigung* (Berlin: Evangelische, 1962), 342–70.

Schwarz, G. 'πιστιν ως κοκκον σιναπεως', *Biblische Notizen* 25 (1984), 27–35.

Schweizer, E. *The Good News According to Mark: A Commentary on the Gospel*, trans. D. H. Madvig (Atlanta: John Knox Press, 1970).

The Good News According to Matthew, trans. D. E. Green (Atlanta: John Knox Press, 1975).

'Matthew's Church', trans. R. Morgan, in G. N. Stanton (ed.), *The Interpretation of Matthew*, Issues in Religion and Theology 3 (London: SPCK, 1983), 129–55.

Scott, W. *Hermetica: The Ancient Greek and Latin Writings which contain Religious or Philosophical Teachings Ascribed to Hermes Trismegistus*, 2 vols. (Oxford: Clarendon Press, 1924 and 1925).

Scroggs, R. *The Last Adam: A Study in Pauline Anthropology* (Philadelphia: Fortress Press, 1966).

Seitz, O. J. F. 'Antecedents and Signification of the Term ΔΙΨΥΧΟΣ', *JBL* 63 (1944), 131–40.

Seybold, K. 'חָשַׁב *et al.*', *TDOT*, vol. 5, 228–45.

Shedd, R. P. *Man in Community: A Study of St Paul's Application of Old Testament and Early Jewish Conceptions of Human Solidarity* (London: Epworth, 1958).

Simon, D. W. 'Faith as a Grain of Mustard Seed', *The Expositor* 9 (1879), 307–16.

Smith, W. C. *Belief and History* (Charlottesville: Virginia University Press, 1977).

Faith and Belief (Princeton: Princeton University Press, 1979).

Snodgrass, K. R. 'Justification by Grace – To the Doers: An Analysis of the Place of Romans 2 in the Theology of Paul', *NTS* 32 (1986), 72–93.

Sobrino, J. *Christology at the Crossroads: A Latin American Approach*, trans. J. Drury (London: SCM Press, 1978).

Spicq, C. *L'Épître aux Hébreux*, Etudes bibliques, 2 vols. (Paris: J. Gabalda, 1952 & 1953).

Les Épîtres Pastorales, Etudes bibliques, 4th edn. (Paris: J. Gabalda, 1969).

Stanley, C. D. '"Under a Curse": A Fresh Reading of Galatians 3.10–14', *NTS* 36 (1990), 481–511.

Stanton, G. N. *Jesus of Nazareth in New Testament Preaching*, SNTSMS 27 (Cambridge: Cambridge University Press, 1974).

Stauffer, E. *New Testament Theology*, trans. J. Marsh (London: SCM Press, 1955).

Stead, C. *Divine Substance* (Oxford: Oxford University Press, 1977).

Stein, R. H. 'The Proper Methodology for Ascertaining a Markan Redaction History', *NovT* 13 (1971), 181–98.

Stendahl, K. *Paul among Jews and Gentiles and other Essays* (London: SCM Press, 1977).

Stewart, R. A. *Rabbinic Theology: An Introductory Study* (Edinburgh: Oliver & Boyd, 1961).

Stowers, S. K. 'ΕΚ ΠΙΣΤΕΩΣ and ΔΙΑ ΤΗΣ ΠΙΣΤΕΩΣ in Romans 3:30', *JBL* 108 (1989), 665–74.

Strathmann, H. 'μάρτυς κτλ', *TDNT*, vol. 4, 474–514.

Stuhlmacher, P. *Gerechtigkeit Gottes bei Paulus*, FRLANT 87 (Göttingen: Vandenhoeck & Ruprecht, 1965).

Reconciliation, Law and Righteousness: Essays in Biblical Theology, trans. E. Kalin (Philadelphia: Fortress Press, 1986).

Suhl, A. *Die Wunder Jesu: Ereignis und Überlieferung* (Gütersloh: Gerd Mohn, 1968).

Sutherland, D. D. 'Gen. 15:6 and Early Christian Struggles over Election', *SJT* 44 (1991), 443–56.

Sweet, J. P. M. *Revelation*, Pelican New Testament Commentaries (London: SCM Press, 1976).

'Maintaining the testimony of Jesus: the suffering of Christians in the Revelation of John', in W. Horbury and B. McNeil (eds.), *Suffering and Martyrdom in the New Testament: Studies presented to G. M. Styler by the Cambridge New Testament Seminar* (Cambridge: Cambridge University Press, 1981), 101–17.

Swete, H. B. *The Apocalypse of St John* (London: MacMillan, 1906).

Swetnam, J. *Jesus and Isaac: A Study of the Epistle to the Hebrews in the Light of the Aqedah*, Analecta biblica 94 (Rome: Biblical Institute, 1981).

Swinburne, R. *Faith and Reason* (Oxford: Clarendon Press, 1981).

Taeger, J.-W. *Der Mensch und sein Heil: Studien zum Bild des Menschen und zur Sicht der Bekehrung bei Lukas*, Studien zum Neuen Testament 14 (Gütersloh: Gerd Mohn, 1982).

Talmon, S. 'הַר *et al.*', *TDOT*, vol. 3, 427–47.

Tannehill, R. C. *Dying and Rising with Christ: A Study in Pauline Theology*, BZNW 32 (Berlin: Töpelmann, 1967).

Taylor, G. M. 'The Function of ΠΙΣΤΙΣ ΧΡΙΣΤΟΥ in Galatians', *JBL* 85 (1966), 58–76.

Taylor. J. V. *The Christlike God* (London: SCM Press, 1992).

Taylor, V. *The Gospel According to St Mark: The Greek Text with Introduction, Notes, and Indexes* (London: Macmillan, 1963).

Telford, W. R. *The Barren Temple and the Withered Tree: A redaction-critical analysis of the Cursing of the Fig-tree pericope in Mark's Gospel and its relation to the Cleansing of the Temple tradition*, JSNTSS 1 (Sheffield: JSOT, 1980).

Terveen, J. L. Jesus in Hebrews: An Exegetical Analysis of the References

to Jesus' Earthly Life in the Epistle to the Hebrews, unpublished Ph.D. thesis (Edinburgh University, 1986).
Theissen, G. *The Miracle Stories of the Early Christian Tradition*, SNTW, trans. F. McDonagh (Edinburgh: T. & T. Clark, 1983).
Theunissen, M. ''O αἰτῶν λαμβάνει: Der Gebetsglaube Jesu und die Zeitlichkeit des Christseins', in B. Casper (ed.), *Jesus Ort der Erfahrung Gottes*, 2nd edn. (Freiburg: Herder, 1976), 13–68.
Thiselton, A. C. *The Two Horizons: New Testament Hermeneutics and Philosophical Description with special reference to Heidegger, Bultmann, Gadamer and Wittgenstein* (Exeter: Paternoster, 1980).
Thompson, M. *Clothed with Christ: The Example and Teaching of Jesus in Romans 12.1–15.13*, JSNTSS 59 (Sheffield: JSOT, 1991).
Thüsing, W. 'New Testament approaches to a transcendental Christology', in K. Rahner and W. Thüsing, *A New Christology*, trans. D. Smith and V. Green (London: Burns & Oates, 1980), 43–234.
Tiede, D. L. *The Charismatic Figure as Miracle Worker*, SBLDS 1 (Missoula: Scholars Press, 1972).
Torrance, J. B. 'The Vicarious Humanity of Christ', in T. F. Torrance (ed.), *The Incarnation: Ecumenical Studies in the Nicene-Constantinopolitan Creed A. D. 381* (Edinburgh: Handsel, 1981), 127–47.
Torrance, T. F. 'One Aspect of the Biblical Conception of Faith', *ExpT* 68 (1956), 111–14.
'The Biblical Concept of "Faith"', *ExpT* 68 (1956), 221–2.
'The Hermeneutics of St Athanasius', *'Ἐκκλησιαστικὸς Φάρος* 52 (1970), 89–106, 237–49, 446–68, 53 (1971), 133–49.
Theology in Reconciliation: Essays towards Evangelical and Catholic Unity in East and West (London: Geoffrey Chapman, 1975).
'The Deposit of Faith', *SJT* 36 (1983), 1–18.
The Mediation of Christ (Exeter: Paternoster, 1983).
The Trinitarian Faith: The Evangelical Theology of the Ancient Catholic Church (Edinburgh: T. & T. Clark, 1988).
Towner, P. H. *The Goal of Our Instruction: The Structure of Theology and Ethics in the Pastoral Epistles*, JSNTSS 34 (Sheffield: JSOT, 1989).
Trites, A. A. 'Μάρτυς and Martyrdom in the Apocalypse', *NovT* 15 (1973), 72–80.
The New Testament Concept of Witness, SNTSMS 31 (Cambridge: Cambridge University Press, 1977).
'The Prayer Motif in Luke-Acts', in C. H. Talbert (ed.), *Perspectives on Luke-Acts* (Edinburgh: T. & T. Clark, 1978), 168–86.
Trocmé, E. *Jesus and his Contemporaries*, trans. R. A. Wilson (London: SCM Press, 1973).
Turner, N. *Christian Words* (Edinburgh: T. & T. Clark, 1982).
Twelftree, G. *Christ Triumphant: Exorcism Then and Now* (London: Hodder & Stoughton, 1985).
Urbach, E. E. *The Sages: Their Concepts and Beliefs*, trans. I. Abrahams (Cambridge, Mass: Harvard University Press, 1987).
Vallotton, P. *Le Christ et La Foi: Etude de théologie biblique* (Genève: Labor et Fides, 1960).

Vanhoye, A. 'Jesus "fidelis ei qui fecit eum" (Hebr 3:2)', *Verbum Domini* 45 (1967), 291–305.

La structure littéraire de l'Épître aux Hébreux, Studia Neotestamentica 1, 2nd edn. (Paris: Desclée de Brouwer, 1976).

Vermes, G. 'Hanina ben Dosa', *JJS* 23 (1972), 28–50.

Jesus and the World of Judaism (London: SCM Press, 1983).

Vincent, M. R. *A Critical and Exegetical Commentary on the Epistles to the Philippians and to Philemon*, ICC (Edinburgh: T. & T. Clark, 1897).

Vos, L. A. *The Synoptic Traditions in the Apocalypse* (Kampen: J. H. Kok, 1965).

Wagner, G. *Pauline Baptism and the Pagan Mysteries*, trans. J. P. Smith (Edinburgh: Oliver & Boyd, 1967).

Wainwright, W. J. 'Wilfred Cantwell Smith on Faith and Belief', *Religious Studies* 20 (1984), 353–66.

Wallis, I. G. 'Your Faith has Saved You': A Redaction-Critical Analysis of the Synoptic Logion, unpublished M.Litt. thesis (Cambridge University, 1984).

Watson, F. *Paul, Judaism and the Gentiles*, SNTSMS 56 (Cambridge: Cambridge University Press, 1986).

Wedderburn, A. J. M. 'Some Observations on Paul's Use of the Phrases "In Christ" and "With Christ"', *JSNT* 25 (1985), 83–97.

Weiser, A. 'πιστεύω κτλ (OT Section)', *TDNT*, vol. 6, 182–96.

Weiss, H.-F. *Der Brief an die Hebräer*, KEK (Göttingen: Vandenhoeck & Ruprecht, 1991).

Westcott, B. F. *The Epistle to the Hebrews*, 2nd edn. (London: MacMillan, 1892).

Westermann, C. *Genesis: A Commentary*, 3 vols., trans. J. Scullion (London: SPCK, 1984–87).

Wifall, W. 'David – Prototype of Israel's Future?', *Biblical Theology Bulletin* 4 (1974), 93–107.

Wiles, M. F. 'Miracles in the Early Church', in C. F. D. Moule (ed.), *Miracles: Cambridge Studies in their Philosophy and History* (London: Mowbray, 1965), 221–34.

Faith and the Mystery of God (London: SCM Press, 1982).

Wilckens, U. *Der Brief an die Römer*, EKKNT 6/1–3, 3 vols. (Köln/Neukirchen: Benziger/Neukirchener, 1978).

Williams, J. A. *Biblical Interpretation in the Gnostic Gospel of Truth from Nag Hammadi*, SBLDS 79 (Atlanta: Scholars Press, 1988).

Williams, R. *Arius: Heresy and Tradition* (London: Darton, Longman & Todd, 1987).

Williams, S. K. *Jesus' Death as Saving Event: The Background and Origin of a Concept*, HDS 2 (Missoula: Scholars Press, 1975).

'The "Righteousness of God" in Romans', *JBL* 99 (1980), 241–90

'Again Pistis Christou', *CBQ* 49 (1987), 431–47.

'Justification and the Spirit in Galatians', *JSNT* 29 (1987), 91–100.

'The Hearing of Faith: ΑΚΟΗ ΠΙΣΤΕΩΣ in Galatians 3', *NTS* 35 (1989), 82–93.

Williamson, R. *Philo and the Epistle to the Hebrews*, ALGHJ 4 (Leiden: E. J. Brill, 1970).

Wilson, R. M. *Hebrews*, New Century Bible (Basingstoke: Marshall, Morgan & Scott, 1987).

Wilson, S. G. *Luke and the Pastoral Epistles* (London: SPCK, 1979).

Wissmann, E. *Das Verhältnis von ΠΙΣΤΙΣ und Christusfrömmigkeit bei Paulus*, FRLANT (Göttingen: Vandenhoeck & Ruprecht, 1926).

Wittgenstein, L. *Philosophical Investigations*, trans. G. E. M. Anscombe (Oxford: Blackwell, 1978).

Wolter, M. *Die Pastoralbriefe als Paulustradition*, FRLANT 146 (Göttingen: Vandenhoeck & Ruprecht, 1988).

Wright, N. T. *The Climax of the Covenant: Christ and the Law in Pauline Theology* (Edinburgh: T. & T. Clark, 1991).

'Adam, Israel and the Messiah', in *Climax*, 18–40 [cf. revision of *SBL 1983 Seminar Papers* (Chicago: Scholars Press, 1983), 359–89].

'Jesus Christ is Lord: Phil. 2.5–11', in *Climax*, 56–98.

'Curse and Covenant: Galatians 3.10–14', in *Climax*, 137–56.

'The Seed and the Mediator: Galatians 3.15–20', in *Climax*, 157–74.

Young, F. M. *From Nicea to Chalcedon: A Guide to the Literature and its Background* (London: SCM Press, 1983).

The Making of the Creeds (London: SCM Press, 1991).

Ziesler, J. A. *The Meaning of Righteousness in Paul: A Linguistic and Theological Enquiry*, SNTSMS 20 (Cambridge: Cambridge University Press, 1972).

Paul's Letter to the Romans, Pelican New Testament Commentaries (London: SCM Press, 1989).

Zmijewski, J. 'Der Glaube und Seine Macht: Eine traditionsgeschichtliche Untersuchung zu Mt 17:20; 21:21; Mk 11:23; Lk 17:6', in J. Zmijewski and E. Nellessen (eds.), *Begegnung mit dem Wort: Festschrift für Heinrich Zimmermann*, Bonner Biblische Beiträge (Bonn: Peter Hanstein, 1980), 81–103.

INDEX OF MODERN AUTHORS

INDEX OF PASSAGES

Old Testament

Testament of Isaac

Testament of Jacob

Testament of Moses

Testament of Zebulun

Tobit

Wisdom

Dead Sea Scrolls, Josephus and Philo

Dead Sea Scrolls

Josephus

Philo

Rabbinic texts

Mekilta

Midrashim

Mishnah

Babylonian Talmud

INDEX OF SUBJECTS

Printed in the United States
34057LVS00006B/32

9 780521 018845